G

Eye-tracking in Interaction

Advances in Interaction Studies (AIS)

ISSN 1879-873X

Advances in Interaction Studies (AIS) provides a forum for researchers to present excellent scholarly work in a variety of disciplines relevant to the advancement of knowledge in the field of interaction studies. The book series accompanies the journal *Interaction Studies: Social Behaviour and Communication in Biological and Artificial Systems.*

The book series allows the presentation of research in the forms of monographs or edited collections of peer-reviewed material in English.

For an overview of all books published in this series, please see
http://benjamins.com/catalog/ais

Volume 10

Eye-tracking in Interaction. Studies on the role of eye gaze in dialogue
Edited by Geert Brône and Bert Oben

Eye-tracking in Interaction

Studies on the role of eye gaze in dialogue

Edited by

Geert Brône
Bert Oben
University of Leuven

John Benjamins Publishing Company

Amsterdam / Philadelphia

∞™   The paper used in this publication meets the minimum requirements of
the American National Standard for Information Sciences – Permanence
of Paper for Printed Library Materials, ANSI z39.48-1984.

DOI 10.1075/ais.10

Cataloging-in-Publication Data available from Library of Congress.

ISBN 978 90 272 0152 2   (HB)
ISBN 978 90 272 6346 9   (E-BOOK)

John Benjamins Publishing Company · https://benjamins.com

Table of contents

CHAPTER 1

Introduction

Gaze, interaction and eye-tracking: A multidisciplinary endeavor

Geert Brône and Bert Oben

1.   Eye gaze in interaction

Several subdisciplines and programs in linguistics and psychology have demonstrated a long-standing interest in the study of non-verbal communication in relation to speech. The most widely studied form of non-vocal communication is by far (co-speech) gesture, defined as the use of hands, arms and other body parts, typically in conjunction with speech. Within the broadly defined category of gesture, hand gestures have received most attention because of their broad semiotic potential (see Müller et al., 2013, 2014 for a state-of-the-art). This volume, however, zooms in on a different semiotic channel within the visual modality that has been shown to have multiple communicative functions as well, viz. eye gaze in face-to-face interaction.

Ever since the publication of early pioneering work by Kendon (1967), Argyle & Cook (1976) and Goodwin (1980, 1981), different disciplines have shown an interest in the role of eye gaze in conversation, including conversation analysis, psycholinguistics and research on human-computer interaction. One of the main reasons for this multidisciplinary interest is the key role that eye gaze plays in establishing successful communication as an essentially *joint action* (Clark, 1996; Pickering & Garrod, 2004, 2006; Linell, 2009; Zima and Brône, 2015; Feyaerts, Brône and Oben, 2017). Communication partners coordinate their production and interpretation, that is, they need to be able to react or adjust to their partners as much as they need to be able to anticipate their partners' actions. Establishing and managing this interaction typically requires information from different signal systems simultaneously, and eye gaze seems to play a constitutive role in the different phases of this complex process, including signaling attention and interest, achieving joint attention, organizing the sequential structure of the interaction, reference identification and disambiguation, feedback and feedback elicitation, etc. Teasing apart these different functions, and designing methods to study or implement

https://doi.org/10.1075/ais.10.01bro

them (e.g. in human-computer interaction) is a complex undertaking that – not surprisingly – requires a multidisciplinary approach. This volume aims to present a state-of-the-art collection of chapters on eye gaze in interaction, focusing on theoretical and methodological issues, presenting critical overviews of key phenomena and introducing original empirical studies. What unites the different takes on the phenomenon of eye gaze in interaction in this volume, is a methodological focus on the potential of (mobile) eye-tracking as a tool for gaining high-quality information on the gaze behavior of participants engaged in human-human or human-computer interaction. It is an explicit aim of this volume to bring together different disciplines, which to some extent have an altogether different approach to the use of eye-tracking in interaction. We hope that crossing the disciplinary boundaries may be fruitful and inspire the further development of this new technology-driven endeavor. Before we discuss the introduction of eye-tracking to interaction research in Section 2, the remainder of this section examines, in somewhat more detail, the body of literature that has dealt with the role of eye gaze as a communicative resource in interaction.

The above-mentioned pioneering work is generally referred to as the first truly empirical research on eye gaze in interaction, based on the detailed analysis of video data (and its transcription), and focusing on both the speakers' and hearers' gaze direction while engaging in face-to-face dialogue. These studies provided compelling evidence for the multifunctionality of eye gaze as a communicative instrument and have, in fact, paved the way for more recent work. This work can, broadly speaking, be subdivided into two clusters, relating to the research fields involved. One research line focuses on gaze behavior as an interactional resource in conversation (functioning as a display of (dis)engagement, participation, affiliation, turn allocation, etc.) and is mainly inspired by conversation analysis and interactional linguistics. Another line zooms in on the cognitive import of speakers' and listeners' gaze on language processing and production, spatial mapping (including deixis) and the coordination of joint tasks. Needless to say, there is no strict divide between the two lines, but for organizational reasons we discuss them separately here.

In the more strongly interactional line of research on eye gaze, two key topics can be identified (drawing on Rossano's (2012a) overview), viz. (i) the relation between eye gaze and participation roles in the interaction, and (ii) the regulatory function of eye gaze. The first refers to the relationship among the participants engaged in an interaction, including the distribution and negotiation of speaker and hearer roles (referred to as the participation framework by Goffman, 1981). The early empirical observations on gaze behavior in interaction, in fact, related to this participation framework, as they showed that gaze behavior while speaking differs substantially from gaze while listening. Kendon (1967) and Argyle & Cook (1976) showed that hearers typically displayed longer sequences of uninterrupted gaze towards the speakers, while speakers tended to shift their gaze towards and away from the hearer more frequently. This basic observation has been confirmed in several later studies (Goodwin, 1981, Vertegaal, 1999, Hirvenkari et al., 2013, Brône et al., 2017). Rossano (2012b), however, adds that this distributional pattern is partly dependent on the specific interactional activities of the participants. For instance, during the activities of tellings and questions, a more sustained gaze by the recipient is required, as it is viewed as a display of attention and engagement. Apart from the speakers and their directly addressed recipients, other unaddressed participants engaged in the interaction may display interesting gaze behavior as well. For instance, Holler and Kendrick (2015) show that unaddressed participants seem to anticipate turn shifts between the primary participants: in question-response sequences the unaddressed participants typically shift their gaze towards the projected next speaker before the ongoing turn has been completed.

As for the regulatory functions of eye gaze, i.e. its role in the sequential organization of the ongoing interaction, several studies have shown that speaker gaze can have a 'floor apportionment' function: speakers tend to display gaze aversion briefly after taking the turn and then shift their gaze back to the (primary) recipient shortly before turn completion as a signal of potential turn transition (Duncan, 1975, Kendon, 1967, Streeck, 2014, Rossano, 2010, Jehoul et al., 2017, but also De Ruiter, 2005 for a somewhat different position). Auer (this volume) takes this basic insight and extends it to the interactionally more complex constellation of triadic (and thus multi-party) conversations. He shows that speaker gaze may serve both addressee selection and next-speaker selection, and the sequential position is constitutive in determining this function. Thus, while speakers may shift their gaze between different addressees while speaking, the gaze target at the TCU end seems to determine who will be the next speaker. Apart from its function in the distribution of turns, gaze may also be used by speakers to monitor or elicit responses by the recipients (Goodwin & Goodwin, 1986, Sweetser & Stec, 2016). Face-to-face interactions typically involve gaze windows, i.e. moments during which both participants look at each other, and which allow speakers to elicit and recipients to realize a form of minimal response (which can be verbal back channels such as *mh,* nonverbal signals such as headnods, or combinations of these) (Bavelas et al., 2002). Vranjes et al. (this volume) show, for the specific case of interpreter-mediated interaction, that this multimodal display of recipiency involving gaze may differ depending on the specific role of the participant in the interaction.

What the studies on the relationship between speaker-hearer gaze and feedback show, is that interactants display a synchronized system of multimodal behavior to achieve successful communication. And this brings us to the more cognitively oriented line of work on eye gaze in interaction, which has focused strongly on joint attention and the construction of shared situation models. One correlate of this basic feature of joint attention in interaction is *shared gaze* or the joint focus on relevant objects in the shared visual space (e.g. referents that are the current topic of conversation). This form of gaze coordination is the focus of a series of experiments reported by Richardson and colleagues (Richardson & Dale, 2005; Richardson et al., 2007, 2009), who measured the coupling of eye movements between participants performing joint tasks via a computer screen. The results show that participants display a strong tendency towards joint visual attention as well as an impact of shared background knowledge on this coupling. In a similar vein, Brennan et al. (2008) and Neider et al. (2010) used collaborative visual search tasks for remotely located pairs of people (both wearing head-mounted eye-trackers) to study the relative impact of shared gaze and speech on performance efficiency. The results show that the condition with shared gaze (with participants seeing the gaze cursor generated by the eye-tracker of the other) scored significantly better than (a) solitary search, (b) a condition with only shared voice, and even (c) the condition with both shared gaze and shared voice. Within the realm of human-computer interaction research, for example Staudte and Crocker (2011) show how speaker gaze by a virtual agent plays an important role in complex reference resolution, and Skantze et al. (2014) demonstrate how speaker gaze by a robot has an impact on turn taking and task performance of the human interlocutor.

Apart from participants' shared gaze at relevant objects or other referents, the distribution of visual attention across the interactional space of the conversation is particularly relevant as well for the present volume. Interactants do not only focus on specific referents or on the speakers and/or addressees. Rather, the above-mentioned roles of eye gaze as cues for referent assignment, turn management etc. illustrate the complexity of the phenomenon, which may simultaneously be treated as the cause and effect of specific behavior in interaction. One of the best-known phenomena in this respect is the *gaze cueing effect*, an effect on the gaze behavior of an addressee that is triggered by cueing a target (e.g. by looking at it). Studies on the gaze cueing effect, which date back to early work by Posner et al. (1980), stress its role for joint attention in interaction (Emery, 2000, Frischen et al., 2007). Lachat et al. (2012) are the first to test the gaze cueing effect in a spontaneous face-to-face setting (rather than in on-screen experiments), however without the use of the eye-tracking paradigm. Gullberg & Holmqvist (2006) and Gullberg & Kita (2009) focus on one specific case of gaze cueing, using head-mounted eye-trackers, viz. the effect of a speaker focusing on his/her own gesture on the addressee's gaze behaviour. The studies reveal that a speaker's gaze at own gestures is a powerful cue for addressees to leave the dominant fixation position (i.e. the face of the speaker) and give overt visual attention to the speaker's gesture (Oben, 2015). Amati and Brennan (this volume) discuss how gaze cues by speakers may or may not be treated differently by observers in settings where they have direct access to the gazer's face in comparison to remote settings with shared gaze systems (in which gaze is represented by a dynamic cursor displayed on a screen). Taking a broader perspective, Knoeferle et al. (this volume) show that speaker gaze, in fact, may facilitate language processing and even language learning in socially interactive contexts.

The studies by Gullberg and colleagues show the way in which different modalities may be geared to one another to create cognitive and/or communicative effects (i.e. visual focus on gesture and its relation to information uptake). Building on this line of research, Oben and Brône (2015) observed another interactional effect of gaze fixations on gesture. Based on a dataset of face-to-face interactions recorded with mobile eye-tracking systems, they found that when addressees focus their visual attention on speaker gestures, they are more likely to produce similar gestures in their consecutive turn as speaker after turn transition. In other words, this study provides evidence for a form of multimodal interactive alignment (Pickering & Garrod, 2004): gestural alignment may be induced by gaze fixations on speakers' gestures. Similarly, but in a context of mediated interaction between virtual agents and humans, Wang & Neff (2013) showed that humans are faster at copying a hand gesture made by a virtual agent if that agent is looking at the human participant (compared to the agent producing the gesture without looking at the participant). In addition, Postma et al. (2013) demonstrated the same effect for alignment of intonation: human participants copy more of the intonation produced by a virtual agent if that agent is looking at the participant while producing the utterance.

What this brief overview, which by no means was intended as an exhaustive literature review, shows is the multifunctionality and versatility of eye gaze as a semiotic resource in interaction. To come back to the first paragraph of this section, it can be argued that like any other type of (manual) gesture, eye gaze can be categorized as a form of visible bodily action in Kendon's terminology (Kendon, 2004). That is, eye gaze is not simply to be treated as a form of oculomotoric action functioning as part of the cognitive-perceptual system. Rather, gaze should be perceived as bodily action invested with meaning, both on the part of speakers and their addressees, relevant for the joint action that is human-human (or even human-computer) interaction (Clark, 1996, Brennan, 2005, De Jaegher et al., 2010). This meaning is thus fundamentally grounded in the interaction, as it presupposes the participants' awareness of each others' gaze behavior. To take the example of shared gaze in interaction discussed above, joint attention towards a physically co-present object of interest can be crucial for the interactional success of a joint action and hinges on the participants' awareness of what the other is oriented towards (Brennan et al., 2008; Stukenbrock, 2015, this volume). In a similar vein, averting one's gaze as a turn holding mechanism in interaction can only be truly interactionally successful if this gaze event is observed by the other participant(s) and is treated by the latter as a communicative resource.

What we have not discussed so far, is how to deal with this complex and often highly-dynamic resource from a methodological point of view. In the following section, we deal with some of the technological innovations that have sparked an increased interest in eye gaze in interaction in recent years, with a particular focus on unobtrusive eye-tracking.

2.   Eye-tracking in interaction

Getting a fine-grained picture of the different participants' gaze behavior in ongoing interaction is a complex methodological issue, and in fact has been a challenge that has refrained researchers for a long time from doing empirical research on this topic. As an illustration, the above-mentioned pioneering study by Kendon (1967) was based on first-acquaintance face-to-face interactions and made use of a set-up with one camera and a mirror so that both participants' eye gaze could be captured simultaneously. The analysis of such data is a painstaking task that requires the estimation of gaze behavior on a (milli)second-by-(milli)second basis. This may, at least in part, be the reason why there is a significant gap in the empirical literature after the early studies by Kendon, Argyle & Cook and Goodwin. But how, then, was the interest of linguists and psycholinguists sparked again after more than two decades of relative 'radio silence'? A possible explanation may, in fact, be found in technological innovations that have fueled the field of multimodal interaction analysis. And these innovations pertain to both hardware and software solutions.

The example of Kendon's study with the complex camera constellation is illustrative of early struggles with recording equipment. With the availability of compact, high-definition camera systems it has become substantially easier to record slices of face-to-face interaction from multiple camera angles, the combination of which allows for the analysis of multiple participants' eye gaze patterns. In fact, several video corpus projects aiming at the disclosure of spoken interaction data have adopted such a multi-angle approach, with either a speaker or a scene-oriented focus. In a speaker-oriented design, the primary focus is on capturing the individual speakers in as much detail as possible, whereas in a scene-oriented setting, the cameras are set up in such a way that the analyst can obtain a 360° perspective on the interactional landscape. For the study of eye gaze in interaction, most notably the speaker-oriented design may be fruitful. Examples of such speaker-oriented multi-angle corpora are the Nottingham Multimodal Corpus (NMMC corpus, and more specifically the data recorded as part of the HeadTalk project, Knight et al., 2008, 2009), the Spontal Corpus of Swedish dialogues (Edlund et al., 2010) and the IFADV corpus of Dutch two-party interactions (Van Son et al., 2008). In the case of IFADV, the corpus has, in fact, been annotated for the gaze direction of the participants and these annotations are made freely available for research purposes.

Some of the recent multimodally oriented research in conversation analysis investigates eye gaze based on high-quality video data. These data are then transcribed in great detail, including information on the different participants' gaze direction. Studies in this field include the above-mentioned work by Rossano on sequence organization (Rossano, 2010, 2012b), and Oloff's work on overlapping talk and withdrawal in conversation (Oloff, 2012, 2013), among others. Despite the potential of modern camera equipment and the availability of datasets with annotated gaze information, studying gaze behavior only on the basis of such 'external' video data of a participant's face is still problematic for specific research questions. The main issue is that external video data only allow for gaze target estimations and cannot pinpoint the exact focus of attention (this issue was raised among others by Kendon, 2004, Paggio et al., 2010, Streeck, 2009). In addition, video data alone do not provide information on more subtle eye movements that may have interactional relevance as well, such as short moments of gaze aversion (Weiß & Auer, 2016, Brône et al., 2017) and specific visual scan paths (Pfeiffer & Weiß, 2017). To overcome this issue of accuracy and reliability, researchers increasingly rely on unobtrusive forms of eye-tracking to track participants' gaze behavior during face-to-face conversation. The exact type of eye-tracking that is used, and tied to this the type of interaction that is being recorded, may differ significantly, as we will describe in the following.

The methodological paradigm of eye-tracking has a long-standing tradition in the fields of psychology and psycholinguistics, where it has been used for questions relating to the cognitive processing and production of language for more than fifty years (for overviews see Rayner, 1998, Duchowski, 2007, Kreysa & Pickering, 2011 and other chapters in Liversedge, et al. 2011). Traditional lab-based eye-tracking equipment allows for studies on eye movements as a measure of cognitive processing on the part of an individual cognizer (who is given a particular stimulus, e.g. a text or image), but given its relatively obtrusive nature (e.g. participants are in a fixed head position while performing experimental tasks), it is not particularly suited for studying eye gaze in interactional settings. Only with the advent of unobtrusive eye-tracking technology, this field of inquiry has opened up. Based on the specific type of eye-tracking equipment being used (and test design being implemented), two main settings can be distinguished (both of which are represented in this volume): mediated interactions recorded using remote eye-tracking systems and face-to-face interaction recorded using mobile eye-tracking systems (typically eye-tracking glasses or table-top eye-trackers).

In the case of mediated interactions, the recordings typically involve collaborative tasks that participants perform on a computer, which not only record the participant's own gaze behavior on the screen, but may also provide real-time information on the other participant's current gaze fixation (see e.g. Bailly et al., 2010, this volume; Barisic et al., 2013; Neider et al., 2010; Brennan et al., 2012; Broz et al., 2012). This specific interactional design allows for experimental control and provides a solid method for measuring gaze coordination in natural collaborative tasks. The specific set-up of two remote eye-tracking devices used for interactive tasks has been referred to as the *dual eye-tracking paradigm* and has generated a significant body of studies (DUET, see Clark & Gergle, 2011 for an overview). Next to the more controlled mediated settings, a small but steadily growing body of research has applied mobile eye-tracking devices to real face-to-face interactions, either with table top eye-tracking devices (Jokinen et al., 2009, Jokinen, 2010) or with eye-tracking glasses (Holler & Kendrick, 2015; Brône & Oben, 2015; Oben & Brône, 2015; Jehoul et al., 2017; Oben, this volume; Weiß & Auer, 2016, Auer, this volume; Stukenbrock, 2015, this volume; Vranjes et al., this volume; Pfeiffer & Renner, this volume). In these studies, the experimental control is often minimal, with participants in dyadic (Oben & Brône, Oben, Pfeiffer & Renner) or triadic interactions (Holler & Kendrik, Weiß & Auer, Jokinen, Vranjes, Auer) engaging in unscripted dialogues. Only a few studies apply this 'multifocal' eye-tracking paradigm in another interactional configuration than the prototypical F-formation of face-to-face interactions (Kendon, 1990). Stukenbrock (2015, this volume) studies dyads, among others, while they are jointly shopping on a market or searching for a book in a library, which not only involves moments of side-by-side constellation (rather than face-to-face) but also a much more dynamic interactional space (with the moving interactants). In a similar vein, Auer (2017) studies pairs of participants while they 'walk and talk', with a specific focus on the interactional role of eye gaze in managing potential obstacles in the dyad's trajectory.

With the more free-range or unscripted face-to-face interactions that are increasingly being collected with mobile eye-tracking systems comes an additional challenge, though. In comparison to external video camera data, scholars no longer need to rely on gaze target estimations (supra), but now they are confronted with a continuous data stream on the participants' gaze distribution in interaction. The output of most mobile eye-tracking systems consists of a video file in which the output of an integrated scene camera is combined with gaze coordinates (represented as a gaze cursor in the video output). But how do we take this information and implement it as part of a multimodal account of eye gaze in interaction? In many of the above-mentioned studies, the gaze information is either treated as an annotation layer among other semiotic channels that are coded (e.g. in annotation software such as ELAN (Wittenburg et al., 2006) or ANVIL (Kipp, 2014)) or is included as part of a rich transcription in the tradition of conversation analysis. In either case, the transfer from the 'raw data' generated by the eye-tracking systems into analyzable data sets for systematic analysis still is a time-consuming undertaking. As a consequence, most studies are based on relatively small data sets, especially in comparison to current practices in corpus linguistics.

One way of dealing with this manual annotation load is to introduce (semi-)automatic annotation practices, based on image processing techniques. De Beugher et al. (2015, 2016, this volume) introduce an attempt at such a system, combining detection algorithms to determine relevant regions of interest on which gaze coordinates can be mapped. More specifically, the system takes the images generated by the scene camera of a mobile eye-tracker and runs a basic semi-automatic annotation for relevant body parts of persons appearing in the video.[1] These include face detection, hand detection, position of hands in gesture space, and basic hand motion features. The resulting annotations can then be mapped onto the gaze coordinates generated by the eye-tracker and can be exported for further analysis in annotation software or other tools. Pfeiffer et al. (this volume) present a method for automatically annotating gaze targets in a more experimental (but nevertheless face-to-face) setting in which participants were involved in a collaborative figure identification task. Their tool, called EyeSee3D, is based on computer vision techniques as well as augmented reality technology and essentially construes a model of the environment as a 3D situation model on which experimental stimuli (in this case small toy figures) as well as gaze information can be mapped.

What this brief overview shows, is that there is a growing and multidisciplinary interest in applying eye-tracking to the study of face-to-face interaction. With the rapid development of eye-tracking systems towards versatile and user-friendly (almost plug-and-play) recording systems, as well as the first attempts at (semi-) automatic annotation support, it is to be expected that the community of researchers using eye-tracking technology for interaction research will expand in the years to come. However, to date there is no publication that brings together the different strands of research in this strongly multidisciplinary program. The present volume is an attempt at filling this gap and is thus envisioned as an 'innovating reader', which addresses key questions of interdisciplinary relevance (e.g. to what extent can the analysis of fine-grained eye gaze data, obtained with eye-tracking technology, inform conversation analysis, and vice versa?), positioning (e.g. what is the semiotic status of eye gaze in relation to linguistic signaling?), and methodology (e.g. can we strike a balance between experimental control and authenticity in setting up dialogue settings with eye-tracking technology?). The exploration of these and other

---

1. The semi-automatic aspect of the procedure resides in the fact that (a) the user needs to manually pinpoint the hands of a person when he/she first appears in a recording, after which the automatic annotation is started, and (b) the system requires manual confirmation or correction if a certain confidence threshold for the automatic annotation has not been reached.

questions contributes to the demarcation of a burgeoning research program. In the following section, we describe how the volume is structured in order to provide a state-of-the-art of the field.

3.   Outline of the volume

The volume is subdivided into three major parts, each of which deals with particular aspects of the multidisciplinary endeavour of eye-tracking in interaction. The first part centers around theoretical considerations on the status of eye gaze in multimodal interaction. The chapters in this section present overviews of existing work on eye gaze in interaction, with a specific focus on its relationship with other semiotic modes such as speech and gesture. In addition, this section zooms in on considerations on how eye-tracking technology can feed into existing theoretical accounts of interaction (including conversation analysis, cognitive science, and human-computer interaction). The second part has a stronger methodological focus on data collection and processing. The chapters in this section present either a comparative analysis of data collection techniques (e.g. controlled tasks vs. free-range interaction; mediated vs. face-to-face) or technical solutions that may facilitate post-processing and annotation. The third section presents a representative sample of case studies in which eye-tracking is used in different ways and in different interactional settings. In this sense, this section presents illustrations of the considerations in the previous sections, based on empirical analysis. Thus, although the volume is subdivided into three thematically motivated parts, there is a strong cross-section interaction.

Part 1: Theoretical considerations

In the first chapter of this volume, Amati and Brennan consider the contribution of eye gaze to recognizing intentions and coordinating joint action in spatial contexts. They discuss evidence about how observers use gaze cues (whether interactively or non-interactively) in contexts where they can see the gazer's face, as well as during remote electronic communication via a shared gaze system where each partner's gaze is represented to the other by a dynamic cursor displayed over a shared screen. This overview tries to reveal how decoding human intentions from eye gaze can be virtually effortless in spontaneous social interaction, explicitly informative about cognition and perception in experimental contexts, and quite challenging in the implementation in human-machine interaction.

In a second chapter, Knoeferle, Kreysa and Pickering discuss the role of speaker gaze on a listener's language processing, short-term memory for new information, and child language learning. Speaker gaze appears to facilitate the listener's performance in all of these domains, which suggests that it plays an important role in communication. Indeed, many findings indicate that speaker gaze can facilitate not just referential but also compositional processes such as syntactic structuring and thematic role assignment. Its effects on adult short-term memory appear weaker: gaze seems to rapidly guide attention and enhances immediate but not long-lasting semantic memory. In addition, a speaker's gaze between a caregiver and child is beneficial for language learning. These observations converge the evidence that speaker gaze effects are important for both language processing and learning, and are potentially boosted in a socially interactive context.

Third, Dale and Spivey review a range of findings that show how eye movements (and other body movements) exhibit correlated behaviour across two or more people during natural interactions. The authors synthesise these different results into a more general account of how people's cognitive, sensory and motor systems become coordinated with one another during natural dialogue. They argue that treating conversational partners as parts of one integrated system is a useful explanatory strategy for understanding interaction. Eye-tracking, alongside many other tools to measure the complexity of multimodal behaviour, can assist in empirically underpinning such, quite radical, theory development.

In the final chapter of this section, Crocker and Staudte present work that has investigated he role of speaker gaze for language comprehension. A first issue they address is whether this role is unique to gaze. Secondly, they distinguish between the role and effects of speaker gaze and listener gaze. Speakers tend to fixate objects they are about to mention, while listeners inspect those objects they believe to be the intended referents of the speaker. These production- and comprehension-contingent gaze behaviours appear to further form an integral part of the signal itself, making it inherently reciprocal: listeners monitor speaker gaze for intended referents. Listener gaze, in turn, allows speakers to exploit it and enhance communicative success.

Part 2: Methodological considerations

Section 2 unites contributions with a focus on methodological innovations from which research on eye gaze in an interactional setting might benefit. First, Pfeiffer and Renner demonstrate ways of measuring and representing gesture and gaze behaviour in 3D space. Using motion capturing to measure participants' movements, they have developed tools to represent deictic gestures using pointing rays or to represent gesture space using 3D heat maps. More relevant to this volume, the authors exemplify how they automatically annotated fixations on predefined objects. Their annotation method, EyeSee3D, first generates a 3D situation model of the items present in the visual field (in their case e.g. LEGO figures) and then uses the information from the eye-tracker to automatically annotate which items participants are fixating. The fact that this method works in real-time is a feat that allows for actual interaction between human and computer or for assistive systems that provide help based on real-time gaze behaviour.

Second, Bailly, Mihoub, Wolf and Elisei demonstrate how gaze patterns correlate with the cognitive states of the interlocutors (speaking, listening, thinking), their respective roles in the conversation (instruction giver, respondent) and their social relationship (colleague, supervisor). This information is then modelled into conversational agents and the authors provide evidence of how a meticulous design of gaze behaviour in those agents is crucial for the communicative efficiency between human and computer.

Finally, De Beugher et al. discuss a model for the (semi-)automatic annotation of mobile eye-tracking data based on computer vision techniques. On the basis of a number of case studies they highlight the possibilities and limitations of using object recognition algorithms to automate the tedious process of analysing mobile eye-tracking data. To maximally fit in with the topic of this volume they zoom in on the automatic recognition of the human body and its relevant articulators (head, torso, arms, hands). Taking several data sets that were manually coded as ground truth, they show the reliability of their tool and discuss various output formats for their annotations (e.g. fixations on a timeline, ELAN-files and CSV-files).

Part 3: Case studies

In the third section we present a number of case studies in which eye gaze during face-to-face interaction is key. In a first contribution, Auer focusses on addressee selection and turn-taking in three-party interaction. His data suggest that gaze is a powerful tool in managing next-speakership: the addressee that a speaker is focussing on at the end of a TCU (turn constructional unit) will be the most likely next speaker, especially when co-occurring with a long silence after the TCU. However ubiquitous this 'next-speaker-selection-by-gaze' may be, the cases where a participant takes the floor even though he was not being looked at towards the end of the current speaker's TCU do not seem to violate any rules in the turn-taking machinery. In this vein, the status of gaze in turn-taking should be treated as inviting rather than an obliging technique for next-speaker selection.

The second chapter in this section demonstrates the role gaze might have in behaviour at another multimodal level, viz. alignment (or copying behaviour) of hand gestures and lexical items. In a corpus of dyadic interactions Oben demonstrates that gaze behaviour affects alignment behaviour differently at the lexical than at the gestural level: if a speaker is looking at an addressee's face while uttering a target word, this significantly increases the probability that the addressee will use that same word later in the conversation. If a speaker is looking at an addressee's face while performing a target gesture, there is no correlation with subsequent gesture production by that addressee. However, if an addressee looked at a gesture made by a speaker, this gesture was significantly more often used by that addressee later in the conversation (compared to situations in which the addressee was not looking at that gesture).

Third, Stukenbrock discusses the role of eye gaze in deictic referencing by using eye-tracking data recorded during every-day activities (e.g. visiting a market or a library). The author provides detailed analyses on gaze practices in deictic reference from a conversational-analytical perspective and points out that deictic reference in face-to-face interaction occurs systematically at specific moments in the accomplishment of joint attention. More specifically, three relevant types of establishing joint attention are distinguished:

i.   the object-eye link: both speaker and addressee are looking at the same object
ii. the gesture-eye link: the addressee is looking at the speaker's deictic gesture
iii. the eye-eye link: addressee and speaker are looking at each other, mutually signalling the referent has been found

In the final chapter, Vranjes, Bot, Feyaerts and Brône focus on listeners' multimodal displays of recipiency in a naturally occurring interpreter-mediated psychotherapeutic interaction. Because the primary interlocutors have no or limited access to each other's languages they have to rely on the interpreter and other modalities for the successful accomplishment of the social action. The authors show that backchannel signals are found on different levels of communication and that multimodal feedback patterns exist between the interpreter and the two primary speakers, but also between the primary participants themselves. For example, gestural feedback signals by the interpreter (e.g. head nods or smiles) often co-occur with mutual gaze between interpreter and patient, and therapists use gaze to establish intersubjective ground between themselves and the patient (even though they do not understand each other).

References

Argyle, M. & Cook, M. (1976). *Gaze and mutual gaze*. London: Cambridge University Press.

Auer, P. (2017). Walking and talking. How speakers jointly manoeuvre in space. Invited talk at the international conference on "Spatial Boundaries and Transitions in Language and Interaction". Monte Veritá, April 2017.

Bailly, G., Raidt, S. & Elisei, F. (2010). Gaze, conversational agents and face-to-face communication. *Speech Communication* – special issue on Speech and Face-to-Face Communication 52, 598–612. https://doi.org/10.1016/j.specom.2010.02.015

Barisic, I., Timmermans, B., Pfeiffer, U., Bente, G., Vogeley, K., & Schilbach, L. (2013). In it together: using dual eyetracking to investigate real-time social interactions. Presented at the Proceedings from SIGCHI Conference on Human Factors in Computing Systems, Paris.

Bavelas, J. B., L. Coates & T. Johnson. (2002). Listener responses as a collaborative process: The role of gaze. *Journal of Communication*, 52, 566–580. https://doi.org/10.1111/j.1460-2466.2002.tb02562.x

Brennan, S. E. (2005). How conversation is shaped by visual and spoken evidence. In J. C. Trueswell & M. Tanenhaus (Eds.), *Approaches to studying world-situated language use: Bridging the language-as-product and language-action traditions* (pp. 95–129). Cambridge, MA: MIT Press.

Brennan S. E., Chen X., Dickinson C., Neider M. & Zelinsky G. (2008). Coordinating cognition: The costs and benefits of shared gaze during collaborative search. *Cognition*, 106, 1465–1477. https://doi.org/10.1016/j.cognition.2007.05.012

Brennan, S. E., Hanna J., Zelinsky G. & Savietta, K. (2012). Eye gaze cues for coordination in collaborative tasks. *Proceedings of the DUET Workshop*. Seattle, Feb. 2012.

Brône, G. & Oben, B. (2015). InSight Interaction. A multimodal and multifocal dialogue corpus. *Language Resources and Evaluation*, 49, 195–214. https://doi.org/10.1007/s10579-014-9283-2

Brône, G., Oben, B. & Feyaerts, K. (2010). Introducing the InSight Interaction Corpus. *Proceedings of the 7th International Conference on Language Resources and Evaluation*. Workshop on Multimodal Corpora. Malta, 17–18 May 2010.

Brône, G., Oben, B., Vranjes, J., Feyaerts, K. (2017). Eye gaze and viewpoint in multimodal interaction management. *Cognitive Linguistics*, 28, 449–483.

Broz, F. et al. (2012). Mutual gaze, personality, and familiarity: Dual eye-tracking during conversation. *Proceedings of HRI 2012*.

Clark, A. T., & Gergle, D. (2011). Mobile Dual Eye-tracking Methods: Challenges and Opportunities. *Paper presented at DUET 2011: Dual Eye Tracking workshop at ECSCW 2011*.

Clark, H. H. (1996). *Using language*, Cambridge: Cambridge University Press. https://doi.org/10.1017/CBO9780511620539

De Beugher, S., Brône, G., Goedemé, T. (2016). Semi-automatic Hand Annotation Making Human-human Interaction Analysis Fast and Accurate. In J. Braz (Ed.), *Proceedings of the 11th Joint Conference on Computer Vision, Imaging and Computer Graphics Theory and Applications: Vol. 4*. VISIGRAPP. Rome,Italy, 27–29 February 2016 (pp. 552–559). Setúbal: Scitepress.

De Beugher, S., Brône, G., Goedemé, T. (2015). Semi-automatic annotation of eye-tracking recordings in terms of human torso, face and hands. In T. Pfeiffer & K. Essig (Eds.), *SAGA 2015 Proceedings*. International Workshop on Solutions for Automatic Gaze Data Analysis. Bielefeld, Germany, 29–30 September 2015. Bielefeld, Germany: CITEC.

De Jaegher, H., Di Paolo, E. & Gallagher, S. (2010). Can social interaction constitute social cognition? *Trends in Cognitive Sciences*, 14(10), 441–447. https://doi.org/10.1016/j.tics.2010.06.009

De Ruiter, J. P. (2005). The role of eye-gaze in visual dialogue tasks. Paper presented at the AMLaP, Ghent, Belgium.

Duncan, S. (1975). Interaction units during speaking turns in dyadic, face-to-face conversations. In A. Kendon, R. M. Harris & M. R. Key (Eds.), *Organization of behavior in face-to-face Interaction* (pp. 199–212). The Hague: Mouton. https://doi.org/10.1515/9783110907643.199

Duchowski, A. (2007). *Eye tracking methodology. Theory and practice.* London: Springer.

Edlund, J., Beskow, J., Elenius, K., Hellmer, K., Strömbergsson, S., House, D. (2010). Spontal: a Swedish spontaneous dialogue corpus of audio, video and motion capture. In: Proceedings of the Seventh International Conference on Language Resources and Evaluation (LREC)

Emery, N. J. (2000). The eyes have it: The neuroethology, function and evolution of social gaze. *Neuroscience and Biobehavioral Reviews*, 24, 581–604. https://doi.org/10.1016/S0149-7634(00)00025-7

Feyaerts, K., Brône, G. & Oben, B. (2017). Multimodality in Interaction. In: B. Dancygier (Ed.), *The Cambridge handbook of cognitive linguistics* (pp. 135–156). Cambridge: Cambridge University Press.

Frischen, A., Bayliss, A. P., & Tipper, S. P. (2007). Gaze cueing of attention: Visual attention, social cognition, and individual differences. *Psychological Bulletin*, 133, 694–724. https://doi.org/10.1037/0033-2909.133.4.694

Goffman, E. (1981). *Forms of talk.* Philadelphia: University of Pennsylvania Press.

Goodwin, C. (1980). Restarts, pauses, and the achievement of a state of mutual gaze. *Sociological Inquiry*, 272–302. https://doi.org/10.1111/j.1475-682X.1980.tb00023.x

Goodwin, C. (1981). *Conversational organization. Interaction between speakers and hearers.* New York, London.

Goodwin, M. H. & Goodwin, C. (1986). Gesture and co-participation in the activity of searching for a word. *Semiotica*, 62(1/2). 51–75.

Gullberg, M. & Holmqvist, K. (2006). What speakers do and what addressees look at. Visual attention to gestures in human interaction live and on video. *Pragmatics & Cognition*, 14, 53–82. https://doi.org/10.1075/pc.14.1.05gul

Gullberg, M. & Kita, S. (2009). Attention to speech-accompanying gestures: Eye movements and information uptake. *Journal of Nonverbal Behaviour*, 33, 251–277. https://doi.org/10.1007/s10919-009-0073-2

Hanna, J. & Brennan, S. (2007). Speakers' eye gaze disambiguates referring expressions early during face-to-face conversation. *Journal of Memory and Language*, 57, 596–615. https://doi.org/10.1016/j.jml.2007.01.008

Hirvenkari, L., Ruusuvuori, J., Saarinen, V. -M., Kivioja, M. & Peräkylä, A. (2013). Influence of turn-taking in a two-person conversation on the gaze of a viewer. *PLoS ONE* 8(8). https://doi.org/10.1371/journal.pone.0071569

Holler, J. & Kendrick, K. (2015). Unaddressed participants' gaze in multi-person interaction: Optimizing recipiency. *Frontiers in Psychology*, 6, 98. https://doi.org/10.3389/fpsyg.2015.00098

Jehoul, A., Brône, G., Feyaerts, K. (2017/forthcoming). Gaze distribution during fillers: empirical data on the difference between Dutch 'euh' and 'euhm'. In: P. Paggio et al. (eds.), *Proceedings of the MMSYM Symposium '16*.

Jokinen, K. (2010). Non-verbal signals for turn-taking & feedback. *Proceedings of the 7th International Conference on Language Resources & Evaluation (LREC)*.

Jokinen, K., Nishida, M. & Yamamoto, S. (2009). Eye gaze experiments for conversation monitor-ing. In: *Proceedings of the 3rd International Universal Communication Symposium*.

Kendon, A. (1967). Some functions of gaze-direction in social interaction. *Acta Psychologica*, 26, 22–63. https://doi.org/10.1016/0001-6918(67)90005-4

Kendon A. (1990). *Conducting interaction: Patterns of behavior in focused encounters*. Cambridge: Cambridge University Press, 1990.

Kendon, A. (2004). *Gesture: Visible action as utterance*. Cambridge: Cambridge University Press. https://doi.org/10.1017/CBO9780511807572

Kipp, M. (2014). ANVIL: A universal video research tool. In: J. Durand, U. Gut & G. Kristofferson (Eds.), *Handbook of corpus phonology* (pp. 420–443). Oxford: Oxford University Press.

Knight, D., Evans, D., Carter R. & Adolphs, S. (2009). HeadTalk, HandTalk and the corpus: towards a framework for multi-modal, multi-media corpus development. *Corpora*, 4: 1–32. https://doi.org/10.3366/E1749503209000203

Knight, D., Adolphs, S., Tennent, P. & Carter, R. (2008). The Nottingham multimodal corpus: a demonstration. In: Proceedings of the Sixth International Conference on Language Resources and Evaluation (LREC).

Kreysa, H. & Pickering, M. (2011). Eye movements and dialogue. In S. Liversedge, D. Gilchrist & S. Everling (Eds.), *The Oxford Handbook of Eye Movements* (pp. 943–959). Oxford: Oxford University Press.

Lachat, F., Conty, L., Hugueville, L. & George, N. (2012). Gaze cueing effect in a face-to-face sit-uation. *Journal of Nonverbal Behavior*, 36, 177–190. https://doi.org/10.1007/s10919-012-0133-x

Linell, P. (2009). *Rethinking language, mind and world dialogically: Interactional and contextual theories of human sense-making*. Charlotte, NC: Information Age Publishing.

Liversedge, D., Gilchrist, I. & Everling, S. (Eds.). (2011). *The Oxford handbook of eye movements*. Oxford: Oxford University Press. https://doi.org/10.1093/oxfordhb/9780199539789.001.0001

Müller, C. et al. (Eds.). (2013). *Body – Language – Communication. An international handbook on multimodality in human interaction*. Vol. 1. Berlin: Mouton de Gruyter.

Müller, C. et al. (Eds.). (2014). *Body – Language – Communication. An international handbook on multimodality in human interaction*. Vol. 2. Berlin: Mouton de Gruyter.

Neider, M., Chen, X., Dickinson, C., Brennan, S. & Zelinsky, G. (2010). Coordinating spatial referencing using shared gaze. *Psychonomic Bulletin & Review*, 17, 718–724. https://doi.org/10.3758/PBR.17.5.718

Novick, D. G., Hansen, B. & Ward, K. (1996). Coordinating turn-taking with gaze. *ICSLP*, 3, 1888–1891.

Oben, B. (2015). Modelling interactive alignment. A multimodal and temporal account. KU Leuven, unpublished PhD dissertation.

Oben, B. & Brône, G. (2015). What you see is what you do. On the relationship between gaze and gesture in multimodal alignment. *Language and Cognition* 7 (4), 546–556. https://doi.org/10.1017/langcog.2015.22

Oertel, C., Wlodarczak, M., Edlund, J., Wagner, P. & Gustafson, J. (2012). Gaze patterns in turn-taking. *Proceedings of Interspeech 2012*.

Oloff, F. (2012). Withdrawal from turns in overlap and participation. In P. Bergmann, J. Brenning, M. Pfeiffer & E. Reber (Eds.), *Prosody and embodiment in interactional grammar* (pp. 207–236). Berlin/Boston: De Gruyter. https://doi.org/10.1515/9783110295108.207

Oloff, F. (2013). Embodied withdrawal after overlap resolution. *Journal of Pragmatics*, 46, 139–156. https://doi.org/10.1016/j.pragma.2012.07.005

Paggio, P., Allwood, J., Ahlsén, E., Jokinen, K. & Navarretta, C. (2010). The NOMCO Multimodal Nordic Resource – Goals and characteristics. In: Proceedings of LREC 2010. Valletta, Malta.

Pfeiffer, M. & Weiß, C. (2017). Speaker gaze during descriptions and reenactments in storytelling. Paper presented at *15th International Pragmatics Conference*. Belfast, 16–21 July 2017.

Pickering, M. & Garrod, S. (2004). Toward a mechanistic psychology of dialogue. *Behavioral and Brain Sciences*, 27, 169–226. https://doi.org/10.1017/S0140525X04000056

Pickering, M. & Garrod, S. (2006). Alignment as basis for successful communication. *Research on Language & Computation*, 203–228. https://doi.org/10.1007/s11168-006-9004-0

Posner, M. I., Snyder, C. R., Davidson, B. J. (1980). Attention and the detection of signals. *Journal of Experimental Psychology*, 109, 160–174. https://doi.org/10.1037/0096-3445.109.2.160

Postma-Nilsenova, M., Brunninkhuis, N. & Postma, E. (2013). Eye gaze affects vocal intonation mimicry. *Proceedings of the Cognitive Science Society*, 35.

Rayner, K. (1998). Eye movements in reading and information processing: 20 years of research. *Psychological Bulletin*, 85, 618–660. https://doi.org/10.1037/0033-2909.85.3.618

Richardson, D. & Dale, R. (2005). Looking to understand: The coupling between speakers' and listeners' eye movements and its relationship to discourse comprehension. *Cognitive Science*, 29, 1045–1060. https://doi.org/10.1207/s15516709cog0000_29

Richardson, D., Dale, R. & Kirkham, N. (2007). The art of conversation is coordination. Common ground and the coupling of eye movements during dialogue. *Psychological Science*, 18, 407–413. https://doi.org/10.1111/j.1467-9280.2007.01914.x

Richardson, D., Dale, R. & Tomlinson, J. (2009). Conversation, gaze coordination & beliefs about context. *Cognitive Science*, 33, 1468–1482. https://doi.org/10.1111/j.1551-6709.2009.01057.x

Rossano, F. (2010). Questioning and responding in Italian. *Journal of Pragmatics*, 42, 2756–2771. https://doi.org/10.1016/j.pragma.2010.04.010

Rossano, F. (2012a). Gaze in conversation. In J. Sidnell & T. Stivers (Eds.), *The Handbook of Conversation Analysis* (pp. 308–329). Chichester: Wiley-Blackwell. https://doi.org/10.1002/9781118325001.ch15

Rossano, F. (2012b). Gaze behavior in face-to-face interaction. Nijmegen, The Netherlands: Max Planck Institute for Psycholinguistics unpublished dissertation.

Skantze, G., Hjalmarsson, A., & Oertel, C. (2014). Turn-taking, feedback and joint attention in situated human-robot interaction. *Speech Communication*, 65, 50–66.

Staudte, M. & Crocker, M. (2011). Investigating joint attention mechanisms through spoken human-robot interaction. *Cognition*, 120, 268–291. https://doi.org/10.1016/j.cognition.2011.05.005

Streeck, J. (2009). *Gesturecraft – The manufacture of meaning*. Amsterdam/Philadelphia: John Benjamins. https://doi.org/10.1075/gs.2

Streeck, J. (2014). Mutual gaze and recognition: Revisiting Kendon's 'Gaze direction in two-person conversation'", In M. Seyfeddinipur & M. Gullberg (Eds.), *From gesture in conversation to visible action as utterance: Essays in honor of Adam Kendon* (pp. 35–56). Amsterdam: John Benjamins.

Stukenbrock, A. (2015). *Deixis in der face-to-face Interaktion*. Berlin: Mouton De Gruyter.

Sweetser, E. & Stec, K. (2016). Maintaining multiple viewpoints with gaze. In B. Dancygier, L. Wei-Lun & A. Verhagen (Eds.), *Viewpoint and the fabric of meaning* (pp. 237–258). Berlin: Mouton de Gruyter.

Van Son, R., Wesseling, W., Sanders, E., Van Der Heuvel, H. (2008). The IFADV corpus: A free dialog video corpus. In: *Proceedings of the Sixth International rossanoConference on Language Resources and Evaluation (LREC)*.

Vertegaal, R. (1999). The GAZE Groupware system: Mediating joint attention in multiparty communication and collaboration. In: M. G. Williams & M. W. Altom (Eds.), *Proceedings of CHI'99* (pp. 294–301). Pittsburgh: ACM.

Wang, Y. & Neff, M. (2013). The Influence of Prosody on the Requirements for Gesture-Text Alignment. In R. Aylett, B. Krenn, C. Pelachaud & H. Shimodaira (Eds), *Intelligent Virtual Agents. IVA 2013. Lecture Notes in Computer Science*, vol 8108. Springer, Berlin, Heidelberg.

Weiß, C. & Auer, P. (2016). Das Blickverhalten des Rezipienten bei Sprecherhäsitationen: eine explorative Studie. *Gesprächsforschung*, 17, 132–167. http://www.gespraechsforschung-online.de/fileadmin/dateien/heft2016/ga-weiss.pdf.

Wittenburg, P., Brugman, H., Russel, A., Klassmann, A. & Sloetjes, H. (2006). ELAN: a Professional Framework for Multimodality Research. In: Proceedings of LREC 2006, Fifth International Conference on Language Resources and Evaluation.

Zima, E. & Brône, G. (2015). Cognitive Linguistics and interactional discourse: time to enter into dialogue. *Language and Cognition*, 7, 485–498. https://doi.org/10.1017/langcog.2015.19

PART 1

Theoretical considerations

CHAPTER 2

Eye gaze as a cue for recognizing intention and coordinating joint action

Franco Amati and Susan E. Brennan
Stony Brook University

People in conversation are highly sensitive to where others are looking. It has been argued that eye gaze is such a compelling social signal that following the gaze of another person is practically reflexive. Others have demonstrated that the role of gaze in interaction is more flexible. The direction of eye gaze can be informative about what a person is searching for, monitoring, orienting toward, referring to, deciding to choose, planning, or intending. But because it can signal all of these things (or none of them, as when attention is captured inadvertently by something sudden or salient), a look is often ambiguous. In this chapter, we consider the contributions of eye gaze to recognizing intentions and coordinating joint action in spatial contexts. To the extent that gazing at an object is instrumental to what the gazer is doing, a look can provide a window for an experimenter into the gazer's cognitive processing, a cue for an interacting partner about the gazer's intention, or a hint for a marketer about the gazer's preference or indecision. Patterns of looks can be interpreted by people engaged in perspective taking, or by automated pattern recognizers engaged in mind-reading. Finally, eye gaze has the potential to be deployed communicatively, as when one person intends that another recognize what she is attending to and use this information to coordinate their behavior. We discuss evidence about how observers use gaze cues (whether interactively or non-interactively) in contexts where they can see the gazer's face, as well as during remote electronic communication by way of a shared gaze system where each partner's gaze is represented to the other by a dynamic cursor displayed over a shared screen.

Keywords: gaze ambiguity, predictability of gaze, intention reading, coordinating behavior

1. Introduction

People in conversation are highly sensitive to where others are looking. Imagine the professor who glances surreptitiously at her watch during office hours; this may be enough to send a shy undergraduate student hurtling toward the door, apologizing for taking up so much time. For many, the intuition is strong that the eyes

https://doi.org/10.1075/ais.10.02ama

are a revealing cue. Eye gaze can be informative about what a person is searching for, monitoring, orienting toward, referring to, deciding to choose, planning, or intending. At the same time, because it can signal all these things (or none of them, as when attention is captured inadvertently by something sudden or salient), a look is often ambiguous. Despite eye gaze being such a noisy signal, people reliably use it to make inferences about the minds of others. In this chapter we discuss the use of gaze cues in non-social and social contexts, both face to face and remotely, in order to take the perspectives of others, to communicate intentions, and to predict behavior – in essence, to read people's minds. We start with examples from human development of the use of eye gaze both as an experimental measure and as a referential cue. The three sections after that discuss gaze as an automatic alerting cue, a cue to a gazer's intentions, and an instrumental cue that can enable an observer to identify what the gazer is doing. We cover the application of gaze monitoring to predicting people's choices, and then discuss how accurate human observers are at decoding the information available in gaze (or "mind reading"). We describe the use of gaze cues in communication, both face-to-face and in a prototype that displays partners' gaze cursors to each other remotely, *shared gaze*. Then we discuss some of the challenges in using gaze as an input signal to machines.

2.   Eye gaze as an interactional cue

2.1   Eye gaze as an output measure and an input cue in development

Eye gaze is a useful output measure for exploring early perception and cognition, as early as in infancy. The timing of gaze toward objects is related to children's developmental level and cognitive capacity; studies of cognitive development have long used preferential looking as a measure to understand how the perceptual system of an infant makes discriminations (e.g., Fantz, 1965; Spelke, 1990). For example, a change in direction of gaze can indicate that a child has perceived a change in the environment, such as a difference between two speech sounds (Jusczyk & Aslin, 1995); gaze duration can indicate that the child's expectation about an action or event has been violated (Baillargeon, Spelke, Wasserman, 1985; Onishi & Baillargeon, 2005). Perhaps paradoxically, an infant's looks toward an object can indicate either that the object is *familiar* or that the object is *novel*, depending on previous experience (e.g., whether the infant has already habituated to the object, Hunter & Ames, 1988). That is, the infant may have pre-existing preferences or pre-experiment exposures that should be carefully considered when determining whether a particular gaze result should be interpreted as a preference for something familar, or an attraction to novelty. Familiarity should be well controlled in studies of looking behavior, whether of infants or adults (Houston-Price & Nakai, 2004). Moreover, it is important to repeatedly measure patterns of looking to see if they change as a result of testing conditions (Hunter & Ames, 1988). Interpretation of eye gaze as a cognitive measure depends on the context; when context is carefully staged, relatively naturalistic studies of looking behavior yield simple measures of visual attention that, even in young children, can provide interpretable evidence about cognitive processing that psychologists would otherwise not have access to if they had to rely solely on verbal or motor responses.

Infants find the eye gaze of others to be a compelling input cue. As young as 10 weeks old, infants are faster to orient toward a target preceded by a face whose gaze has just shifted toward the target rather than shifting away (Hood, Willen, & Driver, 1998). They can follow gaze direction by 18 months, expecting gaze to terminate at an object (Doherty, 2006). Young children learn their early words as they interact with others and achieve a joint focus of attention on objects of interest (Baldwin, 1995; Tomasello, 1995). They quickly learn that if they see a person looking at something, there is a good chance the person wants the thing they are looking at; their understanding of others' desires precedes their understanding of beliefs (Wellman & Wooley, 1990). By age 3, most children begin to appreciate that others have beliefs and that these may or may not be the same as their own, although they may not be able to reliably represent others' false beliefs until a year or two later (Astington & Gopnik, 1991; Apperly & Butterfill, 2009; Doherty, 2006). Together, these component abilities form the foundation for the development of perspective taking (Baron-Cohen, 1995; Bakti, Baron-Cohen, Wheelright, Connelen, & Ahluwalia, 2000).

2.2   Eye gaze as an alerting cue

Adults can reliably use both gaze and non-gaze cues to anticipate spatially presented stimuli. Early spatial attention paradigms (following Posner, 1980; Posner & Cohen, 1984) required observers to fixate on a point in the center of a screen with an empty box on each side. One box was then highlighted or else a dot was presented in one of the boxes as either a valid or an invalid (misleading) alerting cue, followed by a target appearing on the left or the right; the observer responded to the target upon detecting it. Alternatively, a central arrow served as the anticipatory cue. Response times to the targets were faster for validly cued trials than invalidly cued trials (Posner, 1980). The valid cues in Posner (1980) that appeared in the same spatial locations as the targets are considered to be exogenous cues (reflexive or bottom-up, driven by the stimulus; Frischen, Bayliss, & Tipper, 2007), whereas the central arrow cue is considered to be endogenous (top down, or volitional; ibid).

Posner's paradigm was adapted to use another deictic (pointing) cue consisting of a schematic face with left- or right-oriented eyes instead of arrows. This manipulation led to strong cueing effects that were interpreted as an ability to follow social gaze (Driver, Davis, Ricciardelli, Kidd, Maxwell, & Baron-Cohen, 1999; Friesen & Kingstone, 1998; Langton & Bruce, 2000). This *gaze following effect* was presumed to be automatic, in part because it was found even when people know that the gaze cues are entirely non-predictive of where a target will appear (and in fact even when targets are *less* likely to appear in that direction; Driver et al., 1999). Clearly, there is something very compelling about another person's eye gaze, even schematized representations of it; the gaze following effect emerges so strongly in experiments that it is claimed that people cannot help but follow gaze cues (Friesen & Kingstone, 1998; Bayliss, et al., 2010). The power of gaze has been assumed to be derived from its social origin (even though most experimental paradigms that are used to study gaze following lack social context).

While some studies have concluded that gaze following is automatic or reflexive, that may not always be the case. Gaze following may just *seem* to be automatic or reflexive in experimental tasks that rely on exogenously cued objects devoid of social context. That is, when a task is stripped of any intentional context and cued objects appear out of thin air, the situational demands may be such that an observer has no other choice but to follow the gaze direction of a disembodied face because that's simply all there is to do. In contrast, experiments that have examined both bottom-up (exogenous) and top-down (endogenous) effects of eye gaze on behavior favor an account where gaze-following is not always reflexive – that is, observing a shift in another person's direction of gaze need not force an overt orienting of the observer's attention.

2.3   Eye gaze as a cue to intentionality

Engaging in joint actions with other people (such as conversing, playing a team sport, or doing a collaborative task such as cleaning a house or loading a dishwasher together) requires coordinating with another person, and spontaneous coordination requires recognizing intentionality (Sebanz, et al., 2006).[1] Generally, people are good at determining whether or not overt actions are intentional (such as when they see another person reach toward an object, walk toward a door, point, etc.), and this

---

1.   In the meaning of *coordination*, we include contingent behaviors produced by interacting partners in the service of some goal, task, or joint action. These include not only convergent behavior such as *entrainment* in perspective taking, or even more unconsciously, *alignment*, but also *complementary* synchronized behaviors (such as *I'll search here while you search there* (Brennan et al., 2008).

is especially so for actions that they have experienced doing themselves (Romani, Cesari, Urgesi, Facchini, & Aglioti, 2003; Sebanz & Shiffrar, 2009; Shiffrar & Freyd, 1990). But many everyday actions occur instrumentally, so perceiving rapidly performed actions as intentional requires monitoring the details of such actions and making inferences about what a person is trying to do. To the extent that intentions are perceived as causing behavior, then intention recognition can be facilitated by reverse engineering that process (Baker, Saxe, & Tenenbaum, 2009; Dennet, 1987; Gopnik & Metlzhoff, 1997). From observations of the actions of others, inferences about relevant goals can be made and updated on-line as more and more information becomes available. If expectations are violated then predictions are revised (Wolpert, Doya, & Kawato, 2003; Frith & Frith, 2006). This process of "behavior reading" is how people (and some animals) come to accurately infer mental states from actions (Penn & Povinelli, 2007). So even though many social cues such as eye movements might convey intentions, people still have to learn how and when this real-time information is relevant.

Although goals can influence how people move their eyes, eye gaze, both in real life and in the lab, is a noisy behavior. It is not always clear when someone's eye gaze reflects his or her intention. Eyes signal to others what a person finds interesting in the environment, but it is well known that attention is not always under conscious control. Sometimes people look at things that have little to do with their actual intentions (see Henderson 2003 for review). Because the eyes quickly respond to exogenous cues, attention is captured involuntarily by salient aspects of the environment (Kuhn et al., 2008), as well as by sudden onsets (Abrams & Christ, 2003; Frischen et al., 2007). Not only can gaze be driven involuntarily by aspects of the spatial environment, but it can be driven by mental imagery of things that are not physically present, leading the eyes to move in meaningful ways while looking at nothing at all (Altmann, 2004; Altmann & Kamide, 2003; Ferriera, Apel, & Henderson, 2008; Spivey & Geng, 2001).

There are also times when people intentionally try *not* to look at something, rendering their eye movements difficult to interpret. What makes this possible is that people can direct attention covertly while keeping the eyes stationary enabling them to look at one thing, while still processing information from somewhere else. For example, in order to throw off an opponent, a basketball player may look away from a teammate, but still throw an accurate pass to that teammate (Sebanz & Schiffrar, 2009). Nonetheless, there are still many ways in which the eyes *do* reliably (and interpretably) map onto intention. When people are actively searching for particular objects or making choices between alternatives, their eye movements frequently align with their goals.

Thus, eye gaze opens a window onto intention, even if the mapping of looks to meanings can be ambiguous. But when is gaze actually *communicative* – a signal meant to be recognized by others as intentional? The philosopher of language Grice (1957) distinguished two types of meaning: *natural*, in the sense that *smoke means fire* (causal but not communicative), and *non-natural*, in the sense that a smoke *signal* can be produced with an intention to communicate, and recognized as such. The question arises about what sort of cue eye gaze should be considered to be. Gaze behavior seems to range from being entirely instrumental, as when it is shaped entirely by the need to perform a task, to being used intentionally such as when it displays attention or points in a direction expected to be recognized by a conversational partner. To count as communicative, a cue or signal must meet three criteria; (1) it must be informative, (2) the information in the cue must be recoverable by others, and (3) the cue should be flexible, that is, it should be flexibly shaped by its producer's intention (Brennan & Williams, 1995). Spoken utterances typically meet all three criteria, but other potentially communicative signals may be more ambiguous; for instance, a newborn baby's cry is informative to the parent about the baby's distress; but this is not a communicative signal intended to get a response out of the parent until the baby is older; parents of older children can tell the difference. The cue of eye gaze is ambiguous in the same way, in that it can be instrumental (e.g., as one searches for an object), communicative (e.g. as one deliberately points to an object one has found), or both. In the next sections, we will discuss the information available in gaze patterns, the ability of observers to decode such information, and the communicative use of eye gaze by interacting partners.

3.   Identifying tasks from eye movements

The task observers are instructed to do while viewing an image guides their patterns of eye movements (Yarbus, 1967). This claim inspired many to explore the potential for using eye movements as a window into a person's cognitive state or goals. It was established that different tasks generally change patterns of eye movements (Castelhano, Mack, & Henderson, 2009; DeAngelus & Pelz, 2009; Ballard & Hayhoe, 2009). This type of top-down effect exists not only in the visual cognition literature but also in the psycholinguistics literature, particularly in "visual world" studies, which examine how people process visual and auditory information together (e.g., Tanenhaus, Spivey-Knowlton, Eberhard, & Sedivy, 1995). The main finding in many of these studies is that patterns of gaze can be guided by the spoken utterances or narrative heard while viewing characters or a scene. For example, patterns of gaze over the same image differ depending on whether an observer is listening to spatial information expressed as fictive motion or non-figuratively (e.g., "the palm trees *run along* the highway" vs. "the palm trees *are next to* the highway"; Matlock & Richardson, 2004, p. 909). Observers look toward a character's face more often upon hearing a remark offensive to that character when they believe the character can hear the remark than when they believe the character cannot hear it (Crosby, Monin, & Richardson). Basically, a particular task or setting, or the words in a particular utterance, can change the pattern of gaze. The information that needs to be sampled from the visual environment is relevant to the extent that it helps accomplish the goal.

The demands of a task bias eye movements in measurable ways, and recently researchers have begun to systematically investigate whether eye movements can be used to identify the task a person is doing (Zelinsky, Peng, & Samaras, 2013; Haji-Abolhassani & Clark, 2014; Henderson, Shinkareva, Jing Wang, Luke, & Olejarczyk, 2013). Such investigation is sometimes called "reverse Yarbus", because it reverse-engineers the underlying mental state or goal from a pattern of eye movements. This data driven strategy involves examining both the spatial and temporal characteristics of gaze patterns that systematically differ depending upon the instructions (Mills, Hollingworth, Van der Stigchel, Hoffman, & Dodd, 2011). Naturally, this line of work leads to questions about how far the strategy of reverse inference could be pushed in order to decode more complex cognitive tasks, and by extension, the mental states that underlie them (Henderson et al., 2013; Greene, Liu, & Wolfe, 2012). Despite some doubt as to whether it is even possible to decode considerably different tasks from features of eye fixation patterns alone (Greene et al., 2012), recent studies employing machine learning techniques with data classifiers have been able to differentiate observers' tasks using gaze data (Borji & Itti, 2014; Kanan, et al., 2014; Henderson et al., 2013). In addition, patterns of eye blinks have been shown to be useful in distinguishing different types of activities, such as reading, talking, watching television, using tools, and solving problems (Ishimaru, Kunze, Kise, Weppner, Dengel, Lukowicz, & Bulling, 2014). These findings have opened up a host of potential applications and new questions about the usefulness of eye tracking for non-invasively classifying, diagnosing, and predicting many kinds of mental states.

4. **How gaze fixations reveal what people prefer:**
    Applications to predicting choices

Determining what a person is thinking, feeling, or wanting before they ultimately make a decision is the focus of many applied fields. Using eye movements to inform predictions about upcoming choices and other behavior is the aim of many researchers in advertising, marketing, web design, artificial intelligence, and human factors. From predicting whether or not a person will choose one product over another, to determining whether a person is distracted while driving, the use of eye tracking to "read minds" is becoming a reality. The following sections give examples of eye tracking research that is relevant to the question of how gaze fixations relate to choices and preferences.

One of the goals in the domain of marketing research is to understand how the way a buyer visually inspects a product predicts a decision to buy it. Knowing how preferences and knowledge interact with fixation patterns could shed light on how people weigh alternatives and make choices (Van der Lans, 2006; Chandon, Hutchinson, & Young, 2001). The more one knows about what draws consumers' attention, the better one can make such predictions. Generally it has been shown that product display location influences fixations; for example, products in the center of a display attract more attention (Atalay, Bodur, & Rosolofoarison, 2012). Also, consumers appear to dislike having too many or too few options to choose from, as shown by a pattern of many fixations and postponed choices (Reutskaja, Nagel, Camerer, & Rangel, 2011). First fixations are also shown to bias choices, though the first fixation itself is not necessarily indicative of the item that is valued the most. When the best or most highly valued products are positioned in good locations (i.e., visual sweet spots) there is a high likelihood of choosing these objects (Reutskaja, et al., 2011). It has also been found that when people are under time pressure to make choices about products, they shorten their fixation durations in order to increase the number of options that are sampled before making a choice (Suri & Monroe, 2003). So optimizing visual characteristics of product displays can influence the way people look at products, which in turn can influence their decisions.

Much is known about how eye movements reflect a person's decision process in forced choice situations. On preference-based tasks with multiple items to choose from, people tend to make more fixations on items that they end up choosing, to look at them first, and to look at them longer (Glaholt & Reingold, 2011, 2012; Glaholt, Wu, & Reingold, 2009; Pierters & Warlop, 1999; Russo & Leclerc, 1994). This means the gazer accumulates more evidence in favor of the chosen item (Krajbich & Rangel, 2011). Longer fixation durations on the first fixation are associated with a higher probability of choosing the item. Decision makers are more likely to fixate first on the alternative that they will end up choosing (Glaholt & Reingold, 2012), but only when they have previewed the alternatives ahead of time (Krajbach & Rangel, 2011).

Decision makers make repeated fixations on the same object before choosing it (Krajbich, Armel, & Rangel, 2010). The likelihood of fixating on the item that is ultimately chosen increases up until the decision is made (Simion & Shimojo, 2006; Glaholt & Reingold, 2009), because the more an observer looks at the item, the more they are able to tell whether they like it, and the more they like something, the more they look at it. This pattern of continually increasing gaze toward an eventual choice in a preference task is known as the "gaze cascade," (Shimojo, Simion,

Shimoho, & Scheier, 2003; Simion & Shimojo, 2006; Bee, Prendinger, Andre, & Ishizuka, 2006).

People are also very likely to fixate last on the item they end up choosing, immediately before choosing it (Krajbich & Rangel, 2011; Kramer, Lu, Camerer, & Rangel, 2012). But how reliably does the last fixation predict the final choice? Although final fixations are more likely to land on the chosen item than on a non-chosen item, this is not always the case. For example, people do not simply choose the last thing they look at if their subjective rating of another item is higher (Krajbich & Rangel, 2011). Particularly when prices for items are visible, a last fixation on a *non*-chosen item might occur if the person is considering the price (or some other attribute) and then ruling it out in favor of another option that they have readied themselves to choose (Krajbich et al., 2012). Whether final fixations coincide with selection depends on the task. In a search task, a final fixation on a target object is more or less instrumental (assuming that the target is unambiguous); however, for tasks with more subjective decision thresholds (such as personal preference), the final fixation is likely to be less predictive.

Computational models of gaze behavior and decision-making in consumer choice tasks consider the tendency to choose the last item fixated to be a final fixation *bias* (Krajbich, Armel, & Rangel, 2010), although calling it a bias suggests a sort of causality that may not be warranted. Before making a choice, people accumulate evidence about different items as they explore all the possible options. So it seems odd to consider the final fixation to be a source of bias after people have already taken time to examine the environment and are just a button-press away from making their choice.

To what extent can observers use a gazer's final fixation to predict the gazer's behavior? One limitation regarding the presumed utility of the final fixation is that it while it may be a useful cue in the laboratory, it would not be so useful for observers attempting to predict others' behavior in real time. By definition, the final fixation happens too close to the decision itself for it to have the kind of predictive power that is useful in the realm of social interaction. For some applications, particularly involving inferences about intentions, the value of a prediction is more likely to hinge on how *early* the prediction can be made. For example, when an athlete attempts to defend a goal in soccer or block a shot in basketball, it is most useful to consider the opponent's entire repertoire of behavior leading up to the final action to form the basis for a timely response (Tomeo, Cesari, Aglioti, & Urgesi, 2012; Sebanz & Shiffrar, 2009); otherwise the athlete runs the risk of being duped by a last-second deceptive cue. In situations that do not involve competition or time pressures, our athlete-observer could presumably wait a few more moments for the opponent's behavior to actually unfold. However, a choice like the impending release of a ball signals the end of an action; by then it is too late to do anything about it. In most domains there is no clear indication ahead of time that a fixation will be a final look, because it is a final look only if the choice immediately follows. In line with this idea, Foulsham and Lock (2015) modeled the features that human decoders use to predict preferences and found that while final fixations were strongly associated with preference, coding for final fixations did not improve prediction accuracy significantly above and beyond measuring proportion of fixations. Practically speaking, for most tasks in real-word contexts, waiting around to see what people look at last just before they perform an action is not the best strategy for mind reading.

Task instructions and individual differences in indecisiveness or achievement ability also have been shown to influence eye movements on decision-making tasks (Patalano, Juhasz, & Dice, 2010; Glaholt, Wu, & Reingold, 2010; Shimojo et al., 2003). The difficulty of making a choice also plays a role. This has been measured as the difference between subjective preference ratings of the preferred choice and next best item (Krajbich & Rangel, 2011). Furthermore, the extent to which choices require more deliberation can lead to different patterns of eye movements; the more time people are given to make their choice, the more fixations they make, the more re-fixations they make on the preferred item, and the more consistent their overall gaze behavior is from one trial to the next (Maughan, Gutnikov, & Stevens, 2007). These findings highlight the complex ways in which choice constraints, task design, personal preferences, and individual differences can relate to eye movement patterns.

We draw a distinction between the analysis of eye gaze patterns by machines or using algorithms, vs. the kind of mind reading one human being does about another in everyday social interactions. Clearly, a number of eye gaze variables are helpful in predicting preferences, identifying tasks, and recognizing intentions. First and last looks, proportions of fixations, dwell time, and gaze patterns (or "gaze signatures") are all very informative measures, and constitute the parameters that are often used when applying machine learning to an individual's eye gaze behavior in the laboratory – a form of data-driven mind reading. Relatively less is known about which characteristics of eye gaze are used by human observers to intuitively infer the mental states of other people in the world. For example, under what circumstances do people in conversation attend to where their partner looks first, recognize whether their partner looks there for a longer period of time than elsewhere, and recognize this as evidence that the partner wants or is referring to a particular object? We next focus on this issue as it arises in mind reading by people embedded in tasks and social contexts as well as mind reading by machines programmed to facilitate various human tasks.

5. Decoding other people's eye movements

People seem to engage in an intuitive form of mind reading with each social interaction that takes place. Mind reading to the extent that one person can recognize
another's intentions can feel pretty effortless with the right amount of context and
enough familiarity with a partner. While not always accurate, this human ability is
quite flexible. Whether a person is searching for their keys or looking for an item
in the super market, there is seemingly valuable information in the eye gaze signal
itself that other people should be able to pick up on. Yet until recently, researchers
rarely examined human observers' ability to decode this information solely from
eye movements.

Several studies have examined people's ability to use scan paths, or representations of successive fixations connected by lines superimposed over images. In one
decoding study by Greene et al. (2012) human observers were used as intuitive
decoders of eye movement data, employed as a control condition after a machine
classifier failed. The study's goal was to determine whether information about the
task was detectable by humans from the fixations alone. Static depictions of scan
paths were selected randomly from their earlier experiment. The human observers
had to predict which task the subject was doing when the scan path was generated;
the observers were unsuccessful at this decoding task. Their failure to accurately
interpret scan paths did not mean that the eye movements themselves lacked per-
ceptible task-relevant information, especially because static scan paths lack many
of the properties that make eye movements interpretable in real life. These include
temporal dynamics combined with the spatial aspects of gaze, produced in the
context of a gazer's body and facial orientation and expressions. Human observers
can, under some circumstances, decode static scan paths to determine what kind
of category of object a person is searching for (e.g., whether the search is for a bear
or a butterfly in a target absent display) with performance comparable to that of
machine learning (Zelinsky, Peng, & Samaras, 2013).

The evidence about human observers' interpretations of dynamic representations of gaze patters is more consistent. Observers can use dynamic representations
of the eye movements of others superimposed over a display to infer others' judgments. Students of computer programing observed expert programmers' recorded
dynamic gaze cursors superimposed over a page of code that the programmers
were debugging; this speeded the student observers' own identification of bugs
in the code (Stein & Brennan, 2004). And observers were able to identify a gazer's preferences for different fractal image patterns by viewing (and sometimes
re-viewing) the eye movements superimposed over the images (Foulsham & Lock,
2015). Accuracy levels in this study reached upwards of 60% (chance being 25%).
However, these observers were less accurate at guessing gazers' preferences when

the gazers were instructed to be deceptive when choosing which fractal images they preferred (ibid).

Outside of laboratory settings, judging others' gaze in the real world is fraught with factors that make this a complex task. Choices encountered in the real world differ not only in spatial characteristics, but also on high-level semantic properties, which makes the range of individual preferences and possible intended actions far greater than what could be concluded from tracking preferences among simple alternatives. Moreover, there are many potential social attributions that could interact with one's assumptions or attributions about eye gaze. For example, what one person knows about another person's history or preferences might constrain predictions from and interpretations of the other's eye gaze. The extent to which people believe that others share their own preferences might affect their frames of reference when making behavioral predictions from gaze. Whether there is reason to suspect that another person has sincere or disingenuous intentions could also factor in. These are many other factors relevant to attributing meaning to someone's gaze behavior as well; how these attributions factor into perceptual judgments of gaze remains unclear. And while few empirical studies have tested the extent to which such factors interact with the perception of eye movements, the intuition is that people somehow manage to be successful at drawing inferences from social gaze, despite all the noise and complexity. So when it comes to decoding experiments, the interesting thing is not simply whether or not a person or a search classifier *can* decode gaze patterns, but rather what the decoding task tells us about the strategies decoders might be using to make inferences.

Adding to the concern over what humans perceive and actually use when making predictions about gaze is the extent to which strategies generalize to or are consistent with what is known about gaze following in every day life. In face-to-face interaction, people must triangulate their estimations of another person's gaze trajectory in order to map gaze to an object or area of interest. These estimates may be egocentric (Loomis & Knapp, 2003) or systematically distorted as the direction of gaze is departs from the axis from the gazer to the observer (Fukusima & Loomis, 1997). Another hurdle that must be overcome when inferring intentions from the eyes is that typically eye movements, though directly observable, happen very rapidly. Observing another person's face, head, and body orientation (and especially changes in these) can help one orient to the direction of their attention, but it can still be difficult to determine the precise focus of the other's attention (Langton, 2000; Cline, 1967; Argyle & Cook, 1976; Stiefelhagen & Zhu, 2002).

Just as eye gaze is a resource in face-to-face conversation (as we will discuss in the next section), eye tracking technology can be used to project people's gaze cursors onto screens for remotely-located others to see in real time (a *shared gaze* system that we will discuss in the section after that). This enables them to monitor each other's fixations patterns, including timing and duration cues. A gaze cursor superimposed on a screen can be less noisy than monitoring a person's looks in a face-to-face interaction. So when there is a clear eye movement signal in the form of a gaze cursor, the ability to monitor where another person is attending can be much more precise and easy to interpret, especially when it is displayed over imagery that partners know they share. Of course, monitoring gaze in the absence of facial expression or head turning leaves out information that is important in certain contexts, such as when it is relevant to consider the gazer's attitude or emotional reaction toward what they are looking at (people who are interacting face-to-face do not first perceive features of eye movements in isolation and then later integrate this information with tasks or social context). If contextual information is known, then it may affect the interpretation of a gaze pattern. A promising but under-explored area of research is how observers integrate multiple-sources of top-down, contextual information to make inferences about the gaze of others.

6. Eye gaze as a coordination signal in face-to-face communication

Establishing the role that gaze direction plays in the context of everyday human interaction is challenging because communication is a realm in which coordination and rapid predictions are essential. Speakers, while planning and articulating utterances, simultaneously track their addressees' backchannels and other non-verbal responses and make inferences about their understanding and uptake; they do this rapidly, spontaneously, and often implicitly. This informs the process of grounding, by which partners in conversation seek and provide evidence that they understand one another (Clark & Brennan, 1991). In jointly coordinated activities, being able to see what a conversational partner is doing, or monitoring the gaze of one's interactive partner helps establish mutual understanding, especially when partners are mutually aware of this (Brennan, 2005; Richardson & Dale, 2005; Clark & Krych, 2004). This is what makes the ability to jointly attend to the same evidence so pivotal in joint actions (e.g., Baldwin, 1995; Mundy & Lewell, 2007; Böckler & Sebanz, 2013; Sebanz, Bekkering, & Knoblich, 2006).

People in conversation seek to achieve mutual understanding to a degree sufficient for their current purposes (Brennan, 1990, 1995; Clark & Brennan, 1990). Generally speaking, addressees gaze more at speakers than speakers gaze at addressees (Argyle & Cook, 1976). Gaze is a signal for coordinating turn-taking, with speakers gazing away from addressees at points during the utterance and returning gaze to monitor or cue addressees' responses (Ho, Foulsham, & Kingstone, 2015; Sacks, Schegloff, & Jefferson, 1974). Speakers engaged in a matching task tend to look up from their displays and toward each other at times of difficulty with the task

(Boyle, Anderson, & Newlands, 1994). When a speaker begins an utterance, but can see that an addressee is not overtly paying attention, she may interrupt herself in an attempt to get the addressee to look at her (Goodwin, 1981). A speaker may gaze longer at an item she is referring to, in order to get an addressee to look at it too. In these ways, eye gaze is used by people in conversation as a coordination signal and to achieve joint attention.

In face-to-face interaction, a speaker's gaze is a meaningful communicative signal that hearers can incrementally integrate with linguistic information in ways that are guided by their shared context. In one set of experiments (Hanna & Brennan, 2007), pairs of naive interacting subjects sat face-to-face, separated by a low barrier so that they saw each other's faces but not each other's displays on either side of the barrier. They conversed in order to match duplicate sets of cards that were arranged either congruently or non-congruently. That is, their card arrangements on either side of the barrier were either *mirrored*, where the target referent card appeared at the same spatial location on both sides of the display (so that what was to the speaker's left was to the matcher's right), or else *reversed*, where what was at the speaker's left appeared for the addressee to be at the opposite end of the display, toward the addressee's left. In both mirrored and reversed conditions, hearers were able to use the speaker's direction of gaze to identify the intended referent even before hearing the whole expression (e.g., at the color word of expressions like "*the green square with the Q*" when there were two green squares marked with different letters in the display). Hearers integrated the speaker's gaze cues with the unfolding linguistic information in the utterance and rapidly mapped this onto their own displays well before hearing the disambiguating letter, although this took 150–250 ms longer when displays were reversed than mirrored (even though in both conditions, both partners were aware of the relationship between their displays). This suggests a flexible use of gaze cues in face-to-face communication. The question remains as to whether hearers in Hanna and Brennan's (2007) paradigm might learn to inhibit any reflexive constraint in order to automate the re-mapping of a partner's incongruent gaze in order to use it as quickly as congruent gaze (without the 150–250 ms delay), or else to simply ignore the partner's gaze when it's not spatially correspondent.

Cues from the direction of a depicted agent's visual orientation can be ignored or overridden when an attribution is made that these cues are not meaningful. In several experiments where individuals observed a non-interacting agent's gaze direction, reflexive gaze-following to a target was inhibited when observers believed an agent could not see the target because his vision was occluded by closed eyes or opaque goggles (Nuku & Bekkering, 2008; Teufel, Alexis, Clayton, & Davis, 2010), or when a character's intention toward an object is known in advance (Amati & Brennan, 2015). In sum, although humans are quite sensitive to eye gaze, they appear to be able to ignore or inhibit gaze-following to some degree, and to use the direction of another person's attention flexibly when it's a meaningful or communicative signal (Hanna & Brennan, 2007; Senju, & Cisbra, 2008; Böckler, Knoblich & Sebanz, 2011; Nuku & Bekkering, 2008; Teufel et al., 2010; Ricciardelli, P., Carcagno, S., Vallar, G., & Bricolo, E., 2013). This makes sense; there would be no adaptive value to automatically or reflexively following others' gaze at all times, as this would interrupt and interfere with the purposeful deployment of attention. Gaze following in natural communication requires people to recognize when another's gaze is informative, and when it is not, and for their intentions to drive their response to this information.

7.   Eye gaze in electronic communication

Another way in which gaze can be used communicatively is via interfaces that promote awareness of individual and joint attention in real time, when two people collaborate remotely. Pairs of remotely-located partners each wore a head-mounted eye tracker and saw each other's moving gaze cursors displayed in real-time over the same image in a *shared gaze system* (first described in Zelinsky, Dickinson, Chen, Neider, & Brennan, 2005 and deployed for collaborative search tasks in Brennan, Chen, Dickenson, Neider, & Zelinsky, 2008; Neider, Chen, Dickinson, & Brennan, 2010). In the Brennan et al. (2008) study, partners searched together for a target (an O in a field of Qs), a task in which it made sense for them to search different parts of the display in parallel. They were able to coordinate dividing up the labor (e.g., one searched the left-hand side of the display while the other searched the right) without even speaking (in a condition where gaze was the only channel of communication and they could not hear each other speak before or during the task). One of the questions asked by this study was whether partners would be able to use a gaze cursor efficiently right from the start, without attention being hampered by the sudden onsets or peripherally viewed motion from their partner's cursor. Indeed, partners were able to covertly attend to each other's gaze cursor in their visual periphery while searching another part of the display, which suggests that they succeeded in controlling attention dynamically, moment-by-moment. This indicates that eye gaze is such a powerful cue that people who are not physically co-present can adapt quickly to abstract representations of a partner's visuo-spatial attention (even in the absence of facial cues and cues about the progress of a task that are available when people work together in the same room).

Another study from our lab simultaneously recorded two partners' speech along with synchronized gaze and mouse cursors (Churilov, 2014) as they searched together for locations on a map. Having any sort of visual evidence (whether from mouse or gaze cursors) was more efficient than speech alone, replicating previous studies that used mouse cursors or physical gestures (respectively, Brennan, 1990, 2005; Clark & Krych, 2004). A gaze cursor was a noisier cue than a mouse cursor (the latter is more under intentional control as a deictic or pointing signal), but gaze provided more timely information that could be used to infer a partner's intention earlier (Churilov, 2014). Several other labs are using dual-eye tracking to investigate cognition and collaboration in social and interactive contexts (e.g., Carletta, Hill, Nicol, Taylor, De Ruiter, & Bard, 2010; Jermann, Nussli, & Li, 2010; Pfeiffer, Vogeley, & Schilbach, 2013; Trösterer, Gärtner, Wuchse, Maurer, Baumgartner, Meschtscherjakov, & Tscheligi, 2015). As eye tracking becomes more reliable, easier to use, more affordable, and even mobile, it will be increasingly feasible for human-machine interfaces to incorporate shared gaze technology to support joint action and remote social interaction.

8.   Mind reading by machines: Eye gaze as an input signal

Despite the ambiguity and noise inherent in eye gaze, interpreting a partner's gaze does not appear to pose much of a burden to people in conversation. The impact of ambiguity is a different matter altogether when people interact with machines. When eye movements are used as an input signal in human-machine interaction, determining whether a user's gaze should be interpreted as issuing an intentional command (e.g., to position a cursor and to make a selection) vs. instrumentally (e.g., as searching a display) is notoriously difficult (Bednarik, Vrzakova, & Hradis, 2012; Bulling & Gellerson, 2010; Jacob, 1991, 1995). The same action (e.g., a look to a particular object) on the part of a user can map to multiple actions on the part of the system, depending on the task context or *mode*. As appealing as it would be for an interface to empower a user to simply fixate something in order to issue a command, the risk is that the user may happen to look at something *without* wanting to do so, but trigger the command anyway (Bednarik et al., 2012; Bulling & Gellersen, 2010). This problem is not unique to gaze cues of course; there is potential for ambiguity whenever "intelligent" interfaces are at work, such as when a user unintentionally hovers a cursor over a button on a screen and the system ends up activating that button, when a cell phone mistakenly autocorrects a user's text (Wood, 2014), or when a user issues a voice command that is misrecognized, resulting in the wrong command being executed (Brennan & Hulteen, 1995).

The problem with detecting the intended mode or context for an input signal is known as the "Midas Touch" problem (Jacob, 1991; Velichkovsky, Sprenger, & Unema, 1997; Majaranta & Raiha, 2002). Mode problems can be solved by having the user perform an additional action, such as pushing a button to pick up (or release) an object that is fixated, in order to drag it with the eyes (Jacob, 1995). Because it is extremely tiring to intentionally restrict one's gaze in order to use it reliably as a pointing command in a user interface, and because there are many more reliable and precise devices for spatial input, gaze input has been used as an command signal only by those who lacked other options (ibid). Jacob advocated using eye movements to provide *implicit* information rather than explicit commands in human-computer interfaces (ibid).

To understand the information implicitly available in eye gaze (rather than using eye gaze as an explicit pointing or selecting command), it is necessary to better understand how eye gaze fits in with the repertoire of spontaneous behaviors that occur as people collaborate on joint tasks. Future investigations of gaze decoding could incorporate the use of shared gaze systems to examine how eye movement patterns are modulated on-line as partners interact and make predictions in real time. The intentions and meanings behind gaze patterns are likely to change on the fly, depending upon whether goals change during an interactive task and upon whether the partners are temporally and visually co-present with one another.

Advances in machine learning have enabled computer applications to make reliable predictions about mental states from users' eye movements. Eye movements have been used to evaluate users' strategies, such as how they search for information on computer screens; well-organized computer interfaces lead to more efficient scan paths and less time spent searching the display (Goldberg & Kotval, 1999). Similarly, associating errors or long latencies with the gaze signatures that precede them could enable an application to recognize or anticipate a user's confusion, and it could then offer help. Progress in this area could lead to improvements in the way people interact with their personal computers and mobile devices.

Safety concerns open up another category of applications. For example, detecting states of inattention or distraction is a major aim for developers of intelligent driving systems. Eye tracking can be used to monitor the driver's attention and detect when it is disrupted. Using machine learning, in-vehicle systems can recognize both visual distraction (e.g., looking away to change the radio) and cognitive distraction (e.g., talking on a hands-free phone) (Liang, Reyes, & Lee, 2007). Using a combination of eye movement data and simple driving performance measures, a driver's distraction can be detected with over 95% accuracy. It is also possible to use eye tracking to monitor for fatigue (Ji, Zhu, & Lan, 2004) and to identify a driver's intent to change lanes (Doshi & Trivedi, 2009).

Eye gaze data have also been used as input to robotic systems to get them to monitor attention while interacting with humans in dialogue. Recent developments in the designs of humanoid robots have incorporated eye trackers to monitor the attention from multiple users simultaneously (Bennewitz, Faber, Joho, & Behnke, 2007). With an ability to detect and monitor gaze patterns, the machine can monitor and adjust to human reactions, for example, shifting attention from one addressee to another or changing gaze direction to look at another person who is involved in the conversation but in the periphery (ibid).

Even mobile devices and video game consoles have gaze tracking cameras with eye movement analysis capabilities that have the potential to enable users to control applications with their eyes (Drewes, De Luca, & Schmidt, 2007; Smith & Graham, 2006). Applications can automatically pause a video when a user is no longer looking at the screen or advance text in a document while a user is reading (Dickie, Vertegaal, Sohn & Cheng, 2005). While the accuracy of mobile eye tracking continues to improve, one of the biggest obstacles to integrating this technology into human-machine interfaces still involves the Midas Touch or mode problem we highlighted earlier, that is, the difficulty of distinguishing intentional from unintentional eye movement and interpreting it with respect to the intended context (Velichkovsky, Sprenger, & Unema, 1997; Majaranta & Raiha, 2002; Bulling, & Gellerson, 2010).

While detecting people's mental states or intentions sufficiently well for a machine to control an application may differ quite a bit from how humans go about considering the intentions of others, it would help to understand the differences between how both forms of "intelligent" agents read minds. This could be especially true when humans interact with computer systems that are attempting to detect their intentions with the aim of enhancing their experience. People will not be particularly welcoming of eye tracking cameras in their personal devices that monitor their attention and make incorrect assumptions or clumsy guesses about what to do next (Liebling & Preibusch, 2014). Here is the challenge: When people think that their minds are being read by another person, they have the feeling of being understood, but when they think their mind is being read by a computer, they may feel that their privacy is being invaded. Better understanding the potential and different implications for mind reading by humans and machines could support advances in how both systems can naturally work together.

9. Conclusion

From an early age, people learn how to flexibly use the gaze of others to achieve joint attention and to make predictions about others' behavior and mental states. The information available in eye gaze can be instrumental to doing a collaborative task such as searching an environment, or it can be communicative, in the service of coordinating joint activity. Decoding human intentions from eye gaze can be virtually effortless in spontaneous social interaction, explicitly informative about cognition and perception in experimental contexts, and challenging indeed

Brennan, S. E. (2005). How conversation is shaped by visual and spoken evidence. *Approaches to studying world-situated language use: Bridging the language-as-product and language-as-action traditions*, 95–129.

Brennan, S. E., Chen, X., Dickinson, C., Neider, M., & Zelinsky, G. (2008). Coordinating cognition: The costs and benefits of shared gaze during collaborative search. *Cognition*, 106, 1465–1477. https://doi.org/10.1016/j.cognition.2007.05.012

Brennan, S. E., & Hulteen, E. (1995). Interaction and feedback in a spoken language system: A theoretical framework. *Knowledge-Based Systems*, 8, 143–151. https://doi.org/10.1016/0950-7051(95)98376-H

Brennan, S. E., & Williams, M. (1995). The feeling of another's knowing: Prosody and filled pauses as cues to listeners about the metacognitive states of speakers. *Journal of Memory and Language*, 34(3), 383–398 https://doi.org/10.1006/jmla.1995.1017

Bulling, A., & Gellersen, H. (2010). Toward mobile eye-based human-computer interaction. *Pervasive Computing, IEEE*, 9(4), 8–12. https://doi.org/10.1109/MPRV.2010.86

Carletta, J., Hill, R. L., Nicol, C., Taylor, T., De Ruiter, J. P., & Bard, E. G. (2010). Eyetracking for two-person tasks with manipulation of a virtual world. *Behavior Research Methods*, 42(1), 254–265. https://doi.org/10.3758/BRM.42.1.254

Castelhano, M. S., Mack, M. L., & Henderson, J. M. (2009). Viewing task influences eye movement control during active scene perception. *Journal of Vision*, 9(3):6.1–15. https://doi.org/10.1167/9.3.6

Chandon, P., Hutchinson, J. W., & Young, S. H. (2001). *Measuring the value of point-of-purchase marketing with commercial eye-tracking data*. INSEAD.

Churilov, E. (2014). *Speaking, pointing, and gazing: Different communication strategies for different communicative constraints*. Unpublished.Master's thesis, Stony Brook University.

Clark, H. H., & Brennan, S. E. (1991). Grounding in communication. In L. B. Resnick, J. Levine, & S. D. Teasley (Eds.), *Perspectives on socially shared cognition* (pp. 127–149). Washington, DC: APA. Reprinted in R. M. Baecker (Ed.), *Groupware and computer-supported cooperative work: Assisting human-human collaboration* (pp. 222–233). San Mateo, CA: Morgan Kaufman Publishers, Inc. https://doi.org/10.1037/10096-006

Clark, H. H., & Krych, M. A. (2004). Speaking while monitoring addressees for understanding. *Journal of Memory and Language*, 50(1), 62–81. https://doi.org/10.1016/j.jml.2003.08.004

Cline, M. G. (1967). The perception of where a person is looking. *The American Journal of Psychology*, 41–50. https://doi.org/10.2307/1420539

Crosby, J. R. Monin, B., & Richardson, D. (2008). Where do we look during potentially offensive behavior? *Psychological Science*, 19, 226–228). https://doi.org/10.1111/j.1467-9280.2008.02072.x

DeAngelus, M., & Pelz, J. B. (2009). Top-down control of eye movements: Yarbus revisited. *Visual Cognition*, 17(6–7), 790–811. https://doi.org/10.1080/13506280902793843

Dennett, D. C. (1987). *The intentional stance*. Cambridge, MA: MIT press.

Dickie, C., Vertegaal, R., Sohn, C., & Cheng, D. (2005). eyeLook: using attention to facilitate mobile media consumption. In *Proceedings of the 18th annual ACM symposium on User interface software and technology* (pp. 103–106).

Doherty, M. J. (2006). The development of mentalistic gaze understanding. *Infant and Child Development*, 15(2), 179–186. https://doi.org/10.1002/icd.434

Doshi, A., & Trivedi, M. M. (2009). On the roles of eye gaze and head dynamics in predicting driver's intent to change lanes. *Intelligent Transportation Systems, IEEE Transactions on*, 10(3), 453–462. https://doi.org/10.1109/TITS.2009.2026675

Drewes, H., De Luca, A., & Schmidt, A. (2007). Eye-gaze interaction for mobile phones. In *Proceedings of the 4th international conference on mobile technology, applications, and systems and the 1st international symposium on computer human interaction in mobile technology* (pp. 364–371). ACM.

Driver, J., Davis, G., Ricciardelli, P., Kidd, P., Maxwell, E., & Baron-Cohen, S. (1999). Gaze perception triggers reflexive visuospatial orienting. *Visual Cognition*, 6, 509–540. https://doi.org/10.1080/135062899394920

Fantz, R. L. (1965). Visual Perception from birth as shown by pattern selectivity. *Annals of the New York Academy of Sciences, New Issues in Infant Development*, 118, 793–814. https://doi.org/10.1111/j.1749-6632.1965.tb40152.x

Ferreira, F., Apel, J., & Henderson, J. M. (2008). Taking a new look at looking at nothing. *Trends in Cognitive Sciences*, 12(11), 405–410. https://doi.org/10.1016/j.tics.2008.07.007

Foulsham, T., & Lock, M. (2015). How the eyes tell lies: Social gaze during a preference task. *Cognitive Science*, 39, 1704–1726. https://doi.org/10.1111/cogs.12211

Friesen, C. K. & Kingstone, A. (1998). The eyes have it! Reflexive orienting is triggered by nonpredictive gaze. *Psychonomic Bulletin & Review*, 5, 490–495. https://doi.org/10.3758/BF03208827

Frischen, A., Bayliss, A. P., & Tipper, S. P. (2007). Gaze cueing of attention: Visual attention, social cognition, and individual differences. *Psychological Bulletin*, 133(4), 694–724. https://doi.org/10.1037/0033-2909.133.4.694

Frith, C. D., & Frith, U. (2006). How we predict what other people are going to do. *Brain Research*, 1079(1), 36–46. https://doi.org/10.1016/j.brainres.2005.12.126

Fukusima, S. S., Loomis, J. M., & Da Silva, J. A. (1997). Visual perception of egocentric distance as assessed by triangulation. *Journal of Experimental Psychology: Human Perception and Performance*, 23(1), 86.

Glaholt, M. G., & Reingold, E. M. (2009). Stimulus exposure and gaze bias: A further test of the gaze cascade model. *Attention, Perception, & Psychophysics*, 71(3), 445–450. https://doi.org/10.3758/APP.71.3.445

Glaholt, M. G., & Reingold, E. M. (2011). Eye movement monitoring as a process tracing methodology in decision making research. *Journal of Neuroscience, Psychology, and Economics*, 4(2), 125. https://doi.org/10.1037/a0020692

Glaholt, M. G., & Reingold, E. M. (2012). Direct control of fixation times in scene viewing: Evidence from analysis of the distribution of first fixation duration. *Visual Cognition*, 20(6), 605–626. https://doi.org/10.1080/13506285.2012.666295

Glaholt, M. G., Wu, M. C., & Reingold, E. M. (2010). Evidence for top-down control of eye movements during visual decision making. *Journal of Vision*, 10(5), 15. https://doi.org/10.1167/10.5.15

Goldberg, J. H., & Kotval, X. P. (1999). Computer interface evaluation using eye movements: methods and constructs. *International Journal of Industrial Ergonomics*, 24(6), 631–645. https://doi.org/10.1016/S0169-8141(98)00068-7

Goodwin, C. (1981). *Conversational organization: Interaction between speakers and hearers*. New York, NY: Academic Press.

Gopnik, A., Meltzoff, A. N., & Bryant, P. (1997). Words, thoughts, and theories (Vol. 1). Cambridge, MA: MIT Press

Greene, M. R., Liu, T., & Wolfe, J. M. (2012). Reconsidering Yarbus: A failure to predict observers' task from eye movement patterns. *Vision Research*, 62, 1–8. https://doi.org/10.1016/j.visres.2012.03.019

Grice, H. P. (1957). *Meaning*. Philosophical Review, 66, 377–388.

Haji-Abolhassani, A., & Clark, J. J. (2014). An inverse Yarbus process: Predicting observers' task from eye movement patterns. *Vision Research*, 103, 127–142. https://doi.org/10.1016/j.visres.2014.08.014

Hanna, J. E., & Brennan, S. E. (2007). Speakers' eye gaze disambiguates referring expressions early during face-to-face conversation. *Journal of Memory and Language*, 57(4), 596–615. https://doi.org/10.1016/j.jml.2007.01.008

Henderson, J. M. (2003). Human gaze control during real-world scene perception. *Trends in Cognitive Sciences*, 7(11), 498–504. https://doi.org/10.1016/j.tics.2003.09.006

Henderson, J. M., Shinkareva, S. V., Wang, J., Luke, S. G., & Olejarczyk, J. (2013). Predicting cognitive state from eye movements. *PloS One*, 8(5), e64937. https://doi.org/10.1371/journal.pone.0064937

Ho, S., Foulsham, T., & Kingstone, A. (2015). Speaking and Listening with the Eyes: Gaze Signaling during Dyadic Interactions. *PLoS One*, 10(8), e0136905. https://doi.org/10.1371/journal.pone.0136905

Hood, B. M., Willen, J. D., & Driver, J. (1998). Adults' eyes trigger shifts of visual attention in human infants. *Psychological Science*, 9(2), 131–134. https://doi.org/10.1111/1467-9280.00024

Houston-Price, C. & Nakai, S. (2004). Distinguishing novelty and familiarity effects in infant preference procedures. *Infant and Child Development*, 13, 341–348. https://doi.org/10.1002/icd.364

Hunter, M. A. & Ames, E. W. (1988). A multifactor model of infant preferences for novel and familiar stimuli. In Rovee-Collier C., Lipsitt L. P. (Eds.) *Advances in Infancy Research*, Vol. 5 (pp. 69–95). Stamford, CT: Ablex.

Ishimaru, S., Kunze, K., Kise, K., Weppner, J., Dengel, A., Lukowicz, P., & Bulling, A. (2014, March). In the blink of an eye: combining head motion and eye blink frequency for activity recognition with Google Glass. In *Proceedings of the 5th augmented human international conference* (p. 15). ACM. https://doi.org/10.1145/2582051.2582066

Jacob, R. J. (1991). The use of eye movements in human-computer interaction techniques: What you look at is what you get. *ACM Transactions on Information Systems (TOIS)*, 9(3), 152–169. https://doi.org/10.1145/123078.128728

Jacob, R. J. (1995). Eye tracking in advanced interface design. In W. Barfield & T. A. Furness (Eds.), *Virtual environments and advanced interface design* (pp. 258–308). New York: Oxford University Press.

Jermann, P., Nüssli, M. A., & Li, W. (2010, September). Using dual eye-tracking to unveil co-ordination and expertise in collaborative Tetris. In *Proceedings of the 24th BCS Interaction Specialist Group Conference* (pp. 36–44). British Computer Society.

Ji, Q., Zhu, Z. & Lan, P. (2004). Real-Time Nonintrusive Monitoring and Prediction of Driver Fatigue. *IEEE Transactions on Vehicular Technology*, 53, 1052–1068.

Jusczyk, P., & Aslin, R. (1995). Infants' detection of the sound patterns of words in fluent speech. *Cognitive Psychology* 29, 1–23. https://doi.org/10.1006/cogp.1995.1010

Kanan, C., Ray, N. A., Bseiso, D. N., Hsiao, J. H., & Cottrell, G. W. (2014, March). Predicting an observer's task using multi-fixation pattern analysis. In *Proceedings of the Symposium on Eye Tracking Research and Applications* (pp. 287–290). ACM. https://doi.org/10.1145/2578153.2578208

Krajbich, I., Armel, C., & Rangel, A. (2010). Visual fixations and the computation and comparison of value in simple choice. *Nature Neuroscience*, 13(10), 1292–1298. https://doi.org/10.1038/nn.2635

Krajbich, I., Lu, D., Camerer, C., & Rangel, A. (2012). The attentional drift-diffusion model extends to simple purchasing decisions. *Frontiers in Psychology*, 3, 193. https://doi.org/10.3389/fpsyg.2012.00193

Krajbich, I., & Rangel, A. (2011). Multialternative drift-diffusion model predicts the relationship between visual fixations and choice in value-based decisions. *Proceedings of the National Academy of Sciences*, 108(33), 13852–13857. https://doi.org/10.1073/pnas.1101328108

Kuhn, G., Tatler, B. W., Findlay, J. M., & Cole, G. G. (2008). Misdirection in magic: Implications for the relationship between eye gaze and attention. *Visual Cognition*, 16(2–3), 391–405. https://doi.org/10.1080/13506280701479750

Langton, S. R. (2000). The mutual influence of gaze and head orientation in the analysis of social attention direction. *The Quarterly Journal of Experimental Psychology: Section A*, 53(3), 825–845. https://doi.org/10.1080/713755908

Langton, S. R. H. & Bruce, V. (2000). You must see the point: Automatic processing of cues to the direction of social attention. *Journal of Experimental Psychology: Human Perception and Performance*, 26, 747–757.

Liang, Y., Reyes, M. L., & Lee, J. D. (2007). Real-time detection of driver cognitive distraction using support vector machines. *Intelligent Transportation Systems, IEEE Transactions*, 8(2), 340–350. https://doi.org/10.1109/TITS.2007.895298

Liebling, D. J., & Preibusch, S. (2014). Privacy considerations for a pervasive eye tracking world. In *Proceedings of the 2014 ACM International Joint Conference on Pervasive and Ubiquitous Computing: Adjunct Publication* (pp. 1169–1177). ACM.

Loomis, J. M., & Knapp, J. M. (2003). Visual perception of egocentric distance in real and virtual environments. *Virtual and Adaptive Environments*, (11), 21–46.

Majaranta, P., & Räihä, K. J. (2002, March). Twenty years of eye typing: systems and design issues. In *Proceedings of the 2002 Symposium on Eye Tracking Research & Applications* (pp. 15–22). ACM.

Matlock, T., & Richardson, D. C. (2004). Do eye movements go with fictive motion? *Proceedings of the 26th Annual Conference of the Cognitive Science Society* (pp. 909–914). Mahwah, NJ: Lawrence Erlbaum.

Maughan, L., Gutnikov, S., & Stevens, R. (2007). Like more, look more. look more, like more: the evidence from eye-tracking. *Journal of Brand Management*, 14(4), 335–342.

Mills, M., Hollingworth, A., Van der Stigchel, S., Hoffman, L., & Dodd, M. D. (2011). Examining the influence of task set on eye movements and fixations. *Journal of Vision*, 11(8), 17. https://doi.org/10.1167/11.8.17

Mundy, P., & Newell, L. (2007). Attention, joint attention, and social cognition. *Current Directions in Psychological Science*, 16(5), 269–274. https://doi.org/10.1111/j.1467-8721.2007.00518.x

Neider, M. B., Chen, X., Dickinson, C. A., Brennan, S. E., & Zelinsky, G. J. (2010). Coordinating spatial referencing using shared gaze. *Psychonomic Bulletin & Review*, 17(5), 718–724. https://doi.org/10.3758/PBR.17.5.718

Nuku, P., & Bekkering, H. (2008). Joint attention: Inferring what others perceive (and don't perceive). *Consciousness and Cognition*, 17(1), 339–349. https://doi.org/10.1016/j.concog.2007.06.014

Onishi, K. H., & Baillargeon, R. (2005). Do 15-month-old infants understand false beliefs? *Science*, 308(5719), 255–258. https://doi.org/10.1126/science.1107621

Patalano, A. L., Juhasz, B. J., & Dicke, J. (2010). The relationship between indecisiveness and eye movement patterns in a decision making informational search task. *Journal of Behavioral Decision Making*, 23(4), 353–368.

Penn, D. C., & Povinelli, D. J. (2007). On the lack of evidence that non-human animals possess anything remotely resembling a 'theory of mind'. *Philosophical Transactions of the Royal Society of London B: Biological Sciences*, 362(1480), 731–744. https://doi.org/10.1098/rstb.2006.2023

Pfeiffer, U. J., Vogeley, K., & Schilbach, L. (2013). From gaze cueing to dual eye-tracking: novel approaches to investigate the neural correlates of gaze in social interaction. *Neuroscience & Biobehavioral Reviews*, 37, 2516–2528. https://doi.org/10.1016/j.neubiorev.2013.07.017

Pieters, R., & Warlop, L. (1999). Visual attention during brand choice: The impact of time pressure and task motivation. International Journal of Research in Marketing, 16(1), 1–16. https://doi.org/10.1016/S0167-8116(98)00022-6

Posner M. I. (1980). Orienting of attention. *Quarterly Journal of Experimental Psychology*, 32, 3–25. https://doi.org/10.1080/00335558008248231

Posner, M. I. & Cohen, Y. A. (1984). Components of visual orienting. In: Bouma, H.; Bouwhuis, D. G. (Eds.) *Attention and performance XVII: Control of visual processing*. Hillsdale, NJ: Erlbaum; 1984. pp. 531–556.

Reutskaja, E., Nagel, R., Camerer, C. F., & Rangel, A. (2011). Search dynamics in consumer choice under time pressure: An eye-tracking study. *The American Economic Review*, 900–926. https://doi.org/10.1257/aer.101.2.900

Ricciardelli, P., Carcagno, S., Vallar, G., & Bricolo, E. (2013). Is gaze following purely reflexive or goal-directed instead? Revisiting the automaticity of orienting attention by gaze cues. *Experimental Brain Research*, 224(1), 93–106. https://doi.org/10.1007/s00221-012-3291-5

Richardson, D. C., & Dale, R. (2005). Looking to understand: The coupling between speakers' and listeners' eye movements and its relationship to discourse comprehension. *Cognitive Science*, 29(6), 1045–1060. https://doi.org/10.1207/s15516709cog0000_29

Romani, M., Cesari, P., Urgesi, C., Facchini, S., & Aglioti, S. M. (2003). Motor facilitation of the human cortico-spinal system during observation of bio-mechanically impossible movements. *Neuroimage*, 26(3), 755–763. https://doi.org/10.1016/j.neuroimage.2005.02.027

Russo, J. E., & Leclerc, F. (1994). An eye-fixation analysis of choice processes for consumer non-durables. *Journal of Consumer Research*, 274–290. https://doi.org/10.1086/209397

Sacks, H., Schegloff, E. A., & Jefferson, G. (1974). A simplest systematics for the organization of turn-taking in conversation. *Language*, 50, 696–735. https://doi.org/10.1353/lan.1974.0010

Sebanz, N., Bekkering, H., & Knoblich, G. (2006). Joint action: bodies and minds moving together. *Trends in Cognitive Sciences*, 10(2), 70–76. https://doi.org/10.1016/j.tics.2005.12.009

Sebanz, N., & Shiffrar, M. (2009). Bluffing bodies: Inferring intentions from actions. *Psychonomic Bulletin & Review*, 16, 170–175. https://doi.org/10.3758/PBR.16.1.170

Senju, A., & Csibra, G. (2008). Gaze following in human infants depends on communicative signals. *Current Biology*, 18(9), 668–671. https://doi.org/10.1016/j.cub.2008.03.059

Shiffrar, M., & Freyd, J. J. (1990). Apparent motion of the human body. *Psychological Science*, 1(4), 257–264. https://doi.org/10.1111/j.1467-9280.1990.tb00210.x

Shimojo, S., Simion, C., Shimojo, E., & Scheier, C. (2003). Gaze bias both reflects and influences preference. *Nature Neuroscience*, 6(12), 1317–1322. https://doi.org/10.1038/nn1150

Simion, C., & Shimojo, S. (2006). Early interactions between orienting, visual sampling and decision making in facial preference. *Vision Research*, 46(20), 3331–3335. https://doi.org/10.1016/j.visres.2006.04.019

Smith, J. D., & Graham, T. C. (2006, June). Use of eye movements for video game control. In *Proceedings of the 2006 ACM SIGCHI International Conference on Advances in Computer Entertainment Technology* (p. 20). ACM. https://doi.org/10.1145/1178823.1178847

Spelke, E. S. (1990). Principles of object perception. *Cognitive Science*, 14(1), 29–56.
https://doi.org/10.1207/s15516709cog1401_3

Spivey, M. J., & Geng, J. J. (2001). Oculomotor mechanisms activated by imagery and memory:
Eye movements to absent objects. *Psychological Research*, 65(4), 235–241.
https://doi.org/10.1007/s004260100059

Stein, R. & Brennan, S. E. (2004). Another person's eye gaze as a cue in solving programming
problems. *Proceedings, ICMI 2004, Sixth International Conference on Multimodal Interfaces*
(pp. 9–15), Penn State University, State College, PA.

Stiefelhagen, R., & Zhu, J. (2002, April). Head orientation and gaze direction in meetings. In
CHI'02 Extended Abstracts on Human Factors in Computing Systems (pp. 858–859). ACM.

Suri, R., & Monroe, K. B. (2003). The effects of time constraints on consumers' judgments of prices
and products. *Journal of Consumer Research*, 30(1), 92–104 https://doi.org/10.1086/374696

Tanenhaus, M. K., Spivey-Knowlton, M. J., Eberhard, K. M., & Sedivy, J. C. (1995). Integration
of visual and linguistic information in spoken language comprehension. *Science*, 268(5217),
1632–1634. https://doi.org/10.1126/science.7777863

Teufel, C., Alexis, D. M., Clayton, N. S., & Davis, G. (2010). Mental attribution drives rapid,
reflexive gaze-following. *Attention, Perception, & Psychophysics*, 72, 695–705.
https://doi.org/10.3758/APP.72.3.695

Tomasello, M. (1995). Joint attention as social cognition. In C. Moore and P. J. Dunham (Eds.),
Joint attention: Its origins and role in development, 103–130. Laurence Erlbaum Associates,
Hillsdale, NJ.

Tomeo, E., Cesari, P., Aglioti, S. M., & Urgesi, C. (2012). Fooling the kickers but not the goal-
keepers: behavioral and neurophysiological correlates of fake action detection in soccer.
Cerebral Cortex, 279, 1–14.

Trösterer, S., Gärtner, M., Wuchse, M., Maurer, B., Baumgartner, A., Meschtscherjakov, A.,
Tscheligi, M. (2015). Four eyes see more than two: Shared gaze in the car. *Proceedings,
Interact 2015*.

Van der Lans, R. J. A. (2006). *Brand search*, (doctoral thesis). Tilburg University, Netherlands.

Velichkovsky, B., Sprenger, A., & Unema, P. (1997, January). Towards gaze-mediated interaction: Collecting solutions of the "Midas touch problem". In *Human-Computer Interaction
INTERACT'97* (pp. 509–516). Springer US.

Wellman, H. M., & Woolley, J. D. (1990). From simple desires to ordinary beliefs: The early development of everyday psychology. *Cognition*, 35, 245–275.
https://doi.org/10.1016/0010-0277(90)90024-E

Wolpert, D. M., Doya, K., Kawato, M. (2003). A unifying computational framework for motor
control and social interaction. *Philosophical Transactions of the Royal Society of London:
Brain and Biological Sciences*, 358 (1431), 593–602. https://doi.org/10.1098/rstb.2002.1238

Wood, N. (2014). *Autocorrect awareness: categorizing changes and measuring authorial perceptions*
(unpublished honors thesis). Florida State University, 351, Tallahassee, FL.

Yarbus, A. L. (1967). Eye movements during perception of complex objects. In *Eye movements
and vision* (pp. 171–211). Springer US. https://doi.org/10.1007/978-1-4899-5379-7_8

Zelinsky, G. J., Dickinson, C. A., Chen, X., Neider, M. B., & Brennan, S. E. (2005). Collaborative
search using shared eye gaze. Abstract, *Journal of Vision*, 5. p. 700. https://doi.org/10.1167/5.8.700

Zelinsky, G. J., Peng, Y., & Samaras, D. (2013). Eye can read your mind: Decoding gaze fixations to
reveal categorical search targets. *Journal of Vision*, 13(14), 10. https://doi.org/10.1167/13.14.10

CHAPTER 3

Effects of a speaker's gaze on language comprehension and acquisition

Pia Knoeferle[i,ii,iii], Helene Kreysa[iv] and Martin J. Pickering[v]
[i]Humboldt-Universität zu Berlin / [ii]Berlin School of Mind and Brain / [iii]Einstein Center for Neurosciences Berlin / [iv]Friedrich-Schiller Universität Jena / [v]The University of Edinburgh

This chapter discusses the role of a speaker's gaze on a listener's language processing, recall of information, and on child language learning. Speaker gaze facilitates performance in all of these domains, which suggests that it plays an important role in communication. Indeed, the findings indicate that speaker gaze can facilitate not just referential but also compositional processes such as syntactic structuring and thematic role assignment in listeners. Speaker gaze even guided comprehenders' attention to a target object more rapidly than other aspects of the visual context (action event depictions); but unlike the action depictions, it had no beneficial effects on comprehenders' post-experiment memory in socially non-interactive settings (when comprehenders inspect the speaker on a computer display). In socially interactive settings, however, speaker gaze seemed to affect memory in that joint object-based attention between a caregiver and child was beneficial for language learning. We conclude that speaker gaze effects are important for both language processing and learning, and are potentially boosted in a socially interactive context.

Keywords: language processing, language learning, recall and memory, communicative function of gaze

1. Introduction

Without doubt eye gaze plays a central role in our cognitive functioning and our interaction with the world. When watching a ballet performance, our eyes bring objects, people, and dynamic events into the focus of attention. When pouring water into a glass, our gaze precedes our hand movements and can provide guidance during action execution. When we interact with an interlocutor, our gaze can direct the interlocutor to the objects and events we think are relevant for the conversation. And when we share a glass of Prosecco with a good friend in the evening, eye contact asserts our social presence among others. These are only some of the

https://doi.org/10.1075/ais.10.03kno

many situations in which we rely on eye gaze to facilitate our interaction with the environment around us and the people in it.

But how do listeners make use of speaker gaze? In this chapter, we ask whether they use it to help them understand the speaker's utterance, recall information from memory (also measured against the effects of other cues such as action depictions), and learn words. Given that gaze seems to play a central role in situations like the ones described above, we might be tempted to nod in assent and argue that it is pivotal to human-human communication. Indeed, a rich literature on eye tracking in human-human communication corroborates that where a speaker looks (e.g., Hanna & Brennan, 2007) and whether gaze cues are present (Macdonald & Tatler, 2013; Knoeferle & Kreysa, 2012) can influence a listener's gaze behavior (for a summary see Kreysa & Pickering, 2011). For instance, when a listener sees an interlocutor inspect a person or an object, she tends to follow the speaker's gaze to the inspected object within a few hundred milliseconds (Hanna & Brennan, 2007). Listeners can even use the gaze of a robot speaker to rapidly anticipate a referent before the linguistic input permits them to identify which referent will be mentioned next (Staudte & Crocker, 2011).

On the other hand, it is unclear to which extent a listener integrates her representation of the speaker's gaze with her representation of the utterance. Following a speaker's gaze could consume important cognitive resources. Indeed, sometimes people avert their eye gaze when answering complex questions (Glenberg, Schroeder, & Robertson, 1998), perhaps to manage cognitive load (Doherty-Sneddon & Phelps, 2005, 2007). It is thus possible that listeners process speaker gaze only superficially as a pointer to a potentially interesting location, instead of integrating it with their unfolding interpretation of the utterance (*deictic account*). If so, the speaker's gaze would merely signal to the listener where to look but would not otherwise enrich the language-based representations.

One way of testing whether gaze is used merely as a pointer to a location is to compare its effects to those of another cue that functions predominantly as a pointer. Research suggests that speaker gaze has similar effects to arrows, at least in human-robot interaction (Staudte et al., 2014; see also Santiesteban, Catmur, Coughlan Hopkins, Bird, & Heyes, 2014). Santiesteban et al. (2014), for instance, observed that participants treated an avatar's perspective similarly to that of an arrow. The participants judged whether an indicated number of dots was consistent with the number of dots they could see from their own perspective. Response latencies were longer when the number of dots the participants could see matched (vs. mismatched) the number of dots that a depicted avatar was able to see or that an arrow was pointing to, and there was no reliable latency difference between these two situations (avatar perspective versus arrows). It has been shown that behavior in such self-consistency tasks is relatively robust to strategic control, and that the effects of both of these cues manifest themselves even when it is not necessary for the task (e.g., Samson, Apperly, Braithwaite, Andrews, & Bodley, 2010). Staudte et al. (2014) similarly found no qualitative differences in the effects of a robot's gaze compared with an arrow on listeners' visual attention when both cues were similarly precise in timing, suggesting that both function in a similar manner, as location pointers. Additionally, there is good evidence that the presence of eye-like stimuli can rapidly direct an observer's attention (e.g., Driver, Davis, Ricciardelli, Kidd, Maxwell, & Baron-Cohen, 1999; Langton & Bruce, 2000; Langton, Watt, & Bruce, 2000). Moreover, listeners rarely look at the speaker during comprehension when that speaker is talking about objects and events in the immediate environment (e.g., Hanna & Brennan, 2007; Knoeferle & Kreysa, 2012). Taken together, these findings suggest that speaker gaze itself might not carry much meaning, and simply serve as a convenient deictic cue (see the deictic account above).

But it is also possible that speaker gaze could help listeners to better link spoken words to their referents (*referential account*). On this account, it would not only guide a listener's attention to an object but further enrich the mental representations that a listener constructs of that object. For instance, if there are several pianos and the speaker looks at one of them before naming it, reference to the piano is disambiguated and the object and language representations might be enhanced with the features of that particular piano, rendering these representations more salient.

Yet another possibility is that a speaker's gaze could inform not just deictic and referential processes but also other comprehension processes such as syntactic structure building and thematic role assignment (*syntactic-thematic account*). For instance, if following a speaker's gaze boosts referential representations, these might be available earlier for syntactic structuring and thematic role assignment. On a variant of the syntactic-thematic account, an increased activation of referential representations might carry pragmatic implications such as signalling a deviation from the canonical word order. If the listener interprets the speaker's gaze in this way, we might see evidence in the *listener's* gaze pattern or in his/her ensuing communicative behavior. Note that on all of these accounts, the listener would follow the speaker's gaze to an object. But on the deictic and referential accounts, we should not observe that speaker gaze effects on listener gaze or listeners' later sentence judgments vary with the sentential structure and thematic role relations. The syntactic-thematic account, by contrast, would predict such variation. If we obtain evidence in favour of the latter account, we would conclude that speaker gaze plays an important role in language comprehension.

In assessing the above accounts of *speaker* gaze effects, we rely on extant evidence that generally, visual context effects on establishing reference, syntactic structuring, and thematic role assignment can be indexed by the gaze behavior of a listener. That the listener's gaze can provide insight into her unfolding language comprehension was first established by Cooper (1974) and re-activated for use with modern eye-tracking technology by Tanenhaus, Spivey-Knowlton, Eberhard, and Sedivy (1995; for a review see e.g. Huettig, Rommers, & Meyer, 2011; Knoeferle & Guerra, 2016). Experiments using eye-tracking have since provided substantial evidence that objects and actions in a visual context can rapidly affect a listener's referential processes, syntactic structuring and thematic role assignment, as reflected in her gaze record (e.g., Chambers et al., 2004; Dahan & Tanenhaus, 2005; Knoeferle et al., 2005; Spivey et al., 2002; Tanenhaus et al., 1995; see Knoeferle, Habets, Crocker, & Münte, 2008 for corroborative results from neuroscientific methods). To the extent that speaker gaze also elicits these sorts of processes in a listener, they should be reflected in the listener's gaze behavior.

Beyond the question of the function of speaker gaze for *real-time* listener comprehension (deictic, referential, and/or syntactic-thematic), we assess the role of speaker gaze by asking whether it can also benefit later recall and how it holds up when compared to another cue that has robustly influenced comprehension (action depictions). Above, we had argued that speaker gaze might enhance the representation of an object in the listener's interpretation, strengthening the link between the spoken word form and an object (representation). Persistence of these effects on the listener beyond momentary attentional guidance (perhaps facilitating transfer of word-object relations into short- or long-term memory), would suggest that a speaker's gaze is an important factor in relating language to the world. A related consideration is how speaker gaze effects compare to other robust visual context effects, such as those of depicted action events. The latter can rapidly modulate the listener's visual attention and comprehension, as well as immediate recall of information about who-is-doing-what-to-whom (e.g., Zhang & Knoeferle, 2012). We will compare how these two distinct cues (gaze and action events) affect both real-time listener attention and ensuing recall of processed content. If speaker gaze is indeed an important information source for communication, then it should hold its own against other visual context effects that emerge robustly in communication.

Finally, if speaker gaze (including joint attention) is fundamental to communicative processes, then it should affect both language processing and language learning. It has been argued that perception of the non-linguistic context (of which the speaker is a part, see Knoeferle & Guerra, 2012; Münster & Knoeferle, 2018) does not influence language processing in children (e.g., Gleitmann, 1990; Trueswell et al., 1999; but see Nappa et al., 2009). On the other hand, many researchers argue that the visual context, including a social context that permits joint attention between a child and her caregiver, is critical for language learning (Kuhl et al., 2003, Kuhl, 2007, see also Tomasello, Carpenter, Call, Behne, & Moll, 2005). We consider how children's acquisition of vocabulary can benefit from joint object-based attention with a caregiver and how their inspection of objects during the learning of word-object mappings relates to their success in learning the object names. To the extent that a speaker's gaze affects structural processes in the listener, has long-lasting effects, holds its own when compared to the effects of other visual contextual cues, and facilitates language learning also in the form of joint attention, we can conclude that it plays a central role for communication, perhaps especially in interactive face-to-face contexts when objects are around us and speaker gaze is readily available.

In the remainder of this chapter we focus on the effect of the speaker's gaze on the listener's unfolding interpretation of the utterance and its subsequent recall, as well as on language development in socially interactive situations. Section 2 asks whether speaker gaze informs syntactic structuring and thematic role assignment. Section 3 discusses whether speaker gaze (compared with action depictions) also benefits later recall of inspected objects. While Sections 2 and 3 focus on adult language processing, Section 4 assesses the role of speaker gaze as well as of joint visual attention in young infants and their caregivers (also in socially interactive contexts).

2. The role of speaker eye gaze: Syntactic structuring and thematic role assignment

When considering the literature on speaker gaze, it is clear that gaze has benefits for communication. The present section assesses which function(s) speaker gaze can have for a listener's real-time language comprehension. As already mentioned, following a speaker's gaze can permit a listener to figure out which referent(s) are likely to be named even before the actual naming occurs (Hanna & Brennan, 2007; Staudte & Crocker, 2011). One reason for the beneficial effects of speaker gaze is that speakers tend to look at objects they are about to mention (Meyer et al., 1998; Griffin & Bock, 2000). In fact, the systematic link between a speaker's locus of visual attention and her reference to it may in part be the reason why listeners tend to look at objects in the line of other people's gaze (e.g., Driver et al., 1999; Ricciardelli Bricolo, Aglioti, & Chelazzi, 2002).

However, while a speaker's gaze is beneficial for the listener, facilitating conversation, we know little about the extent of its effects. Recall that we considered whether a speaker's gaze could – in addition to functioning as a deictic or referential cue – contribute towards syntactic structuring and thematic role assignment in the listener. Here we will discuss the case of non-canonical German object-verb-subject (OVS) sentences. For these sentences, a speaker inspecting referents that correspond to the sentential object (patient) and subject (agent) would likely first inspect the object referent, name it, and then, while producing the verb, shift her gaze to the subject referent just before naming it. In such a situation, the speaker's gaze when perceived by a listener could speed up the availability of that listener's referential representations, thus benefitting also processes such as thematic role assignment, as outlined in the introduction. Alternatively, or in addition, the higher activation of referential representations might carry pragmatic implications.

Knoeferle and colleagues have examined such effects of speaker gaze on thematic role assignment and syntactic structuring (Knoeferle & Kreysa, 2012; Kreysa & Knoeferle, 2011; Kreysa, Knoeferle, & Nunnemann, 2014). In these studies, participants inspected videos in which a speaker looked at three characters displayed on a computer screen (Figure 1). She referred to the depicted characters using a sentence in either SVO or OVS order (e.g., *Der/Den Kellner beglückwünscht den/ der Millionär...*, 'The waiter (subj /obj) congratulates the millionaire (obj/subj)...'). Filler sentences contained a range of further structures (e.g., dative-initial, passive, and prepositional constructions).

Figure 1. Snapshot from one of the videos used by Knoeferle and Kreysa (2012) for the sentence *Der (subj) /Den (obj) Kellner beglückwünscht den (obj) /der (subj) Millionär...,* ('The waiter (subj/obj) congratulates the millionaire (obj/subj)...').

While uttering the verb, the speaker shifted gaze from the first-mentioned character (the waiter) to the target character (the millionaire) and then named him. The authors assessed whether the speaker's gaze and head shifts would permit an onlooker to anticipate the target (object or subject) referent prior to his mention (the speaker was either visible, as in Figure 1, or obscured behind a grey bar). To this end, they recorded the listeners' eye movements. In addition, the experiment examined post-sentence verification time depending on speaker gaze to see how long-lasting such gaze effects might be. Following each video, participants saw a template such as Figure 2a. They had been told in the instructions that the stick figures stood for the characters in the previous video (i.e., the middle stick figure stands for the waiter in Figure 1). In one task, the participants then judged whether the two circled figures had been mentioned in the sentence. In another task, a different set of participants viewed an image such as Figure 2b and judged whether who-did-what-to-whom as depicted by the arrow matched who-did-what-to-whom in the sentence (e.g., for Figure 1 and the SVO sentence variant followed by Figure 2(b) they would respond "yes"). The obtained response latencies served as a post-trial measure of speaker gaze effects on the processing of the SVO and OVS sentences by the listener.

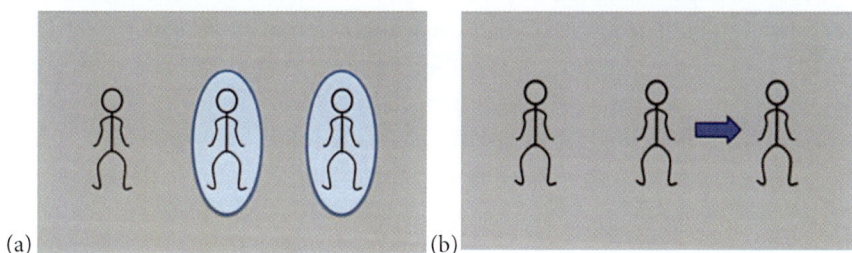

(a)   (b)

Figure 2. Response templates for verifying (a) the mentioned referents and (b) the role relations of the previously heard sentence.

Being able to see the speaker shift gaze to the target referent before its mention influenced how quickly the listeners themselves shifted gaze to that referent: They made more anticipatory fixations to that referent (i.e., on average 200 ms before the onset of *millionaire*) when the speaker was present (and her gaze thus available, as in Figure 1) than when she was absent (and gaze following was not possible); in this case, listeners' gaze to the millionaire only increased midway during *millionaire*). Both tasks also elicited more anticipatory listener fixations to the target referent during SVO than OVS sentences, though this facilitation was greater when listeners verified role relations (Figure 2b) than when they verified referents (Figure 2a).

Speaker gaze also affected the post-trial verification response times, at least when the task required role relations verification (see above). Here, participants were faster when they had seen the speaker shift gaze than when she had not been visible, and faster for SVO than OVS sentences. However, when verifying role relations, they were equally fast in verifying OVS and SVO sentences when the sentence matched the template (Figure 2a) if they had previously followed the speaker's gaze to the target referent (but not if they had failed to do so). Thus, the effect of speaker gaze persisted at least until the task had been completed, several seconds after sentence presentation.

In summary, speaker gaze did appear to affect the listeners' syntactic structuring and thematic role assignment within a few hundred milliseconds after the speaker had shifted gaze to an upcoming referent and before she mentioned that referent. Here, the speaker's gaze likely adds emphasis that makes the referential representations available earlier and more salient for the later processing of both SVO and OVS sentences. The specific sentence structure contributed to the gaze effect, permitting us to argue that speaker gaze does tie in with the unfolding structural representations (i.e., supporting the syntactic-thematic account). For SVO sentences, the enhanced object representation could permit listeners to better differentiate which of the two available object referents to attend to. Indeed, this benefit was stronger than the comparable enhancement for OVS sentences. For the latter, however, enhancement of the post-verbal referent could signal a deviation from the canonical SVO word order, effectively rendering the final noun phrase in an OVS sentence a more felicitous subject. In the latter case, the greater felicity appears to assist even downstream verification judgements. Overall thus, speaker gaze appears to play an important role for adult listeners' syntactic structuring and thematic role assignment.

3.   Immediate attention and later recall: Speaker gaze vs. action depictions

In asking whether speaker gaze plays a fundamental role for language processing, we next consider its influence on short-term memory and visual attention compared with that of another cue already mentioned above, depicted actions. Much like speaker gaze to a character (e.g., the millionaire in Figure 2 for 'The waiter congratulates the millionaire…'), action depictions can facilitate syntactic structuring and thematic role assignment. When an action is depicted by means of an object (e.g., the waiter in Figure 2 might congratulate the millionaire by handing him balloons), the verb in NP1-V-NP2 sentences can relate to that action depiction; by linking the verb to the action depiction (and its agent and patient in the scene), listeners can rapidly anticipate the upcoming patient (the millionaire in Figure 2).

A series of experiments by Knoeferle et al. (2005), for instance, revealed rapid effects of action event depictions on listeners' incremental language processing and visual attention to objects. When listening to a sentence about action event depictions (e.g., a princess depicted as washing a pirate; a fencer depicted as washing the princess), case marking would usually disambiguate the thematic role relations. But for feminine nouns such as *die Prinzessin* ('the princess'), case marking in German is identical for the accusative (object) and nominative (subject) case. Both subject-object and object-subject ordering is grammatical (subject-first is preferred), resulting in temporary thematic role ambiguity for sentences starting with a feminine noun phrase such as *die Prinzessin* … (literally: 'the princess washes'). But action depictions can rapidly disambiguate the syntactic structure and thematic role ambiguity. As listeners hear *Die Prinzessin wäscht* ('The princess washes'), they first look at her, suggesting they have established reference; but hearing *wäscht* ('washes'), they begin to inspect the pirate (perhaps they have already noticed he is the patient of the depicted washing action). If they hear 'paints', however, they rapidly re-direct their gaze to the fencer (the agent of the painting action) and anticipate him as the agent. The latter gaze pattern suggests the listeners have assigned a patient role to the princess character and its referring expression *die Prinzessin* ('the princess').

Action effects on syntactic and semantic processes have been replicated across eye-tracking studies (e.g., Knoeferle & Crocker, 2006, 2007; Knoeferle et al., 2011) and studies using event-related brain potentials (e.g., Knoeferle et al., 2008, Knoeferle et al., 2014). Depicted actions were moreover prioritized over stereotypical knowledge in guiding comprehenders' visual anticipation during sentence listening (Knoeferle & Crocker, 2006). For example, when hearing that someone is being arrested, comprehenders rapidly look for a stereotypical person (e.g., a sheriff or policeman). But when no policeman is present, they rapidly relate the verb *verhaftet* ('arrests') in an object-verb sentence beginning to a depicted arresting action, even if its agent is non-stereotypical (e.g., a scholar). In fact, when they see both a policeman (doing something unrelated) and a scholar (depicted as arresting someone), they inspect the scholar more than the policeman (perhaps because they had noticed the scholar's action in previewing the scene).

Both the robustness and the rapidity with which such actions affect listeners' visual attention and language processing make it interesting to compare their effects with that of a speaker's gaze. Actions mediated by the verb (e.g., *washes* referring to a washing action; *congratulates* referring to a congratulatory action depicted as handing over balloons) might be integrated with the verb's argument structure and thematic roles, such that the action and verb representations become closely linked with the representations of (agent and patient) event participants. Through such event representations, the actions would then be closely integrated with the unfolding utterance.

Gaze might well hold its own in such a comparison, since it has likewise been shown to lead to strong and early effects in some paradigms: While Staudte et al. (2014) did not find preferential processing of a virtual agent's gaze over simple arrow cues, Neider, Chen, Dickinson, Brennan, and Zelinsky (2010) showed that a cursor symbolizing a speaker's gaze location led to faster collaborative spatial search than verbal input alone (see also, e.g., Hanna & Brennan, 2007; Macdonald & Tatler, 2013). However, unlike actions – which are referenced by verbs – gaze behavior is not directly reflected in language. As a result, its influence might be less closely tied to language processing than that of action depictions (though recall the modulation of speaker gaze effects by sentence structure, discussed in Section 2).

Kreysa et al. (2014; see also Kreysa, Nunnemann, & Knoeferle, 2018) directly compared the effects of action depictions with those of speaker gaze and head shifts, using the paradigm established in Knoeferle and Kreysa (2012, see Figure 1). As in the earlier studies, the speaker was present on half of the trials and obscured by a grey bar in the other half of the trials. In addition, objects representing the action referred to by the verb were either depicted or not (e.g., balloons were used as objects to stand for the action of congratulating with a sentence such as 'The waiter congratulates the millionaire…'). The logic was the same as before: how rapidly would listeners anticipate the target character (the millionaire)? In a first experiment, one action was depicted: to continue with the previous example, some balloons appeared on the screen between the waiter and the millionaire at the same time as the onset of the speaker gaze shift. In a second experiment, two competing action tools appeared (e.g., balloons between the waiter and millionaire, and a pistol between the waiter and the musician). The presence of two competing action depictions forced listeners to process the action in greater depth, since they had to establish reference from the verb to the correct action. Four conditions were compared: Participants listened to sentences either with both the speaker and (either one or two) action depictions present, or with just the action depiction(s) or just the speaker present, or neither of these cues.

As in the earlier studies (e.g., Knoeferle & Kreysa, 2012), when only the speaker was visible, participants increased their fixations to the target character (the millionaire) immediately after the speaker had shifted her gaze to it; the speaker herself was hardly ever inspected. The sudden appearance of the action depictions, by contrast, did not lead to such an immediate fixation of the millionaire. Instead, listeners first inspected the action depictions in both experiments. Although they then did move their gaze to the millionaire, this occurred later than when the speaker's gaze shift prompted the listeners to anticipate the millionaire. Thus, the processing of different scene-sentence relations (i.e., the different ways in which speaker gaze and action depictions related to language) elicited distinct listener gaze responses. Nonetheless, both types of cues did enable the listener to visually anticipate the millionaire.

The authors also assessed whether listeners would benefit from this anticipation during later recall of the sentence content (Kreysa et al., 2018). When participants were asked to recall the target character of individual trials after the experiment, they were actually worse for trials in which the speaker had been present than for trials in which she had been obscured. By contrast, depicted actions slightly improved recall of the target character, compared to a no-cue baseline.

In summary, based on the eye-movement record during comprehension, we might conclude that speaker gaze had a more immediate effect than depicted actions on listeners' visual attention and language comprehension. Consequently, we might be tempted to rate its contribution towards communication as more rapid (and perhaps more substantial) than that of actions. However, this advantage of gaze over actions was short-lived: At least with regard to post-experiment recall, the early anticipation of the target character following the speaker's gaze shift did not lead to a closer integration and greater accessibility of the unfolding sentence and scene representations. Thus, while peripherally processed gaze cues may be fast in guiding listeners' attention to relevant objects, they may not necessarily benefit a listener's short term memory of the sentence content to the same extent as referentially-mediated cues such as action depictions.

If this is true, then speaker gaze may be of limited importance for slower processes such as consolidating word-object relations in memory. Alternatively, experiencing another person's gaze behavior and sharing their attentional focus (e.g., during episodes of joint interaction or communication) could enrich object representations in such a way that these are encoded better than in the absence of such social attention (e.g., Kuhl, Tsao, & Liu, 2003). If so, this would suggest that speaker gaze – when available – can enrich the representation of the unfolding interpretation and ensuing memory of its content. On that account, the absence of speaker gaze benefits on post-experiment recall of sentence content in Kreysa et al. (2018) might be attributed to the absence of real social interaction in their experiments. We will assess these possibilities by considering evidence from research on child language learning in socially interactive settings.

4. Speaker gaze and joint attention in child language processing and learning

We consider (a) the extent to which speaker gaze affects a child's visual attention, and (b) the relation between joint attention of a child and caregiver to an object and the acquisition of that object's name. Children are sensitive to eye gaze from very early on. For instance, newborns tend to orient towards photographs of faces more and look at them longer when the depicted face appears to look at them than when its eyes are averted (Farroni, Csibra, Simion, & Johnson, 2002). Infants tend to follow the direction of an adult's gaze from approximately six to nine months onwards; 12-month-olds will follow an adult's gaze towards an object, and somewhat older infants can use the adult's gaze to determine which of two objects is being named (e.g., Baldwin, 1993a, 1993b). Also at around 12 months, infants begin to understand that gaze relates an inspected object to the person inspecting it (Woodward, 2003), and both gaze and emotion cues can inform their expectations as to what somebody is going to do next (Phillips, Wellman, & Spelke, 2002). Infants' gaze-following can thus implicate intentional relations of a speaker to an object, such that when an adult inspects a location or an object, the infant may understand this behavior as a link to communicative intentions (see also Woodward, 1998).

Convincing evidence for the effect of speaker gaze on learning about objects comes from a study by Wu et al. (2011, Experiment 1). The scientists familiarized 9-month-olds with how novel objects split into parts by showing them two instances of an object's splitting behavior (e.g., during training, an abstract geometric object composed of three differently coloured parts would split in the same way twice, replacing, for instance, the right upper part with another part each time). During testing, the infants saw the same object split in a manner consistent (right upper part splits) or inconsistent (one of the other two parts splits) with the splits observed during training; they gazed longer at objects that split in an inconsistent way. Crucially, in follow-up studies, the infants used a video-taped speaker's eye gaze for learning the object features. Their learning improved and children preferred the object with the inconsistent (vs. consistent) split only when the speaker had inspected it during training (compared to when no speaker had been visible during training, Wu et al., 2011). This occurred both when only one object was present and when two objects (a target and a distractor) competed for the infant's attention.

In addition to speaker gaze effects, the situation of a caregiver and child gazing at an object together may play a pivotal role for child learning of object names. Tomasello and Farrar (1986) examined effects of joint object-directed attention in interactions between children (15 months and 21 months) and their mothers. The mother played with the child using a set of toys. The mother's references to objects that had been the focus of joint attention were positively correlated with the child's vocabulary size at 21 months. By contrast, outside of joint attention episodes, object references that attempted to re-direct child attention to a new object were negatively correlated with the child's vocabulary size at 21 months of age (see also Tomasello & Todd, 1983). Overall, infants' word learning success has been robustly linked to joint attention to a referent during interaction with a caregiver (e.g., Baldwin, 2000; Brooks & Meltzoff, 2005; Carpenter, Nagell, & Tomasello, 1998; see also Yu, Ballard, & Aslin, 2005 for a study which used a cursor representing a speaker's gaze to facilitate adult listeners' learning of Mandarin words).

A link between the infant's gaze shifts (from a social partner to the object of conversation) and her language learning has also been observed for second language learning of phoneme discrimination. The important finding is that learning the phonemes of a new language benefits from social interaction (Kuhl et al., 2003; Conboy, Brooks, Meltzoff, & Kuhl, 2015). Conboy et al. (2015) analyzed eye-movements of infants (9.5–10.5-month-olds) from monolingual English families, following a Spanish-speaking tutor's introduction of new toys (e.g., stuffed animals) to the child. During these exposure sessions, the scientists recorded instances of joint attention of the tutor and the child to the toys. In a test session several weeks after this exposure, the same infants' brain responses were recorded to gain insight into their phonemic discrimination in Spanish and in English. Crucially, the infants' social gaze behavior correlated with their brain response at 11 months as they discriminated Spanish phonemes (but not when they discriminated native English phonemes). Thus, a social aspect of gaze behavior such as joint attention may play a role in learning new linguistic information.

Overall, a speaker's gaze to objects can affect learning about objects, object features, and object names in children. In addition, episodes of joint attention between a caregiver and an infant appear to play a fundamental role for language learning, even including subtle aspects of language such as new phonemic contrasts. Clearly then, an adult speaker's gaze behavior and focus of attention, as well as ensuing instances of joint attention between speaker and listener, play an important role for language learning and for relating language to the world.

5.   The role of speaker gaze: Social and pragmatic considerations

We have assessed the role of a speaker's gaze behavior for language processing and learning. Section 2 discussed the role of speaker gaze during real-time language processing in adults. This discussion contributed the insight that a speaker's gaze, in addition to rapidly disambiguating reference, can also affect syntactic structuring and thematic role assignment within a few hundred milliseconds. Section 3 suggested that the effect of speaker gaze on referential disambiguation may predominantly be momentary, and that it seems not to extend into benefits for encoding the representations of attended objects into memory. Perhaps then a speaker's gaze primarily points to an object (deictic account). Staudte et al. (2014) also found that listeners responded to a virtual agent's gaze no differently than to an arrow pointing to a target object. Their results support the view that gaze merely acts as a visual cue. Findings from Knoeferle and Kreysa (2012) added the insight that speaker gaze can indicate a deviation from what is expected (e.g., the upcoming mention of a sentence-final subject in non-canonical sentences; syntactic-thematic account) but does not seem to contribute to forming memories of scene and sentence content (Kreysa et al., 2018).

However, a view of speaker gaze as having purely deictic effects or only short-term effects on referential and thematic processes is contradicted by evidence from language acquisition in socially interactive situations. These studies revealed that a speaker's visual attention can help with learning about objects, that joint attention between a caregiver and a child can facilitate word learning, and that joint attention is positively correlated even with 10-month-olds' learning of phonemic contrast in a new language.

Perhaps the seemingly conflicting insights from the studies reviewed in Sections 3 and 4 can be reconciled by considering the presence vs. absence of social factors and truly interactive contexts? In the studies by Kreysa et al. (2014, 2018), the speaker was video-taped and participants did not actively engage in social interaction with her. The speaker did in fact display emotional signals such as smiling at the participant before each trial, but the brief smile may not have been sufficient to truly engage the participant socially and emotionally. Staudte et al. (2014) also used a paradigm without social interaction between the (virtual agent) speaker and listener.

One possibility is that the results in the studies by Kreysa and colleagues and Staudte et al. can be attributed to the lack of social interaction. In the studies by Tomasello and Farrar (1986) as well as by Kuhl and colleagues (e.g., Conboy et al., 2015), by contrast, the infant interacted with a caregiver while playing with toys. Such direct social interaction may have facilitated the use of the speaker's gaze (though note that Wu et al. 2011 report gaze benefits for learning about objects in a passive listening paradigm, too). Usage-based approaches to language learning emphasize the importance of social interaction and of scaffolding language learning from it (Tomasello, 2003). The early social context is dyadic, whereby infants respond to the caregiver's face and voice within the first few weeks after their birth. They also gaze-follow at an early age (e.g., 11–14 months, Scaife & Bruner, 1975, see Saxton, 2010). Shared attention in adult-child interaction is moreover positively correlated not only with later vocabulary (e.g., Tomasello & Farrar, 1986; Tomasello & Todd, 1983) but also with the development of syntactic knowledge (Rosenthal, Rollins, & Snow, 1998). Towards the end of the first year, triadic interactions emerge, whereby the caregiver and the child jointly attend to a third object (Tomasello et al., 2005). This could be sharing a book, or jointly building a tower made of blocks. Children are sensitive to the social context (e.g., an agent's actions and pointing, see Woodward & Sommerville, 2000) and their behavior suggests that they interpret actions socially (as goal-directed behavior), highlighting the importance of social factors.

Further support for the importance of social and emotional aspects for language learning comes from a proposal by Kuhl (2007). Kuhl proposed a 'social gating' hypothesis to explain why phonetic learning occurs when infants actively interact with an adult tutor, but not when they listen passively to the television set (Kuhl, 2007). According to Kuhl, language learning is enhanced in social settings because the adult's social-communicative intentions boost the saliency of the input (perhaps also increasing arousal and attention, Kuhl, 2011). Similar emotional arousal does not as easily occur in the laboratory without an emotional or social interactive context (though this is not to say that movies and television series cannot also generate arousal such as when we watch the latest Bond movie or hear highly emotional speech on TV). Following a social account, we could attribute the failure to find effects of the speaker's gaze on short-term memory recall (Kreysa et al., 2018) to a lack of social engagement of the listener with the situation. This would predict that we should be able to find effects of speaker gaze on later recall if we succeeded in sufficiently engaging the listener's social and emotional system during the experiment. For instance, let's imagine the speaker, in addition to shifting gaze to the target, would sound surprised or outraged when naming it. To the extent that such emotion would engage the listener's arousal system, we might observe gaze effects not just in the moment but also during later recall of the inspected object.

A connection with social factors also fits well with extant frameworks for language interaction in the psycholinguistic literature: Pickering and Garrod (2004) challenged the overwhelming focus on monologue, and argued that the ease of conversation results from the contextual benefits of dialogue interaction and alignment of the speaker's and listener's representations. While their 'interactive alignment' framework has largely been concerned with alignment at linguistic levels (e.g., phonological, syntactic, and semantic) the ultimate goal during dialogue is alignment at the level of situation models (e.g., referential relations), leading to mutual understanding. Pickering and Garrod (2004) suggest that alignment need not be limited to linguistic processing (Pickering & Garrod, 2004, p. 188). Indeed, their model has since been linked with social perspectives on cognition (Garrod & Pickering, 2009; Pickering & Garrod, 2009). In relation to the social account, one could imagine that the difference in findings (infant phonetic learning occurs during active tutor interaction but not during passive television listening, which Kuhl (2007) accommodates by appealing to emotional factors) might in addition be affected by interactive alignment. Here, listener/learner representations would gradually be more aligned with speaker/tutor representations in interactive than passive settings (perhaps because the former activate production mechanisms to a greater extent, thus strengthening the to-be-learned representations, see Pickering & Garrod, 2007).

Clearly, many details of how a speaker's visual attention ties in with incremental language interpretation and syntactic structure building remain to be uncovered. What the present chapter highlights is that the focus of a speaker's visual attention – as reflected in their gaze behavior – affects both referential and structural processing by the listener, perhaps mediated through social and pragmatic inferences. Similarly, gaze following of adult speakers by children and joint attention during social interaction benefits child language acquisition. In conclusion, we argue that an interlocutor's gaze behavior facilitates communication at many levels and that such facilitation may be enhanced in socially interactive contexts.

Acknowledgements

This research was supported by the DFG project *Focus and thematic role assignment FoTeRo* (SPP 1727 XPrag, German Research Council) and by the European Union's Seventh Framework Programme for research, technological development and demonstration under grant agreement n°31674, both awarded to PK. We further acknowledge support by the Excellence Center 277 for Cognitive Interaction Technology (CITEC, DFG, German Research Council) and Leverhulme Trust Research Project Grant RPG-2014–253.

References

Baldwin, D. (1993a). Infants' ability to consult the speaker for clues to word reference. *Journal of Child Language*, 2, 395–418. https://doi.org/10.1017/S0305000900008345

Baldwin, D. (1993b). Early referential understanding: Young children's ability to recognize referential acts for what they are. *Developmental Psychology*, 29, 1–12. https://doi.org/10.1037/0012-1649.29.5.832

Baldwin, D. A. (2000). Interpersonal understanding fuels knowledge acquisition. *Current Directions in Psychological Science*, 9, 40–45. https://doi.org/10.1111/1467-8721.00057

Brooks, R., & Meltzoff, A. N. (2005). The development of gaze following and its relation to language. *Developmental Science*, 8, 535–543. https://doi.org/10.1111/j.1467-7687.2005.00445.x

Carpenter, M., Nagell, K., & Tomasello, M. (1998). Social cognition, joint attention, and communicative competence from 9 to 15 months of age. *Monographs of the Society for Research in Child Development*, 63, 1–174. https://doi.org/10.2307/1166214

Chambers, C. G., Tanenhaus, M. K., & Magnuson, J. S. (2004). Actions and affordances in syntactic ambiguity resolution. *Journal of Experimental Psychology: Learning, Memory, and Cognition*, 30, 687–696. https://doi.org/10.1037/0278-7393.30.3.687

Conboy, B. T., Brooks, R., Meltzoff, A. N., & Kuhl, P. K. (2015) Social Interaction in Infants' Learning of Second-Language Phonetics: An Exploration of Brain-Behavior Relations, *Developmental Neuropsychology*, 40, 216–229. https://doi.org/10.1080/87565641.2015.1014487

Cooper, R. M. (1974). The control of eye fixation by the meaning of spoken language: A new methodology for the real-time investigation of speech perception, memory, and language processing. *Cognitive Psychology*, 6, 84–107. https://doi.org/10.1016/0010-0285(74)90005-X

Dahan, D., & Tanenhaus, M. (2005). Looking at the rope when looking for the snake: Conceptually mediated eye movements during spoken-word recognition. *Psychonomic Bulletin & Review*, 12, 453–459. https://doi.org/10.3758/BF03193787

Doherty-Sneddon, G., & Phelps, F. G. (2005). Gaze aversion: A response to cognitive or social difficulty? *Memory & Cognition*, 33, 727–733. https://doi.org/10.3758/BF03195338

Doherty-Sneddon, G., & Phelps, F. G. (2007). Teachers' responses to children's eye gaze. *Educational Psychology*, 27, 93–109. https://doi.org/10.1080/01443410601061488

Driver, J., Davis, G., Ricciardelli, P., Kidd, P., Maxwell, E., & Baron-Cohen, S. (1999). Gaze perception triggers reflexive visuospatial orienting. *Visual Cognition*, 6, 509–540. https://doi.org/10.1080/135062899394920

Farroni, T., Csibra, G., Simion, F., & Johnson, M. H. (2002). Eye contact detection in humans from birth. *Proceedings of the National Academy of Sciences of the United States of America*, 99, 9602–9605. https://doi.org/10.1073/pnas.152159999

Griffin, Z. M., & Bock, K. (2000). What the eyes say about speaking. *Psychological Science*, 11, 274–279. https://doi.org/10.1111/1467-9280.00255

Garrod, S., & Pickering, M. J. (2009). Joint action, interactive alignment, and dialog. *Topics in Cognitive Science*, 1, 292–304. https://doi.org/10.1111/j.1756-8765.2009.01020.x

Glenberg, A. M., Shroeder, J. L., & Robertson, D. A. (1998). Averting the gaze disengages the environment and facilitates remembering. *Memory & Cognition*, 26, 651–658. https://doi.org/10.3758/BF03211385

Gleitman. L. R., (1990). The structural sources of verb meaning. *Language Acquisition* 1, 3–55. https://doi.org/10.1207/s15327817la0101_2

Hanna, J., and Brennan, S. (2007). Speaker's eye gaze disambiguates referring expressions early during face-to-face conversation. *Journal of Memory and Language*, 57, 596–615. https://doi.org/10.1016/j.jml.2007.01.008

Huettig, F., Rommers, J., & Meyer, A. S. (2011). Using the visual world paradigm to study language processing: A review and critical evaluation. *Acta psychologica*, 137, 151–171. https://doi.org/10.1016/j.actpsy.2010.11.003

Knoeferle, P., Crocker, M. W., Scheepers, C., & Pickering, M. J. (2005). The influence of the immediate visual context on incremental thematic role-assignment: evidence from eye- movements in depicted events. *Cognition*, 95, 95–127. https://doi.org/10.1016/j.cognition.2004.03.002

Knoeferle, P., & Crocker, M. W. (2007). The influence of recent scene events on spoken comprehension: evidence from eye movements. *Journal of Memory and Language*, 57, 519–543. https://doi.org/10.1016/j.jml.2007.01.003

Knoeferle, P., & Crocker, M. W. (2006). The coordinated interplay of scene, utterance, and world knowledge: evidence from eye-tracking. *Cognitive Science*, 30, 481–529. https://doi.org/10.1207/s15516709cog0000_65

Knoeferle, P. & Guerra, E. (2012). What's non-linguistic visual context? – A view from language comprehension. In: Rita Finkbeiner, Jörg Meibauer, & Petra Schuhmacher (eds) *What is a context? Linguistic approaches and challenges* (pp. 129–149). Amsterdam: John Benjamins. https://doi.org/10.1075/la.196.09kno

Knoeferle, P. & Guerra, E. (2016). Visually situated language comprehension. *Language and Linguistics Compass*, 10, 66–82. https://doi.org/10.1111/lnc3.12177

Knoeferle, P., Habets, B., Crocker, M. W., Muente, T. F. (2008). Visual scenes trigger immediate syntactic reanalysis: evidence from ERPs during situated spoken comprehension. *Cerebral Cortex*, 18, 789–795. https://doi.org/10.1093/cercor/bhm121

Knoeferle, P. & Kreysa, H. (2012). Effects of speaker gaze on syntactic structuring. *Frontiers in Psychology*, 2:376. https://doi.org/10.3389/fpsyg.2011.00376.

Knoeferle, P., Urbach, T, & Kutas, M (2011). Comprehending visual context influences on incremental sentence comprehension: insights from ERPs and picture-sentence verification. *Psychophysiology*, 48, 495–506. https://doi.org/10.1111/j.1469-8986.2010.01080.x

Knoeferle, P., Urbach, T., & Kutas, M. (2014). Different mechanisms for role relations versus verb-action congruence effects: Evidence from ERPs in picture-sentence verification. *Acta Psychologica*, 152, 133–148. https://doi.org/10.1016/j.actpsy.2014.08.004

Kreysa, H., & Knoeferle, P. (2011). Effects of speaker gaze on spoken language comprehension: Task matters. In: L. Carlson, C. Hölscher & T.F. Shipley (Eds.), *Proceedings of the 33rd Annual Conference of the Cognitive Science Society* (pp. 1557–1562), Austin, TX: The Cognitive Science Society.

Kreysa, H., Knoeferle, P., & Nunnemann, E. (2014). Effects of speaker gaze versus depicted actions on visual attention during sentence comprehension. In: Paul Bello, Marcello Guarini, Marjorie McShane & Brian Scassellati (Eds). *Proceedings of the 36th Annual Meeting of the Cognitive Science Society*, (pp. 2513–2518). Austin, TX: Cognitive Science Society.

Kreysa, H., Nunnemann, E., & Knoeferle, P. (2018). Distinct effects of different visual cues on sentence comprehension and later recall: The case of speaker gaze versus depicted actions. *Acta Psychologica*. https://doi.org/10.1016/j.actpsy.2018.05.001

Kreysa, H., & Pickering M. J. (2011). Eye movements in dialogue. In S. P. Liversedge, I. D. Gilchrist, & S. Everling (Eds.), *The Oxford Handbook of Eye Movements* (p. 943–959). Oxford: OUP.

Kuhl, P. K., Tsao, F. -M., & Liu, H. -M. (2003). Foreign-language experience in infancy: Effects of short-term exposure and social interaction on phonetic learning. *Proceedings of the National Academy of Sciences*, 100, 9096–9101. https://doi.org/10.1073/pnas.1532872100

Kuhl, P. K. (2007). Is speech learning "gated" by the social brain? *Developmental Science*, 10, 110–120. https://doi.org/10.1111/j.1467-7687.2007.00572.x

Kuhl, P. K. (2011). Social mechanisms in early language acquisition: Understanding integrated brain systems supporting language. In J. Decety & J. Cacioppo (Eds.), *The Oxford handbook of social neuroscience* (pp. 649–667). Oxford, UK: Oxford University Press.

Langton, S. R. H. and Bruce, V. (2000). You must see the point: automatic processing of cues to the direction of social attention. *Journal of Experimental Psychology: HPP*, 26, 747–757.

Langton, S., Watt, R. J., & Bruce, V. (2000). Do the eyes have it? Cues to the direction of social attention. *Trends in Cognitive Sciences*, 4, 50–59. https://doi.org/10.1016/S1364-6613(99)01436-9

Macdonald, R. G., & Tatler, B. W. (2013). Do as eye say: Gaze cueing and language in a real-world social interaction. *Journal of Vision*, 13, 1–12. https://doi.org/10.1167/13.4.6

Meyer, A. S., Sleiderink, A. M., & Levelt, W. J. M. (1998). Viewing and naming objects: Eye movements during noun phrase production. *Cognition*, 66, B25–B33. https://doi.org/10.1016/S0010-0277(98)00009-2

Münster K. and Knoeferle P. (2018) Extending Situated Language Comprehension (Accounts) with Speaker and Comprehender Characteristics: Toward Socially Situated Interpretation. *Frontiers in Psychology*, 8, 2267. https://doi.org/10.3389/fpsyg.2017.02267.

Nappa, R., Wessel, A., McEldoon, K. L., Gleitman, L., & Trueswell, J. C. (2009). Use of Speaker's Gaze and Syntax in Verb Learning. *Language Learning and Development*, 5, 203–234. https://doi.org/10.1080/15475440903167528

Neider, M. B., Chen, X., Dickinson, C. A., Brennan, S., & Zelinsky, G. (2010). Coordinating spatial referencing using shared gaze. *Psychological Bulletin & Review*, 17, 718–724. https://doi.org/10.3758/PBR.17.5.718

Phillips A. T., Wellman H. M., & Spelke E. S. (2002). Infants' ability to connect gaze and emotional expression to intentional action. *Cognition*, 85, 53–78. https://doi.org/10.1016/S0010-0277(02)00073-2

Pickering, M. J., & Garrod, S. (2004). Toward a mechanistic psychology of dialogue. *Behavioral and Brain Sciences*, 27, 169–225. https://doi.org/10.1017/S0140525X04000056

Pickering, M., & Garrod, S. (2007). Do people use language production to make predictions during comprehension? *Trends in Cognitive Sciences*, 11, 105–110. https://doi.org/10.1016/j.tics.2006.12.002

Pickering, M. J., & Garrod, S. (2009). Language, interaction and embodiment. *European Journal of Social Psychology*, 39, 1178–1179. https://doi.org/10.1002/ejsp.680

Ricciardelli, P., Bricolo, E., Aglioti, S., & Chelazzi, L. (2002). My eyes want to look where your eyes are looking: Exploring the tendency to imitate another individual's gaze. *NeuroReport*, 13, 2259–2264. https://doi.org/10.1097/00001756-200212030-00018

Rosenthal Rollins, P., & Snow, C. (1998). Shared attention and grammatical development in typical children and children with autism. *Journal of Child Language*, 25, 653–673. https://doi.org/10.1017/S0305000998003596

Samson, D., Apperly, I. A., Braithwaite, J. J., Andrews, B. J., & Bodley Scott, S. E. (2010). Seeing it their way: evidence for rapid and involuntary computation of what other people see. *Journal of Experimental Psychology: Human Perception and Performance*, 36, 1255–1266.

Santiesteban, I., Catmur, C., Hopkins, S. C., Bird, G., & Heyes, C. (2014). Avatars and arrows: Implicit mentalizing or domain-general processing? *Journal of Experimental Psychology: Human Perception and Performance*, 40, 929–937. https://doi.org/http://dx.doi.org/10.1037/a0035175

Saxton, M. (2010). *Child Language: Acquisition and Development*. London: Sage Publications.

Scaife, M., & Bruner, J. S. (1975). The capacity for joint visual attention in the infant. *Nature*, 253, 265–266. https://doi.org/10.1038/253265a0

Spivey, M., Tanenhaus, M., Eberhard, K., & Seidvy, J. (2002). Eye movements and spoken language comprehension: Effects of visual context on syntactic ambiguity resolution. *Cognitive Psychology*, 45, 447–481. https://doi.org/10.1016/S0010-0285(02)00503-0

Staudte, M., and Crocker, M. W. (2011). Investigating joint attention mechanisms through spoken human–robot interaction. *Cognition* 120, 268–291. https://doi.org/10.1016/j.cognition.2011.05.005

Staudte, M., Crocker, M. W., Heloir, A., & Kipp, M. (2014). The influence of speaker gaze on listener comprehension: Contrasting visual versus intentional accounts, *Cognition*, 133, 317–328. https://doi.org/10.1016/j.cognition.2014.06.003

Tanenhaus, M. K., Spivey-Knowlton, M. J., Eberhard, K., & Sedivy, J. C. (1995). Integration of visual and linguistic information in spoken language comprehension. *Science*, 268, 632–634. https://doi.org/10.1126/science.7777863

Tomasello, M. (2003). *Constructing a language: A usage-based theory of language acquisition*. Cambridge, MA: Harvard University Press.

Tomasello, M., Carpenter, M., Call, J., Behne, T., & Moll, H. (2005). Understanding and sharing intentions: The origins of cultural cognition. *Behavioral and Brain Sciences*, 28, 675–691. https://doi.org/10.1017/S0140525X05000129

Tomasello, M., & Farrar, J. (1986). Joint attention and early language. *Child Development*, 57, 1454–1463. https://doi.org/10.2307/1130423

Tomasello, M. & Todd, J. (1983). Joint attention and lexical acquisition style. *First Language*, 4, 197–211. https://doi.org/10.1177/014272378300401202

Trueswell, J. C., Sekerina, I., Hill, N. M., & Logrip, M. L. (1999). The kindergarten-path effect: Studying on-line sentence processing in young children. *Cognition*, 73, 89–13. https://doi.org/10.1016/S0010-0277(99)00032-3

Woodward, A., & Sommerville, J. (2000). Twelve-month-old infants interpret actions in context. *Psychological Science*, 11, 73–77. https://doi.org/10.1111/1467-9280.00218

Woodward, A. (1998). Infants selectively encode the goal object of an actor's reach. *Cognition*, 69, 1–34. https://doi.org/10.1016/S0010-0277(98)00058-4

Woodward, A. L. (2003). Infants' developing understanding of the link between looker and object. *Developmental Science*, 6, 297–311.

Wu, R., Gopnik, A., Richardson, D. C., & Kirkham, N. Z. (2011). Infants learn about objects from statistics and people. *Developmental Psychology*, 47, 1220–1229. https://doi.org/10.1037/a0024023

Yu, C., Ballard, D. H., & Aslin, R. N. (2005). The role of embodied intention in early lexical acquisition. *Cognitive Science*, 29, 961–1005. https://doi.org/10.1207/s15516709cog0000_40

Zhang, Lu & Knoeferle, P. (2012). Visual Context Effects on Thematic Role Assignment in Children versus Adults: Evidence from Eye Tracking in German. In: Naomi Miyake, David Peebles, & Richard P. Cooper, *Proceedings of the Annual Meeting of the Cognitive Science Society* (pp. 2593–2598), Boston, USA: The Cognitive Science Society.

CHAPTER 4

Weaving oneself into others
Coordination in conversational systems

Rick Dale and Michael J. Spivey
University of California, Los Angeles / University of California, Merced

We review a range of findings that show how eye movements (and other body movements) exhibit correlated behavior across two or more people during natural interactions. We then synthesize these different results into a more general account of how people's cognitive, sensory and motor systems become coordinated with one another during natural dialogue. We argue that treating conversants as parts of one integrated *system* is a useful explanatory strategy for understanding interaction. We end by describing explicit quantitative conditions for seeking "systemhood" in human interaction. These conditions motivate future research questions on social eye movements and other behaviors.

Keywords: behavioral synchrony, interaction as coupled multi-person system, dense-sampling measures, social gaze

1. Introduction: The eyes of social systems

When two people interact, they reveal widespread interdependence. This interdependence happens in many ways. The words used by one interlocutor are partly a function of the words that their conversation partner just used. Conversation partners choose words that facilitate understanding given what they know of each other (Clark & Wilkes-Gibbs, 1986). They even combine words into sentences in a manner that adapts to the information flow that might help a comprehender (Jaeger, 2010). This interdependence occurs in other subtler behaviors, too. Their phonological tendencies may become more similar – or less similar – depending on the social goals they have with each other (Manson et al., 2013; Coupland, 1985). The subtle body sway that they reveal may also become correlated, and this correlation may reflect the kind of social interaction they are having (Paxton & Dale, 2013). Under particular conditions, their heart rate may even fluctuate in similar ways (Fusaroli et al., 2016). Sometimes these patterns are powerful indices of a shared understanding, other times they may be a soft but detectable background "hum" of shared multimodal structure (Louwerse et al., 2012).

https://doi.org/10.1075/ais.10.04dal

We do not yet have a good understanding of the processes that govern this interdependence. Some of these similarities between people may be merely correlational, an outcome of other functional correspondences. For example, the precise words chosen by partners may drive shared posture dynamics, suggesting that the bodily signals themselves may not be in a direct causal relationship (Shockley et al., 2007). However, it is unlikely to be so simple a story. For example, eye-movement correspondence can facilitate memory, which in turn may influence eye-movement correspondence – forming a kind of causal circuit or feedback loop (D. Richardson & Dale, 2005). In addition, there may be multiple causal forces driving these correspondences between two people. Shared topics and words in conversation may drive bodily correlation; but so may a desire to be more socially affiliated, such as by occupying similar bodily stances or to nod in understanding in a similar way (e.g., Lakin & Chartrand, 2003).

Because of this complexity, it is important to improve our understanding of how, in natural conversation, the various processes involved work in concert. Though we focus on eye movements in this chapter, we will consider their relationship to the overall system, to other behaviors and cognitive processes. We situate work on visual attention during interaction in this broader landscape of research on language and social interaction.

A first goal of this chapter is a theoretical one. In order to unpack the complexity of interaction, we argue that it is advantageous to consider two people in interaction as constituting their own kind of unitary system. By understanding the dyad as a kind of coupled system, we can investigate relationships between its different parts and processes, whether they are attached to a single interlocutor, or whether they reflect information flowing bi-directionally between two people.

Our second goal is to show that eye movements are an especially fruitful source of data to test this "system" premise. By now, more than a decade of research has been devoted to how two visual attentional systems can become interdependent in the manner described above. We argue that this research has resulted in an important central observation: The dynamics of visual attention between two people reveal that they *can* become a coupled system.

In what follows, we first develop what we mean by "system," in the next section. After this, we provide an extensive empirical review, showing that eye movements and other behavioral signatures indeed reveal patterns of rich social interdependence, even in very basic experimental tasks. In the concluding section of the chapter, we elaborate on the criteria for determining whether two people form a unitary system, and describe how this motivates future research questions.

1.1 Three types of system

As a theoretical commitment, it is insufficient to say simply that two people form a "system." There are many senses of the word "system," and these can be broken down into at least three types: mechanical, computational, and complex. These definitions are not completely independent. Computational systems can also be considered complex dynamic systems (Simon, 1992), and complex systems can certainly, in a way, carry out computation (Crutchfield, 1994). But these notions of "system" offer terminological and conceptual distinctions that are useful for supporting empirical research questions (for an early review and discussion, see: Shenhar, 1990).

The simplest sense of system is a *mechanical system*. A mechanical system is one composed of elementary parts, and these parts have very particular and fixed purposes. These parts carry out such functions amidst other parts, and result in particular behaviors in response to specific states or conditions. If one of these parts is disrupted in some way, it can have an immediate detrimental effect on the functioning of the system. A car's engine, a thermostat, and a typewriter are classic examples of such a system. Even in their modern instantiations, these systems have parts of relatively fixed function, and when these parts are disrupted, the system is not especially adaptive – its operation is disrupted in some fashion. In the parlance of cognitive modeling, these systems do not show "graceful degradation" (Bechtel & Abrahamsen, 1991).

A *computational system* is more flexible. It has components such as variable states and algorithms that can take on more diverse sorts of input/output transformations. In fact, the classical mechanical systems mentioned above can be made more flexible by integrating new computational hardware and software to make these devices more adaptive. For example, a smart thermostat may adapt to the occupants of a home by learning what temperatures they set – even if the thermostat's temperature meter is miscalibrated. Classic examples of computational systems are exemplified by symbolic cognitive models (Newell, 1980; Anderson, 1996). Cognitive models can be highly adaptive. They can deploy context-specific computational rules of operation that can help the system overcome rapid changes in its environment, or to generalize to new environments.

Finally, a *complex system* is one in which its parts may not even have strictly designated functions; these functions may change within the overall system in response to conditions the system finds itself in (M. Richardson et al., 2014). Such systems are highly adaptive (Mitchell, 2009). In fact, adaptive complex systems have been referred to as "anti-fragile," in the sense that they thrive on perturbations (Taleb, 2012). Some have argued that in complex systems, the parts themselves may not be neatly structurally or functionally distinguishable from the whole or its environment (Chemero & Turvey, 2008). Consider a simple, single gesture embedded in linguistic interaction. In form and function, that gesture requires its relationships to other aspects of interaction to bring it significance. The gesture and its context are, in an important sense, mutually reliant (Enfield, 2013).

This system taxonomy has a complicated and sometimes provocative history, which we've synthesized here (for useful review see Adams & Aizawa, 2001; Bechtel & Abrahamsen, 2010; Eliasmith, 1996; Spivey, 2008; Van Orden et al., 2003; Van Orden & Stephen, 2012). Indeed, the three types of system are not unrelated, and not even always mutually exclusive. There is considerable debate about the difference between computational and complex systems (e.g., Eliasmith, 2012; Van Orden & Stephen, 2012). There are deep similarities between these concepts, such that any complex dynamic system can be characterized as computational in some sense or another (e.g., Crutchfield, 1994; Edelman, 2008; Mitchell, 2009; and of course Wiener, 1961). In addition, mechanical systems can be regarded as kinds of very simple computational systems (e.g., Ashby, 1956; Van Gelder, 1998). We therefore do not pretend that these concepts perfectly designate systems that interest cognitive scientists.

However, adopting one of these system concepts can facilitate (or deter) research questions by favoring particular causal narratives. For example, researchers who highlight computational systems often strictly delimit the internal states of the system from the environment in which it functions (Adams & Aizawa, 2001). Those who highlight complex systems, however, see elements of the environment as important parts of the system itself (Chemero, 2011). In cognitive terms, the arrangement of tools or artifacts in our environment, including the position and behavior of other *individuals* in our environment, involve exchanges of information that are an active part of processing (Hutchins, 1995; Tollefsen, 2006).

When one embraces the complex-systems concept, it motivates considering all the exchanges of information – whether within and across individuals and artifacts – as a coherent system that can be investigated. This is the system concept that inspires the current chapter. We hope to convince the reader that this system concept is especially useful in the case of eye movements. Eye movements are *both* a continuous perceptual medium *and* behavioral signal that others can see (Risko et al., 2016). Their semi-continuous dynamics make social eye movements a fruitful signal for investigating "systemhood" between two or more interacting individuals.

Eye-movement research is also an archetype of an emerging general research strategy among those interested in complex and dynamic systems. Eye movements provide semi-continuous dynamics of a system. These dynamics can be investigated for their shared structure across individuals, how processing is perturbed or stabilized in real-time, and more. In general, these behavioral dynamics can reveal the co-variation among parts of a system. The eyes are not alone in this respect. We begin the next section by considering the wealth of data that can be gathered on the dynamics of cognitive systems. This also includes speech, body movement, and more. In order to pursue a complex and dynamic systems approach to cognition, researchers have lately taken on strategies for designing experiments, measuring behavior semi-continuously, and framing their analysis under new techniques. In the next sections, we showcase the wide variety of research that takes on this dynamic approach. We then situate eye-movement research within it.

2.   Collecting samples from the temporal dynamics of a cognitive process

In order to measure a complex dynamical system properly, one needs a sequence of samples from the system while it is functioning. Too often, traditional cognitive psychology methods have been designed to collect a single measurement at the end of the process carried out by the cognitive system (e.g., reaction time and/or accuracy). If the dynamics of the process are key to understanding the mechanisms of the system – because it is a *dynamical* system – then that single sample collected after the process is complete does not provide much insight into those mechanisms.

The research paradigms for developing sequences of multiple samples during a cognitive-motor process may be carved up into three basic categories: a) devise a cyclic motor behavior that can be measured continuously, b) treat a series of discrete separated tasks (experimental trials) as though it were one long more-general cognitive performance, and c) develop a methodology that can collect multiple samples within the few seconds that make up each experimental trial: dense-sampling methods.

2.1   Devise a cyclic motor behavior

The first, and perhaps oldest, approach involves designing a behavioral task that is repetitive and cyclic so that the human system can be measured many times during this lengthy process. This could be something as basic as walking on a treadmill while the leg and body movements are recorded with motion capture methods (Hove & Keller, 2015), or something as simple as tapping your finger to the beat of a metronome (Hove, Spivey, & Krumhansl, 2010; Repp, 2005), or it could be as contrived as a bimanual coordination task where one's index fingers are supposed to waggle up and down in anti-phase with one another (one index finger going up while the other index finger is going down; see Kelso, 1984, 1997).

In the case of bimanual coordination, the Haken, Kelso, and Bunz (1985) model provides an elegant mathematical account of the circumstances under which anti-phase synchrony could be maintained in the finger waggling, and those conditions under which the fingers would involuntarily fall into in-phase synchrony (both fingers up at the same time, and then both down at the same time). The fingers can maintain that anti-phase finger waggling at slow and medium speeds. But when the frequency speeds up, these two connected networks naturally slip into in-phase synchrony, where they both produce essentially identical activity patterns at the same time. This pull toward synchrony among systems that are informationally connected with one another is a common phenomenon in an extremely wide variety of contexts, including superconductors, pendulum clocks, fireflies, and neural networks (Strogatz, 2003).

In fact, that natural pull toward synchrony even happens when the two limbs that are trying to coordinate in anti-phase repetition belong to two different brains. Following up on the work of Kelso and colleagues, Schmidt, Carello and Turvey (1990) had *two people* sit on a table and each of them swung one leg in anti-phase synchrony with the other person's leg (e.g., one person's leg swung forward while the other person's leg swung backward). Just as with bimanual coordination, at slow and medium frequencies, this anti-phase pattern could be maintained. But at higher frequencies, the two legs tended to involuntarily slip into in-phase synchrony.

Obviously, this pull toward synchrony was not due a corpus callosum connecting the motor cortices. It was due to the shared perception-action loop connecting the left motor cortex in one person's brain to the right motor cortex in the other person's brain. While each person was producing their own motor output, they were simultaneously perceiving the motoric results of the other person's motor cortex, and this perceptual information continuously influenced their own motor cortex. The continuous information flow between the two people allowed the two of them to function as a single two-legged complex system. Importantly, the same Haken-Kelso-Bunz mathematical model of attractor basins in a relative-phase landscape, which described how a system with two fingers waggling would settle into certain patterns of behavior, also fit the data from two people's legs swinging. That is, the model that treated a person's two fingers like they were *one complex system* also successfully treated two people's different legs like they were *one complex system*.

2.2   A series of experimental trials as dynamics

The second paradigm that allows one to collect many samples from the temporal dynamics of a cognitive process is one where the traditional cognitive psychology experiment remains the same, but the data undergo a very different treatment. In many traditional cognitive experiments, a series of experimental trials are randomized in order, and one data point is collected at the end of each trial. The order of trial types is usually randomized with the intent of ruling out any sequential effects from one trial to the next. The experimenter hopes that, when one trial is over, the participant's brain goes back to a neutral resting state in preparation for the next trail. Any deviations from that expectation will turn into "random noise" in the data once many participants have contributed data to many different sequencings of those experimental trials. But what if there are intrinsic fluctuations in the participant's overall performance of the cognitive task across the duration of the experiment? What if the "noise" in the data wasn't purely random?

When each participant's sequence of reaction times is treated as one long time series of cognitive performance, it turns out that the fluctuations do not exhibit uncorrelated noise, but instead the noise has correlations with itself over time (Gilden, 2001; Kello, Anderson, Holden, & Van Orden, 2008; Van Orden & Holden, 2002). This correlated "pink" noise tends to show an abundance of long-range correlations, as is often observed in the power law distributions of behaviors from self-organized complex systems, such as avalanches, earthquakes, animal swarming behaviors, heart function, and neural networks. Thus, the ubiquitous presence of 1/f power law scaling of the variance (i.e., "pink" noise) in reaction times and other sequential behaviors was taken as evidence that human cognition may not be well described by a traditional *computational system* composed of processing modules linked up with linear signal transmission (i.e., the box-and-arrow computer metaphor for the mind, where variance comes only from white uncorrelated noise). Instead, human cognition may be better described as a self-organized *complex system* in which coherent mental processes emerge, or "soft-assemble", dynamically as a result of many simple sensory and motor processes interacting (Kello et al., 2010; Kloos & Van Orden, 2010; Van Orden, Holden, & Turvey, 2003).

Dotov, Nie and Chemero (2010) offer an example application of this to test whether a person and her environment are acting as a "system." These authors tracked smooth use of an artifact (computer mouse) in an extended task. They found this correlation (pink) noise under conditions when a participant was smoothly utilizing the artifact, and inferred that the artifact had become, in a sense, a participant in those cognitive dynamics.

2.3   Dense-sampling methods

The third paradigm that allows one to collect many samples from the temporal dynamics of a cognitive process is one where laboratory devices are used that can record multiple measurements per second: dense-sampling methods. There are several such methods, and we will mention two here before turning to this chapter's focus: eyetracking methods. For example, electroencephalography (EEG) and magnetoencephalography (MEG) typically collect a thousand or more samples per second of brain activity, and when those data are examined with time series analysis methods, they can reveal the sequence of influences between cortical regions (e.g., Gow & Olson, 2015; see also Spivey, 2016).

Though brain imaging techniques can constrain the experimental task environment, many dense-sampling methods can allow for the experimental task to become more ecologically valid (i.e., more applicable to real-life circumstances). Rather than interrupting a participant's cognitive process and forcing them to provide some explicit meta-cognitive report of their internal processes (e.g., speed-accuracy tradeoff methods), or asking them to perform an unusual observation on what would otherwise be their normal everyday language processing (e.g., phoneme-monitoring tasks, or lexical decision tasks), dense-sampling methods often allow a person to go about their cognitive task in a normal fashion without interruptions. The samples are collected (multiple times per second) as a by-product of the person's natural behaviors while carrying out the cognitive task.

For example, Shockley, Santana, and Fowler (2003) recorded two people's postural sway while they engaged in a joint puzzle-solving task. Each person stood on a pressure plate, and changes in the x,y location of each person's center of mass were recorded 60 times per second. The natural conversation and body language during the 30-minute task were uninterrupted by this dense-sampling measure, and yet millions of data points were collected across the 26 participants. Buried in those millions of data points, Shockley et al. found that when the two people are conversing with each other to solve the puzzle, their postural sway (as a simple index of their body language) gets coordinated in a way that shows recurrent patterns with one another (see also M. Richardson, Marsh, & Schmidt, 2005). By contrast, when each participant is conversing with an unrelated confederate to solve the same puzzle, that coordination in postural sway is not present.

In fact, in those situations where two people become entrained with one another, even with something as simple as tapping together to the beat of a metronome, they can develop an increased affiliation for one another. Hove and Risen (2009) had pairs of participants tap their fingers in synchrony with a visual metronome, and under circumstances where synchrony was greater between the two people, their reported affiliation with one another was also greater.

The direction of causality can go the other way as well. Having that affiliation already, such as with a family member, can in turn cause more synchrony between the two people. For example, Konvalinka et al. (2011) demonstrated that when a person watches their family member do a fire-walking ritual, both the fire-walker's heart rate and the family member's heart rate become coordinated in a way that shows recurrent patterns with one another. By contrast, non-related spectators did not show that heart rate coordination with the fire walker. Thus, similar to Kelso's (1984) waggling fingers and Schmidt et al.'s (1990) swinging legs, a dyad of two people engaged in a conversation or a joint task, or even just sharing a profound moment together, often begin to function in a way that looks a bit more like *one complex system* than two.

3.   Eyetracking as a dense-sampling measure of human interaction

Among the various dense-sampling measures that are used to study cognition, the most widespread dense-sampling measure of human linguistic interaction is perhaps eyetracking. Originally called the Visual World Paradigm, this approach started out focusing significantly on adapting traditional experimental frameworks from psycholinguistics into the dense-sampling context. By collecting multiple samples (i.e., visual fixations) during the process of each trial – rather than a solitary data point at the end of a trial – the Visual World Paradigm was also able to use somewhat more ecologically valid tasks that did not involve meta-linguistic queries, the way lexical-decision tasks or phoneme-monitoring tasks do. Instead, the participant could simply follow natural spoken instructions to move objects around in a display, and the eye movements were recorded as a natural by-product of the language comprehension process.

One of the first reported results with this spoken language eyetracking paradigm demonstrated that a visual context could influence the real-time resolution of a syntactic ambiguity (Tanenhaus, Spivey-Knowlton, Eberhard, & Sedivy, 1995; see also Farmer, Cargill, Hindy, Dale, & Spivey, 2007). The accepted wisdom of that time suggested that only syntactic principles could influence the syntactic decisions made in the face of a temporary structural ambiguity (Ferreira & Clifton, 1986; Frazier, 1995). For example, while hearing "on the towel" in sentences (1) and (2), there's no way to know whether this prepositional phrase is part of the verb phrase in curly brackets, telling you where to put the apple (as in sentence 1), or whether it is part of the noun phrase in square brackets, telling you where the apple currently is (as in sentence 2). Tanenhaus et al. (1995) showed that when there was one apple in the visual display, the eyetracker recorded people's eyes looking at the irrelevant extra towel, suggesting that people were briefly mis-parsing sentence (2) as initially instructing them to relocate the apple onto that empty towel. By contrast, when the display contained two apples (so that the pragmatics of the situation required further specification for "the apple"), that same syntactically ambiguous sentence no longer elicited eye movements to that other towel.

(1) {Put [the apple] on the towel}.

(2) {Put [the apple (on the towel)] in the box}.

The VWP showed not only that visual context can influence syntactic processing over several seconds of speech, but also that it can influence reference resolution over the one or two seconds it takes to utter a single noun phrase. For
example, with sentence (3), when the display has only one starred object, Eberhard,
Spivey-Knowlton, Sedivy, and Tanenhaus (1995) found that people would often
fixate that correct object before the noun "square" was even uttered. Due to their
incremental comprehension of the sentence as it unfolded, and mapping of those
adjectives onto the available objects in the display, they were able to determine the
object to which that noun phrase referred *without even having to hear its head noun*
(see also Reali, Spivey, Tyler & Terranova, 2006).

(3) Touch the starred yellow square.

Altmann and Kamide (1999) showed that a similar kind of linguistic anticipation
works for transitive verbs as well. When there was only one edible object in the
display (e.g., a cake) and the participant heard sentence (4), participants were often
fixating the cake before the word "cake" had even been spoken. Not only does visual
context influence these real-time predictions, but so do the semantic relationships
between the verb and the relevant nouns (Knoeferle & Crocker, 2006).

(4) The boy ate the cake.

At the finer-grain temporal scale of a few hundred milliseconds, the VWP was even
able to show that visual context could influence processing during the recognition
of a single spoken word. Partway through hearing the word "candle" in sentence
(5), participants frequently fixated a candy when one was in the display (Allopenna,
Magnuson, & Tanenhaus, 1998; Spivey-Knowlton, 1996). This highly-replicated
finding reveals two key insights about spoken language comprehension: (1) the
process of spoken word recognition accrues acoustic-phonetic information continuously over the time scale of dozens of milliseconds, such that objects with similar
sounding names can draw one's attention while hearing one of the words, and
(2) visual context can influence this speech perception process.

(5) Pick up the candle.

In addition to having inanimate objects in the visual environment that can serve as
context for real-time language comprehension, there are frequently people in the
environment who can serve as context as well (Brown-Schmidt, Yoon, & Ryskin,
2015; Fitneva & Spivey, 2005). However, in contrast to the inanimate objects as

context, people do a lot more than simply help a listener comprehend the linguistic stimuli, they help *co-create* the linguistic stimuli in the first place via natural unscripted conversation. Compared to the unidirectional scripted instructions typically used in the early experiments with the VWP, natural unscripted conversation makes for a significantly different language environment. So different, in fact, that some of the temporary ambiguities that psycholinguists have identified in language processing don't really behave like they are ambiguous.

In an example of this, Brown-Schmidt, Campana and Tanenhaus (2005) used an unscripted joint task that required coordination and conversation, and recorded participants' eye movements. They found that when sentences with complex noun phrases, such as (3), naturally occurred in the conversation (436 of them), the listener at that moment exhibited exactly the incremental comprehension that had been previously observed in the scripted experiments (e.g., Eberhard et al., 1995). However, when Brown-Schmidt et al. identified the 75 times that a spoken word in this unscripted conversation was potentially temporarily ambiguous between two objects, such as a candle and a candy, not a single one of those instances involved the listener making distracted eye movements to the competitor object.

More detailed explorations in this unscripted language scenario revealed that two specific pragmatic factors naturally provide the disambiguation of these potentially ambiguous linguistic events (Brown-Schmidt & Tanenhaus, 2008). Proximity of the potential referents and relevance to the task are two pragmatic factors that tend to constrain the referential domain to a subset of objects in the visual environment. Thus, in natural unscripted conversation, as two people are co-creating their dialog, the dyad routinely uses these pragmatic factors to prevent confusing ambiguities from even happening in the first place.

A dyad develops this ability to behave as one complex system by way of enabling a variety of entrainment processes across the two people; not just postural sway and heart rate, as mentioned above, but even brain activity. Kuhlen, Allefeld, and Haynes (2012) recorded continuous EEG activity from a man and then from a woman while they each retold common fairytales from memory on camera. The video and audio recordings were then replayed, overlaid on one another, for participants who were instructed to either attend to the female speaker or attend to the male speaker. While seeing and hearing the exact same stimulus, but attending to only one of the speakers, these participants' had their brain activity recorded with continuous EEG. The listeners who attended to the female speaker produced EEG time series data that correlated more with the female speaker's EEG time series data, and the listeners who attended to the male speaker produced EEG time series data that correlated more with the male speaker's EEG time series data. Thus, a listener's brain activity becomes similar to a speaker's brain activity (see also Hasson, Nir, Levy, Fuhrmann, & Malach, 2004).

It should not be surprising that when brain activity becomes entrained across two people, eye movements also become entrained across those two people. For example, D. Richardson and Dale (2005) had a participant look at a display of six characters from a television sitcom and tell the unscripted story of their favorite episode into the microphone while their eye movements were tracked. Later, this audio track was played back into the headphones of other participants whose eyes were being tracked. Using time series recurrence analysis in a fashion similar to how Shockley et al. (2003) analyzed postural sway, Richardson and Dale found that listeners produced eye movement sequences that showed substantial similarity to the eye movement sequences that were produced by the speaker – with about a 2-second lag in the time series. That 2-second lag is roughly accounted for by the time it takes for the speaker to look at a face and then utter the name of that face, plus the time it takes for the listener to comprehend that spoken name and then program an eye movement to that face. When that 2-second lag is adjusted for, the eye movements of the speaker and the listener show remarkable synchrony, such that the listener's oculomotor behavior was becoming entrained with the speaker's oculomotor behavior.

Now consider the more common scenario of two people having a two-way live conversation, where the dialog that gets produced is a real-time co-creation of the two people. D. Richardson, Dale, and Kirkham (2007) used two eyetrackers in two separate rooms with the participants each wearing a telecommunication headset. The participants engaged in spontaneous unscripted dialog about the same visual display, and each dyad's eye movements exhibited the same kind of recurrence of sequential patterns as before – but with one important difference. Instead of the peak coordination in eye movements happening at a 2-second lag between the two time series, the peak in eye movement coordination for these live two-way interlocutors happened at zero lag in the time series. Essentially, because the dialog was being co-created, a listener was often able to anticipate the speaker's words and attention enough that they were usually looking at the same thing that the speaker was looking at, at the same time.

Of course, eye movements are not the only behaviors that result from brain activity. And when brain activity gets entrained across two people during conversation, many behaviors will become coordinated. Louwerse, Dale, Bard, and Jeuniaux (2012) recorded a variety of facial and manual gestures, as well as speech acts, while two people participated face-to-face as an Instruction Giver and an Instruction Follower, using a shared cartoon map that had some occasional differences in their landmarks, forcing the two people to discuss and identify the differences between their two maps. At a variety of timescales within the duration of the conversation – be it within a second, or over dozens of seconds, or even minutes – each dyad routinely exhibited temporally coordinated behaviors of all kinds (e.g., smiles, head-nods, pointing gestures, queries and clarifications, etc.). Some of these coordinated behaviors were nearly synchronized, within a second of each other, whereas others exhibited a 20-second lag in their entrainment. Notably, this ubiquitous motor and linguistic coordination tended to increase as the dyad acquired more experience as a team.

By having a shared visual information resource – whether it be a line-up of six faces (D. Richardson et al., 2007), a cartoon map (Louwerse et al., 2012), or an actual nautical map that sailors are looking at together during a boat race (see Hutchins, 1995) – each person that manipulates that co-present visual resource to aid their own cognitive processes winds up also aiding the cognitive processes of the other viewers and interlocutors. As a result, their individual perception-action loops (Neisser, 1976) become entangled with one another via those shared actions and shared language (Spivey, 2012).

3.1   Human interaction as systemic coupling

The research reviewed in the prior section shows that eye movements serve as powerful indices of language comprehension, including when that comprehension takes place in unscripted conversation between two people. Additionally, that tight coupling in eye movements seen in D. Richardson and Dale (2005), D. Richardson et al. (2007) and in other behaviors (e.g., Kuhlen et al., 2012; Louwerse et al., 2012), suggests that the dense-sampling measures are indexing the interdependence of two cognitive systems.

Similar research using this dense-sampling technique aims to show precisely this – that a task analysis of human interaction is best explained as a kind of emergent system. This goal again holds across a variety of measures and behavioral signals. For example, Mønster, Håkonsson, Eskildsen, and Wallot (2016) had three-person teams figure out how to build as many origami boats as possible in assembly-line style, while recording their facial muscles (with electromyography) and sweating (with a galvanic skin response measure). Rather than simply analyzing one time series from one of the team members, Mønster et al. looked at the temporal coordination of those measures across team members. Teams that smiled in synchrony a lot tended to exhibit good team cohesion and positive affect toward the group. Teams that sweated in synchrony a lot tended to exhibit poor team cohesion and negative tensions within the group. Importantly, the key indicators of team success or failure were not merely in the recordings of physiological measures themselves. What provided the index of how coordinated and successful the team was at their joint task was analyzing the degree of synchrony among those physiological measures. Similarly, Fusaroli, Bjorndahl, Roepstorff and Tylén (in press) found that a team of people building with LEGO blocks showed an increase in shared heart rate dynamics as they developed more practice with the task. Improvements in behavioral coordination among the team resulted in increases heart rate synchrony and also produced increases in rapport and group competence.

In addition to this ecologically valid strategy, some have also sought to distill critical ingredients of this two-person complex system in basic experimental designs. One such distillation is from the work of Jordan, Knoblich and colleagues, who designed game-like interfaces for participants to jointly control an icon on a computer screen (Jordan & Knoblich, 2004). A dyad would control an object by sharing the responsibility of its movement (e.g., separate direction vs. velocity keys). In their original findings, Jordan and Knoblich (2003) discovered that smooth dynamic control over the computer icon came from participants coordinating predictive behaviors with each other. The overt actions of one partner served to anticipate or signal to the other what was going to happen next. This meant that not only were participants interdependent in a weak sense (i.e., one affects the other), but that the actions *possible* by another person were being integrated and responded to by a partner. These participants are, one could argue, co-representing the task. Not only do the *actions* of each person tacitly anticipate the competitive response options confronting their partner (Knoblich & Jordan, 2003; Sebanz, Knoblich & Prinz, 2003), but their *neural activity* also reveals this compensation for the partner's challenges at early stages of perceptual processing (Sebanz, Knoblich, Prinz, & Wascher, 2006). In certain circumstances, the pair can become like a two-brained, two-bodied meta-person.

In another example of how eye movements demonstrate this tendency for interaction to "weave" two people into one complex system, Dale et al. (2011) analyzed eye-movement correlation between people playing the so-called tangram game. The tangram game is a psycholinguistic task in which participants learn to refer to unfamiliar objects ("tangrams") to more efficiently pick them out as a team of two. The authors described the coupling of visual attention between two people as reflecting an emerging "tangram recognition system" that comprises two people. They analyzed eye movements of both interaction partners, and also the mouse-movement dynamics of the person tasked with clicking the shape that they were hunting for.

After participants did this over a few rounds, they became highly efficient, picking out tangrams in less than a second. In these expert dyads, eye movements became tightly coupled between the two people. These pairs showed increased maximum correlation between eye movements, in highly compressed periods of time (< 1 s), suggesting that their interaction was organizing their visual attention into bursts of matching. Meanwhile, the computer mouse exhibited a kind of "fixed" lag behind the eyes (approximately 500 ms). These two-person systems had parts with different temporal relationships to each other. Visual attention became coupled, but the manual components of the system (the computer mouse) had a "delay line" that was invariant even in the expert performers.

These results suggest that the task is a critical feature of interacting systems and how they meld. Participants learn how to solve tasks together, and from the simplest anticipation tasks (Knoblich & Jordan, 2003) to complex referential tasks (Dale et al., 2011), they organize their behavior in ways that achieve what the task prescribes. The resulting "two-person system" that emerges is a function of the task parameters.

This can be seen in other interactive experiments in which distinct patterns of joint behavior occur, dependent on task features. For example, when participants are in conflict or argue, the correlation between their body movements may diminish (Paxton & Dale, 2013a,b). In other tasks, participants may even take on complementary patterns of behavior. Fusaroli et al. (2012) find that pairs of participants who perform best on a joint perceptual task do not just copy each other, but become similar in language in task-oriented ways. In fact participants who showed too much copying tended to perform worse. This suggests that participants may sometimes *complement* each other in their dynamics. This can be confirmed by a clever analysis of the time series carried out by Fusaroli and Tylén (2015). They find that dyadic behavior in an interactive task is best accounted for by treating their transcript as a *single time series*, rather than two separate time series.

All this is to say that pairs of participants adapt to a task together. The dense-sampling of their behaviors shows interdependence, and shared dynamics encourage treating them as a kind of system, even if it is only momentary, for the duration of that particular exchange. The parts of this system – whether linguistic, bodily, visual, manual, etc. – come to take on different relative dynamics depending on the task parameters. It is the interaction in these tasks, and the shared goals of the participants, that shape their relative dynamics. This is indicative of the "complex system" concept described in the introduction to his chapter.

But so far, even after this extensive review, we have not fleshed out the explanatory value of describing the two participants as a system. Admittedly, computational systems could account for most behavioral results reviewed above. In the next section, we argue that explicit quantitative conditions can be specified for "systemhood." These conditions are inspired by complex systems, and perhaps more uniquely frame next steps for theoretical and empirical development.

4.   Concluding discussion: Criteria for systemhood

We have showcased an array of findings suggesting that two conversants are acting much as a coherent, interdependent unit of two parts. Eye movements and other dynamic behaviors show interdependence during interaction. But this is not quite enough, of course. To a reader who prefers the so-called intracranial "mark of the cognitive" (Adams & Aizawa, 2001), these many indirect or correlational findings are insufficiently convincing.

In this concluding section, we offer further support for this complex systems formulation. Until now we've focused on high-level implications of our three system types, and focused on empirical review. But putting these pieces together, we find some concrete recommendations for cognitive experimentation as it bears on the "systemhood" of two people. The subtle differences suggested by complex nonlinear systems can cash out in empirical studies and theory development. We identify two sets of conditions for systemhood: one weak, and the other strong. Each recommends *specific* conditions in empirical analysis, and hold in eye movement data in particular.

4.1   Implications for research: Weak and strong conditions for systemhood

There are quantitative implications of taking a complex-systems approach to cognitive systems generally, and language use in particular. The first of these weak conditions is that the two-person system shows (WC1) <u>real-time coordination and potential for behavioral reorganization</u>. If we dense-sample behaviors in a natural task, their behaviors become statistically related, demonstrated via some quantitative analysis such as cross-correlation or cross recurrence or lag sequential analysis (see Bakeman & Quera, 2011, for review). The manner in which this correlation unfolds suggests that there is adaptation or short-term learning, in response to cognitive, environmental and social conditions.

When two people are faced with an interactive goal, such as identifying strange tangram shapes (Dale et al., 2011), their visual attentional systems become tightly time locked at 0 ms (see also D. Richardson et al., 2007). If the task changes, such as rendering communication unidirectional (speaker/listener), then the temporal function changes, showing distinct lags (D. Richardson & Dale, 2005). In the example of Brown-Schmidt et al. (2005), real-time two-way conversation leads to a complete absence of the effects of temporary ambiguity of a spoken word that are otherwise routinely observed with decontexualized scripted instructions. This is not just a simple change in the systems, but a reorganization of their patterns of behavior relative to an interlocutor. This reorganization is evident even when no interaction is taking place between people. For example, Crosby et al. (2008) have shown that the expectation that another person is present in a task changes visual attentional strategy (cf. Risko & Kingstone, 2011).

The second quantitative implication is how the eyes participate with the rest of the system. A complex systems approach predicts that (WC2) <u>the many potentially varying dimensions of behavior get compressed in their dynamics</u>. Though there are a large number of degrees of freedom in behavior, they are interdependent in a way that their "true" dimensionality is lower (see discussion in Riley et al., 2011). In Louwerse et al. (2012), we find that there is a cascade of constraint over the diverse patterns of behavior. Coordinated gestures become time locked. Coordinated head nods have a distinct temporal organization. Even incidental touching of the face becomes coordinated with its own particular temporal structure. Overall, this suggests there is "correlation structure" across the system. In the case of eye movements, this can be seen again in the tangram task, in which eye movements become tightly constrained alongside the language that participants come to use to identify the unfamiliar shapes (Dale et al., 2011). In fact, one could argue that the eye movements and referential terminology come to form a coupled circuit. As the eyes become better organized together, they better succeed at the task, which amplifies the linguistic strategy that was used, which again further couples the eyes, etc.

The prior two conditions represent weaker inferential conditions because they are easy to establish even in interacting individuals that are obviously not "systems." WC1 would be expected in single channels of behavior that show merely correlated patterns of behavior, and WC2 is simply to say that the correlation structure holds across a variety of behaviors. However weak they may be, they are pervasively observed in natural conversation. The problem, to echo a familiar statistics cliché, is that "correlation does not imply systemhood." Two further conditions strengthen the sense in which two people form a system. The following two strong conditions represent important next steps for research on eye movements in natural interaction and beyond.

First, in order to call two people a system, their behavior does not exhibit only reorganization in observed behavior, but primarily *functional* reorganization. The parts of the two-person system reveal a (SC1) <u>mutual adaptivity that is accounted for by a systematic account of the task constraints</u>. This is perhaps best demonstrated by the goal-oriented alignment that participants show at the linguistic level (Fusaroli et al., 2012). Here we find that participants are not merely reorganizing their behavior but also that it is best accounted for by the constraints from the task. In this sense, the reorganization observed in the two-person systems is in the service of succeeding in their joint task together. This stronger condition requires a solid theoretical understanding of the experimental task. Other examples are audience design tasks, such as those of Brown-Schmidt, Brennan and colleagues, which shows that knowledge of, or experience with, a task partner can sharply influence the pattern of behavior taking place in the task (for review see Brennan et al., 2010).

The second strong condition is that (SC2) the parts that coalesce to support system behavior respond to each other's changes. This is sometimes referred to as *reciprocal compensation* in the motor control literature in which multiple muscles or joints work together as one integrated system (see discussion in M. Richardson et al., 2014 and Riley et al., 2011). In the domain of natural conversation, one person should compensate for the other, or some aspects of each other's behavior should do so, too. Something like this can be seen in the distilled experimental conditions of Knoblich and Jordan (2003), where one participant's actions are in direct response to *anticipated* actions by his or her partner. Similarly, in social attention, Crosby et al. (2008; see also D. Richardson et al., 2012) show that participants anticipate the potential social discomfort of particular conversation topics by looking to potentially offended parties; the eyes are showing a kind of adaptation to the social-cognitive expectations that people have of each other. In general, this is a less attested pattern at the level of natural linguistic interaction, and is an open question: Does behavior, from visual attention to gesture and other linguistic contributions, respond dynamically in reciprocal compensation with one another, including those very behaviors *across* individuals?

These stronger conditions are often offered in other literatures to exemplify system-level operation, from physics (e.g., Haken, 1977) to motor control (e.g., Kelso et al., 1984; Latash et al., 2002). If the latter two conditions could be better attested in ongoing work in social eye movements and other behaviors, it would draw exciting bridges between the performance of two people in interaction with well-developed process theories in other domains.

4.2   Conclusion

The strongest "intracranial" accounts of cognition come perhaps from philosophers of mind. In particular, Rupert (2011) and Adams and Aizawa (2001) argue at length against extending cognitive systems beyond their traditional locus in the head (for counterpoint, see Noë, 2009). We would agree that this traditional boundary is a critical ingredient for cognitive theory. However, we are convinced that multi-person systems offer exciting possibilities for new theory development. By looking upon interaction through a complex-systems lens, it may offer provocative reframing of conversation and other forms of natural interaction as the operation of a single system. Such multi-person systems would be, of course, labile and loosely-coupled – people form ephemeral systems. But as it becomes coupled, what is the system capable of? How does it perform, and how do the parts work together to support that performance?

In the prior section we described some quantitative conditions that support systemhood. Elaborating the relationships within and between interaction partners will help us gain a clearer understanding of social interaction itself. Consider again visual attention, the focus of this chapter. Finding the cognitive processes and behaviors that act in a "causal circuit" with visual attention – such as memory, word choice, social affiliation and so on – are critical for understanding how two people stabilize each other's behavior, and support their interactive goals.

This search for principles could reveal new lines of questioning. For example, once two people form their own complex system, we can then subject it to all sorts of quantitative investigation. This investigation would include the several lines of inquiry that began this chapter, including the computational approach itself (cf. Beer & Williams, 2015). What computations do teams carry out? How can we maximize the computational abilities of a dyad, its transactive memory, or its affect and affiliation? What are the dynamic signatures of the formation and dissolution of dyadic systems, and can we predict their onset? These are questions others have already asked, of course (among many: Fitneva & Spivey, 2005; Fusaroli et al., 2014; Gallagher & Crisafi, 2009; Hutchins, 1995; Spivey, 2008; Tollefsen & Dale, 2012; Wegner, 1987). At minimum, we hope to have convinced the reader that eyetracking research, and related findings in experimental psychology, have much to offer to such theory development.

References

Adams, F., & Aizawa, K. (2001). The bounds of cognition. *Philosophical psychology*, 14(1), 43–64. https://doi.org/10.1080/09515080120033571

Allopenna, P. D., Magnuson, J. S., & Tanenhaus, M. K. (1998). Tracking the time course of spoken word recognition using eye movements: Evidence for continuous mapping models. *Journal of memory and language*, 38(4), 419–439. https://doi.org/10.1006/jmla.1997.2558

Altmann, G. T., & Kamide, Y. (1999). Incremental interpretation at verbs: Restricting the domain of subsequent reference. *Cognition*, 73(3), 247–264. https://doi.org/10.1016/S0010-0277(99)00059-1

Anderson, J. R. (1996). ACT: A simple theory of complex cognition. *American Psychologist*, 51(4), 355. https://doi.org/10.1037/0003-066X.51.4.355

Ashby, W. R. (1956). *An introduction to cybernetics*. London: Chapman & Hall.

Bakeman, R., & Quera, V. (2011). *Sequential analysis and observational methods for the behavioral sciences*. Cambridge: Cambridge University Press. https://doi.org/10.1017/CBO9781139017343

Bechtel, W., & Abrahamsen, A. (1991). *Connectionism and the Mind*. Backwell, Cambridge, MA.

Bechtel, W., & Abrahamsen, A. (2010). Dynamic mechanistic explanation: Computational modeling of circadian rhythms as an exemplar for cognitive science. *Studies in History and Philosophy of Science Part A*, 41(3), 321–333. https://doi.org/10.1016/j.shpsa.2010.07.003

Beer, R. D., & Williams, P. L. (2015). Information processing and dynamics in minimally cognitive agents. *Cognitive science*, 39(1), 1–38. https://doi.org/10.1111/cogs.12142

Brennan, S. E., Galati, A., & Kuhlen, A. K. (2010). Two minds, one dialog: Coordinating speaking and understanding. *Psychology of Learning and Motivation*, 53, 301–344. https://doi.org/10.1016/S0079-7421(10)53008-1

Brown-Schmidt, S., Campana, E., & Tanenhaus, M. K. (2005). Real-time reference resolution by naïve participants during a task-based unscripted conversation. In J. Trueswell & M. Tanenhaus (Eds.), *World Situated Language Use: Psycholinguistic, Linguistic and Computational Perspectives on Bridging the Product and Action Traditions*, (pp. 153–171) Cambridge, MA: MIT Press.

Brown-Schmidt, S., Yoon, S. O., & Ryskin, R. A. (2015). People as contexts in conversation. *Psychology of Learning and Motivation*, 62, 59–99. https://doi.org/10.1016/bs.plm.2014.09.003

Brown-Schmidt, S., & Tanenhaus, M. K. (2008). Real-time investigation of referential domains in unscripted conversation: A targeted language game approach. *Cognitive Science*, 32(4), 643–684. https://doi.org/10.1080/03640210802066816

Chemero, A. (2011). *Radical embodied cognitive science*. MIT press.

Chemero, A., & Turvey, M. T. (2008). Autonomy and hypersets. *Biosystems*, 91(2), 320–330. https://doi.org/10.1016/j.biosystems.2007.05.010

Clark, H. H., & Wilkes-Gibbs, D. (1986). Referring as a collaborative process. *Cognition*, 22(1), 1–39. https://doi.org/10.1016/0010-0277(86)90010-7

Coupland, N. (1985). 'Hark, hark, the lark': social motivations for phonological style-shifting. *Language & Communication*, 5(3), 153–171. https://doi.org/10.1016/0271-5309(85)90007-2

Crosby, J. R., Monin, B. & Richardson, D. C. (2008). Where Do We Look During Potentially Offensive Behavior? *Psychological Science*, 19 (3), 226–228. https://doi.org/10.1111/j.1467-9280.2008.02072.x

Crutchfield, J. P. (1994). The calculi of emergence: computation, dynamics and induction. *Physica D: Nonlinear Phenomena*, 75(1), 11–54. https://doi.org/10.1016/0167-2789(94)90273-9

Dale, R., Kirkham, N. Z. & Richardson, D. C. (2011). The dynamics of reference and shared visual attention. *Frontiers in Psychology*, 2. https://doi.org/10.3389/fpsyg.2011.00355

Dotov, D. G., Nie, L., & Chemero, A. (2010). A demonstration of the transition from ready-to-hand to unready-to-hand. *PLoS One*, 5(3), e9433.

Eberhard, K. M., Spivey-Knowlton, M. J., Sedivy, J. C., & Tanenhaus, M. K. (1995). Eye movements as a window into real-time spoken language comprehension in natural contexts. *Journal of psycholinguistic research*, 24(6), 409–436. https://doi.org/10.1007/BF02143160

Edelman, S. (2008). On the nature of minds, or: truth and consequences. *Journal of Experimental & Theoretical Artificial Intelligence*, 20(3), 181–196. https://doi.org/10.1080/09528130802319086

Eliasmith, C. (1996). The third contender: A critical examination of the dynamicist theory of cognition. *Philosophical Psychology*, 9(4), 441–463. https://doi.org/10.1080/09515089608573194

Eliasmith, C. (2012). The complex systems approach: rhetoric or revolution. *Topics in cognitive science*, 4(1), 72–77. https://doi.org/10.1111/j.1756-8765.2011.01169.x

Enfield, N. J. (2013). *Relationship thinking: Agency, enchrony, and human sociality*. Oxford University Press. https://doi.org/10.1093/acprof:oso/9780199338733.001.0001

Farmer, T. A., Cargill, S. A., Hindy, N. C., Dale, R., & Spivey, M. J. (2007). Tracking the continuity of language comprehension: Computer mouse trajectories suggest parallel syntactic processing. *Cognitive Science*, 31(5), 889–909. https://doi.org/10.1080/03640210701530797

Ferreira, F., & Clifton, C. (1986). The independence of syntactic processing. *Journal of memory and language*, 25(3), 348–368. https://doi.org/10.1016/0749-596X(86)90006-9

Fitneva, S. A. & Spivey, M. J. (2005). Context and language processing: The effect of authorship. In J. Trueswell & M. Tanenhaus (Eds.), *World Situated Language Use: Psycholinguistic, Linguistic and Computational Perspectives on Bridging the Product and Action Traditions*, (pp. 317–328) Cambridge, MA: MIT Press.

Frazier, L. (1995). Constraint satisfaction as a theory of sentence processing. *Journal of Psycholinguistic Research*, 24(6), 437–468. https://doi.org/10.1007/BF02143161

Fusaroli, R., & Tylén, K. (2015). Investigating conversational dynamics: Interactive alignment, Interpersonal synergy, and collective task performance. *Cognitive Science*, 40, 145–171.

Fusaroli, R., Bahrami, B., Olsen, K., Roepstorff, A., Rees, G., Frith, C., & Tylén, K. (2012). Coming to terms quantifying the benefits of linguistic coordination. *Psychological Science*, 23(8), 931–939. https://doi.org/10.1177/0956797612436816

Fusaroli, R., Bjørndahl, J. S., Roepstorff, A., & Tylén, K. (2016). A Heart for Interaction: Shared Physiological Dynamics and Behavioral Coordination in a Collective, Creative Construction Task. *Journal of Experimental Psychology: Human Perception & Performance*, 42(9), 1297–1310.

Fusaroli, R., Rączaszek-Leonardi, J., & Tylén, K. (2014). Dialog as interpersonal synergy. *New Ideas in Psychology*, 32, 147–157. https://doi.org/10.1016/j.newideapsych.2013.03.005

Gallagher, S., & Crisafi, A. (2009). Mental institutions. *Topoi*, 28(1), 45–51. https://doi.org/10.1007/s11245-008-9045-0

Gilden, D. L. (2001). Cognitive emissions of 1/f noise. *Psychological review*, 108(1), 33–56. https://doi.org/10.1037/0033-295X.108.1.33

Gow, D. W. & Olson, B. B. (2015): Sentential influences on acoustic- phonetic processing: a Granger causality analysis of multimodal imaging data, *Language, Cognition and Neuroscience*. https://doi.org/10.1080/23273798.2015.1029498

Haken, H. (1977). *Synergetics. Physics Bulletin*, 28(9), 412. https://doi.org/10.1088/0031-9112/28/9/027

Haken, H., Kelso, J. S., & Bunz, H. (1985). A theoretical model of phase transitions in human hand movements. *Biological cybernetics*, 51(5), 347–356. https://doi.org/10.1007/BF00336922

Hasson, U., Nir, Y., Levy, I., Fuhrmann, G., & Malach, R. (2004). Intersubject synchronization of cortical activity during natural vision. *Science*, 303(5664), 1634–1640.

Hove, M. J., & Keller, P. E. (2015). Impaired movement timing in neurological disorders: rehabilitation and treatment strategies. *Annals of the New York Academy of Sciences*, 1337(1), 111–117. https://doi.org/10.1111/nyas.12615

Hove, M. J., & Risen, J. L. (2009). It's all in the timing: Interpersonal synchrony increases affiliation. *Social Cognition*, 27(6), 949–960. https://doi.org/10.1521/soco.2009.27.6.949

Hove, M. J., Spivey, M. J., & Krumhansl, C. L. (2010). Compatibility of motion facilitates visuomotor synchronization. *Journal of Experimental Psychology: Human Perception and Performance*, 36(6), 1525–1534.

Hutchins, E. (1995). *Cognition in the Wild*. MIT press.

Hutchins, E. (1995). How a cockpit remembers its speeds. *Cognitive science*, 19(3), 265–288. https://doi.org/10.1207/s15516709cog1903_1

Jaeger, T. F. (2010). Redundancy and reduction: Speakers manage syntactic information density. *Cognitive psychology*, 61(1), 23–62. https://doi.org/10.1016/j.cogpsych.2010.02.002

Jordan, J. S., & Knoblich, G. (2004). Spatial perception and control. *Psychonomic Bulletin & Review*, 11(1), 54–59. https://doi.org/10.3758/BF03206460

Kello, C. T., Anderson, G. G., Holden, J. G., & Van Orden, G. C. (2008). The pervasiveness of 1/f scaling in speech reflects the metastable basis of cognition. *Cognitive Science*, 32(7), 1217–1231. https://doi.org/10.1080/03640210801944898

Kello, C. T., Brown, G. D., Ferrer-i-Cancho, R., Holden, J. G., Linkenkaer-Hansen, K., Rhodes, T., & Van Orden, G. C. (2010). Scaling laws in cognitive sciences. *Trends in Cognitive Sciences*, 14(5), 223–232. https://doi.org/10.1016/j.tics.2010.02.005

Kelso, J. A. S. (1984). Phase transitions and critical behavior in human bimanual coordination. *American Journal of Physiology-Regulatory, Integrative and Comparative Physiology*, 246(6), R1000–R1004.

Kelso, J. A. S. (1997). *Dynamic patterns: The self-organization of brain and behavior*. MIT press.

Kelso, J. S., Tuller, B., Vatikiotis-Bateson, E., & Fowler, C. A. (1984). Functionally specific articulatory cooperation following jaw perturbations during speech: evidence for coordinative structures. *Journal of Experimental Psychology: Human Perception and Performance*, 10(6), 812.

Kloos, H., & Van Orden, G. (2010). Voluntary behavior in cognitive and motor tasks. *Mind and Matter*, 8(1), 19–43.

Knoblich, G., & Jordan, J. S. (2003). Action coordination in groups and individuals: learning anticipatory control. *Journal of Experimental Psychology: Learning, Memory, and Cognition*, 29(5), 1006–1016.

Knoeferle, P., & Crocker, M. W. (2006). The coordinated interplay of scene, utterance, and world knowledge: Evidence from eye tracking. *Cognitive Science*, 30(3), 481–529. https://doi.org/10.1207/s15516709cog0000_65

Konvalinka, I., Xygalatas, D., Bulbulia, J., Schjødt, U., Jegindø, E. M., Wallot, S., Van Orden, G., & Roepstorff, A. (2011). Synchronized arousal between performers and related spectators in a fire-walking ritual. *Proceedings of the National Academy of Sciences*, 108(20), 8514–8519. https://doi.org/10.1073/pnas.1016955108

Kuhlen, A. K., Allefeld, C., & Haynes, J. D. (2012). Content-specific coordination of listeners' to speakers' EEG during communication. *Frontiers in Human Neuroscience, 6*, Article 266.

Lakin, J. L., & Chartrand, T. L. (2003). Using nonconscious behavioral mimicry to create affiliation and rapport. *Psychological science*, 14(4), 334–339. https://doi.org/10.1111/1467-9280.14481

Latash, M. L., Scholz, J. P., & Schöner, G. (2002). Motor control strategies revealed in the structure of motor variability. *Exercise and sport sciences reviews*, 30(1), 26–31. https://doi.org/10.1097/00003677-200201000-00006

Louwerse, M. M., Dale, R., Bard, E. G., & Jeuniaux, P. (2012). Behavior matching in multimodal communication is synchronized. *Cognitive Science*, 36(8), 1404–1426. https://doi.org/10.1111/j.1551-6709.2012.01269.x

Manson, J. H., Bryant, G. A., Gervais, M. M., & Kline, M. A. (2013). Convergence of speech rate in conversation predicts cooperation. *Evolution and Human Behavior*, 34(6), 419–426. https://doi.org/10.1016/j.evolhumbehav.2013.08.001

Mitchell, M. (2009). *Complexity: A guided tour*. Oxford University Press.

Mønster, D., Håkonsson, D. D., Eskildsen, J. K., & Wallot, S. (2016). Physiological evidence of interpersonal dynamics in a cooperative production task. *Physiology & Behavior*, 156, 24–34. https://doi.org/10.1016/j.physbeh.2016.01.004

Neisser, U. (1976). *Cognition and reality: Principles and implications of cognitive psychology*. San Francisco, California: W. H. Freeman.

Newell, A. (1980). Physical symbol systems*. *Cognitive science*, 4(2), 135–183. https://doi.org/10.1207/s15516709cog0402_2

Noë, A. (2009). *Out of our heads: Why you are not your brain, and other lessons from the biology of consciousness*. Macmillan.

Paxton, A., & Dale, R. (2013). Argument disrupts interpersonal synchrony. *The Quarterly Journal of Experimental Psychology*, 66(11), 2092–2102. https://doi.org/10.1080/17470218.2013.853089

Paxton, A., & Dale, R. (2013a). Frame-differencing methods for measuring bodily synchrony in conversation. *Behavior Research Methods*, 45(2), 329–343. https://doi.org/10.3758/s13428-012-0249-2

Paxton, A., & Dale, R. (2013b). Argument disrupts interpersonal synchrony. *The Quarterly Journal of Experimental Psychology*, 66(11), 2092–2102. https://doi.org/10.1080/17470218.2013.853089

Reali, F., Spivey, M. J., Tyler, M. J., & Terranova, J. (2006). Inefficient conjunction search made efficient by concurrent spoken delivery of target identity. *Perception & psychophysics*, 68(6), 959–974. https://doi.org/10.3758/BF03193358

Repp, B. H. (2005). Sensorimotor synchronization: A review of the tapping literature. *Psychonomic bulletin & review*, 12(6), 969–992. https://doi.org/10.3758/BF03206433

Richardson, D. C., & Dale, R. (2005). Looking to understand: The coupling between speakers' and listeners' eye movements and its relationship to discourse comprehension. *Cognitive science*, 29(6), 1045–1060. https://doi.org/10.1207/s15516709cog0000_29

Richardson, D. C., Dale, R. & Kirkham, N. (2007). The art of conversation is coordination: common ground and the coupling of eye movements during dialogue. *Psychological Science*, 18, 407–413. https://doi.org/10.1111/j.1467-9280.2007.01914.x

Richardson, D. C., Street, C. N. H., Tan, J. Y. M., Kirkham, N. Z., Hoover, M. A., & Ghane Cavanaugh, A. (2012).Joint perception: gaze and social context. *Frontiers in Human Neuroscience*, 6. https://doi.org/10.3389/fnhum.2012.00194

Richardson, M. J., Dale, R. & Marsh, K. (2014). Complex dynamical systems in social and personality psychology: theory, modeling and analysis. In H. T. Reis & C. M. Judd (Eds.), *Handbook of Research Methods in Social and Personality Psychology* (pp. 253–282). Cambridge University Press.

Richardson, M. J., Marsh, K. L., & Schmidt, R. C. (2005). Effects of visual and verbal interaction on unintentional interpersonal coordination. *Journal of Experimental Psychology: Human Perception and Performance*, 31(1), 62–79.

Riley, M. A., Richardson, M. J., Shockley, K., & Ramenzoni, V. C. (2011). Interpersonal synergies. *Frontiers in psychology*, 2, 38. https://doi.org/10.3389/fpsyg.2011.00038

Risko, E. F., & Kingstone, A. (2011). Eyes wide shut: implied social presence, eye tracking and attention. *Attention, Perception, & Psychophysics*, 73(2), 291–296. https://doi.org/10.3758/s13414-010-0042-1

Risko, E. F., Richardson, D. C., & Kingstone, A. (2016). Breaking the Fourth Wall of Cognitive Science Real-World Social Attention and the Dual Function of Gaze. *Current Directions in Psychological Science*, 25(1), 70–74.

Rupert, R. D. (2011). Cognitive systems and the supersized mind. *Philosophical Studies*, 152(3), 427–436. https://doi.org/10.1007/s11098-010-9600-6

Schmidt, R. C., Carello, C., & Turvey, M. T. (1990). Phase transitions and critical fluctuations in the visual coordination of rhythmic movements between people. *Journal of experimental psychology: human perception and performance*, 16(2), 227–247.

Sebanz, N., Knoblich, G., & Prinz, W. (2003). Representing others' actions: just like one's own?. *Cognition*, 88(3), B11–B21. https://doi.org/10.1016/S0010-0277(03)00043-X

Sebanz, N., Knoblich, G., Prinz, W., & Wascher, E. (2006). Twin peaks: An ERP study of action planning and control in coacting individuals. *Journal of Cognitive Neuroscience*, 18(5), 859–870. https://doi.org/10.1162/jocn.2006.18.5.859

Shenhar, A. (1990). On system properties and systemhood. *International Journal Of General System*, 18(2), 167–174. https://doi.org/10.1080/03081079008935136

Shockley, K., Baker, A. A., Richardson, M. J., & Fowler, C. A. (2007). Articulatory constraints on interpersonal postural coordination. *Journal of Experimental Psychology: Human Perception and Performance*, 33(1), 201.

Shockley, K., Santana, M. V., & Fowler, C. A. (2003). Mutual interpersonal postural constraints are involved in cooperative conversation. *Journal of Experimental Psychology: Human Perception and Performance*, 29(2), 326–332.

Simon, H. A. (1992). What is an "explanation" of behavior?. *Psychological Science*, 3(3), 150–161. https://doi.org/10.1111/j.1467-9280.1992.tb00017.x

Spivey-Knowlton, M. J. (1996). *Integration of visual and linguistic information: Human data and model simulations*. Ph.D. Dissertation, U. Rochester, NY.

Spivey, M. (2008). *The continuity of mind*. Oxford University Press.

Spivey, M. J. (2012). The spatial intersection of minds. *Cognitive Processing*, 13, 343–346. https://doi.org/10.1007/s10339-012-0520-6

Spivey, M. J. (2016). Semantics influences speech perception: commentary on Gow and Olson (2015). *Language, Cognition and Neuroscience*, 31(7), 856–859.

Strogatz, S. (2003). *Sync: The emerging science of spontaneous order*. New York, NY: Hyperion.

Taleb, N. N. (2012). *Antifragile: Things that gain from disorder* (Vol. 3). Random House Incorporated.

Tanenhaus, M. K., Spivey-Knowlton, M. J., Eberhard, K. M., & Sedivy, J. C. (1995). Integration of visual and linguistic information in spoken language comprehension. *Science*, 268(5217), 1632–1634. https://doi.org/10.1126/science.7777863

Tollefsen, D. P. (2006). From extended mind to collective mind. *Cognitive systems research*, 7(2), 140–150. https://doi.org/10.1016/j.cogsys.2006.01.001

Tollefsen, D. & Dale, R. (2012). Naturalizing joint action: a process-based approach. *Philosophical Psychology*, 25, 385–407. https://doi.org/10.1080/09515089.2011.579418

Van Gelder, T. (1998). The dynamical hypothesis in cognitive science.*Behavioral and brain sciences*, 21(05), 615–628. https://doi.org/10.1017/S0140525X98001733

Van Orden, G. C., & Holden, J. G. (2002). Intentional contents and self-control. *Ecological Psychology*, 14(1–2), 87–109. https://doi.org/10.1080/10407413.2003.9652753

Van Orden, G. C., Holden, J. G., & Turvey, M. T. (2003). Self-organization of cognitive performance. *Journal of Experimental Psychology: General*, 132(3), 331. https://doi.org/10.1037/0096-3445.132.3.331

Van Orden, G., & Stephen, D. G. (2012). Is cognitive science usefully cast as complexity science?. *Topics in cognitive science*, 4(1), 3–6. https://doi.org/10.1111/j.1756-8765.2011.01165.x

Wegner, D. M. (1987). Transactive memory: A contemporary analysis of the group mind. In *Theories of group behavior* (pp. 185–208). Springer New York. https://doi.org/10.1007/978-1-4612-4634-3_9

Wiener, N. (1961). *Cybernetics or Control and Communication in the Animal and the Machine* (Vol. 25). MIT press.

CHAPTER 5

On the role of gaze for successful and efficient communication

Maria Staudte and Matthew W. Crocker
University of Saarland

Speakers tend to fixate objects they are about to mention, while listeners inspect those objects that they believe to be intended referents of the speaker. These production- and comprehension-contingent gaze behaviors may form an integral part of the signal itself, making it inherently reciprocal. Here, we present work that has investigated the interplay of gaze and language and assessed the role of speaker gaze for language comprehension as well as the utility of listener gaze for an instruction giver. Both lines of research make use of artificial interaction partners which increases experimental control while maintaining a dynamic interactive setting. Thus, the reciprocal nature of situated dialogue becomes a tractable aspect in the enterprise of dealing with human (gaze) behavior.

Keywords: speaker gaze as communicative signal, listener gaze monitoring, real-time language comprehension, artificial agents

1. Introduction

Eye-tracking has enabled a number of profoundly productive experimental methodologies for investigating real-time language processing, whether for the investigation of reading processes (Rayner, 1998), or visually situated spoken language processing (Tanenhaus et al., 1995; see also Knoeferle et al. (eds), 2016, for a thorough review of the Visual World Paradigm). In the Visual World Paradigm, researchers have observed – and later exploited – the fact that a listener's visual attention is tightly linked to what she is currently understanding. Simply speaking, listeners look at what they hear, but what they see may in return also influence how a given utterance is understood (Knoeferle & Crocker, 2006). Traditionally, however, these methods have focused on investigating the linguistic signal alone.

In contrast, much of our everyday language use is not only situated, but also *face to face*: In such settings, communication is qualitatively different from isolated language processing: Not only is there a co-present visual scene, but the utterances we produce and comprehend are also accompanied by co-speech signals in the

https://doi.org/10.1075/ais.10.05sta

form of gaze and gesture. To illustrate the potential contribution of gaze to situated communication, imagine sitting next to someone at the breakfast table. From experiments using the Visual World Paradigm, we know that someone who says "We're almost out of jam", will likely shift their gaze to the jam shortly before mentioning it (Griffin & Bock, 2000; Meyer et al., 1998). Correspondingly, the person listening to this utterance will also begin looking at the jam within a few hundred milliseconds of the onset of the word "jam" (Allopena et al., 1998). Indeed, if the sentence is sufficiently constraining, as in "Can you help Billy spread his toast with …", the listener may even anticipate that jam is likely to be mentioned, and inspect it before it is even mentioned (Altmann & Kamide, 1999).

While these kinds of behaviors demonstrate how the visual context informs and grounds on-line comprehension (see e.g. Knoeferle & Crocker, 2006, 2007, for discussion of these mechanisms), they still focus on the spoken linguistic signal. But imagine now that you are not sitting *next* to your interlocutor, but rather *across* from them. Now, the listener may also notice the speaker's gaze towards the jam even before they mention it, and assume that this is the object they are about to refer to. Assuming the speaker's synchronized gaze to objects they are about to mention is systematic and reliable, it seems plausible to suggest that such non-linguistic cues may assist the listener in both (a) identifying the intended referent earlier, before it is even mentioned, and (b) providing disambiguation, in the event that there is more than one kind of jam. Indeed, evidence that listeners exploit speaker gaze has been found in studies by Hanna & Brennan (2007).

Taking the possible consequences of this behavior further, if listeners rapidly and reliably gaze at the objects they believe the speaker is referring to, the speaker may in turn exploit this listener gaze to assess communicative success. If the listener looks at the raspberry jam – but the speaker means the peach jam – the speaker can immediately elaborate their utterance to ensure the listener identifies the intended referent. Some evidence for such use of listener gaze by speakers comes from Clark & Krych (2004).

The close temporal synchronization of speech and gaze, and the potential utility of gaze to both speaker and listener, leads us to hypothesize that gaze may function as an important part of the communicative signal – one that can potentially speed and disambiguate the identification of referents, and provide speakers with an index of communicative success. In this chapter, we summarize a collection of studies that seek to evaluate this hypothesis, and in particular address the following three questions:

1. Does speaker gaze improve real-time comprehension?
2. What mechanisms likely underlie any such benefit due to gaze?
3. Does listener gaze offer potential benefits for improving a speaker's communicative success?

One challenge to a controlled investigation of the role gaze plays in communication, is that it is difficult to undertake without examining what happens when gaze behavior is deviant in some way. That is, responses to *unnatural* behaviors are often essential in order to understand the benefit of some *natural* behavior and for understanding what underlies any such benefit. While it is possible to achieve this in human-human interaction, e.g. by hiding interlocutors' gaze with sunglasses, or manipulating the objects each interlocutor sees, a person's behavior can be manipulated and controlled only to a limited extent. Artificial agents and language generation systems, in contrast, are fully controllable and also have more "reason" to behave unnaturally: People typically have experience of less than successful interactions with artificial systems, and are less surprised to encounter aberrant behaviors. For this reason, all the studies we review here employ artificial speakers in the investigation of speaker and listener eye-movements in spoken interaction. At the same time, we always aim to relate the findings back to human-human interaction for validation.

In the next section, we examine the influence of speaker gaze on comprehension in human-robot interaction, in order to determine the influence of speaker (robot) gaze on listener gaze, as well as on comprehension itself. While clear evidence is found for the facilitatory influence of gaze (1. above), the question arises as to whether or not this is due purely to the visual cueing of relevant referents, or to the deeper referential intentions such gaze cues may signal. To address this issue (2. above) we present a set of studies conducted using a virtual character, to contrast gaze cues with a purely visual arrow cue. Finally, we consider the potential benefit of listener gaze for a language production system (3. above). Specifically, we examine whether an incremental language generation system, that produces directions in a treasure hunting game, can exploit listener gaze to improve communicative success. Beyond the individual contributions of each of these studies, we argue that – taken together – they provide broad support to the hypothesis that gaze is an important dimension of the communicative signal in situated interaction.

2.   The benefit of speaker gaze

Speech planning and eye-movements have been examined, for instance, by Griffin and Bock (2000) who showed that speakers looked at an object ~800–1000 ms before uttering the object's name. This result was observed in a study in which participants viewed and described action scenes containing line drawings of an event involving an agent and a patient character. These experiments were conducted with speakers in isolation, i.e. without a potential listener being present, and it thus remained unclear whether such gaze patterns were strictly for the speaker's

own sake (e.g. for planning and retrieval purposes) or whether they may also provide useful information for a potential listener. Hanna and Brennan (2007) thus
conducted an interactive study in which speakers were instructing listeners about
specific objects in (more or less) shared view. They observed that listeners exploited
the referential speaker gaze, which preceded the verbal target reference, and that
they were able to disambiguate the target referent clearly *before* the linguistic point
of disambiguation.

In order to further elaborate on this result and to explore the benefit of speaker
gaze in more detail, we examine the influence of speaker gaze effect on language
comprehension when it either correctly identified the referenced object as compared to when it was directed to a different, non-mentioned object (see Staudte &
Crocker 2011). Imagine, once again, the breakfast table situation and the speaker
saying "We're almost out of raspberry jam". The above mentioned evidence suggests
that speaker gaze to the raspberry jam preceding the verbal reference will help
listeners to anticipate, referentially ground, and comprehend this utterance. But in
order to assess the nature of this benefit – how much this gaze really "helps" – we
need to know how the utterance is understood when the speaker does not look at
the raspberry jam at all – or even looks at the peach jam instead! This discrepancy
between the target of the speaker's gaze, and hence what the listener potentially
anticipated to be mentioned soon, and the actually mentioned object allows us to
quantify the benefit of speaker gaze and to examine more closely how listeners
integrate referential information coming from the linguistic signal and from gaze.

We thus designed an experiment in which we video-taped a robot speaker that
produced utterances about a co-present array of objects, such as "The cylinder is
taller than the pyramid that is pink". 1000 ms before mentioning the "pyramid",
the robot either looked at a small pink pyramid (congruent gaze), at a big brown
pyramid (non-congruent gaze), or straight ahead (neutral gaze). Listeners were
eye-tracked as they watched these videos and were told to determine whether the
statements were accurate descriptions of the given visual scene, and press a button
as soon as they could to indicate whether they thought the utterance was true or
not. We assessed comprehension difficulty, and hence benefit of congruent gaze in
comparison to neutral and non-congruent gaze, via button press latency.

We found a clear disruption effect of speaker gaze to the non-mentioned pyramid compared to the neutral gaze cue, and a clear facilitation effect of speaker
gaze to the mentioned pyramid compared to the neutral gaze cue. Moreover, we
observed a rather typical phenomenon reflecting the tight link between language
comprehension and eye-movements in the *absence* of speaker gaze cues: Upon
hearing "is taller than", listeners already began inspecting nearby objects that were
smaller than the mentioned cylinder. Such anticipatory eye-movements, however,
were eliminated by the robot gaze movement which listeners preferentially followed

when present. These results suggest that speaker gaze does indeed have a strong influence on listener's expectation of what the speaker will say next and that appropriate gaze cues induce a real benefit for language comprehension. At the same time, these results indicate that incongruence between verbal references and the preceding gaze cues have a disruptive effect on comprehension and may cause misunderstandings.

3.   Mechanisms underlying gaze benefit

At this point it remains unclear whether speaker gaze simply grabs the listener's attention which then simply facilitates or interferes with the attention shift induced by the linguistic signal (we have called this the "Visual Account"), or whether speaker gaze additionally signals some sort of intention by the speaker to now refer to that particular object (the so-called "Intentional Account"). Under the Visual Account, a gaze cue to the raspberry jam in our breakfast example would shift the listener's attention to it shortly before it is actually mentioned. The simple co-incidence of already attending to the right object when "raspberry jam" is uttered would then facilitate the processing of the reference and, thus, the full utterance. Under the Intentional Account, the active expectation that the gazed-at peach jam is what the speaker intends to say next would facilitate comprehension of the referring expression.

Of course, there is evidence for both accounts in the literature. Reflective attention shifts have been examined in depth (e.g. Driver et al., 1999; Friesen & Kingstone, 1998; Langton & Bruce, 1999). Also, the important influence of bottom-up attention shifts on further processing has become evident in studies reported by Gleitman, January, Nappa, & Trueswell (2007) or Tomlin (1997). At the same time, several studies support the hypothesis that people follow gaze *because* – or only when – they believe that the gaze cue reflects the gazer's intentions (e.g. Bayliss, Paul, Cannon, & Tipper, 2006; Becchio et al., 2008; Castiello, 2003; Meltzoff, Brooks, Shon, & Rao, 2010). It is therefore not surprising that we were faced with the question whether our results were caused by low-level effects based on visual attention shifts of the listener only, or whether the benefit really originates from the belief that the robot had *intended* to talk about an object.

Consequently, we conducted a follow-up study in which we asked participants to produce a corrected utterance (when the robot had given a wrong description of the visual scene) of what they thought had been the "intended" description. When the robot had uttered "The cylinder is taller than the pyramid that is brown" even though the cylinder was clearly smaller than the brown pyramid but indeed taller than a co-present pink pyramid, participants were free to either correct (a) the predicate with "is smaller than" or (b) the reference with "pyramid that is pink". We found that where the robot gaze had looked modulated people's choices of how they corrected those utterances. That is, robot speaker gaze to the pink pyramid led to more (b)-corrections than gaze to the brown pyramid or to no object at all.

These results provide some indication that listeners take the speaker's gaze into account when reconstructing their originally intended utterance. But one could also argue that this is the only way in which listeners can not only correct the utterance but also match it up with the produced gaze cue thereby making it the overall most coherent (multimodal) utterance.

We therefore set up a series of slight modified experiments in which we contrasted speaker gaze to an arrow cue that directed listeners' attention instead of the speaker's gaze (Staudte et al., 2014). This contrast was set out to examine to what extent the effect of speaker gaze is specific to a gaze cue and/or speaker intentions and to what extent this can be achieved by other means that also induce the corresponding shifts in visual attention. This set of experiments was conducted using an artificial agent as speaker (called "Amber") in order to better accommodate arrow cues in the scene. The agent's utterances were of the form "The egg is taller than the box." (see also Figure 1).

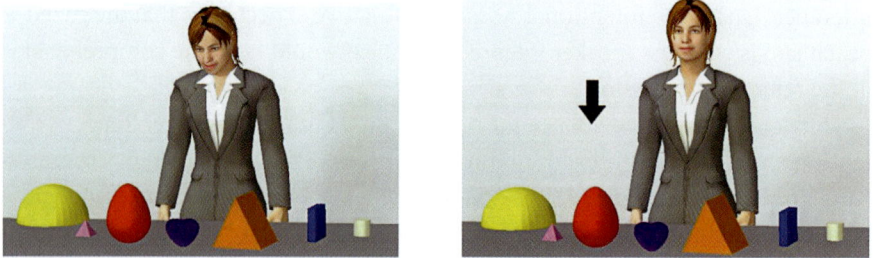

Figure 1. Gaze by "amber" towards egg versus arrow pointing at egg

The first experiment examined whether the agent's gaze cues need to be sequentially aligned with corresponding referential speech cues (as is typically the case for human speakers) in order to be beneficial. That is, whether the agent needs to first look at the egg and then at the box. In contrast, if gaze was a purely visual cue, a "misaligned" sequence of cues might also be beneficial since agent gaze still draws attention to mentioned objects in the scene, generally increasing those objects' salience. Such a misaligned, or reversed cueing pattern, occurs when the agent looks at the box before mentioning "egg" and only then looks at the egg just before mentioning "box". It is interesting to note that, in the misaligned case, the initial gaze cue together with the first noun provides all referential information occurring in this sentence which is earlier than in the congruently aligned condition. The "reverse" graph in Figure 2 also clearly shows that participants do indeed follow the initial agent gaze cue to the box and then follow the linguistic signal to the egg, so both relevant objects have been looked at by the time the comparative "taller than" is heard.

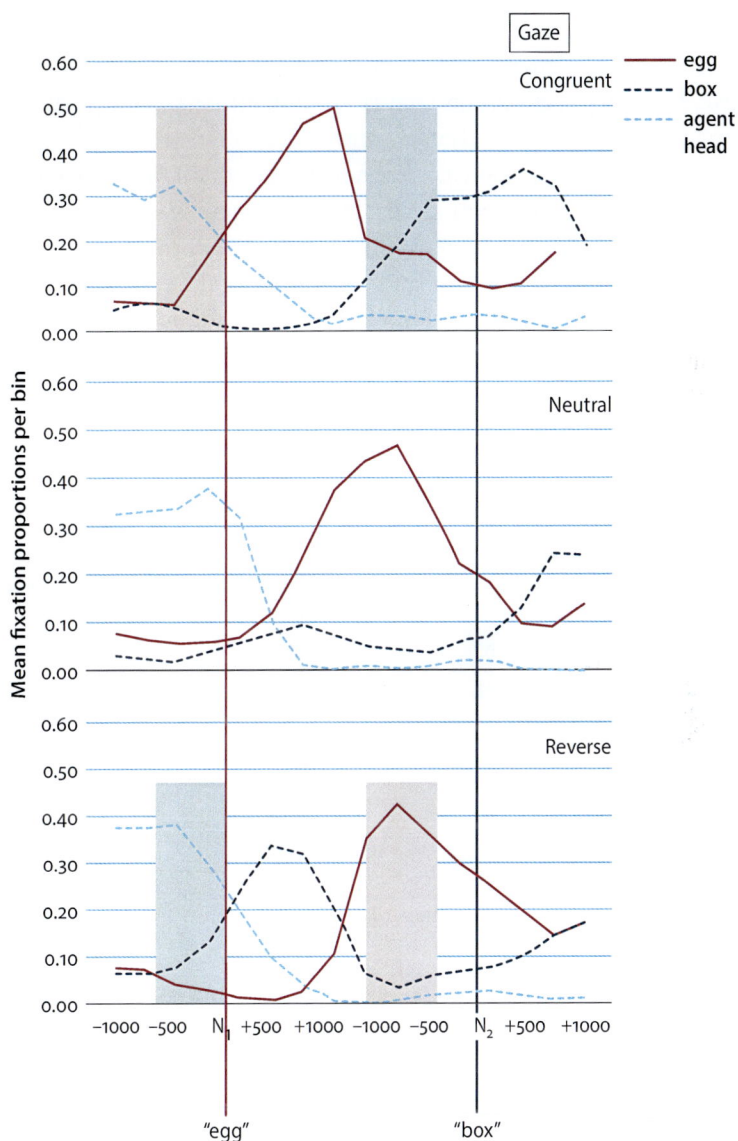

Figure 2. Listener fixations following speaker gaze and speech, time-locked to the onset of "egg" and of "box". Shaded regions indicate the occurrence of the gaze cue that corresponds to the similarly colored referent

In sum, we created again three gaze conditions: The sequence of two referential gaze cues and two referential nouns was either congruent, reverse to each other, or neutral (gaze straight ahead). In the second experiment, agent gaze was replaced with an arrow appearing above the corresponding object in order to reveal whether arrows do, in principle, elicit the same kind of attention shifts with the same or different effect onto language comprehension.

We found that listeners were again slower in the incongruent (though this time reversed) cueing condition compared to neutral gaze, and that they were faster when gaze was congruently cueing the two mentioned objects (see Figure 3). These results suggest that listeners were not able to exploit the reversed gaze cues to facilitate sentence validation. To exclude that there was a learning effect of listeners throughout the experiment with improved performance only in the second half, we also looked at the first and second half of the experiment separately. Results showed that listeners became faster in general but, more importantly, there was no interaction of the experimental half and the gaze condition, i.e., no learning effect.

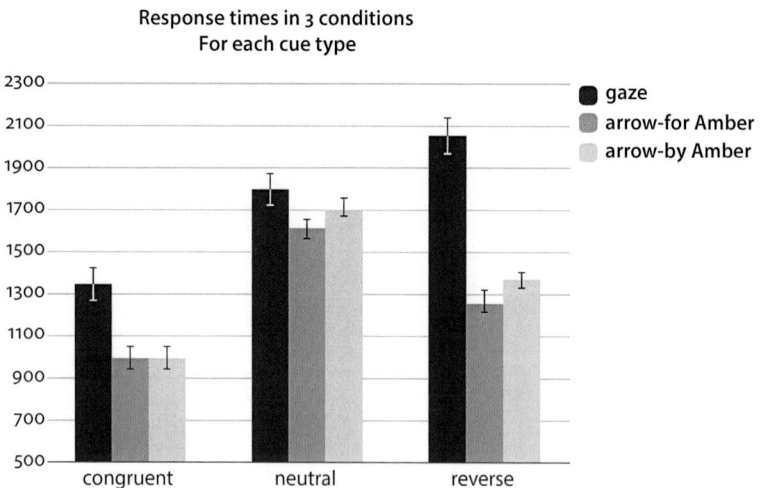

Figure 3. Response times in all three agent experiments

The response times in the arrow experiment show a different pattern: This time listeners were faster in both the congruent as well as the reverse condition compared to the neutral condition. Further, we now observed an interaction of experimental half with gaze condition. This interaction was carried by a significant speed up in the reverse condition: From a mean of 1,477 ms in the first experimental block to 1,123 ms in the second block (t = −4.71, p < 0.001). This suggests that, in contrast with gaze cues, listeners were able to learn to exploit the counter-predictive utility of the arrow cues.

Note that we replicated the results for arrows in a third study with modified instructions that assign different intentions to the arrow cues. While the arrows were initially introduced as an experimenter's device to signal Amber which objects she *should* describe, the modified version introduced the arrows as a means by which Amber herself highlights objects that she finds relevant. This, however, did not result in any difference in behavior.

Summing up, the results of the gaze experiment replicate and extend previous findings concerning the relevance of gaze cue order for comprehension, while the arrow cue turned out to be visually more precise and was (potentially therefore) used more effectively and flexibly to support utterance comprehension.

The design of the arrow cues necessitated a change in cue position relative to the referents, which may have resulted also in a change in cue *precision*. An additional experiment was therefore designed in which the precision of the gaze cue was enhanced to better match that of the arrow cues. The higher precision was achieved (a) by simplifying the visual scene, i.e., reducing the number of objects and by introducing more space between them, and (b) by decreasing the space between the table top and the agent head such that its gaze and head movements were more pronounced and more distinguishable (see Figure 4).

Figure 4. Simplified scene for precise gaze

The response time results of this experiment, in fact, matched that found in the arrow study. That is, there is a significant difference between the neutral and the congruent condition and, just as in the arrow experiment, between the neutral and the reverse condition (with reverse being *faster* than neutral). Congruent and reverse gaze trials did not differ significantly. As in the arrow experiment, we also found a marginally significant interaction of experiment half and gaze condition. Thus, the final experiment in this series shows that a visually precise gaze cue in a simplified scene can also be exploited in a flexible and efficient manner by the listener.

Together, these findings suggest that gaze and arrows direct attention and visually highlight the cued objects in a *similar* way. That is, the effects of gaze-following, that we observed on language comprehension when gaze is a clear and easy cue, also arise when listeners' visual attention shifts are induced by arrows instead. However, speaker gaze may frequently be spatially imprecise, as was the case in the initial gaze experiment, such that it is more difficult to exploit speaker gaze for utterance comprehension when the concurrent utterance does not match the cueing order. This disadvantage can be overcome when speaker gaze is as visually precise as the arrow baseline. Both cues can then be used similarly by listeners to infer and anticipate an upcoming verbal reference. Thus, the predictive effect of speaker gaze for a listener seems to be solely a (learnable) effect of cueing a given object at a given time which is *independent* of the potential intention or mental state attributed to the gazing speaker. This does not rule out that arrows may convey (different) intentions, e.g. by the experimenter. But the results show that temporal alignment is enough to elicit similar results, no matter whether speech, cue and intentions are all assigned to the same entity.

4.   The benefit of listener gaze

As mentioned above, much is already known about how listeners resolve referring expressions and how their eye-movements reflect that in a relatively static environment. However, it is less clear to which extent a (human or artificial) speaker in such a situation might be able to exploit these listener eye-movements as a direct index of whether or not the listener has understood a given referring expression. To call on our breakfast table example one last time, this means that it is unclear whether the speaker would detect the listener's gaze to (a) the raspberry jam or (b) the peach jam after having said "Please pass me the raspberry jam." In situation (a) the speaker might already say "Yeah, thanks." while in situation (b) the speaker could quickly say "No, I mean the *raspberry* jam!"

A speaker reaction so time-locked to listener gaze presupposes two fundamental mechanisms, namely (i) that listener gaze is reliably and rapidly directed towards understood referents in a manner that speakers can detect, and (ii) that speakers can process and react to them quickly enough to timely resolve misunderstandings or uncertainty, for instance, by providing immediate feedback. While studies from the visual world paradigm provide evidence for (i), such findings may not transfer to a highly dynamic and complex environment to the extent that listener gaze can retain its potential utility for speakers.

Previous studies emphasized the average gaze behavior over many trials; but in order to exploit listener gaze in real-time interactions, the speaker must be able to (timely) decode listener gaze in response to a single utterance. Evidence for (ii) remains at best suggestive. While Clark & Krych (2004) present clear evidence that interlocutors pay attention to each other's gaze as part of coordinating their dialog and requesting help, they offer no systematic evidence regarding the use of referential gaze. One reason for this is that it is difficult to simultaneously make the setting truly dynamic, accurately relate listener gaze to specific but varying verbal and visual content, and determine the influence of this gaze behavior on *subsequent* speaker behavior.

In addition, there are challenges in eliciting sufficiently consistent and numerous referring expressions – and gaze-driven feedback – to make a quantitative assessment of the hypothesis.

In order to overcome these problems, we developed an experimental setting in which a natural language generation (NLG) system autonomously creates instructions for a human user to guide her through a virtual environment (see Garoufi et al., 2016, Koller et al., 2012). For instance, the speaker (i.e. the NLG system) might navigate the user to the next target location in this world and then instruct the user to "Push the red button", as in Figure 5b. We then equipped one instance of the system with the capability of monitoring whether the listener subsequently looked at the red (target) button or at any other button such that it could generate feedback accordingly: "Yes, that one!" or "No, not that one". We compared communicative success in terms of correct button presses and users' performance in terms of task completion time between interactions with this eye-movement based NLG system and interactions with two base-line systems. Those systems either generated no feedback at all or feedback that was based on the user's motion towards a visible button. This setup allowed us to create a truly interactive setting with a "confederate" speaker and a human listener while being able to control and, more importantly, manipulate how and when the speaker reacts to listener eye-movements.

As a result, we found that the NLG system that provided eye-movement based feedback, outperformed the other two systems. We also found very typical listener eye-movement patterns reflecting reference resolution, despite the complex task and the quickly changing virtual environment (which really was a prerequisite for being able to give useful feedback). This indicates that communicative success and efficiency are enhanced when the speaker can monitor referential listener gaze and provide feedback to it. More generally, this suggests that speakers *can in principle* exploit those eye-movements and react quickly enough in order to encourage correct or prevent wrong reference resolution and any resulting actions (such as pressing the identified button).

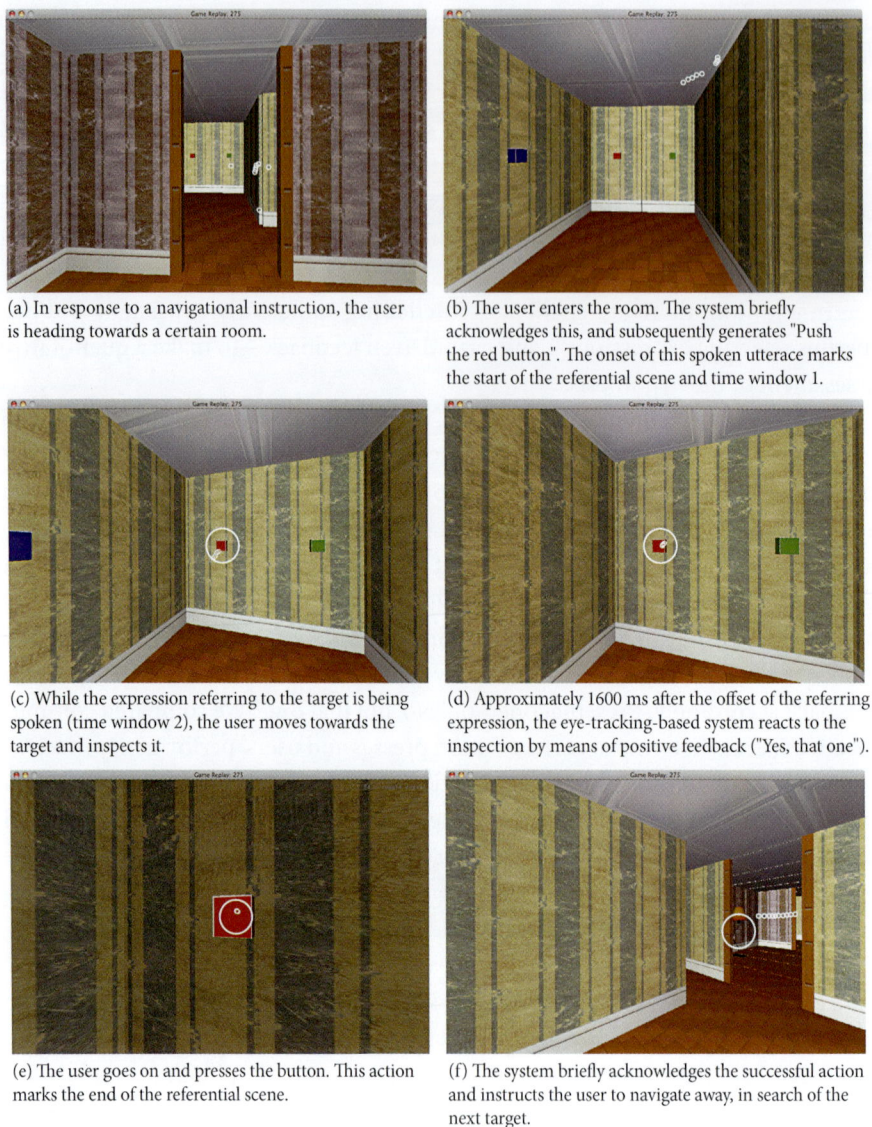

(a) In response to a navigational instruction, the user is heading towards a certain room.

(b) The user enters the room. The system briefly acknowledges this, and subsequently generates "Push the red button". The onset of this spoken utterace marks the start of the referential scene and time window 1.

(c) While the expression referring to the target is being spoken (time window 2), the user moves towards the target and inspects it.

(d) Approximately 1600 ms after the offset of the referring expression, the eye-tracking-based system reacts to the inspection by means of positive feedback ("Yes, that one").

(e) The user goes on and presses the button. This action marks the end of the referential scene.

(f) The system briefly acknowledges the successful action and instructs the user to navigate away, in search of the next target.

Figure 5. Sample scene with the gaze-based NLG-system

5. Discussion

In this chapter we have explored the extent to which gaze can serve as important aspect of the communicative signal in situated spoken language interaction. In particular we find clear evidence that listener eye movements respond rapidly and similarly to both the speaker's gaze and their utterance. Furthermore, the benefits of gaze – and the disruption caused by inappropriate gaze – are robustly indexed in the sentence verification reaction times. Importantly, these effects are observed despite the fact that the verification task does not require participants to pay attention to gaze behavior at all.

Regarding the nature of the mechanisms that underlie the benefit of speaker gaze, the picture remains less clear. The present robot study provided evidence suggesting listeners attribute referential intentions to speaker gaze. These results are also in line with results from Hanna and Brennan (2007). In fact, the similarity between those two investigations strengthens the assumption that human listeners treat robot/agent gaze like another human speaker's gaze (but see also Nass and Moon, 2000, for the more general discussion of whether and when humans treat machines like human partners). However, findings regarding the processing of substitute cues, such as arrows or exogenous capture cues, is less conclusive. Nappa and Arnold (2014), for instance, found different effects on pronoun resolution depending on the cue type (gaze versus black capture cue) and whether the intentions behind the cue were somehow associated with the speaker. At the same time, however, the 'precise gaze' versus arrows study described above revealed that these two cues can also have a very similar effect on listener eye-movement and verification behavior. While these results do not falsify the *Intentional Account*, they seem to suggest instead that speakers can use gaze and other cues flexibly and strategically and for the same purposes.

Finally, we presented evidence that listener gaze can in principle be exploited by a speaker to improve communicative success in real-time, as an indicator of whether listeners have correctly understood the intended referent of an utterance. This sort of study is particularly difficult to realize with two human interlocutors since the listener's eye movements are no longer only the dependent variable (a result of the spoken utterance indexing understanding) but they become also an input variable to influence the speaker's behavior. Thus, most previous studies of human spoken interaction have focused on listener gaze as a cue to comprehension processes, e.g. during the establishment of conceptual pacts (Metzing & Brennan, 2003), perspective-taking in conversation (Keysar et al., 2000; Yoon, Koh, & Brown-Schmidt, 2012), the integration of common ground during production and comprehension (Brown-Schmidt & Hanna, 2011; Hanna, Tanenhaus, & Trueswell, 2003), or word learning in children (Nappa et al., 2009; Yu & Smith, 2012). Few studies have allowed for a true, dynamic interaction where the listener behavior influenced the speaker (but see e.g. Brown-Schmidt & Tanenhaus, 2008; Clark & Krych, 2004). Because of the mutual and dynamic interplay of speaker and listener gaze, the quantitative assessment of how such gaze cues impact human-human interaction remains difficult. Thus, using and controlling an NLG system as a substitute for a real speaker, as described in Section 3, yields a real advantage for investigating those mechanisms that relate to online gaze and speech production and comprehension. At the same time, however, such generation systems behave far from human-like and are still relatively slow while human speakers, in contrast, may not be as sensitive to listener gaze at all times. This makes it difficult to directly compare the results to performance in human-human scenarios.

From a methodological perspective all the studies presented here share their use of artificial agents as "speakers" in our interactions. One immediate and indisputable benefit of this approach is that atypical behaviors, such as incongruent gaze, can be straightforwardly elicited, and are also more plays to listeners. In the case of the final study, this approach reveals further advantages, in that it enables experiments in which participants directly and dynamically interact with agents that embody and instantiate the theories with wish to evaluate. This is of particular importance when investigating participant contingent behaviors, also as an ideal exemplar for artificial interlocutors, in the kinds of multi-modal, situated, and task-oriented settings that human communication epitomizes.

References

Allopenna, P., Magnuson, J., & Tanenhaus, M. (1998). Tracking the time course of spoken word recognition using eye movements: Evidence for continuous mapping models. *Journal of Memory and Language*, 38, 419–439. https://doi.org/10.1006/jmla.1997.2558

Altmann, G., & Kamide, Y. (1999). Incremental interpretation at verbs: restricting the domain of subsequent reference. *Cognition*, 73, 247–264. https://doi.org/10.1016/S0010-0277(99)00059-1

Bayliss, A., Paul, M., Cannon, P., & Tipper, S. (2006). Gaze cueing and affective judgments of objects: I like what you look at. *Psychonomic Bulletin & Review*, 13, 1061–1066. https://doi.org/10.3758/BF03213926

Becchio, C., Bertone, C., & Castiello, U. (2008). How the gaze of others influences object processing. *Trends in Cognitive Science*, 12, 254–258. https://doi.org/10.1016/j.tics.2008.04.005

Brown-Schmidt, S., & Hanna, J. E. (2011). Talking in another person's shoes: Incremental perspective-taking in language processing. *Dialogue and Discourse*, 2, 11–33. https://doi.org/10.5087/dad.2011.102

Brown-Schmidt, S., & Tanenhaus, M. K. (2008). Real-time investigation of referential domains in unscripted conversation: A targeted language game approach. *Cognitive Science*, 32(4), 643–684. https://doi.org/10.1080/03640210802066816

Castiello, U. (2003). Understanding Other People's Actions: Intention and Attention. *Journal of Experimental Psychology*, 29, 416–430.

Clark, H. H., & Krych, M. A.(2004). Speaking while monitoring addressees for understanding. *Journal of Memory and Language*, 50, 62–81. https://doi.org/10.1016/j.jml.2003.08.004

Driver, J., Davis, G., Ricciardelli, P., Kidd, P., Maxwell, E., & Baron-Cohen, S. (1999). Gaze Perception Triggers Reflexive Visuospatial Orienting. *Visual Cognition*, 6(5), 509–540. https://doi.org/10.1080/135062899394920

Friesen, C., & Kingstone, A. (1998). The eyes have it! Reflexive orienting is triggered by nonpredictive gaze. *Psychonomic Bulletin & Review*, 5(3), 490–495. https://doi.org/10.3758/BF03208827

Garoufi, K., Staudte, M., Koller, A. & Crocker, M. W. (2016). Exploiting listener gaze to improve situated communication in dynamic virtual environments. *Cognitive Science*, 40:1671–1703.

Gleitman, L. R., January, D., Nappa, R., & Trueswell, J. C. (2007). On the *give* and *take* between event apprehension and utterance formulation. *Journal of Memory and Language*, 57, 544–569. https://doi.org/10.1016/j.jml.2007.01.007

Griffin, Z. M., & Bock, K. (2000). What the eyes say about speaking. *Psychological Science*, 11, 274–279. https://doi.org/10.1111/1467-9280.00255

Hanna, J., & Brennan, S. (2007). Speakers' eye gaze disambiguates referring expressions early during face-to-face conversation. *Journal of Memory and Language*, 57(4), 596–615. https://doi.org/10.1016/j.jml.2007.01.008

Hanna, J. E., Tanenhaus, M. K., & Trueswell, J. C. (2003). The effects of common ground and perspective on domains of referential interpretation. *Journal of Memory and Language*, 49(1). https://doi.org/10.1016/S0749-596X(03)00022-6

Keysar, B., Barr, D. J., Balin, J. A., & Brauner, J. S. (2000). Taking perspective in conversation: The role of mutual knowledge in comprehension. *Psychological Science*, 11, 32–38. https://doi.org/10.1111/1467-9280.00211

Koller, A., Garoufi, K., Staudte, M., & Crocker, M. W. (2012). Enhancing referential success by tracking hearer gaze. In Proceedings of the 13th Annual Meeting of the Special Interest Group on Discourse and Dialogue. Seoul, South Korea.

Knoeferle, P. & Crocker, M. W. (2006). The coordinated interplay of scene, utterance, and world knowledge: evidence from eye tracking. *Cognitive Science*, 30(3):481–529. https://doi.org/10.1207/s15516709cog0000_65

Knoeferle, P. & Crocker, M. W. (2007). The influence of recent scene events on spoken comprehension: evidence from eye-movements. *Journal of Memory and Language* (Special issue: Language-Vision Interaction); 57(2):519–543. https://doi.org/10.1016/j.jml.2007.01.003

Knoeferle, P., Pyykkönen-Klauck, P. & Crocker, M. W. (Eds.). Visually Situated Language Comprehension. *John Benjamins Publishing Company*, (2016).

Langton, S. R. & Bruce, V. (1999). Reflexive Visual Orienting in Response to the Social Attention of Others. *Visual Cognition*, 6(5), 541–567. https://doi.org/10.1080/135062899394939

Meyer, A., Sleiderink, A., & Levelt, W. (1998). Viewing and naming objects: Eye movements during noun phrase production. *Cognition*, 66, B25–B33. https://doi.org/10.1016/S0010-0277(98)00009-2

Meltzoff, A. N., Brooks, R., Shon, A. P., & Rao, R. P. (2010). Social robots are psychological agents for infants: A test of gaze following. *Neural Networks*, 23(8–9), 966–972. (Social Cognition: From Babies to Robots) https://doi.org/10.1016/j.neunet.2010.09.005

Metzing, C., & Brennan, S. E. (2003). When conceptual pacts are broken: Partner-specific effects on the comprehension of referring expressions. *Journal of Memory and Language*, 49(2), 201–213. https://doi.org/10.1016/S0749-596X(03)00028-7

Nappa, R. & Arnold, J. (2014). The road to understanding is paved with the speaker's intentions: Cues to the speaker's attention and intentions affect pronoun comprehension. *Cognitive Psychology*, 70, 58–81. https://doi.org/10.1016/j.cogpsych.2013.12.003

Nappa, R., Wessel, A., McEldoon, K. L., Gleitman, L. R., & Trueswell, J. C. (2009). Use of speaker's gaze and syntax in verb learning. *Language Learning and Development*, 5(4), 203–234. https://doi.org/10.1080/15475440903167528

Nass, C., & Moon, Y. (2000). Machines and mindlessness: Social responses to computers. *Journal of Social Issues*, 56, 81–103. https://doi.org/10.1111/0022-4537.00153

Rayner, K. (1998). Eye movements in reading and information processing: 20 years of research. *Psychological Bulletin & Review*, 124 (3), 372–422. https://doi.org/10.1037/0033-2909.124.3.372

Staudte, M., & Crocker, M. W. (2011). Investigating joint attention mechanisms through spoken human-robot interaction. *Cognition*, 120, 268–291. https://doi.org/10.1016/j.cognition.2011.05.005

Staudte, M., Crocker, M. W., Heloir, A. & Michael Kipp (2014). The influence of speaker gaze on listener comprehension: Contrasting visual versus intentional accounts. *Cognition*, 133(1): 317–328. https://doi.org/10.1016/j.cognition.2014.06.003

Tanenhaus, M. K., Spivey-Knowlton, M., Eberhard, K., & Sedivy, J. (1995). Integration of visual and linguistic information in spoken language comprehension. *Science*, 268, 1632–1634. https://doi.org/10.1126/science.7777863

Tomlin, R. S. (1997). Mapping conceptual representations into linguistic representations: The role of attention in grammar. In J. Nuyts, & E. Pederson (Eds.), *Language and conceptualization* (pp. 162–189), Cambridge: Cambridge University Press. https://doi.org/10.1017/CBO9781139086677.007

Yoon, S. O., Koh, S., & Brown-Schmidt, S. (2012). Influence of perspective and goals on reference production in conversation. *Psychonomic Bulletin and Review*, 19, 699–707. https://doi.org/10.3758/s13423-012-0262-6

Yu, C., & Smith, L. B. (2012). Embodied attention and word learning by toddlers. *Cognition*, 125, 244–262. https://doi.org/10.1016/j.cognition.2012.06.016

PART 2

Methodological considerations

CHAPTER 6

Quantifying the interplay
of gaze and gesture in deixis using
an experimental-simulative approach

Thies Pfeiffer and Patrick Renner
Bielefeld University

Gaze and gestures have been studied qualitatively, e.g., by Kendon and others (Kendon, 1990; McNeill, 1992; Kendon, 2004; McNeill, 2006). A quantitative assessment of gaze and gestures in dialogue, in particular regarding precise orientations, positions and timings, however, has only been possible with the advent of advanced measuring technologies, such as motion capturing or eye tracking. Especially in dynamic natural environments, when interlocutors are concerned with their surrounding three-dimensional environment, a precise three-dimensional reconstruction of the set-up is required to analyze the produced multimodal utterances.

In this article we review several of our past projects with a focus on our experimental-simulative approach in which we combine state-of-the-art tracking technologies with 3D representations and computer simulations to test different hypotheses in the context of deixis in human-human interaction.

Keywords: gaze, speech, gestures, eye tracking, motion capturing, 3D simulation

1. Introduction

When we are thinking about the modalities we are using to refer to the objects in our environment, speech and, most likely, gestures come to our mind. These are the modalities we, as a speaker, are making explicit use of. As an addressee, however, we intuitively make use of the signals sent by an additional modality when interpreting the speaker's utterance: gaze. Speakers tend to orient themselves towards the objects they are talking about. In most cases, this behaviour seems to be driven purely by personal needs of the speaker, e.g., to achieve a better perception of the referent, to support memory processes or to assess spatial information. For the addressee,

https://doi.org/10.1075/ais.10.06pfe

however, the gaze direction of the speaker provides additional valuable information that helps in disambiguating the utterance.

In our own research, we are aiming at modelling similar behaviours on artificial systems, such as robots. However, to do so, we require quantitative data of a high precision. This is why in the past 10 years we have used tracking technologies to assess different aspects of deixis, answering questions such as: How precise is pointing? How is the direction of pointing constructed? What is the interplay between gaze and gesture? Can we predict pointing targets by observing gaze? What gaze patterns do humans follow when communicating references?

In this article, we will review three of our larger explorative studies we have done in the past, but this time with a strong focus on the methods we have applied in conducting and analyzing these studies. The rationale behind this is that we want to provide examples on how state-of-the-art technology could be used to collect quantitative data and what kind of analyses can be done. We thus have tried to find examples with different foci and alternative ways of combining data.

Example A is primarily concerned with gesture tracking of a single participant and the identification of the pointing target. It also shows how different hypotheses can be tested based on the collected tracking data using simulation techniques. Example B presents a similar case but for the analysis of eye gaze. This example also shows how tracking technology can be used to speed up the annotation processes normally required for this kind of research. In addition to that, example B demonstrates that multiple participants can be tracked using the same technology. The last example C demonstrates that gaze and gesture tracking can be combined in a shared representation and how the interaction of the two modalities can be analyzed, also in the interaction of two interlocutors.

Before we start with the three examples, we will explain the experimental-simulative approach we are following in the next section, to provide a general overview. The presentations of the three examples will be in line with the structure of this approach.

2.   An experimental-simulative approach

In our line of research on different aspects of human behaviour, we follow an experimental-simulative approach inspired by Rickheit and Strohner (1993) and apply it to interaction analysis. The basic idea is that empirical experiments and computer-based simulations can complement each other to incrementally refine scientific models (see Figure 1).

A specialty of our particular approach is that we use an abstract representation of an interaction for describing the empirical data gathered in the experiment and

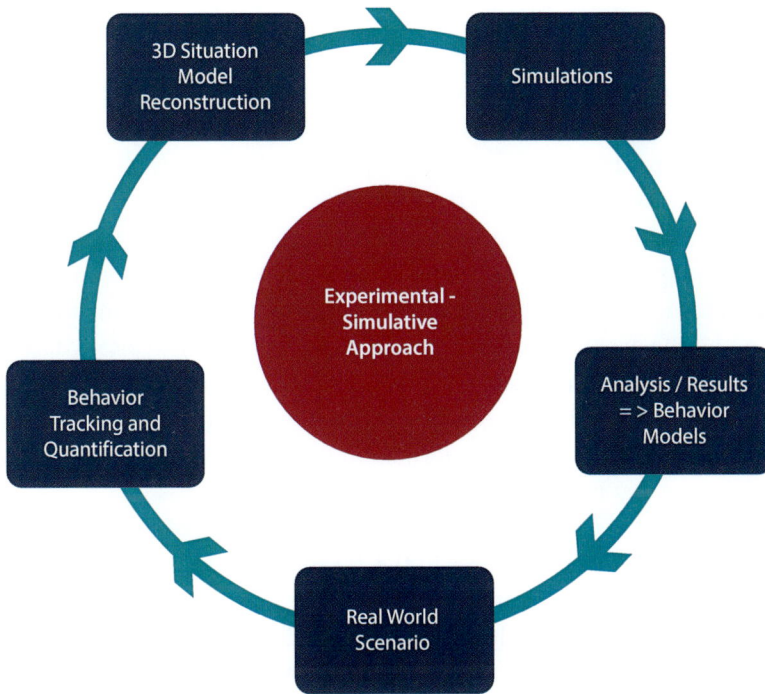

Figure 1. The procedure model of the experimental-simulative approach

as basis for the data-driven simulations. As we are focusing on spatiality aspects of interacting humans, this representation employs a 3D model of the relevant aspects of human interlocutors and their environment, as well as the temporal sequence of an interaction within this environment. We call this model a 3D situation model, because ultimately it should contain the essence of an interaction and thus everything that is required to construct a situation model in the sense of Van Dijk and Kintsch (1983). In reality, our 3D situation model differs to the mental situation model in several aspects. Most importantly, it has a strong focus on spatiality and less so on social aspects, and in contrast to mental models it may contain huge amounts of highly precise spatial data.

2.1   Quantification using tracking technology

Creating 3D situation models requires two steps. The first step is the integration of the actual behavioural data in the 3D situation model. For this, we make use of different tracking technologies (see e.g. Duchowski, 2007; Pfeiffer, 2013b,a for an overview). Such technologies measure for example the position and orientation of optical markers that can be attached to body parts or movable objects (Vicon Motion Systems Ltd., 2016; Advanced Realtime Tracking GmbH, 2016; NaturalPoint, Inc., 2016). Such markers are small target objects which can be easily identified by camera systems and for which the location and orientation can be computed. Alternative solutions can directly assess certain movements, e.g. mobile eye-tracking systems can directly measure the pupil of the wearer (SensoMotoric Instruments GmbH, 2016; Tobii AB, 2016; Kassner and Patera, 2012).

The tracking systems typically operate on a discrete frame-by-frame basis and provide their data at different frame rates. If multiple tracking systems are used, e.g. when combining eye tracking with motion capturing, one is typically faced with several technical problems: the synchronization between the systems, a potentially resampling to provide the recorded data with a consistent frame rate for the 3D situation model, as well as the transformation in a common coordinate system are the major issues that need to be solved.

After all tracking data is converted into a consistent set of coordinate systems, it has to be linked to 3D structures in the 3D situation model that represent the tracked elements (see Figure 2). For a tracked user in a motion capturing suit this could be a simple stick figure with links and joints. It could also be a pair of eye balls which rotate around their axis and fly around at the locations identified using the eye-tracking system. If eye tracking is paired with motion capturing, the eye balls will be located in the head of the representation of the tracked user, e.g. the head of the stick figure, and change their position according to the head movements.

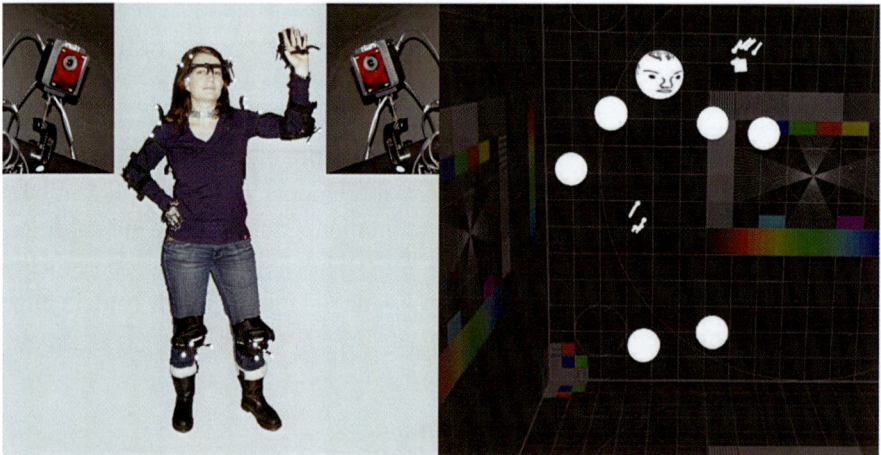

Figure 2. Using motion capturing technology, the movement of interesting body parts can be tracked by attaching visually salient markers (left). The such recorded data can be used to create an abstract representation of a participant in the 3D situation space (right) (Pfeiffer, 2013b)

2.2   Reconstructing a 3D situation model

As a second step, an approximative 3D model of the environment has to be created. This model should cover objects relevant for the interaction domain, but also other spatial aspects that could become relevant for the interaction. It should, for example, contain spatial structures that might occlude target objects, such as walls or furniture, because this affects the behaviour of the humans, e.g. when constructing a referring expression. For typical environments, in particular such environments that are used for studies under a high-level of experimental control, these models can be either hand-crafted or modern technologies, such as 3D scanning and structure-from-motion approaches can be employed. For most situations a coarse geometric model would be sufficient. The descriptions of our studies to follow later in this chapter will provide examples for this.

2.3   Simulations in the 3D situation model

The result of the reconstruction of the real world interaction scenario is a 3D situation model that is an abstract representation of the interaction scenario including the interacting humans and their interaction domain. To be precise, this 3D situation model is actually a model template, which only includes the structural representations of the tracked elements and the approximative 3D model of the environment. Only once this template is filled with real interaction data, we can speak of a real 3D situation model. In a typical experiments, one will thus have one 3D situation model for each recorded experimental session (template + data). These 3D situation models can now be subject to different simulations.

One typical example of such a simulation in the context of deixis is, that different models for the referential scope of a modality can be added to the 3D situation model and tested against the recorded data. In the case of a pointing gesture, this could be a pointing cone that is attached to the tip of the extended index finger of the stick figure which is representing the pointing participant. This cone is meant to describe the area, or in this case we better speak of a volume, within the 3D situation model that would likely contain the target being pointed at (see Figure 3). Similar models can be added for the volume in space attended to via eye gaze. In addition to these more direct mappings, an analysis of the speech of a speaker could identify spatial propositions such as "left of", which could be modelled as spatial constraints in relation to the speaker, the addressee, or any other frame of reference.

Other alternatives are classifiers that can be constructed to generate automatic annotations for specific situations or sequences of events, for example for certain gesture trajectories (Pfeiffer et al., 2013), on basis of the recorded data and the data generated by the simulations.

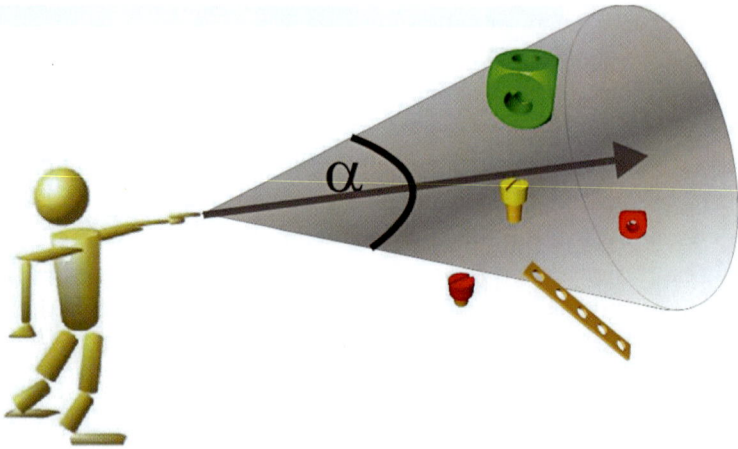

Figure 3. To estimate the opening angle of a pointing cone as a model for describing the referential scope of pointing gestures, a 3D situation model including motion capturing data of pointing gestures has been used. (Pfeiffer, 2010)

2.4   Analysis and results

The 3D situation model provides many different opportunities for analysis: spatial mappings (e.g. identify locations being pointed at), temporal patterns, synchronicity between different interlocutors, and many more. We provide specific examples in the following sections in which we report on different studies that have been conducted following this method.

We have followed different paths in analyzing the data of the simulations. In some cases, our simulations provide annotations complementary to a larger corpus of data, e.g. transcripts of speech. In this case we feed the results back into the traditional process chain of manual annotation of multimodal corpora using tools such as ELAN (Wittenburg et al., 2006). The simulations will provide us either with data that could not have been annotated by humans based on the recorded audio or video material alone (e.g. see the precision of pointing acts in Section 3), or the simulations simply help us speeding up the annotation process, e.g., by providing pre-annotations or full annotations of certain annotation tiers (see the automatic annotation of areas of interest for gaze analysis in Section 4). One advantage in this case is, that the simulations are done automatically and consistently over all recorded sessions.

Another path is creating sets of tabular data files, e.g. in CSV format, for statistical analysis in tools such as R, SAS, SPSS or STATA. This path will typically be the one followed towards the end of the analysis, when preparing the results for publication. In this context, we prefer to use a combination of R[1] and LaTeX[2] using the SWeave[3] or knitr[4] packages, which allow us to integrate the verbal description of our data with R code fragments required for analysis to create a coherent document, including graphics and diagrams which are automatically created based on the data whenever the document is recompiled to produce the pdf output file.

Both manual annotations and the results of a statistical analysis can also be integrated back into the simulation, e.g. to incrementally refine and update the data. For example, a first simulation run could provide automatically identified areas of interest based on a reconstructed 3D gaze ray cast in the 3D situation model. However, as this simulation is data driven and thus based on the recorded motion capturing data, it will be affected by typical problems of motion capturing, such as data loss when markers are temporarily occluded. This means that there could be drop-outs during which an automatic assignment of areas of interest is not possible. After feeding the results of the first simulation run into the annotation pipeline, human raters can assess those critical parts in which markers have been lost (these sequences in the data can be easily identified) and assign the correct areas of interest based on recorded video material. The thus completed assignment of areas of interest can then be picked up by the next simulation run, e.g. to automatically identify patterns of shared attention of two interlocutors on the same areas of interest.

2.5   Summary

By introducing the abstraction step of creating a 3D situation model for a situation under inspection, we make the particular situations subject to computational simulations, which allow us to incrementally and iteratively evaluate and refine scientific models in a data-driven manner. In the following, we elaborate this approach on three distinct examples.

3.   Example A: A study on deixis

The first example we want to address is a study on pointing gestures that has been conducted in a research project in the frame of the Collaborative Research Center 360 (CRC 360), "Situated Artificial Communicators", at Bielefeld University. The

---

1.   https://www.r-project.org/

2.   http://www.dante.de/

3.   https://www.statistik.lmu.de/leisch/Sweave/

4.   http://yihui.name/knitr/

overarching topic of this CRC was the creation of robotic interaction partners that can be instructed using natural language and gestures to conduct certain assembly tasks. The particular research has been conducted in cooperation with Hannes Rieser, Andy Lücking and Alfred Kranstedt in the time between 2003 and 2006 during the last funding period of the CRC 360 (Kranstedt et al., 2006b,c,a).

3.1   Background

In a study on deixis preceding this one, in which participants played "pointing games" while being video-taped, it became apparent that it is difficult to assess a precise direction of pointing based on 2D video recordings (Kühnlein and Stegmann, 2003). At that time, linguists and computer scientists at Bielefeld University were working closely together on topics such as situated dialog for communication with robots. The scope of research was thereby not tied to physical robots but included virtual agents, such as the virtual agent Max (Kopp et al., 2003), as well. This is where virtual reality came into play as a methodology for supporting basic research in linguistics (Pfeiffer, 2012).

The central question asked in the project was whether pointing gestures construct a pointing ray that is casted in the environment to designate the pointing target, or whether less rigid approaches, for example a pointing cone with a larger opening angle, better describe the observable behaviour. To answer this question, precise data on the position and orientation of the hand and in particular of the pointing finger were required, and video-based annotations failed to provide this data with the required accuracy.

This study on deixis was actually the first study in which we made use of technologies from the field of virtual reality, in particular real-time motion capturing and 3D visualization, to collect and fuse the behavioural data of the participants with a previously unmatched level of precision (Pfeiffer et al., 2006).

3.2   Scenario

The basic scenario we used for our series of studies consisted of two non-confederate participants, each playing one of two roles: either description giver or object identifier. The interaction domain consisted of 32 potential target objects placed in a grid-layout on a table. The objects had different colors, sizes and were of different types. However, not a single feature was sufficient to identify the object directly.

The task of the description giver was to communicate the target object that was presented to him or her on a personal screen to the object identifier.

Depending on different conditions, the description giver was either allowed to use speech and gestures or was restricted to use gestures only. The task of the object identifier was to find out the target referenced by the description giver. Depending on the condition, the object identifier was either placed to the left side of the description giver (see Figure 4 a) or at the other end of the table (see Figure 4 c).

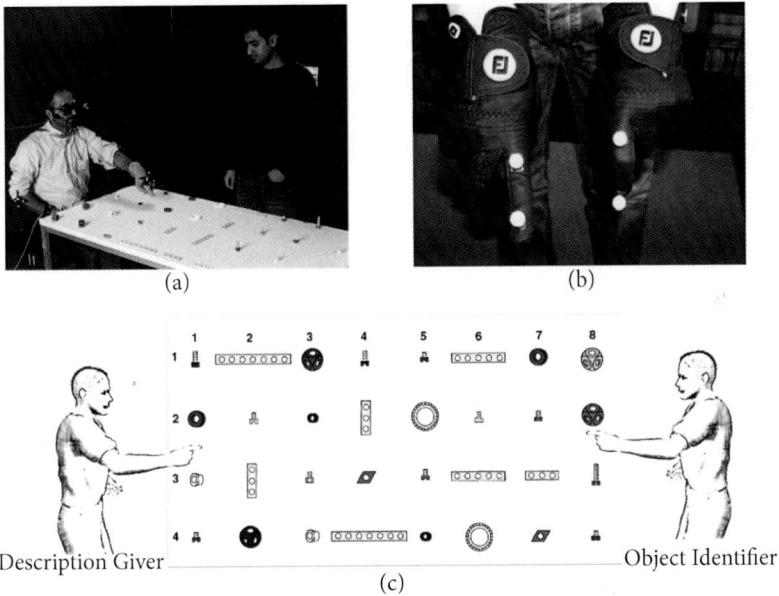

(a)

(b)

Description Giver

Object Identifier

(c)

Figure 4. In a study on deixis using speech and gesture, motion capturing was used to track the position and orientation of the index finger and a 3D reconstruction of the scenario was created to measure the accuracy of the pointing gestures in the simulations. (Pfeiffer, 2010)

3.3 Tracking setup

Relevant features of the interacting interlocutors considered in the 3D situation model were the position and orientation of the index fingers of the left and the right hand of the description giver, as well as his or her head. These we tracked using an optical tracking system (see Figure 2). The object identifier remained untracked (which we regretted later). To be able to get precise data for the index finger, we designed special gloves and attached tracking markers (see Figure 4). As tracking hardware we used an optical tracking system providing tracking data with a frequency of 60 Hz.

3.4   Reconstructed 3D situation model

Besides the representation of the description giver, the 3D situation model we created contained also the table and the set of objects we have used as target domain. The 3D model was carefully designed to match exactly the positions of the objects in the real world.

3.5   Simulations in the 3D situation model

Figure 5 shows a visualization of the constructed 3D situation model. It includes a virtual model of the table and 32 virtual objects located at exactly the same positions as the original ones in the real world setting. As the data visualized in Figure 5 aggregate data of a full recording session, the head and hand positions are not shown. Instead, we chose to add a visualization of the annotation schema introduced by McNeill (1992) as an abstract representation of the description giver in this case. The figure shows the results of a simulation run in which we reconstructed virtual pointing rays constructed on basis of the recorded data. Position and orientation of hand and index finger were taken from the motion capturing data, the timespans during which the strokes occurred were manually annotated based on the videos and both data were fused for the simulation.

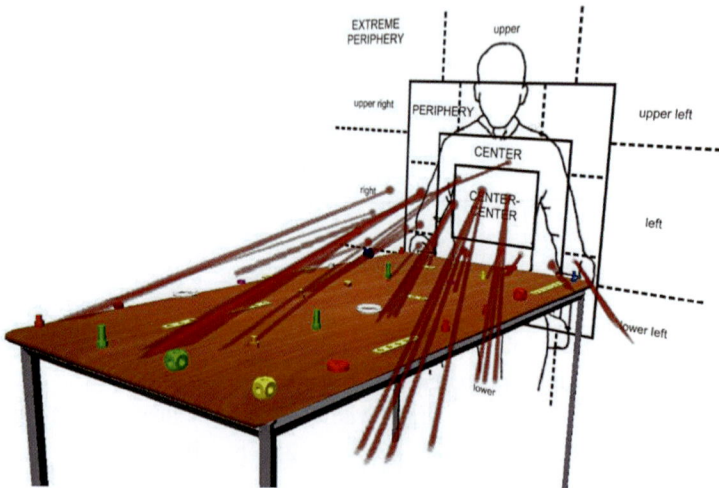

Figure 5. This visualization shows the pointing rays that have been simulated for all pointing acts of a certain participant. Origin and direction of the pointing rays are given by the motion capturing data. (Pfeiffer, 2010)

It can easily be imagined that using these simulations, different models for the extension of pointing can be constructed (pointing ray, pointing cone), including different ways on how the direction of pointing is derived (extended index finger, aiming with gaze over the finger). This is what we did and what is presented in the following section. The model also allows us to measure the deviation between a postulated pointing ray for a specific demonstration game and the optimal ray towards the known target object. This provides a measure for quantifying the precision of pointing gestures.

In addition to that, it would also easily be possible to represent, visualize, and analyze multimodal models of deixis, e.g. by adding simulations of the line of sight for each eye (given that eyes had been tracked) or the visual field of the description giver (based on head tracking) to the simulation.

3.6   Results

From the many different aspects we have investigated with this exploratory study, we have reviewed two that used quite unique methods of analysis in this context and at that time.

3.6.1   Distribution of hand positions

We aggregated the tracked hand positions represented in the 3D situation model for each participant and created a 3D heatmap (see Figure 6). This heatmap representation is more commonly known in the area of attention analysis. The metaphor is that the areas that are marked with red color have received a higher amount of attention, while for the areas that have received lower amounts of attention the colors are changed until they become transparent for areas that have been completely unattended. In our case we used a similar mapping, but instead of attention we accounted for the presence of the hand during the stroke of the pointing act. In a 2D condition, this would have resulted in an image overlay of the original image, but in the 3D case, the result is a 3D voxel image, similar to those produced by brain and body scanners used in neurosciences.

Using this method, we could nicely reveal the different search strategies that had been used by the different participants (see Figure 6; Pfeiffer, 2010, 2011). We observed strategies that tried to move the pointing finger as closely to the object as possible, or that increased the height of the pointing hand in accordance with the distance of the target (the more distant, the higher the hand).

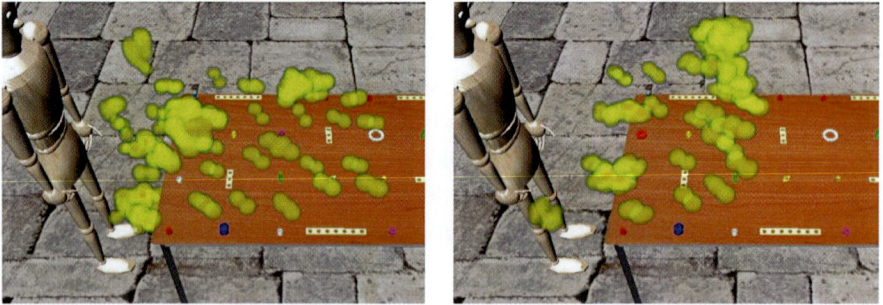

Figure 6. An aggregation of the spatial positions of the hands during the stroke of the pointing acts revealed different strategies: reaching as closely as possible (left), raising the hands higher when pointing to distant objects (right). (Pfeiffer, 2010, 2011)

3.6.2   *Direction of pointing gestures*

In later work we re-analyzed the data by running simulations with different models on how the direction of a pointing gesture is actually constructed (Pfeiffer, 2010). We proposed several models, such as an index-finger-as-a-vector approach in which we measured the orientation of the index finger and projected the pointing ray as an extension of the finger in space. We called this index-finger-pointing (IFP). The alternative models took an aiming of the pointing description giver into account by constructing the direction of pointing using the difference vector between the eye of the description giver and the tip of the index finger. We called this gaze-finger-pointing (GFP). For GFP we already had several alternatives, either using the left (GFP/left) or the right eye (GFP/right), using a cyclopean eye in the middle of both eyes (GFP/cyc) and the dominant eye (GFP/dom). The results of these simulation runs are shown in Figure 7. It turned out that the lowest deviation from the ideal pointing direction straight to the target is achieved by orienting the projected pointing ray along the vector starting in the dominant eye and aiming over the tip of the index finger (GFP/cyc), which is thus the most plausible model for pointing direction given our data.

Distribution of angular errors (S+G trials)

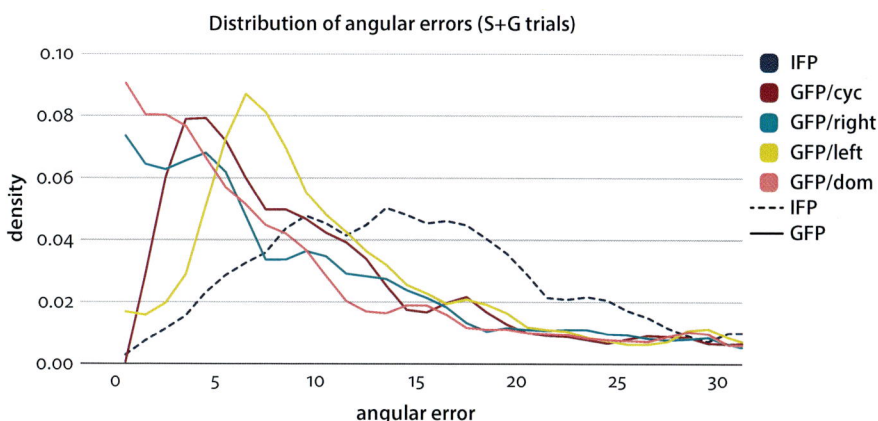

Figure 7. A simulation of different models for constructing the direction of pointing revealed that the most plausible model considered the position of the dominant eye aiming over the tip of the index finger. (Pfeiffer, 2010)

4. Example B: Deictic gaze of two interlocutors in a search scenario

In the second example, we explored referential gaze in a scenario with two interlocutors who both were equipped with mobile eye-tracking glasses. This study has its background in the project "Modelling Partners" of the Collaborative Research Center 673 (CRC 673; 2006–2014) named "Alignment in Communication", which was located at Bielefeld University. Alignment means subconscious adaptation processes which are important for flawless human-human communication. The aims of this CRC were on the one hand to explore these alignment processes and on the other hand to investigate whether they can be used to enhance human-robot communication. The study was originally presented in Renner et al. (2015).

4.1 Background

Eye gaze plays an important role in human communication. One foundational skill in human social interaction is joint attention which is receiving increased interest in particular in the area of human-agent or human-robot interaction. Joint attention can be defined as simultaneously allocating attention to a target as a consequence of attending to each other's attentional states (Deak et al., 2001). In other words: Interlocutors have to deliberatively focus on the same target while being mutually aware of sharing their focus of attention (Tomasello et al., 2005; Hobson, 2005).

4.2   Scenario

In order to investigate patterns of visual joint attention, we created an experimental condition in which two participants in a cooperative task were only allowed to use gaze for communication. Also, information required to solve the cooperative task was distributed between the interlocutors, making communication crucial for solving the task. This was realized by creating a setup where the interlocutors were facing each other sitting at a table where 26 different LEGO Duplo figures were placed in five rows. Each figure was facing one of the interlocutors, thus revealing information necessary for disambiguation only to either participant. In each trial, the participants' were given a verbal specification of a figure to be found. They themselves, however, were not allowed to make use of speech or hand gestures. By experimental design, they were thus forced to negotiate by gaze which figure was the correct one. An example of the study setup can be found in Figure 8.

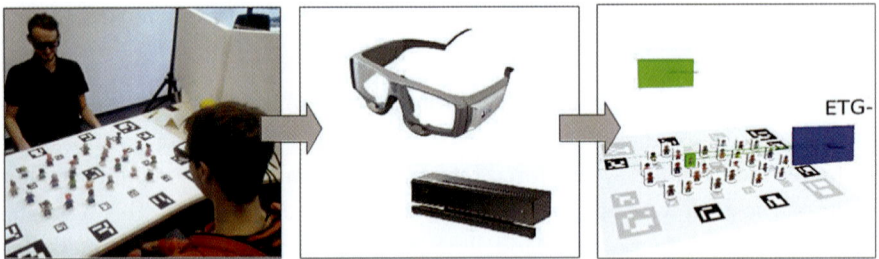

Figure 8. Left: real world figure identification task; middle: choice of tracking devices, such as eye-tracker or Kinect; right: situation model including areas of interest for all figures and the heads of the interlocutors (boxes). (Pfeiffer et al., 2016)

4.3   Method

The analysis of eye-movement data gathered under mobile conditions is difficult and requires large resource investments. Following our experimental-simulative approach, we developed a tool called EyeSee3D (Pfeiffer and Renner, 2014; Pfeiffer et al., 2016) to automatically annotate the areas of interest in our study. The aim of our EyeSee3D approach is to enable automatic analysis of experiments in real-world scenarios where mobile eye tracking is involved. However, it is also applicable for pure virtual reality scenarios, when the position and orientation towards the visualized content is known. The central idea is modelling the environment as an abstract 3D situation model where the relevant stimuli are represented (see Figure 8, right) and then cast a ray along the line of sight into the model and check for intersections with proxy models of the objects of interest. It is the same idea that has been used in Example A to identify the targets of pointing gestures.

Tracking

The mobile eye-tracking system can be used during experiment recording to update the situation model (see Figure 8, middle), e.g. by using computer vision technology. This includes the head position and orientation as well as the orientation of the eye(s). The head position and orientation can be determined either by an external tracking system or by our integrated fiducial marker tracking based approach (see Figure 8, left). For the integrated approach, which was used for this study, markers have to be placed in the environment in such a way that at least one marker is visible in the scene camera image of the eye-tracker whenever a stimulus is fixated. Fiducial markers that are detected in the scene camera image can be used to calculate the position and orientation of the camera and thus the eye-tracking device. As this approach requires an instrumentation of the environment with markers, it cannot be applied to every research scenario. However, this approach is cost-efficient, because it only adds the cost of printed markers and is easy to set-up. In our experiments, we have observed that participants notice the marker during the preparation, but as soon as they are occupied with the experiment task, for them the markers disappear in the background and we do not observe noticeable numbers of fixations on any of the markers.

Reconstructed 3D situation model

For analysing the interactions which occurred during the study, a 3D situation model was created, which included the figures as primary stimuli. They were modelled using small proxy boxes, which was a sufficient granularity for analysis. Both interlocutors were equipped with mobile eye-tracking glasses from SMI. The head positions of the interlocutors were then also integrated into the situation model as proxy boxes in order to be able to analyze gaze on the interaction partner as well. So altogether the study featured 28 areas of interest, 26 figures and the heads of two interlocutors. Data from both mobile eye-tracking systems were integrated in the same 3D situation model, which allowed us to asses mutual gaze on areas of interest, which is at the essence of determining joint attention.

Figure 9 shows the modelled scenario: On the left-hand side, the view from the scene camera of one participant's eye-tracking glasses is shown. The participant's fixation is depicted by the 2D gaze cursor as it is normally generated by mobile eye-tracking software. On the right, the same picture is overlaid with the 3D situation model matched to the perspective of the scene camera by our software.

Figure 9. Study scenario from the view of one interlocutor. On the left, the current fixation is depicted in the gaze video. On the right, the 3D situation model is aligned to the perspective of the eye-tracker and the target figure is determined and highlighted. Pfeiffer et al. (2016)

Simulations in the 3D situation model

Based on the updated situation model, a 3D gaze ray for each participant wearing an eye-tracking system can be constructed. It then can be casted into the situation model. In a second step we can identify the objects of interest being gazed at by intersecting these gaze rays with the 3D models (see Figure 9).

The right-hand side of Figure 9 shows this procedure: The gaze cursor is replaced by the 3D gaze rays. To highlight that a fixation on a stimulus is ongoing, the fixated figure is highlighted in green in our analysis software. The large green box in the upper part of the image is the area of interest representing the interlocutor. Its position and orientation is updated according to the tracking information gathered from the corresponding participant's scene camera.

4.4   Results

Using our EyeSee3D method, gaze on areas of interest (i.e. the figures and the partner) was automatically annotated. This was done for both interlocutors at the same time. Based on this data, the course and interplay of fixations during each task could be analysed, including fixations on the different figures as well as on the interlocutor. In Figure 10, fixations of one trial are shown, where fixations on the distractor figures were aggregated to one virtual area of interest called "other figure".

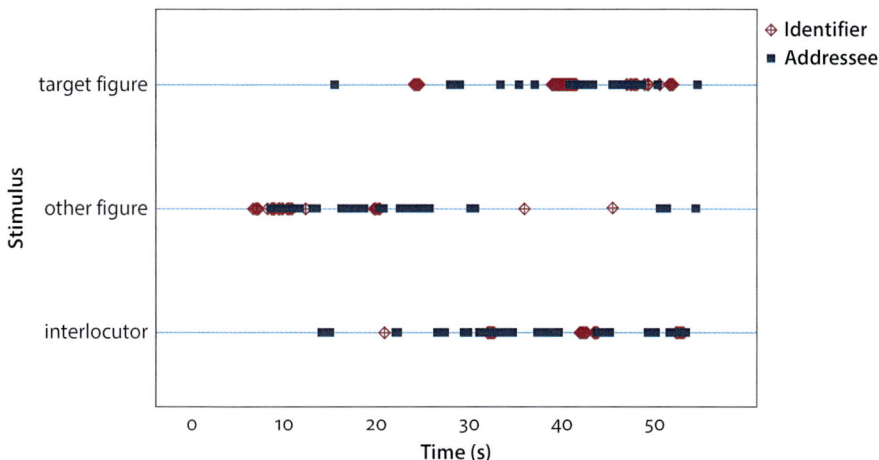

Figure 10. Fixations of both interlocutors during one trial. Gaze on figures which were distractors was aggregated as "other figure", the searching target is called "target figure"

4.4.1   *Automatic annotation of gaze targets*

When developing tools for an automatic annotation, the standard baseline to compare the performance of the algorithms with is defined by human annotators. The determined interrater agreement reliability between two human annotators for our scenario was Kappa = 0.8314, which is considered to be almost perfect (Landis and Koch, 1977). Then the annotation of each human annotator was compared with those of our software. For one annotator Kappa was 0.7691, which is considered to be a substantial agreement and it is quite close to 0.8, from which on almost perfect agreement starts. For the second annotator, Kappa was 0.7343, which is still in the range of substantial agreement.

We have to note that a disagreement with human annotators does not always or necessarily mean wrong annotations. E.g., there were fixations outside the field-of-view of the scene camera of the eye tracker. In these cases, the automatic annotation may still use the scene camera image for locating the eye-tracking device in space and in combination with the gaze direction determined by the eye-tracking cameras may reconstruct the three-dimensional gaze-ray to test for hits with the areas of interest. The human annotator, however, will not be able to make proper annotations during such periods of off-screen fixations. These fixations could thus only be annotated using the EyeSee3D software – but this then leads to a disagreement and thus has a negative impact on Kappa.

4.4.2   Identifying patterns of shared gaze

From these aggregated data, gaze patterns could be calculated. The different patterns to be found were "Searching" for the correct figure, "Identifying" the target figure, "Looking at the Partner", "Looking for Focus" (i.e. trying to get help from the interlocutor) and "Offering Focus" (i.e. trying to help the partner). For finding the patterns, simple equations were applied to the data using a sliding-window approach. E.g. for the searching pattern, the equation was:

$$\frac{|\ \textit{fixations (other stimuli) }|}{|\ \textit{fixations (all) }|} \quad \rightarrow 1$$

So if, in a data window of e.g. two seconds, the majority of all fixations targeted distractor stimuli, the "Searching" pattern was conducted. The calculated patterns for the identifier and for the addressee could then be compared over the course of all trials. Figure 11 shows the shares of calculated patterns for the addressee and the interlocutor. The identifier who had the necessary disambiguation information conducted the identifying, the offering focus and the looking at partner pattern more often than the addressee who conducted more searching and looking for focus.

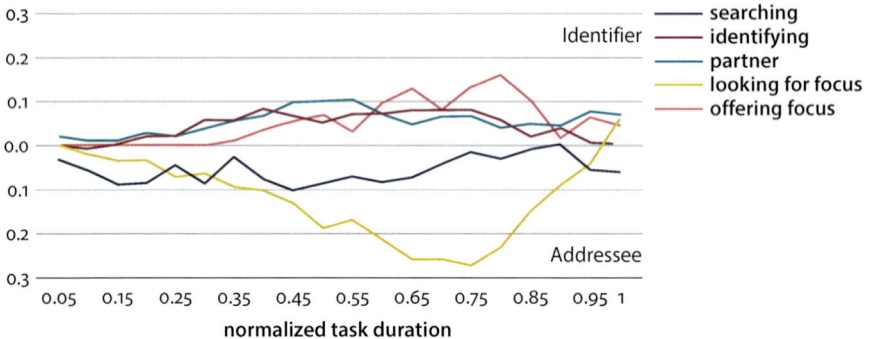

Figure 11. The share of conducted gaze patterns of the addressee and the identifier over all trials (normalized). The patterns *identifying*, *offering focus* and *looking at partner* were more often conducted by the identifier, the patterns searching and looking for focus more often by the addressee

4.5   Summary

This example shows that 3D situation models are a powerful tool that may also be used for the analysis of multiple interaction partners and in particular their interactions in a coherent way. In addition to that, we have seen that using 3D situation models sometimes enables us to analyse data that is not directly accessible in the recorded data, as in the example of the fixations to off-screen targets.

5.   Example C: Gaze and deixis in shared space of two interlocutors

The third example study combines the exploration of pointing gestures and gaze in a route planning scenario. It also origins from the CRC 673 "Alignment in Communication" and was conducted in the subproject "Interaction Space". The aim of this subproject was to investigate spatial alignment of gestures during interaction of a human and a robot. In this context, the presented study was conducted for exploring the interplay between gaze and referential gestures in shared space of two interlocutors (Renner et al., 2014).

5.1   Background

When cooperating in shared space, we have to coordinate our actions well to avoid harm and to ensure a successful and swift completion of our task. In the context of a robotic scenario, where a human interlocutor interacts with a robot in a shared space, the behaviour of the robot could be improved if the robot were able to recognize the focus of attention of its interaction partner. This way, e.g. gesture trajectories could be anticipated and considered during action planning to avoid potentially occupied areas. In an experiment of two human interlocutors, the interplay of gaze and deixis in shared-space interactions was observed. The focus of the experiment was on the spatial distribution of hand-pointing targets as well as on the interplay between manual pointing gestures and fixations.

The scenario of the experiment was anchored in a route planning context, motivated by former work of Holthaus et al. (2011). Gaze and pointing directions as well as the head positions of the participants were recorded.

5.2   Scenario

In order to ensure valid results for natural interaction, a relatively unconstrained interaction scenario of two interacting, non-confederate participants, was used instead of a rigid experimental design with a high level of control. In the route planning scenario, the two interlocutors were sitting at a table facing each other. Placed between them was a map on which they performed several joint planning tasks. To record eye movements, one participant was equipped with a mobile eye tracker. This participant is in the following called P1, the interlocutor without the eye-tracking system is called P2.

To elicit spatial references to their own peripersonal space (the space surrounding them closely) as well as to the space shared by both participants, we used three different floor plans (see Figure 12): ground floor, first and second floor. They were placed between the participants so that there is one within each peripersonal space.

The middle floor plan was placed in the interaction space. The scenario was designed to yield a lively interaction facilitating frequent pointing gestures to enable joint planning of routes, which was verified in a small pilot study.

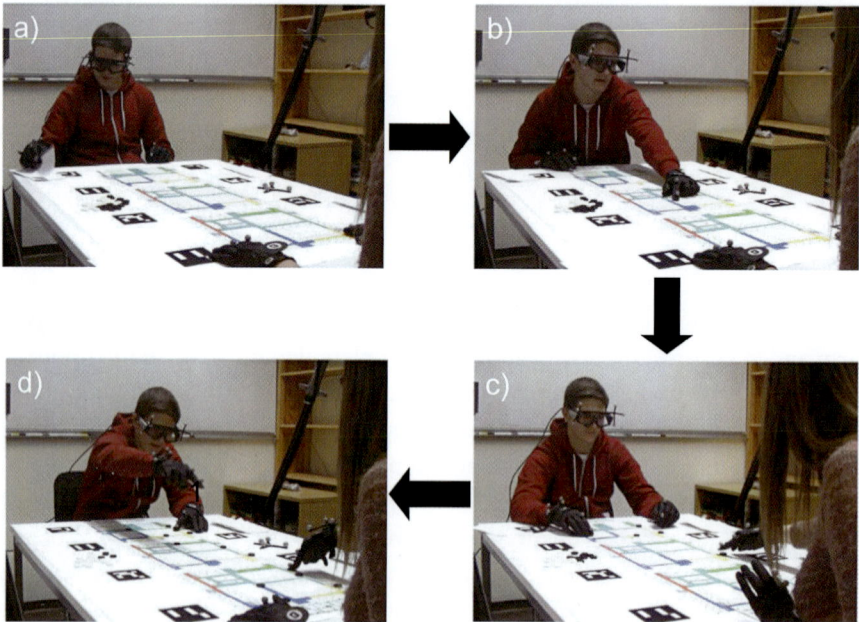

Figure 12. The main steps of the first task type: (a) Drawing a subtask card, (b) explaining the route, (c) placing blockages and (d) jointly planning the remaining route. (Renner et al., 2014)

The main hypothesis in that setup was that given the onset of a hand movement, the target of a pointing gesture can be predicted by looking at the location of preceding fixations. Following up, the distribution of fixations and pointing movements in the different spatial areas was evaluated.

Task

In general, the participants' task was to plan routes from a point A to a point B distributed over the three floor plans. Figure 12 shows the four important steps of the first task type: (a) The task began with P1 drawing a card where starting point and target room were marked. (b) P1 then demonstrated these to the interlocutor and described the fastest route. (c) The interlocutor P2 then drew a card with blockages and indicated them on the floor plans using gaming tokens. (d) Finally,

P1 and P2 jointly planned the remaining route. The roles of P1 and P2 in the tasks were switched every second repetition.

5.3   Method

In order to analyze the experiment including eye-tracking data as well as pointing gestures without the effort of manual annotation, the EyeSee3D toolkit was used and extended. The main issue here was to integrate gaze and pointing on the one hand and including the high amount of rooms in the floor plans without increased modelling effort.

Tracking

During the experiments we collected multimodal data: As explained above, one participant (P1) was equipped with mobile eye-tracking glasses to record binocular eye movements and the own field of view of using the HD scene camera.

For a precise tracking of the index finger positions of both hands of both participants, an optical tracking system was used. Based on experiences from the previous study on deixis we attached the tracking markers for the index fingers to soft golfing gloves which do not compromise the hands' freedom of action (see Figure 4).

Reconstructed 3D situation model

The three floor plans contained a high number of rooms to be included into the situation model. Instead of modelling each of these separately (which normally would be necessary as each room is a separate area of interest) as 3D objects, a technique from web design was made use of: The plans were represented as webpages with HTML image maps mapped on the surface of the 3D table model. Each annotated area of the image map represented a room or floor and could be tagged with a specific text that was output when the user fixated the area on the floor plan. This approach reduced modelling effort and increased system performance.

For modelling the hands of the interlocutors, simple boxes were created. We were also interested in fixations on the interlocutor's face, but in this free kind of interaction the partners show large head movements. A static representation was thus not reliable. To overcome this issue, we adapted dynamic position changes by detecting faces in the scene camera images of the mobile eye tracker using the Viola/Jones algorithm (Viola and Jones, 2004). To complete the 3D model, the face position was approximated in 3D as well, which can be seen in Figure 13.

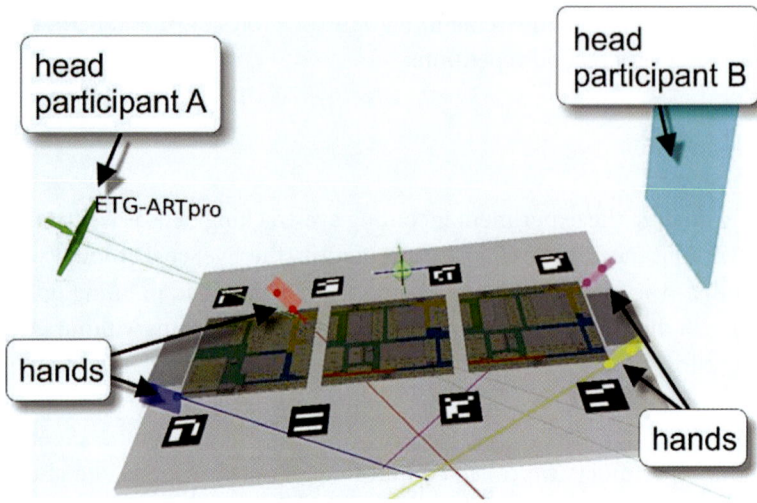

Figure 13. The 3D representation of the scenario including three floor plans, the fiducial markers, participants' hands with highlighted pointing direction as well as the positions of the interlocutors' faces. (Renner et al., 2014)

Simulations in the 3D situation model
For this specific study, in addition to using gaze directions, an external tracking system was integrated to accurately detect pointing gestures. The link between marker tracking and external tracking was established by placing a tracking target with known position and orientation relative to the fiducial markers (see Figure 12(a), next to the middle floor plan). This way, both inputs could be fused in the situation model of the interaction scenario.

Simulations could thus be applied similarly to the second example study: Rays were simulated originating from the eyes in gaze directions and from the fingertips of the index fingers in pointing directions. These rays could then be intersected with the modelled areas of interest and this way annotations of the fixated stimuli or stimuli which were pointed at were generated.

5.4   Results

By the combination of recording eye movements and pointing gestures, it was possible to analyse the course of the interactions considering both modalities. In most of the tasks, participants had to visit all three floor plans. Figure 14 shows a typical interaction pattern of one task, including the fixations of one participants and pointing gestures of both. Both participants pointed to locations near themselves and to the middle floor plan.

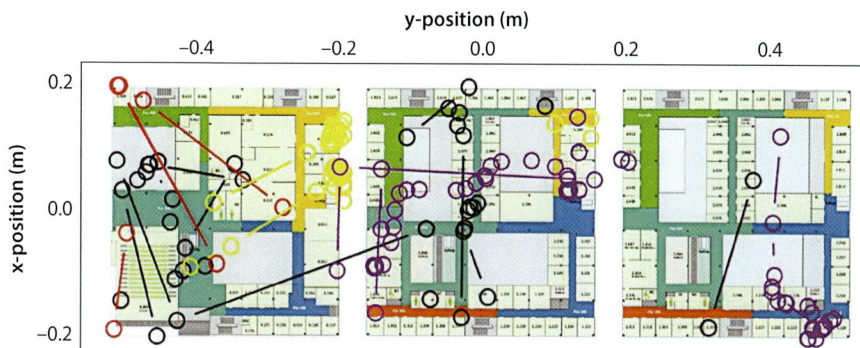

Figure 14. A typical interaction in a route planning task: Communicative fixations are inscribed in black, pointing directions of P1 in red and yellow, those of P2 in blue and purple. The lines represent events that occurred after one another. (Renner et al., 2014)

We measured when and where fixations were made before the stroke of a pointing gesture. In particular we measured whether these fixations targeted the area around the pointing target. As performing a pointing gesture took on average 511 ms (sd: 225 ms) from onset to stroke, gaze could be a hint for the target as soon as the hand starts moving. Figure 15 illustrates the observed fixations on the pointing target of participants P1 before the stroke of the gesture. While fixations were widely spread around the target 2000 ms before the apex, 500 ms before the apex the target area was most frequently fixated.

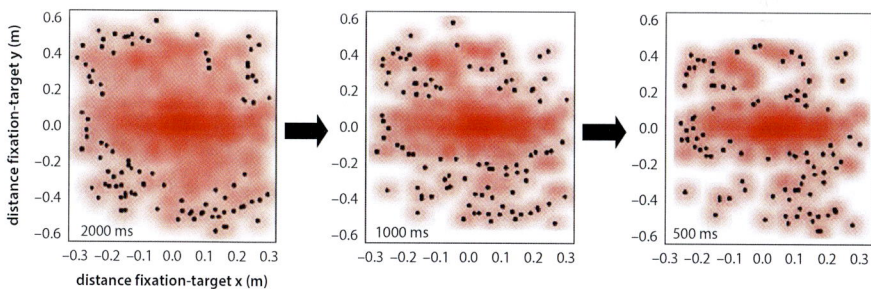

Figure 15. Focusing the pointing target: From left to right, the distribution of all fixations (relative to the pointing target) up to the pointing gesture apex are shown for 2000 ms, 1000 ms and 500 ms (each for an interval of the next 1000 ms), averaged over all participants. (Renner et al., 2014)

5.5   Summary

This example combines the tracking of eye movements and the tracking of gestures in a complex dyadic scenario. The 3D situation model is used to integrate the different modalities and evaluate their spatial co-occurrence and their timing, both within interlocutors and between.

6.   Conclusion

In the past ten years we have been using motion capturing, eye tracking and virtual reality technology for research on gaze and gesture use in human communication and in human-machine interaction. The work presented in this chapter was chosen to give examples on how these technologies could be used to support basic research in getting quantitative spatio-temporal data of a high precision and, in addition to that, how annotation times can be significantly reduced in some cases.

Just recently, we made a re-simulation of the data collected in example A (Section 3) to test different hypotheses on the interface between speech and gesture (Lucking et al., 2015). Based on the already collected data, we were able to simulate the effect of different hypotheses on the referential strength of a manual pointing act on the performance of the participants. This is one important advantage of the intermediate step of constructing a 3D situation model before making the concrete data annotation and/or interpretation steps required for the particular research question: with traditional video annotations, whenever we come up with a new hypothesis, it is quite likely that we would have to go through manual annotation over all the recorded material once again. This is a very time consuming task and requires a high level of quality control regarding the human annotators. In contrast, testing hypotheses based on the already constructed 3D situation model only requires the formulation of some constraints or the construction of helper-geometries (e.g. proxy geometries reconstructing a pointing ray or pointing cones of different opening angle).

The analysis of mobile eye-tracking data is usually a very time-consuming task. The common way of annotating the data is using the scene camera video of the eye tracker where an overlaid gaze cursor represents the current fixation. Thus, for each fixation, the target area of interest has to be identified manually, stepping frame-by-frame over the recorded video. This typically takes about 10-times the actual experiment duration. By using the EyeSee3D method (Section 4) for automatically annotating the eye-tracking data, this effort could be reduced to practically zero. A comparison to annotations created by humans attested a high quality of the automatic annotations. It was even possible to correctly annotate fixations that are outside of the field of view of the scene camera. Moreover, the virtual overlay over the scene camera video (see Figure 9) allows for an online quality control during study conduction, which is a valuable feedback for the experimenter.

Using the automatic annotation combined with a detection of gaze interaction patterns brings another advantage: The calculation of the patterns can now be applied in real-time. This way, they can be used for recognizing the current state of interaction, which in turn is helpful, e.g., for assistive systems or collaboration with robots.

Also shown in Example B was that the approach followed can easily be extended to support multiple participants. While in the example we only had two, in principle the approach supports a virtually unlimited number of participants: most of the relevant analysis is done locally on the machine hosting the eye-tracking software and only matrices representing head position and orientation as well as eye orientations are transmitted and fused in the 3D situation model. All of this happens in real-time.

Last but not least, in Example C (Section 5) we combined our methods for tracking pointing gestures and gaze into an integrated 3D situation model. This way, we were able to analyze the complete interactions during study conduction in real-time. This enabled us to analyze the course of interactions in each trial for both participants, knowing which target room or floor was fixated or pointed at (like in Figure 12). By tracking the positions and orientations of the index fingers as well as the head and eyes, we could moreover analyze these more raw data. This way, it was possible to analyze pointing gestures in the context of fixations.

7.   Outlook: Affordable tracking solutions

The presented approaches come at a cost: at the time being, the required tracking technologies for motion capturing or eye tracking are expensive. However, as similar solutions are slowly taken up by the consumer market, prices go down. There are already some inexpensive mobile eye-tracking devices (Kassner and Patera, 2012) and low-cost tracking systems (Microsoft, 2016), with even better solutions to be expected following the current renaissance of virtual reality technology in the consumer market.

In many research questions, e.g. regarding human-human interaction, not only fixations on areas of interest in the environment, but also fixations on the interlocutor are of relevance. Gaze on the interlocutor's face can be determined by marker tracking if each participant is wearing mobile eye-tracking glasses, as has been shown in the Example B described above, or using computer vision (Example C). For cases where other body parts are relevant, we also integrated basic marker-less body tracking of the Microsoft Kinect v2 into our system.

Figure 16 shows a scenario where one person is wearing an eye tracker. He is observing another person while conducting a task. The depth camera of the Microsoft Kinect sensor is used to detect the body of the interlocutor. In order to integrate eye tracking and body tracking in the 3D situation model, optical marker tracking using fiducial markers is applied for both systems, using the scene camera of the eye-tracking system and the RGB camera of the Kinect. This way, the abstract skeleton representation of the interlocutor can be mapped to the local coordinate system of the scene camera of the eye tracker and even overlaid correctly on the image of the scene camera, as shown in Figure 16 to the right. In the figure, the hands of the observed person are modelled as 3D area of interest and thus the fixation of the observer on the right hand of the observed can be detected automatically.

Figure 16. Dynamic areas of interest are supported using auxiliary tracking technologies. In the example above a Microsoft Kinect v2 is used to track areas of interest on body parts. Left: A scenario where one person is watching the movements of his interlocutor. Right: The live preview shows the 3D model of the interlocutor's skeleton, detected by the Kinect, and the area of interest that has been attached to the skeleton's right hand. Coordinate systems of eye-tracking system and Kinect are synchronized using the marker on the wall. The gaze (green rays) of the observer is currently targeted at the right hand, which is detected by the software and given as Target ID. (Pfeiffer et al., 2016)

The integration in the fused 3D situation model thereby works in real-time, as does the overall system. In comparison to tracking the body using an optical tracking system (ART, OptiTrack, VICON), using Microsoft Kinect v2 renders this approach low-cost and portable. The Kinect can also be used during the preparation of the study to create 3D scans from the stimuli to have the geometries of the areas of interest in the situation model match the real-world objects more closely.

Acknowledgment

This work has been partially supported by the German Research Foundation (DFG) in the Collaborative Research Center 673 Alignment in Communication and the Cluster of Excellence Cognitive Interaction Technology 'CITEC' (EXC 277) at Bielefeld University.

References

Advanced Realtime Tracking GmbH (2016). ART Advanced Realtime Tracking Company Website. http://www.ar-tracking.com/home/, last checked October 2016.

Deak, G. O., Fasel, I., & Movellan, J. (2001). The emergence of shared attention: Using robots to test developmental theories. In *Proceedings 1st International Workshop on Epigenetic Robotics: Lund University Cognitive Studies*, volume 85.

Duchowski, A. (2007). *Eye Tracking Methodology*. Springer London, London.

Hobson, R. P. (2005). What puts the jointness into joint attention? *Joint Attention: Communication and Other Minds: Issues in Philosophy and Psychology*, page 185. https://doi.org/10.1093/acprof:oso/9780199245635.003.0009

Holthaus, P., Pitsch, K., & Wachsmuth, S. (2011). How can I help? Spatial attention strategies for a receptionist robot. *International Journal of Social Robots*, 3:383–393. https://doi.org/10.1007/s12369-011-0108-9

Kassner, M. P. & Patera, W. R. (2012). *PUPIL: constructing the space of visual attention*. PhD thesis, Massachusetts Institute of Technology.

Kendon, A. (1990). *Conducting interaction: Patterns of behavior in focused encounters*, volume 7. CUP Archive.

Kendon, A. (2004). *Gesture: Visible action as utterance*. Cambridge University Press, Cambridge, UK. https://doi.org/10.1017/CBO9780511807572

Kühnlein, P. & Stegmann, J. (2003). Empirical issues in deictic gesture: Referring to objects in simple identification tasks. Technical Report, SFB 360, Bielefeld University.

Kopp, S., Jung, B., Leßmann, N., & Wachsmuth, I. (2003). Max – a multimodal assistant in virtual reality construction. *KI – Künstliche Intelligenz*, 4(03):11–17.

Kranstedt, A., Lücking, A., Pfeiffer, T., Rieser, H., & Staudacher, M. (2006a). Measuring and Reconstructing Pointing in Visual Contexts. In Schlangen, D. & Fernandez, R. (Eds.), *Proceedings of the Brandial 2006 – The 10th Workshop on the Semantics and Pragmatics of Dialogue*, pages 82–89, Potsdam. Universitätsverlag Potsdam.

Kranstedt, A., Lücking, A., Pfeiffer, T., Rieser, H., & Wachsmuth, I. (2006b). Deictic object reference in task-oriented dialogue. In Rickheit, G. & Wachsmuth, I. (Eds.), *Situated Communication*, pages 155–207. Mouton de Gruyter: Berlin.

Kranstedt, A., Lücking, A., Pfeiffer, T., Rieser, H., & Wachsmuth, I. (2006c). Deixis: How to Determine Demonstrated Objects Using a Pointing Cone. In Gibet, S., Courty, N., & Kamp, J. -F. (Eds.), *Gesture Workshop 2005*, LNAI 3881, pages 300–311, Berlin/Heidelberg: SpringerVerlag GmbH.

Landis, J. R. & Koch, G. G. (1977). The Measurement of Observer Agreement for Categorical Data. *Biometrics*, 33(1),159. https://doi.org/10.2307/2529310

Lücking, A., Pfeiffer, T., & Rieser, H. (2015). Pointing and reference recon-sidered. *Journal of Pragmatics*, 77, 56–79. https://doi.org/10.1016/j.pragma.2014.12.013

McNeill, D. (1992). *Hand and Mind: What Gestures Reveal about Thought*. University of Chicago Press, Chicago.

McNeill, D. (2006). Gesture, gaze, and ground. *Lecture Notes in Computer Science*, 3869:1. https://doi.org/10.1007/11677482_1

Microsoft (2016). Kinect for Windows Website. WWW: https://dev.windows.com/en-us/kinect, last checked October 2016.

NaturalPoint, Inc. (2016). OptiTrack Motion Capture Systems Company Website. WWW: http://www.optitrack.com/, last checked October 2016.

Pfeiffer, T. (2010). *Understanding Multimodal Deixis with Gaze and Gesture in Conversational Interfaces*. Dissertation to acquire the doctor rerum naturalium, Bielefeld University, Bielefeld, Germany.

Pfeiffer, T. (2011). Interaction between Speech and Gesture: Strategies for Pointing to Distant Objects. In: E. Efthimiou & G. Kouroupetroglou (Eds.), *Gestures in Embodied Communication and Human-Computer Interaction, 9th International Gesture Workshop, GW 2011*, pages 109–112, Athens: National and Kapodistrian University of Athens.

Pfeiffer, T. (2012). Using virtual reality technology in linguistic research. In *Proceedings of the IEEE Virtual Reality 2012*, pages 83–84, Orange County, CA, USA. IEEE, IEEE. https://doi.org/10.1109/VR.2012.6180893

Pfeiffer, T. (2013a). Documentation of gestures with data gloves. In C. Müller, A. Cienki, E. Fricke, S. Ladewig, D. McNeill & S. Teßendorf (Eds.), *Handbücher zur Sprach- und Kommunikationswissenschaft / Hand- books of Linguistics and Communication Science*, volume 1 of *Handbooks of Linguistics and Communication Science* (pp. 868–879). Berlin: Mouton de Gruyter.

Pfeiffer, T. (2013b). Documentation of gestures with motion capture. In C. Müller, A. Cienki, E. Fricke, S. Ladewig, D. McNeill & S. Teßendorf (Eds.), *Handbücher zur Sprach- und Kommunikationswissenschaft / Hand- books of Linguistics and Communication Science*, volume 1 of *Handbooks of Linguistics and Communication Science* (pp. 857–868). Berlin: Mouton de Gruyter.

Pfeiffer, T., Hofmann, F., Hahn, F., Rieser, H., & Röpke, I. (2013). Gesture semantics reconstruction based on motion capturing and complex event processing: a circular shape example. In M. Eskenazi, M. Strube, B. D. Eugenio & J. D. Williams (Eds.), *Proceedings of the SIGDIAL 2013 Conference* (pp. 270–279). Metz: Association for Computational Linguistics.

Pfeiffer, T., Kranstedt, A., & Lücking, A. (2006). Sprach-Gestik Experimente mit IADE, dem Interactive Augmented Data Explorer. In S. Müller & G. Zachmann (Eds.), *Dritter Workshop Virtuelle und Erweiterte Realität der GI-Fachgruppe VR/AR*, pages 61–72, Aachen: Shaker.

Pfeiffer, T. & Renner, P. (2014). EyeSee3D: A low-cost approach for analyzing mobile 3D eye-tracking data using computer vision and augmented reality technology. In *Proceedings of the Symposium on Eye Tracking Research and Applications*, ETRA '14, pp. 195–202, New York: ACM. https://doi.org/10.1145/2578153.2578183

Pfeiffer, T., Renner, P., & Pfeiffer-Leßmann, N. (2016). EyeSee3D 2.0: Model-based Real-time Analysis of Mobile Eye-Tracking in Static and Dynamic Three-Dimensional Scenes. In *Proceedings of the Ninth Biennial ACM Symposium on Eye Tracking Research & Applications*, pp. 189–196. New York: ACM Press.

Renner, P., Pfeiffer, T., & Pfeiffer-Leßmann, N. (2015). Automatic analysis of a mobile dual eye-tracking study on joint attention. *Abstracts of the 18th European Conference on Eye Movements*, pages 116–116.

Renner, P., Pfeiffer, T., & Wachsmuth, I. (2014). Spatial references with gaze and pointing in shared space of humans and robots. In C. Freksa, B. Nebel, M. Hegarty & T. Barkowsky (Eds.), *Spatial Cognition IX: Volume 8684 of Lecture Notes in Computer Science* (pp. 121–136).

Rickheit, G. & Strohner, H. (1993). *Grundlagen der kognitiven Sprachverarbeitung: Modelle, Methoden, Ergebnisse*. Francke.

SensoMotoric Instruments GmbH (2016). SensoMotoric Instruments GmbH Company Website. WWW: http://www.smivision.com/en.html, last checked October 2016.

Tobii AB (2016). Tobii. WWW: http://www.tobii.com/, last checked October 2016.

Tomasello, M., Carpenter, M., Call, J., Behne, T., & Moll, H. (2005). Understanding and sharing intentions: The origins of cultural cognition. *Behavioral and brain sciences*, 28(05), 675–691. https://doi.org/10.1017/S0140525X05000129

Van Dijk, T. A. & Kintsch, W. (1983). *Strategies of discourse comprehension*. Academic Press.

Vicon Motion Systems Ltd. (2016). VICON Company Website. WWW: http://www.vicon.com/, last checked October 2016.

Viola, P. & Jones, M. J. (2004). Robust real-time face detection. *International Journal of Computer Vision*, 57(2), 137–154. https://doi.org/10.1023/B:VISI.0000013087.49260.fb

Wittenburg, P., Brugman, H., Russel, A., Klassmann, A., & Sloetjes, H. (2006). ELAN: a professional framework for multimodality research. In *Proceedings of LREC*, volume 2006, page 5th.

CHAPTER 7

Gaze and face-to-face interaction
From multimodal data to behavioral models

Gérard Bailly[i], Alaeddine Mihoub[i,ii], Christian Wolf [ii,iii]
and Frédéric Elisei[i]
[i]GIPSA-Lab, Univ. Grenoble-Alpes & CNRS, St Martin d'Hères / [ii]INSA-Lyon,
Villeurbanne – France / [iii]Université de Lyon & CNRS, Villeurbanne

This chapter describes experimental and modeling work aiming at describing gaze patterns that are mutually exchanged by interlocutors during situated and task-directed face-to-face two-ways interactions. We will show that these gaze patterns (incl. blinking rate) are significantly influenced by the cognitive states of the interlocutors (speaking, listening, thinking, etc.), their respective roles in the conversation (e.g. instruction giver, respondent) as well as their social relationship (e.g. colleague, supervisor).

This chapter provides insights into the (micro-)coordination of gaze with other components of attention management as well as methodologies for capturing and modeling behavioral regularities observed in experimental data. A particular emphasis is put on statistical models, which are able to learn behaviors in a data-driven way.

We will introduce several statistical models of multimodal behaviors that can be trained on such multimodal signals and generate behaviors given perceptual cues. We will notably compare performances and properties of models which explicitly model the temporal structure of studied signals, and which relate them to internal cognitive states. In particular we study Semi-Hidden Markov Models and Dynamic Bayesian Networks and compare them to classifiers without sequential models (Support Vector Machines and Decision Trees).

We will further show that the gaze of conversational agents (virtual talking heads, speaking robots) may have a strong impact on communication efficiency. One of the conclusions we draw from these experiments is that multimodal behavioral models able to generate co-verbal gaze patterns of interactive avatars should be designed with great care in order not to increase the cognitive load of human partners. Experiments involving an impoverished or irrelevant control of the gaze of artificial agents (virtual talking heads and humanoid robots) have demonstrated its negative impact on communication (Garau, Slater, Bee, & Sasse, 2001).

Keywords: gaze patterns, coordination, multimodal signals, statistical models, conversational agents

https://doi.org/10.1075/ais.10.07bai
© 2018 John Benjamins Publishing Company

1.   Introduction

The social relevance of eyes in a visual scene has been largely investigated. If visually salient objects attract attention, cognitive demands of the visual search easily override contrastive properties – i.e. spatiotemporal multimodal salience – of the objects (Henderson, Malcolm, & Schandl, 2009). This is particularly the case for faces (Bindemann, Burton, Hooge, Jenkins, & de Haan, 2005) and notably of faces having direct eye contact – see Senju et al (Senju & Hasegawa, 2005) for a review. Võ et al (Võ, Smith, Mital, & Henderson, 2012) argue for a functional, information-seeking use of gaze allocation during dynamic face viewing.

The proper replication of the movement and appearance of the human eye is a challenging issue when building virtual agents or social robots able to engage into believable and smooth communication with human partners (Marschner, Pannasch, Schulz, & Graupner, 2015; Ruhland et al., 2014). We here review some key issues that pave the way towards context-aware gaze models. The chapter is organized as follows. We first argue for the importance of getting multimodal interactive motion capture data that will enable us to study multi-party interactions as dynamically coupled systems. We then review statistical models that can capture regularities and generate context-aware behaviors. We finally draw the reader's attention to the impact of the appearance of the avatar's eye on gaze perception by human viewers and the need for taking care of every processing stage of the perception-action loop, namely the active multimodal scene analysis and comprehension, the behavior planning and execution, as well as the final rendering of movements.

2.   Interactive gaze

2.1   Eyes in the visual scene

Since the seminal works of Yarbus (Yarbus, 1967), Langton (S. R. H. Langton, 2000) and Itti et al (Itti, Dhavale, & Pighin, 2003), numerous studies have questioned visual attention and proposed models to capture the lawful control parameters of scan paths of static images and videos. Visual saliency – the set of perceptual quality which makes some regions of our visual field stand out from their neighborhood – and its interplay with other senses, such as audition (Coutrot, Guyader, Ionescu, & Caplier, 2012) or touch (Van der Burg, Olivers, Bronkhorst, & Theeuwes, 2009) – has drawn much of attention from disciplines such as experimental psychology, image and signal processing or machine vision (Duffner & Garcia, 2015). Modeling bottom-up visual saliency has been the subject of numerous research efforts during the past 20 years, with many successful applications in computer vision and robotics. Recently, Borji et al (Borji, Sihite, & Itti, 2013) performed an exhaustive comparison of 35 state-of-the-art saliency models over challenging synthetic and natural image vs. video datasets. Evaluation scores typically consist in comparing human heat maps – computed by pooling gaze data from several subjects watching the data – with saliency maps computed by the competing models. Top-down factors driven by the cognitive demand (Goferman, Zelnik-Manor, & Tal, 2012) – and notably the task – as well as the presence of agents (Schauerte & Stiefelhagen, 2014) do also strongly influence the scan paths. Borji et al notably evidence that eye fixations in video clips with many actors and moving objects get lowest scores and suggest that gaze patterns are often driven in this context by complex cognitive processes that necessitate a minimum understanding of what is going on in the (audio)visual scene.

2.2 Conversational gaze

Speaking faces are effectively salient and relevant regions of interest in a visual scene – in particular when the audio channel is available (Coutrot & Guyader, 2014; Li, Tian, & Huang, 2014). The scan path to speaking faces mainly goes through the mouth, the eyes, the nose ridge and the forehead (Buchan, Paré, & Munhall, 2007; Vatikiotis-Bateson, Eigsti, Yano, & Munhall, 1998). The proportion of eye- vs. mouth-directed fixations has been shown to depend on cognitive demand: as an example, Lansing et al (Lansing & McConkie, 1999) have evidenced that observers spend more time looking at and direct more gazes toward the upper part of the talker's face when asked to make decisions about intonation patterns than about the words actually being spoken.

While most of the work about gaze and attention has been performed using non interactive stimuli – individual minds and brains observing representations of other people through essentially pre-recorded natural or synthetic videos – several studies have been performed on interactive gaze, i.e. in situations of sensorimotor reciprocity, i.e. situated face-to-face conversations where speakers can see and hear each other. The fact that the observer's actions cannot influence the individuals when watching static images or movies has in fact a strong impact on joint behaviors. Gaze patterns are known to differ between in situ two-ways interaction settings vs. video replay or video simulation. Foulsham et al. (2011) have shown that people were more likely to be gazed at in a video condition than in a live condition when they were close to the observer in the scene (e.g., were approaching in order to pass by). Using more intimate settings, Laidlaw et al. (2011; 2012) further demonstrated that participants sitting in a waiting room looked at a videotaped confederate more often and for a longer duration than at a live confederate: videotaping elicits unlimited screening while live interactions respect the elementary social ground rules. Risko et al. (2016) give numerous examples showing that the presence of another person can substantially alter patterns of gaze in social contexts. Studies of social attention *in the wild* have been favored by the recent availability of light-weight – and more and more discrete – mobile eye trackers.

When engaging in overt attention such as the one required during face-to-face interaction, the cognitive activity matters. Lee et al. (2002) collected gaze data from one female speaker during informal face-to-face conversation. They showed that the distribution of the magnitudes of gaze shifts in listening mode is much narrower than that of talking mode, indicating that, when the subject is speaking, eye movements are more dynamic and active. Conversely, gaze of listeners is much more likely to be focused on the source of information, i.e. the speaker. Vertegaal et al. (2001) measured subjects' gaze at the faces of their conversational partners during four-person conversations. They show that speakers gazed at their interlocutors about 1.6 times less than listeners. More recently, Otsuka et al (2014; 2011) have shown that conversational regimes – namely convergence, dyad-link, and divergence among multiparty conversations – as well as participants status – addressed/unaddressed participants, overhearing/eavesdropping bystanders – strongly influence gaze patterns and head directions between participants.

Most of these studies consider faces in the visual field as dynamic stimuli and potential regions of interest that can attract fixations of a target speaker according to his/her cognitive demand and his/her role in the conversation. Few studies have nevertheless considered gaze patterns as the by-product of a coordinated action, i.e. sensible consequences of an underlying coupled system in which the interlocutors play an active role and coordinate behaviors for sharing common grounds and goals (see notably the importance of the speech channel in Richardson, Dale, & Kirkham, 2007).

2.3   Mutual gaze patterns

Settings where gaze patterns of all parties involved in the conversation are monitored in parallel with other modalities (e.g. voice, body, head, face and hand gestures) are rare. Several studies have of course examined mutual multimodal behaviors using synchronous videos (Cummins, 2012) and manual annotations, but the accuracy of gaze estimation by human viewers can hardly go beyond the basic contrast between eye contact vs. gaze aversion. Bailly et al (G. Bailly et al., 2010; Raidt, Bailly, & Elisei, 2007) designed a computer-mediated face-to-face interaction with two pinhole cameras and two Tobii® eye-trackers both embedded onto two computer screens that displayed live videos of the interlocutors (see Figure 1). Using a similar setup, Barisic et al. (2013) used dual eye-tracking to investigate real-time social interactions: they eliminated the problem of live video capture by tele-representing the interlocutors by virtual avatars (see also the experiment performed by Boker et al., 2009 where they manipulate the control parameters of Active Appearance Models). The Barisic et al system was inspired by Carletta et al. (2010) who demonstrated a dual-tracking system using an experimental paradigm for cooperative on-screen assembly of two-dimensional models. More recently, Brône and Oben (2015) recorded several face-to-face interactions with two head-mounted eye-trackers and associated scene cameras.

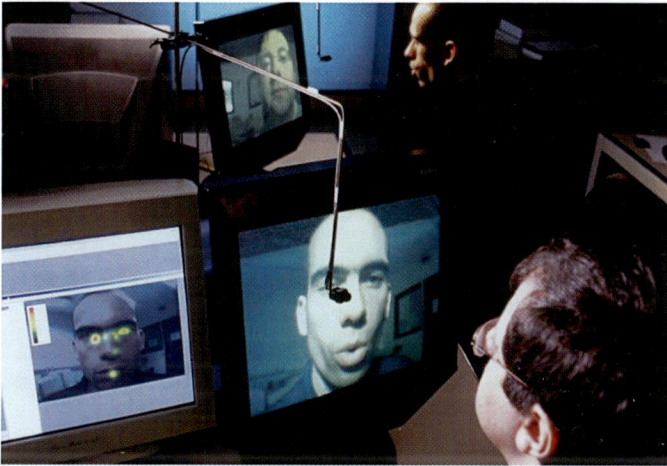

Figure 1. First experimental setting used by Bailly et al. (G. Bailly, Raidt, & Elisei, 2010) to study mutual gaze patterns using computer-mediated face-to-face interactions

In our experiments with dual videos and eye-trackers (G. Bailly et al., 2010), we analyzed the typical distributions of the fixations and blinking rates of one target female participant over the facial elements (eyes, mouth, nose ridge, other parts of the face) of the face of her 10 different interlocutors and the mirror distributions of the interlocutors' gaze on her own facial parts. We showed that these distributions depend on their joint cognitive states, e.g. speaking turns are almost always associated with an eye contact and more specifically with a saccade of the speaker's gaze towards the right eye of the interlocutor, speakers mainly monitors the eyes of their interlocutor while listeners monitors their lips, etc. The interaction scenario was a speech game where interlocutors have to read, utter and repeat so called Semantically Unpredictable Sentences (SUS) (Benoît, Grice, & Hazan, 1996) such as "the hammer fires the cake that spikes". These utterances are quite difficult to understand: when the speaker reads aloud a sentence for the first time, the speaker and the listener have respectively to speak clearly, lip-read and monitor the others' gaze to ensure that the message is correctly passed over. When the listener repeats back what he/she has understood, the respective speaking and listening conditions differ: the text giver knows the textual content and "only" listens to check if the text is correctly spelled out by the receiver. The role of the speaker or listener in the conversation has an impact on the a priori knowledge of what will be exchanged and we expect the role to influence the multimodal behaviors of the speakers. Each member of the dyad was thus text giver and receiver in alternation. We showed that their respective roles and a priori knowledge on the exchanged linguistic content both impact the gaze patterns and the blinking rate, e.g. blinking frequency is much higher while speaking (here an average of 0.6 blinks per seconds) than while listening (0.1 blinks per seconds) and blinking frequency is almost null when receivers listen to the giver's first reading. Note that large head shifts (such as occurring when the text giver finishes reading the target sentence and gets ready to speak to the receiver) are also systematically accompanied by a blink.

3. Learning & generating gaze patterns

3.1 Grounding gaze patterns

Several generative models of gaze patterns have been proposed. The most long-winded line of research has been initiated by Itti et al (Itti et al., 2003; Itti, Dhavale, & Pighin, 2006) who proposed a photorealistic attention-based gaze animation that is grounded on a model of saliency and a biological model of the eye/head saccade subsystem. Itti et al propose a winner-takes-all strategy for allocating the current fixation to the most salient region of a map that combines bottom-up saliency with top-down task-relevance and attention guidance. Sun (Sun, 2003) proposed a hierarchical saliency model that first decomposes the scene into a pyramid of regions of interest and further constraints the fixations to first exhaust salient sub-regions of an image before switching to another region. Picot et al (Picot, Bailly, Elisei, & Raidt, 2007) augmented the Inhibition of Return (IoR) mechanism proposed by Itti et al for attention guidance with a stack of attention – in which are stored the position and local appearance of the most recent N (= 4) regions of interest that have been fixated – and added an object recognizer that triggers object-specific scrutinization mechanism, in particular when detecting a face. *A priori* knowledge about important regions of interest (objects, faces, etc.) is then easily recruited and ad hoc gaze patterning can be triggered.

Note that generation of gaze patterns can also be grounded on speech signals. A number of systems use speech as an input from which to generate facial expressions involving the mouth, head, eyes, and eyebrows (Albrecht, Haber, & Seidel, 2002) – for a review of data-driven mapping techniques addressing this problem see (Ruhland et al., 2014).

We mentioned in Section 2.2 that the structure of conversation has a strong impact on gaze patterns. The generation of gaze paths should thus benefit from an incremental estimation of the cognitive, psychological and physiological state of the interlocutor(s) as well as the locutionary and illocutionary contents of the speech acts. Several authors have proposed statistical models that generate gaze patterns in context. Lee et al (Lee et al., 2002) proposed a statistical eye movement synthesis model for gazing at faces that exploits empirical distributions of durations of fixations and amplitudes of saccades depending on the talking/listening mode of the speaker. Vinayagamoorthy et al (Vinayagamoorthy, Garau, Steed, & Slater, 2004) and Gu et al (Gu & Badler, 2006) further refined the model for virtual characters. There is a rich set of models that exploit empirical distributions for various mechanisms related to the conversational structure (e.g. topic-signaling, turn-taking, etc.) or participant characteristics (e.g. roles, social status, etc.) Gaze patterns are typically described as automata (Mutlu, Kanda, Forlizzi, Hodgins, & Ishiguro, 2012) or belief networks (Pelachaud & Bilvi, 2003) and trigger saccades according to empirical means and standard deviations of spatial and temporal gaze parameters.

Gaze is thus both conditioned by both bottom-up information (i.e. multimodal input) and top-down cognitive demands, especially for establishing and monitoring socio-communicative relations.

3.2 Learning joint behaviors

If several researchers have studied the conversational dynamics (Cummins, 2012; Dale, Fusaroli, Duran, & Richardson, 2013; Fusaroli & Tylén, 2016; Schmidt, Morr, Fitzpatrick, & Richardson, 2012), few works have tried to actually model the links between multimodal behaviors of interlocutors mediated by the structure of their conversation and use these models to predict multimodal joint behaviors. The seminal work of Pentland and colleagues on social signal processing (Pentland, 2004, 2007) has opened the route to both the inference of paralinguistic information from raw signals exchanged during social interaction but also to the generation of such social signals for recommendation systems or autonomous agents. They built a computational model based on Coupled Hidden Markov Models (CHMMs) to characterize the dynamics of dyadic interactions. The degree of coupling was shown to correlate with the success of the intended goals. The work of Otsuka et al. (2011;

2005) is also a very inspiring landmark: they proposed to use a Dynamic Bayesian Network (DBN) to estimate addressing and turn taking ("who responds to whom and when?") and predict gaze shifts between participants of a multi-party conversation. Speech activity, head and gaze shifts across participants were here mediated by the conversational regime (see Section 2.2).

The progress of machine learning techniques offers very powerful tools to mine multimodal scores. They offer elegant and efficient ways to perform decision or regression tasks. It is quite tempting to use regression tools to perform a direct mapping between input features (observed behaviors, a priori contextual knowledge) and desired output behaviors. Thus, Ishii et al. (2014) proposed a support vector machine (SVM) to establish a direct mapping between gaze transition patterns and the timing of speech turns in multi-party meetings. In this context, interaction sequences are represented as temporal sequences where one temporal unit is often the "frame", i.e. one instant of time in an (audio-)visual sequence whose duration depends on the acquisition frequency, typically around 40ms. Frame-based classifiers are very sensitive to the placement of the analysis window and often exhibit noisy temporal output sequences when the window is sliding over the input. These drawbacks are also exhibited by non-deterministic mapping techniques such as Gaussian Mixture Regressors (GMR).

Sequential models such as Hidden Markov Models (HMM) or Dynamic Bayesian Networks (DBN) partially resolve these issues by mediating the correspondence between input/output observations via hidden states or latent variables. These elementary temporal units segment the interaction into homogenous spatio-temporal patterns that can be then combined into larger interaction units. These interaction units can then combine these elementary patterns according to a task-specific syntax and model complex joint sensorimotor behaviors by splitting the regression problem into task-dependent subspaces.

For an introduction to these regression techniques that link input to output observations, see the I/O HMM proposed by Bengio & Frasconi two decades ago (Bengio & Frasconi, 1996). Semi-Hidden Markov Models (Mihoub, Bailly, & Wolf, 2014) have interesting properties for modeling and controlling the durations of these joint sensorimotor states – i.e. the hidden states of the Markov chains that link input observations with desired output features. Moreover, Dynamic Bayesian Networks combine time dependency and structural constraints (with latent variables) with direct causal relations between multimodal features.

3.3 A sample interactive game

We illustrate these concepts through results of recently performed experiments on multimodal face-to-face interaction (Mihoub, Bailly, Wolf, & Elisei, 2016), where gaze was studied together with other signals, such as gesture and speech. Gestural deixis usually involves the combination of "what" information – using deictic words (this, that,...) or the name of the object/agent – and "where" information – using deictic gestures such as head, gaze, body or finger pointing. For that purpose, we designed a game inspired by the famous "put that there" paradigm (Bolt, 1980). This interactive scenario – simple as it can appear at first sight – is a very interesting benchmark for studying and learning human strategies used to maintain mutual attention and coordinate multimodal deixis of objects and places – similar to the visual worlds used by Tanenhaus and colleagues (Allopenna, Magnuson, & Tanenhaus, 1998) and Clark (2003).

The interaction consists in a cube game involving an instructor and a manipulator (Figure 2), the latter following orders of the former, which are typically formulated like *"Put the red dotted cube at the left of the one with the green cross"*. The task is collaborative: the instructor is secretly informed (via a sketch displayed on a tablet) about the pattern to be reproduced by asking the manipulator to move cubes from a source manipulator space to a target chessboard (see Figure 2). The objective

Figure 2. Ego-centric view as seen from the instructor and extracted from the cube game experiment. The current fixation point of the right eye – monitored by a Pertech® head-mounted eyetracker – is cued by a back circle (here surrounding the red cube pointed by the hand of the instructor). Time stamps are used to synchronize multimodal streams

of the statistical model is to learn and reproduce the instructor's coverbal behaviors in terms of gaze and gesture given his/her speech and behavior of the interlocutor. This statistical model may be then transferred to a conversational agent (virtual avatar, lamp avatar or humanoid robot) capable of instructing a human manipulator.

The signal flow between the two participants is modeled by capturing several social signals: the manipulator gestures (MP), instructor speech (SP), instructor gesture (GT) and instructor gaze (FX). In order to learn generic behaviors, all signals are discrete and refer to a limited set of possible references:

- *manipulator gestures* are distinguished as: rest, grasp, manipulate, end, none
- *instructor gestures* are discretized through a dictionary of 5 regions of interest: rest, cube to be displaced, position of target tile, position of the reference cube, none
- *gaze* also refers to one of 8 possible regions of interest: manipulator's face, source manipulator space, chessboard, cube to be displaced, position of target tile, position of the reference cube, tablet, none
- *verbal instructions* are discretized into 5 elements corresponding to the key lexical elements: cube to be displaced, position of target tile, position of the reference cube, else, none

These discrete variables were annotated semi-automatically by only one expert: FX and GT were segmented automatically but labelled by-hand in order to avoid the unnecessary development of target identification algorithms; SP was first aligned with speaker-independent phonetic models and further checked by hand; MP strokes are completely segmented and annotated by hand. Consistency of this multi-stream labelling is essentially post-hoc checked using so-called coordination histograms (Mihoub, Bailly, Wolf, & Elisei, 2016). Modality-specific micro-controllers are then supposed to generate continuous segment-specific (i.e. arm, eye, head) movements as well as speech from these discrete instructions (see our recent evaluation of such a framework in Nguyen, Duc-Anh, Bailly, Gérard, & Elisei, Frédéric, 2016).

We also suppose that the underlying cognitive task follows a specific syntax, which is related to the structure of the interactive task. This syntax is modeled through an intermediate layer, mediating between low-level observations, called *interaction unit (IU)* in line with Ford et al (Ford, 2004), which takes 6 values in our experiments: getting instructions, seeking cube, pointing the cube, pointing the destination position, verification, validation.

In the following, we analyzed a set of 30 game plays in which the instructor interacted with 3 different partners (10 game plays with each one). Each game play consists in placing 10 cubes given an entirely filled manipulator space (16 cubes) and an empty task space. The first cube should be placed in the center tile of the chessboard. The mean duration of a single game is around 1 minute and 20 seconds (~2000 frames, 40ms per frame).

3.4   Learning joint behaviors with dynamic Bayesian networks

Given this experimental setting, the question arises how these different – observed or latent – variables interact and whether causal relations exist between them. The motivation for this analysis is twofold. First, the derivation of a relational graph is an interesting scientific result in itself, which can provide valuable insights into the underlying cognitive process. Secondly, with respect to the goal of this study, causality graphs can be used as a modeling tool for the design of efficient inference algorithms capable of predicting desired variables (here coverbal actions) given observed quantities (here verbal actions).

Of course, the contingent causality relations between the underlying cognitive processes are hidden and as such cannot be retrieved with absolute certainty. Statistical models provide estimations for these relations, which are derived using different mathematical concepts such as correlation and mutual information. The resulting so-called causality graphs provide information on conditional independence properties of the variables of the system. In particular, for each variable A of the model, the graph provides the so-called Markov blanket ∂A, defined as the set of variables which, when conditioned on it, make all other variables independent of A.

In the case of time series, where each considered variable is present for each time instant of a sequence, dynamic Bayesian networks (DBN) have been established as an important tool for modeling structured problems, for learning and inference. They are particularly attractive and useful for modeling the dynamics of multimodal behaviors in face-to-face interactions (Huang & Mutlu, 2014). DBNs are directed acyclic graphs in which nodes represent random variables and edges represent conditional dependencies. Semantically and intuitively an edge from a parent node X to a child node Y means that node X has influence over node Y. An exact description of how independence statements can be derived from the graph is beyond the scope of this chapter. The interested reader is referred to (Koller & Friedman, 2009) and (K. Murphy, 2002).

In some situations and depending on the application, this dependency structure may be manually provided by an expert of the target domain. Alternatively, several statistical methods have been introduced to learn the graphical structure of a DBN automatically from data (Trabelsi, Leray, Ben Ayed, & Alimi, 2013). In our application, our DBN structure (see Figure 3) has been entirely learned from training data. The intra-slice structure is learnt using the K2 algorithm (Cooper & Herskovits, 1992). The inter-slice structure is learned using the REVEAL algorithm (Liang, Fuhrman, Somogyi, & others, 1998). We employed the Bayes Net Toolbox (K. P. Murphy, 2001) for training and inference. The resulting causality network (see Figure 3) presents very interesting intra-slice properties such as:

- The interaction units influence both perception and action streams (black arrows), and thus paces the joint behaviors
- The instructor reacts to the manipulator actions (MP impacts SP, GT and FX) (blue arrows)
- The speech activity (SP) of the instructor influences his co-verbal behavior (GT and FX) (green arrows). This is consistent with co-verbal contingency (McNeill, 1992)
- Each random variable (slice t + 1) is influenced by its history (slice t) (gray arrows)
- as well as inter-slice properties that cue the causal relations within the perception-action loop, notably:
    - The deictic chain that chains gaze, pointing gesture and verbal indexing (FX → GT→ SP) leads to an effective manipulation (→ MP)

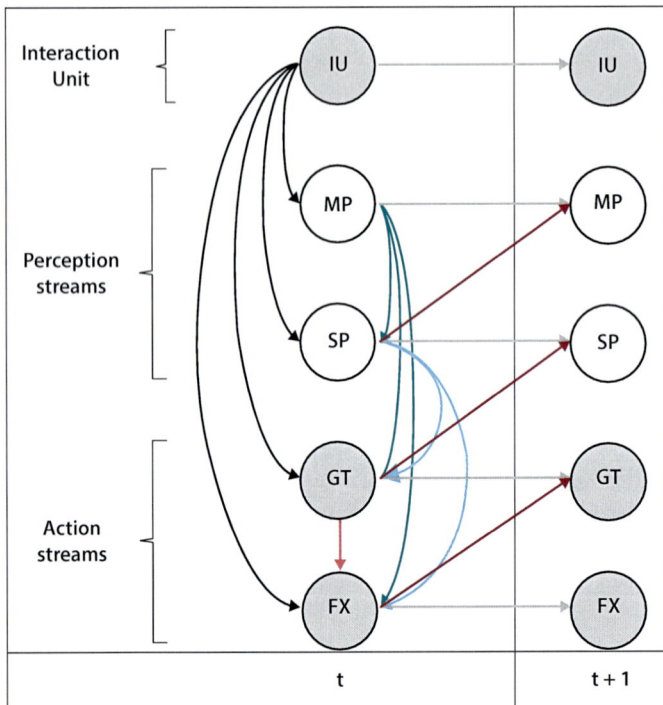

Figure 3. The DBN model learned from training data. Variables in gray circles are to be predicted in the inference stage

The second goal of our work is to be able to infer desired hidden quantities from observed quantities, in particular in a real-time setting with low latency (i.e. limited look-ahead observations) so that these behavioral models can be used to control artificial agents engaged in effective interactions with humans. To this end, the proposed models should be able (1) to estimate the interaction units from perceptual observations (speech activity/ manipulation of the partner); when the two partners cooperate, the sequential organization of the interaction units should ideally reflect the shared mental states of the conversation partners at that particular moment; (2) to generate suitable actions (hand gestures of the instructor and his own gaze fixations) that reflect his current awareness of the evolution of the shared plan. We used the junction tree algorithm (Jensen, Lauritzen, & Olesen, 1990) to perform offline estimation by computing the MPE (most probable explanation) of IU, GT and FX given the whole sequence of MP and SP. The junction tree algorithm gives an exact solution of the estimation problem, i.e. the inferred variable is the most probable one according the probabilistic formulation.

Table 1 gives the results of the proposed method compared to a more classical setting with Hidden Markov Models (HMMs). For all models, 30-fold cross validation was applied. The Levenshtein distance (Levenshtein, 1966) is adopted for the evaluation because it computes a warped distance between predicted and original signals, which is tolerant to minor misalignments. In particular, this avoids getting extremely low scores (near zero) in presence of small latencies.

Table 1. Estimation performance of the DBN model compared to classical hidden Markov models

	IU	GT	FX
DBN	85%	87%	71%
HMM	72%	85%	60%

While the graphical structure was entirely learned in the DBN setting, HMMs are characterized by an imposed structure consisting of (i) hidden variables satisfying the Markov property and (ii) observed variables, which are conditionally independent from each other given the hidden variables. Relaxing these restrictions translates into higher classification rates, as can be seen in Table 1. While the improvement of the estimation of instructor deixis (direction of finger) is minor, large gains are obtained with respect to the estimation of the interaction unit, and the gaze direction. In particular, this shows that gaze is a complex phenomenon whose estimation can be significantly improved if the conditional dependencies on other variables are taken into account correctly. The fixed dependency structures of classical HMMs seem to be too restrictive in this context.

Because of the Levenshtein distance, these results neglect minor misalignments between the reference and the generated scores. We also compared inter-modal synchronization patterns using so-called coordination histograms (Mihoub et al.,

2016). We showed that DBN also better reproduce the natural micro-coordination between multimodal streams. In fact, HMM impose to model all transitions between discrete observations at onsets of hidden states.

HMM and DBN may be improved to cope with interactive and highly rhythmical patterns. We have shown (Mihoub, Bailly, & Wolf, 2015) that semi-HMM that explicitly model the duration of hidden units – so called state occupancy – better capture sensorimotor loops. Similar proposals have been recently done for DBN (Donat, Bouillaut, Aknin, & Leray, 2008). Note finally that Deep Neural Networks (DNN) able to cope with highly structured sequences such as Long Short-Term Memory (LSTM) or Clockwork Recurrent Neural networks (CW-RNN). DNN (Hochreiter & Schmidhuber, 1997) (Sak et al., 2014) offer performative alternatives to Graphical models when large training data is available.

3.5   Adapting joint behaviors

One challenge of the original proposal of Pentland et al. (Pentland, 2004) was to observe and characterize the dynamics of the social glue – i.e. activities or interactions that strengthen the relational ties in a group of people (Lakin, Jefferis, Cheng, & Chartrand, 2003) – via dynamical models of multimodal joint behaviors. We have shown (Mihoub, Bailly, Wolf, & Elisei, 2015) that models of mutual gaze patterns can in fact implicitly capture social features that are encoded via very shallow signals that may escape to human expertise. For instance, for the speech game described in Section 2.3 where a female speaker interacted with 10 different interlocutors, we computed distances between datasets and models of gaze behaviors of different dyads (i.e. applying model trained on interlocutor A to the dataset of interlocutor B). We then performed multidimensional scaling (MDS) on the distance matrix. Analysis evidenced the significant impact of pre-existing social relationships (colleagues vs. students) between interlocutors. Such data mining techniques can be used to detect meaningful dimensions that structure the interactive human behaviors. By using repertoires of behavioral models – or more comprehensive statistical models – trained on multiple dyads or social groups, one may expect to faithfully select and adapt autonomous systems to their audience, notably the role it has to play in the conversation and the social relationship it wants to establish. As an example, De Kok et al. (2013) used so-called "speaker descriptors" (mean and standard deviation of pitch and energy, speech rate and average gaze shift per minute) to select an appropriate model of back channeling – trained as Conditional Random Fields (CRF) models – amongst a collection of pre-analyzed dyadic interactions.

3.6   Effective gaze tracking and generation

Note that the behavioral models proposed above rely on (1) an active visual scene analysis that should deliver estimations of the gaze direction of the conversational partners as well as track the positions of potential objects of interest and (2) a faithful gaze generator that effectively direct the agent's gaze towards the intended targets. Section 4 sketches the current state of the art concerning non-invasive gaze estimation. Section 5 further underlines the importance of accurate gaze control and rendering.

4.   Active gaze estimation from images and videos: Gaze patterns and interaction models

If behavioral models can be trained using data collected on interlocutors with invasive motion capture systems – such as head-mounted eyetrackers or other wearable sensors – autonomous agents should rely on egocentric sensors such as embedded cameras.

The direct estimation of gaze direction from images or videos can be a hard challenge according to the chosen experimental setup. The best standard solutions use special hardware with multiple head-mounted cameras often operating in the infrared spectrum. Although complex, these solutions can now be miniaturized enough to be integrated into mobile devices, and latest technologies allow eye-tracking to be integrated into head-mounted gears like the Google® or SMI® glasses.

Gaze estimation *in the wild* tries to solve this problem from RGB images or images taken from RGB-D (consumer depth) cameras. A major challenge here is to be able to generalize to different head poses and to different individuals. Calibration to the subject at hand is a preponderant methodology, although auto-calibration and calibration free methods are on the rise. Estimation in the wild requires preliminary face detection or head tracking. This estimation is greatly enhanced by depth information such as provided by RGBD sensors such as the Kinect®. As an example, Funes-Mora and Odobez (2014) learn a user-specific 3D head model in an off-line stage. During on-line estimation, the 3D head pose is tracked by aligning new 3D data with the model using iterated closest points (ICP) initialized with a Viola-Jones face detector.

Methods on gaze estimation itself can roughly be classified into two families of approaches. Geometric methods fit a 2D or 3D model of the eye to data, as for instance in (Valenti & Gevers, 2012). These methods are often chosen when specific hardware is available in a multi-camera setup and/or when data quality is high.

Appearance based methods, on the other hand, use direct regression of gaze from appearance features learned from training samples. Issues are the quality of training data in terms of the resolution of the input eye images, and in terms of number of subjects; the ability to generalize; and the problem of obtaining reliable training labels in the case of supervised learning. As an example, Sugano et al (Sugano et al. 2014) proposed a regression plus synthesis approach, where random forests are trained in an offline stage on a mixture of real and synthetic data, which has been created by 3D reconstruction from multiple cameras. In Funes-Mora and Odobez (2014), gaze direction is estimated in the head coordinate system (after head tracking) using regression from histogram of oriented gradient (HoG) features and then mapped back to the global coordinate system. In Duffner and Garcia (2015), visual focus of attention (VFOA, i.e. discrete gaze information restricted to a set of chosen focal points) is inferred with an HMM. In a sequential setting, particle filtering tracks faces and VFOA jointly. Again, the observation model resorts to image primitives such as HoG features or color histograms.

Note that recent methods augment image-based information with contextual cues, such as multimodal contingency, visual saliency, learned gaze patterns and other interaction models. The objective is to leverage the strong linkage between gaze and other verbal and non-verbal signals in human interactions. These contextual features are exploited to improve the quality of gaze estimation or, alternatively, to contextualize training labels.

In Sugano et al. (2013), gaze is estimation is combined with visual saliency, i.e. *a priori* information on the attractiveness of certain locations in the image. Saliency is extracted through face detection, as faces are more likely to be looked at, and additional low-level information calculated from texture. The saliency information is accumulated into Gaze probability maps, which are used as input (soft targets) to train Gaussian process regressors. Alnajar et al. (2013) exploit human gaze patterns, which are learned in an offline stage. The goal is to perform gaze estimation in an uncalibrated setting: initial gaze sequences are first estimated through classical regression and then aligned with known template gaze patterns.

Such signal-dependent bottom-up information are often complemented with a priori top-down information such as the possible regions of interest (RoI) in the scene, the dialog structure, the respective roles of the speakers, the possible conversational regimes, etc. As an example, Sheiki and Odobez (Sheiki and Odobez, 2014) modeled gaze patterns during multi-party meetings and exploit the very properties of these interaction scenarios, notably speaking activity – i.e. people tend to look at speakers –, verbal content – i.e. people tend to look at verbally referenced objects, with a mean delay of 2s (Richardson, Dale, & Shockley, 2008) – and topic – gaze mirrors mental state (Teufel, Alexis, Clayton, & Davis, 2010).

Furthermore, gaze estimation may benefit from other modalities. The kinematic chain of attention involves the whole body, from the orientation of feet and body to the orientation of head and eyes. Conversely, the orientation of all these segments contribute to gaze estimation (Hietanen, 1999) (S. R. Langton, Honeyman, & Tessler, 2004). Thus, the so-called Midline effect (Fuller, 1992) (Hanes & McCollum, 2006) rules the relation between gaze and head orientation.

Finally, gaze estimation should be linked to action and scene comprehension. Active perception refers to the ability of agents to act to better perceive (see Bajcsy, 1988 for a general theoretical framework for active perception). Such actions comprise self-motion (e.g. moving away from interfering sources or near to sources of interest), verbal (e.g. asking interlocutors to play again) as well as nonverbal communication (e.g. displaying facial expressions expressing doubt or surprise) so that to renew percepts. Ferreira et al. (2013) have notably proposed a Bayesian framework for multimodal perception through an active attentional and behavioral exploration of the environment. Optimal exploration can be then expressed in terms of various criteria such as entropy minimization or maximization of reward such as *a posteriori* probability of given events.

Active visual perception also refers to the fact that humans should move eyes to perform a fine-grained analysis of a given region of interest (RoI). In fact, the 6 to 7 million cones that provide the eye's color sensitivity are much more concentrated in the central spot known as the macula. In the center of that region is the "fovea centralis", a 0.3 mm diameter rod-free area with very thin, densely packed cones. Saccades are performed to bring the RoI into the fovea. There are thus major consequences: (1) the input vision stream that delivers information on the actual state of possible ROI is full of *missing data* since this information is only renewed by overt attention shifts: estimation of the gaze of others is thus performed on demand of behavioral models (see early work conducted by Yarbus, 1967), i.e. when such information is necessary to keep track of another's intentions; (2) this action-for-perception is one of the basic mechanism for shared attention mechanisms and, more generally, theory of mind models (ToM) (Baron-Cohen, Jollife, Mortimore, & Robertson, 1997) that conversely enable others to infer our own intentions. Mutual gaze reading is thus a perquisite for effective intelligent interaction. Easing gaze reading for the conversational partners is a key issue for the development of social avatars and androids.

5.   Easing gaze reading

The generation of task-relevant and interlocutor-adaptive gaze patterns is of course a crucial step towards building credible human-agent interactions. These high-level control strategies should not conceal the low-level control and embodiment issues. The embodiment of the artificial agent matters and may bias the perception of the intended movements by human viewers.

As outlined previously, the estimation of the gaze direction of others is a complex by-product of multiple cues that involve eye-related features – notably the position of the iris in the eyelid opening – as well as features related to other deictic features including low-level cues such as body and head posture and high-level cues such as a priori information on potential targets. We demonstrate below that several eye-related features impact the gaze reading.

5.1   Eye appearance

Trutoiu et al (Trutoiu, Carter, Matthews, & Hodgins, 2011) studied temporal and spatial deformations of eyelids when blinking and showed that viewers are quite sensitive to the dynamics of eye blinking. Elisei et al (Elisei, Bailly, & Casari, 2007) showed empirically that gaze shifts are accompanied with eyelids movements (see Figure 4). Oyekoya et al (Oyekoya, Steed, & Steptoe, 2010) confirmed that eyelid movements play an important part both in conveying accurate gaze direction and improving the visual appearance of virtual characters.

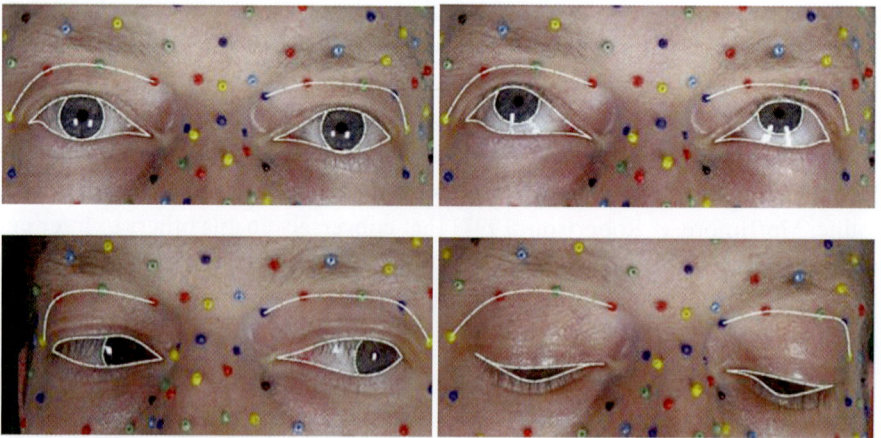

Figure 4. Photogrammetric data showing the deformation of eyelids according to gaze direction (from Gérard Bailly, Elisei, Raidt, Casari, & Picot, 2006)

In a series of books (M. Tomasello, 2009; Michael Tomasello, 2008), Tomasello and his colleagues notably propose that the phylogenetic specificity of humankind rests in its species-specific adaptation for sociability. The account offered by Tomasello contrasts human cooperation and altruism with nonhuman primate competition, and proposes that human altruism leads to shared intentionality (the ability to share attention to a third party – object or agent – and, more generally, to share beliefs and intentions). Tomasello (Michael Tomasello, Hare, Lehmann, & Call, 2007) further proposed the cooperative eye hypothesis (CEH). The CEH suggests that the eye's visible characteristics evolved to ease gaze following. Kobayashi & Kohshima (Kobayashi & Kohshima, 2001) have notably shown that humans have the smallest iris proportion in the eye opening and the largest contrast between iris and sclera colors among the primate and non-primate species with eyes.

Conversely in HAI, humans expect social agents to offer back cooperation, altruism and share goals and plans. Such cooperative behavior will also be favored by the agents' gaze readability. This readability is both a control and a design issue: the eyes should be controlled and move in an appropriate and predictive way but should also be designed so that the eye's visible characteristics are similar to those that humans have developed for the sake of social interaction.

5.2   Estimating gaze direction of avatars

Several studies have shown that multiple cues influence the estimation of gaze direction. Gaze direction is a complex by-product of body, head and eye orientation. Contextual features combine with these bottom-up cues to direct attention. There is surprisingly few works assessing the perception of the gaze of virtual or robotic agents by human observers (see however Cuijpers & van der Pol, 2013 experiments with the Nao). Remarkable experiments have been conducted by Al Moubayed et al (S. Al Moubayed, Edlund, & Beskow, 2012; Samer Al Moubayed, Skantze, & Beskow, 2012) with a lamp avatar called Furhat. They notably compared the estimation by human observers of the gaze of Furhat, its virtual model and the video of its performance both displayed on screen. They showed that Furhat is the only display escaping from the Mona Lisa effect[1] (Gregory, 1997) and delivering very accurate gaze direction, independently of the observer's viewing angle. Similar experiments have been conducted by Delaunay et al. (Delaunay, Greeff, & Belpaeme, 2010). Onuki et al. (Onuki, Ishinoda, Kobayashi, & Kuno, 2013) compared the

---

1.   A person depicted in portrait paintings does not appear slanted even when observers move around. Moreover its gaze seems to follow you when its gaze is facing the original view.

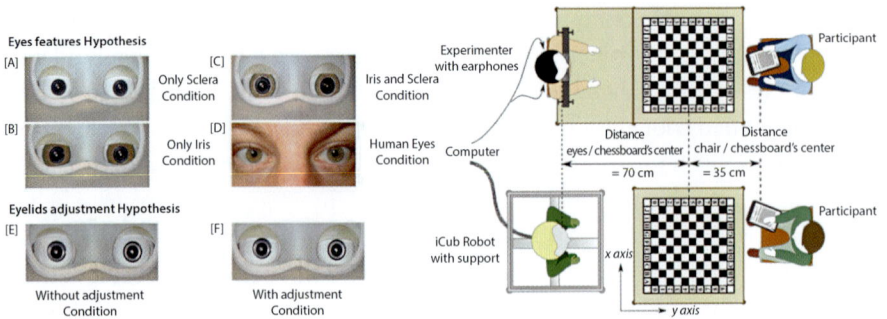

Figure 5. The robot's and human's eyes and robot's eyelids used for the eye direction experiment, accordingly to our hypotheses. [A]: eyes with no iris; [B] eyes with large colored iris caps; [C] eyes with human-sized colored iris caps; [D] human eyes; [E] robot's eye gaze without adjustment of eyelids position; [F] robot's eye gaze with eyelids position adjusted. Right: the interaction set-ups where the participants are either faced to a robot with 3 different iris sizes or a human informer gazing at given tile of a chessboard that they were asked to guess

impression given by mechanical eyes and a lamp avatar: they concluded that eyes with a round outline shape and a large iris were most suitable for precision and subjective agreement.

We also performed (Foerster, Bailly, & Elisei, 2015) a comparative evaluation of the impact of the iris size and the coordination between eye direction and eyelid aperture for the estimation of gaze direction of our iCub humanoid robot Nina by human viewers (see Figure 5). We show that the coordination between eye direction and eyelid aperture significantly contribute in reducing estimation errors. We confirmed the findings of Onuki et al. for the benefit of endowing avatars with large irises. We also compared the performance of the robot with that of a human informer: surprisingly the robot outperformed the human challenger!

6. Future trends

We addressed the challenge of endowing avatars with social gaze. We have demonstrated that these avatars should pay attention to the analysis of audiovisual scene they step in but also to the overt behaviors and estimated intentions of the other agents sharing the environment and conversing with them. We argue for the benefits of building statistical models of multimodal behaviors from human demonstrations, i.e. by collecting traces of exemplary interactions comprising gaze tracks and behavioral signals of all interlocutors together with the estimation of underlying organization of conversational structure and goals.

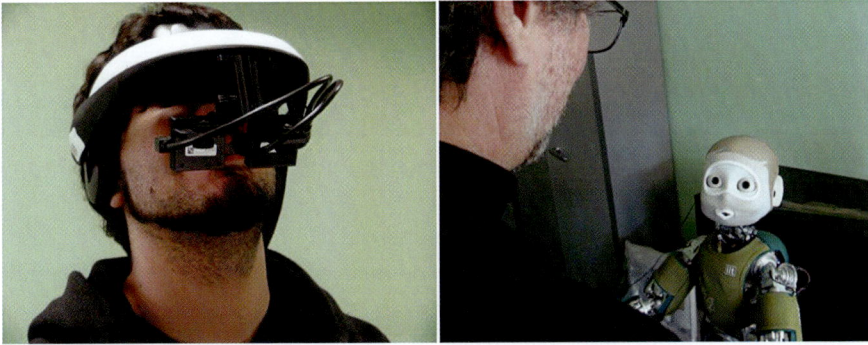

Figure 6. Beaming the GIPSA-Lab iCub: the human tutor (left) monitors the head and eyes of the iCub robot (right) while perceiving (viewing and listening) the remote scene via a head mounted display that plays back the audiovisual streams captured by the cameras and microphones embedded into its eyes and ears. This cognitive gift artificially provides the robot with situated social skills

Such a supervised training faces numerous issues. When performing off-line on collected traces, the performance of current statistical models – even on simple and controlled scenarios involving a reduced set of conversational units – is still far from perfect. Big data is certainly required to inspect the multiple factors that may influence behaviors, along the ever-changing linguistic, paralinguistic and nonlinguistic dimensions of social interactions. But the use of such off-line models for monitoring one-line interactions is still an issue. Moreover the retargeting of human behavior on artificial embodiments faces two main challenges: (a) the source and target degrees of freedom have different properties in terms of dynamics, kinematics and appearance; (b) the expected behaviors of human interlocutors – that are heavily conditioning the input features of predictive behaviors – will be impacted in an unpredictable way by the retargeted behavior and appearance of the avatar. We are presently exploring an original way of coping with this double challenge by immersive teleoperation (Gérard Bailly, Elisei, & Sauze, 2015): the human tutor provides a robot with social behaviors by perceiving and acting in the scene though its robotic effectors (see Figure 6). The human tutor provides the cognitive abilities and the robot the sensorimotor affordances. The robot stores these passively-experienced behaviors into a behavioral memory it will then mine to build socially-effective models. More autonomous strategies – such as developmental learning or learning by curiosity – should take over such a human bootstrapping procedure and replace direct supervision with indirect reward.

We believe that off-line learning of behavior models from massive amounts of data (big-data) will further boost the recognition and predictive performance of the discussed data-driven methodologies. Recently, deep neural networks have been rediscovered in computer vision and machine learning and proven to be extremely efficient, in particular for sequential data (Karpathy et al., 2014) . Handling multi-modality is increasingly shown to be important in these models, where combining and modeling audio and video channels can provide significant gains in applications like audio-visual speech recognition (Ngiam et al., 2011) and audio-visual gesture recognition (Neverova, Wolf, Taylor, & Nebout, 2016).

While the availability of massive amounts of training data has been beneficial to various fields of research, it can be argued that supervised learning using annotated data had most impact in a majority of cases, e.g. in visual object recognition trained on > 1 million annotated images (Krizhevsky, Sutskever, & Hinton, 2012). These amounts of data are currently unavailable in face-to-face interaction, and it might be argued that a large effort by the community is necessary in order to create a corpus of sufficient size.

In scientific terms, we conjecture that research in data-driven learning of behavior models from massive amounts of data will require tackling the task of learning hierarchical models capable of learning interactions in several layers of abstraction: high level components addressing the important cognitive aspects we also dealt with in this chapter (turn taking, back-channeling etc.), low level components modeling information related to the scene, which is often of geometric nature (spatial arrangements between the actors in the scene and their body parts, positions of various objects of interest in the scene etc.), as well as intermediate levels of representations between these two extremes. We believe that semi-supervised learning and weakly-supervised learning of DNN will bring advances to this field.

Acknowledgments

This research supported by ANR (SOMBRERO ANR-14-CE27-0014, Robotex ANR-10-EQPX-44-0 and Persyval ANR-11-LABX-0025), the Rhone-Alpes region (ARC6) and the UJF (EMSOC 2012084RECF991). We also want to thank François Foerster, Carole Plasson and Miquel Sauzé for their valuable contributions. A special thanks to Ghatfan Hasan for keeping Nina alive. We thank the two anonymous peer reviewers whose comments and suggestions greatly improved the initial draft of this paper.

References

Al Moubayed, S., Edlund, J., & Beskow, J. (2012). Taming Mona Lisa: communicating gaze faithfully in 2D and 3D facial projections. *ACM Transactions on Interactive Intelligent Systems*, 1(2), article 11 (25 pages). https://doi.org/10.1145/2070719.2070724

Al Moubayed, S., Skantze, G., & Beskow, J. (2012). Lip-reading: Furhat audiovisual intelligibility of a back-projected animated face. *Intelligent Virtual Agents – Lecture Notes in Computer Science*, 7502, 196–203. https://doi.org/10.1007/978-3-642-33197-8_20

Albrecht, I., Haber, J., & Seidel, H. -P. (2002). Automatic Generation of Non-Verbal Facial Expressions from Speech. In J. Vince & R. Earnshaw (Eds.), *Advances in Modelling, Animation and Rendering* (pp. 283–293). Springer London. Retrieved from https://doi.org/10.1007/978-1-4471-0103-1_18

Allopenna, P. D., Magnuson, J. S., & Tanenhaus, M. K. (1998). Tracking the time course of spoken word recognition using eye movements: Evidence for continuous mapping models. *Journal of Memory and Language*, 38(4), 419–439. https://doi.org/10.1006/jmla.1997.2558

Alnajar, F., Gevers, T., Valenti, R., & Ghebreab, S., (2013). Calibration-free gaze estimation using human gaze patterns (pp. 137–144). Presented at the Computer Vision (ICCV), 2013 IEEE International Conference on, Sydney, Australia: IEEE.

Bailly, G., Elisei, F., Raidt, S., Casari, A., & Picot, A., (2006). Embodied conversational agents : computing and rendering realistic gaze patterns. In *Pacific Rim Conference on Multimedia Processing* (Vol. LNCS 4261, pp. 9–18). Hangzhou – China.

Bailly, G., Elisei, F., & Sauze, M. (2015). Beaming the gaze of a humanoid robot. In *Human-Robot Interaction (HRI)* (pp. 47–48). Portland, OR.

Bailly, G., Raidt, S., & Elisei, F. (2010). Gaze, conversational agents and face-to-face communication. *Speech Communication – Special Issue on Speech and Face-to-Face Communication*, 52(3), 598–612.

Bajcsy, R. (1988). *Active Perception. IEEE, Special Issue on Computer Vision*76(8), 996–1005.

Barisic, I., Timmermans, B., Pfeiffer, U., Bente, G., Vogeley, K., & Schilbach, L. (2013). Using dual eyetracking to investigate real-time social interactions. *Proceedings from SIGCHI Conference on Human Factors in Computing Systems*.

Baron-Cohen, S., Jollife, T., Mortimore, C., & Robertson, M. (1997). Another advanced test of theory of mind: evidence from very high functioning adults with autism or Asperger syndrome. *Journal of Child Psychology and Psychiatry*, 38(7), 813–822. https://doi.org/10.1111/j.1469-7610.1997.tb01599.x

Bengio, Y., & Frasconi, P. (1996). Input-output HMMs for sequence processing. *IEEE Transactions on Neural Networks*, 7(5), 1231–1249. https://doi.org/10.1109/72.536317

Benoît, C., Grice, M., & Hazan, V. (1996). The SUS test: A method for the assessment of text-to-speech synthesis intelligibility using Semantically Unpredictable Sentences. *Speech Communication*, 18, 381–392. https://doi.org/10.1016/0167-6393(96)00026-X

Bindemann, M., Burton, A. M., Hooge, I. C., Jenkins, R., &de Haan, E. F. (2005). Faces retain attention. *Psychonomic Bulletin & Review*, 12(6), 1048–1053. https://doi.org/10.3758/BF03206442

Boker, S. M., Cohn, J. F., Theobald, B. -J., Matthews, I., Brick, T. R., & Spies, J. R. (2009). Effects of damping head movement and facial expression in dyadic conversation using real-time facial expression tracking and synthesized avatars. *Philosophical Transactions of the Royal Society – Biological Sciences*, 364(1535), 3485–3495. https://doi.org/10.1098/rstb.2009.0152

Bolt, R. A. (1980). "Put-that-there": Voice and gesture at the graphics interface. *ACM SIGGRAPH Computer Graphics* 14, 262–270.

Borji, A., Sihite, D. N., & Itti, L. (2013). Quantitative Analysis of Human-Model Agreement in Visual Saliency Modeling: A Comparative Study. *Image Processing, IEEE Transactions on,* 22(1), 55–69. https://doi.org/10.1109/TIP.2012.2210727

Brône, G., & Oben, B. (2015). InSight Interaction: a multimodal and multifocal dialogue corpus. *Language Resources and Evaluation,* 49(1), 195–214. https://doi.org/10.1007/s10579-014-9283-2

Buchan, J. N., Paré, M., & Munhall, K. G. (2007). Spatial statistics of gaze fixations during dynamic face processing. *Social Neuroscience,* 2(1), 1–13. https://doi.org/10.1080/17470910601043644

Carletta, J., Hill, R. L., Nicol, C., Taylor, T., de Ruiter, J. P., & Bard, E. G. (2010). Eyetracking for two-person tasks with manipulation of a virtual world. *Behavior Research Methods,* 42(1), 254–265. https://doi.org/10.3758/BRM.42.1.254

Clark, H. H. (2003). Pointing and placing. In S. Kita (Ed.), *Pointing: Where Language, Culture, and Cognition Meet* (pp. 243–268). New York: Lawrence Erlbaum Associates Publishers.

Cooper, G. F., & Herskovits, E. (1992). A Bayesian method for the induction of probabilistic networks from data. *Machine Learning,* 9(4), 309–347. https://doi.org/10.1007/BF00994110

Coutrot, A., & Guyader, N. (2014). How saliency, faces, and sound influence gaze in dynamic social scenes. *Journal of Vision,* 14(8), 5. https://doi.org/10.1167/14.8.5

Coutrot, A., Guyader, N., Ionescu, G., & Caplier, A. (2012). Influence of soundtrack on eye movements during video exploration. *Journal of Eye Movement Research,* 5(4), 2.

Cuijpers, R. H., & van der Pol, D. (2013). Region of eye contact of humanoid Nao robot is similar to that of a human. In G. Herrmann, M. J. Pearson, A. Lenz, P. Bremner, A. Spiers, & U. Leonards (Eds.), *Social Robotics* (Vol. 8239, pp. 280–289). Springer International Publishing. Retrieved from https://doi.org/10.1007/978-3-319-02675-6_28

Cummins, F. (2012). Gaze and blinking in dyadic conversation: A study in coordinated behaviour among individuals. *Language and Cognitive Processes,* 27(10), 1525–1549. https://doi.org/10.1080/01690965.2011.615220

Dale, R., Fusaroli, R., Duran, N., & Richardson, D. C. (2013). The self-organization of human interaction. *Psychology of Learning and Motivation,* 59, 43–95. https://doi.org/10.1016/B978-0-12-407187-2.00002-2

de Kok, I. (2013). *Listening heads* (PhD Thesis). University of Twente, Enschede, The Netherlands.

Delaunay, F., Greeff, J., & Belpaeme, T. (2010). A study of a retro-projected robotic face and its effectiveness for gaze reading by humans. In *ACM/IEEE International Conference on Human-Robot Interaction (HRI)* (pp. 39–44). Osaka, Japan.

Donat, R., Bouillaut, L., Aknin, P., & Leray, P. (2008). Reliability analysis using graphical duration models (pp. 795–800). Presented at the Availability, Reliability and Security, 2008. ARES 08. Third International Conference on, IEEE.

Duffner, S., & Garcia, C. (2015). Visual Focus of Attention estimation with unsupervised incremental learning. *IEEE Transactions on Circuits and Systems for Video Technology,* to appear.

Elisei, F., Bailly, G., & Casari, A. (2007). Towards eyegaze-aware analysis and synthesis of audiovisual speech. In *Auditory-visual Speech Processing* (pp. 120–125). Hilvarenbeek, The Netherlands.

Ferreira, J. F., Lobo, J., Bessiere, P., Castelo-Branco, M., & Dias, J. (2013). A Bayesian framework for active artificial perception. *IEEE Transactions on Cybernetics,* 43(2), 699–711. https://doi.org/10.1109/tsmcb.2012.2214477

Foerster, F., Bailly, G., & Elisei, F. (2015). Impact of iris size and eyelids coupling on the estimation of the gaze direction of a robotic talking head by human viewers. In *Humanoids* (pp. 148–153). Seoul, Korea.

Ford, C. E. (2004). Contingency and units in interaction. *Discourse Studies* 6, 27–52.

Foulsham, T., Walker, E., & Kingstone, A. (2011). The where, what and when of gaze allocation in the lab and the natural environment. *Vision Research*, 51(17), 1920–1931. https://doi.org/10.1016/j.visres.2011.07.002

Fuller, J. H. (1992). Head movement propensity. *Experimental Brain Research*, 92(1), 152–164. https://doi.org/10.1007/BF00230391

Funes Mora, K. A., & Odobez, J. -M. (2014). Geometric generative gaze estimation (G3E) for remote RGB-D cameras (pp. 1773–1780). Presented at the IEEE Conference on Computer Vision and Pattern Recognition (CVPR), Columbus, OH: IEEE.

Fusaroli, R., & Tylén, K. (2016). Investigating conversational dynamics: Interactive alignment, Interpersonal synergy, and collective task performance. *Cognitive Science*, 40(1), 145–171.

Garau, M., Slater, M., Bee, S., & Sasse, M. A. (2001). The impact of eye gaze on communication using humanoid avatars. In *SIGCHI conference on Human factors in computing systems* (pp. 309–316). Seattle, WA.

Goferman, S., Zelnik-Manor, L., & Tal, A. (2012). Context-aware saliency detection. *Pattern Analysis and Machine Intelligence, IEEE Transactions on*, 34(10), 1915–1926. https://doi.org/10.1109/TPAMI.2011.272

Gregory, R. (1997). *Eye and Brain: The Psychology of Seeing*. Princeton, NJ: Princeton University Press.

Gu, E., & Badler, N. I. (2006). Visual attention and eye gaze during multiparty conversations with distractions (pp. 193–204). Presented at the Intelligent Virtual Agents, Springer.

Hanes, D. A., & McCollum, G. (2006). Variables contributing to the coordination of rapid eye/head gaze shifts. *Biological Cybernetics*, 94, 300–324. https://doi.org/10.1007/s00422-006-0049-9

Henderson, J. M., Malcolm, G. L., & Schandl, C. (2009). Searching in the dark: Cognitive relevance drives attention in real-world scenes. *Psychonomic Bulletin & Review*, 16(5), 850–856. https://doi.org/10.3758/PBR.16.5.850

Hietanen, J. K. (1999). Does your gaze direction and head orientation shift my visual attention? *Neuroreport*, 10(16), 3443–3447. https://doi.org/10.1097/00001756-199911080-00033

Hochreiter, S., & Schmidhuber, J. (1997). Long short-term memory. *Neural Computation*, 9(8), 1735–1780. https://doi.org/10.1162/neco.1997.9.8.1735

Huang, C. -M., & Mutlu, B. (2014). Learning-based Modeling of Multimodal Behaviors for Humanlike Robots. In *Proceedings of the 2014 ACM/IEEE International Conference on Human-robot Interaction (pp. 57–64).* New York, NY, USA: ACM. https://doi.org/10.1145/2559636.2559668

Ishii, R., Otsuka, K., Kumano, S., & Yamato, J. (2014). Analysis and modeling of next speaking start timing based on gaze behavior in multi-party meetings. In *IEEE International Conference on Acoustics, Speech and Signal Processing (ICASSP)* (pp. 694–698). Florence, Italy.

Itti, L., Dhavale, N., & Pighin, F. (2003). Realistic avatar eye and head animation using a neurobiological model of visual attention. In *SPIE 48th Annual International Symposium on Optical Science and Technology* (Vol. 5200, pp. 64–78). Bellingham, WA.

Itti, L., Dhavale, N., & Pighin, F. (2006). Photorealistic attention-based gaze animation. In *IEEE International Conference on Multimedia and Expo* (pp. 521–524). Toronto, Canada.

Jensen, F., Lauritzen, S., & Olesen, K. (1990). Bayesian updating in recursive graphical models by local computations. *Computational Statistics Quaterly*, 4(1), 269–282.

Karpathy, A., Toderici, G., Shetty, S., Leung, T., Sukthankar, R., & Fei-Fei, L. (2014). Large-scale video classification with convolutional neural networks (pp. 1725–1732). Presented at the Computer Vision and Pattern Recognition (CVPR), 2014 IEEE Conference on, IEEE.

Kobayashi, H., & Kohshima, S. (2001). Unique morphology of the human eye and its adaptive meaning: comparative studies on external morphology of the primate eye. *Journal of Human Evolution*, 40(5), 419–435. https://doi.org/10.1006/jhev.2001.0468

Koller, D., & Friedman, N. (2009). *Probabilistic Graphical Models: Principles and Techniques – Adaptive Computation and Machine Learning*. Boston, MA: MIT Press.

Krizhevsky, A., Sutskever, I., & Hinton, G. E. (2012). ImageNet Classification with Deep Convolutional Neural Networks. In *Advances in Neural Information Processing (NIPS)*. Lake Tahoe, NV.

Laidlaw, K. E. W., Foulsham, T., Kuhn, G., & Kingstone, A. (2011). Social attention to a live person is critically different than looking at a videotaped person. *PNAS*, 108, 5548–5553. https://doi.org/10.1073/pnas.1017022108

Lakin, J., Jefferis, V., Cheng, C., & Chartrand, T. (2003). The chameleon effect as social glue: evidence for the evolutionary significance of nonconscious mimicry. *Nonverbal Behavior*, 27(3), 145–162. https://doi.org/10.1023/A:1025389814290

Langton, S. R. H. (2000). The mutual influence of gaze and head orientation in the analysis of social attention direction. *Quarterly Journal of Experimental Psychology*, 53A(3), 825–845. https://doi.org/10.1080/713755908

Langton, S. R., Honeyman, H., & Tessler, E. (2004). The influence of head contour and nose angle on the perception of eye-gaze direction. *Perception & Psychophysics*, 66(5), 752–771. https://doi.org/10.3758/BF03194970

Lansing, C. R., & McConkie, G. W. (1999). Attention to facial regions in segmental and prosodic visual speech perception tasks. *Journal of Speech, Language, and Hearing Research*, 42(3), 526–539. https://doi.org/10.1044/jslhr.4203.526

Lee, S. P., Badler, J. B., & Badler, N. (2002). Eyes alive. *ACM Transaction on Graphics*, 21(3), 637–644. https://doi.org/10.1145/566654.566629

Levenshtein, V. (1966). Binary Codes Capable of Correcting Deletions, *Insertions and Reversals*. *Soviet Physics Doklady*, 10(8), 707–710.

Li, J., Tian, Y., & Huang, T. (2014). Visual saliency with statistical priors. *International Journal of Computer Vision*, 107(3), 239–253. https://doi.org/10.1007/s11263-013-0678-0

Liang, S., Fuhrman, S., Somogyi, R., & others. (1998). Reveal, a general reverse engineering algorithm for inference of genetic network architectures. In *Pacific symposium on biocomputing* (Vol. 3, pp. 18–29).

Marschner, L., Pannasch, S., Schulz, J., & Graupner, S. -T. (2015). Social communication with virtual agents: The effects of body and gaze direction on attention and emotional responding in human observers. *International Journal of Psychophysiology*, 97(2), 85–92. https://doi.org/10.1016/j.ijpsycho.2015.05.007

McNeill, D. (1992). *Hand and Mind. What Gestures Reveal about Thought*. Chicago: Chicago University Press.

Mihoub, A., Bailly, G., & Wolf, C. (2014). Modelling perception-action loops: comparing sequential models with frame-based classifiers. In *Human-Agent Interaction (HAI)* (pp. 309–314). Tsukuba, Japan.

Mihoub, A., Bailly, G., & Wolf, C. (2015). Learning multimodal behavioral models for face-to-face social interaction. *Journal on Multimodal User Interfaces*, 9(3), 195–210. https://doi.org/10.1007/s12193-015-0190-7

Mihoub, A., Bailly, G., Wolf, C., & Elisei, F. (2016). Graphical models for social behavior modeling in face-to face interaction. *Pattern Recognition Letters*, 74, 82–89. https://doi.org/Graphical models for social behavior modeling in face-to face interaction

Murphy, K. (2002). *Dynamic bayesian networks: representation, inference and learning* (PhD Thesis). UC Berkeley, Computer Science Division, Berkeley, CA.

Murphy, K. P. (2001). The Bayes Net Toolbox for MATLAB. *Computing Science and Statistics*, 33, 2001.

Mutlu, B., Kanda, T., Forlizzi, J., Hodgins, J., & Ishiguro, H. (2012). Conversational gaze mechanisms for humanlike robots. *ACM Transactions on Interactive Intelligent Systems (TiiS)*, 1(2), 12.

Neverova, N., Wolf, C., Taylor, G. W., & Nebout, F. (2016). ModDrop: adaptive multi-modal gesture recognition. *IEEE Transactions on Pattern Analysis and Machine Intelligence (PAMI)*, 38(8), 1692–1706.

Ngiam, J., Khosla, A., Kim, M., Nam, J., Lee, H., & Ng, A. Y. (2011). Multimodal deep learning (pp. 689–696). Presented at the International conference on machine learning (ICML), Bellevue, WA.

Nguyen, D.-A., Bailly, G., & Elisei, F. (2016). Conducting neuropsychological tests with a humanoid robot: design and evaluation. In *IEEE International Conference on Cognitive Infocommunications – CogInfoCom* (pp. 337–342). Wroclaw, Poland.

Onuki, T., Ishinoda, T., Kobayashi, Y., & Kuno, Y. (2013). Designing robot eyes for gaze communication. In *IEEE Korea-Japan Joint Workshop on Frontiers of Computer Vision (FCV)* (pp. 97–102). Fukuoka, Japan. https://doi.org/10.1109/FCV.2013.6485468

Otsuka, K. (2011). Multimodal Conversation Scene Analysis for Understanding People's Communicative Behaviors in Face-to-Face Meetings. In *International Conference on Human-Computer Interaction (HCI)* (Vol. 12, pp. 171–179). Orlando FL.

Otsuka, K., Takemae, Y., & Yamato, J. (2005). A probabilistic inference of multiparty-conversation structure based on Markov-switching models of gaze patterns, head directions, and utterances. In *International Conference on Multimodal Interfaces (ICMI)* (pp. 191–198). Seattle, WA.

Oyekoya, O., Steed, A., & Steptoe, W. (2010). Eyelid kinematics for virtual characters. *Computer Animation and Virtual Worlds*, 21(3–4), 161–171.

Pelachaud, C.&Bilvi, M., (2003). Modelling gaze behavior for conversational agents. In *International Working Conference on Intelligent Virtual Agents* (Vol. LNAI 2792). Kloster Irsee, Germany. https://doi.org/10.1007/978-3-540-39396-2_16

Pentland, A. S. (2004). Social dynamics: Signals and behavior. Presented at the International Conference on Developmental Learning, La Jolla, CA.

Pentland, A. S. (2007). Social Signal Processing. *IEEE Signal Processing Magazine*, 24(4), 108–111. https://doi.org/10.1109/MSP.2007.4286569

Picot, A., Bailly, G., Elisei, F., & Raidt, S. (2007). Scrutinizing natural scenes: controlling the gaze of an embodied conversational agent. In *International Conference on Intelligent Virtual Agents (IVA)* (pp. 272–282). Paris, France. https://doi.org/10.1007/978-3-540-74997-4_25

Raidt, S., Bailly, G., & Elisei, F. (2007). Mutual gaze during face-to-face interaction. In *Auditory-visual Speech Processing* (paper P23, 6 pages). Hilvarenbeek, The Netherlands.

Richardson, D. C., Dale, R., & Kirkham, N. Z. (2007). The art of conversation is coordination common ground and the coupling of eye movements during dialogue. *Psychological Science*, 18(5), 407–413. https://doi.org/10.1111/j.1467-9280.2007.01914.x

Richardson, D. C., Dale, R., & Shockley, K. (2008). Synchrony and swing in conversation: co-ordination, temporal dynamics, and communication. In I. Wachsmuth, M. Lenzen, & G. Knoblich (Eds.), *Embodied Communication* (pp. 75–93). Oxford, UK: Oxford University Press.

Risko, E. F., Laidlaw, K. E. W., Freeth, M., Foulsham, T., & Kingstone, A. (2012). Social attention with real versus reel stimuli: toward an empirical approach to concerns about ecological validity. *Frontiers in Human Neuroscience*, 6, 143.   https://doi.org/10.3389/fnhum.2012.00143

Risko, E. F., Richardson, D. C., & Kingstone, A. (2016). Breaking the Fourth Wall of Cognitive Science Real-World Social Attention and the Dual Function of Gaze. *Current Directions in Psychological Science*, 25(1), 70–74.

Ruhland, K., Andrist, S., Badler, J., Peters, C., Badler, N., Gleicher, M.&R. Mcdonnell (2014). Look me in the eyes: A survey of eye and gaze animation for virtual agents and artificial systems (pp. 69–91). Presented at the Eurographics State-of-the-Art Report.

Sak, H., Vinyals, O., Heigold, G., Senior, A., McDermott, E., Monga, R., & Mao, M. (2014). Sequence discriminative distributed training of long short-term memory recurrent neural networks. *Entropy*, 15(16), 17–18.

Schauerte, B., & Stiefelhagen, R. (2014). "Look at this!" learning to guide visual saliency in human-robot interaction (pp. 995–1002). Presented at the Intelligent Robots and Systems (IROS 2014), 2014 IEEE/RSJ International Conference on, IEEE.

Schmidt, R., Morr, S., Fitzpatrick, P., & Richardson, M. J. (2012). Measuring the dynamics of interactional synchrony. *Journal of Nonverbal Behavior*, 36(4), 263–279.   https://doi.org/10.1007/s10919-012-0138-5

Senju, A., & Hasegawa, T. (2005). Direct gaze captures visuospatial attention. *Vision Cognition*, 12, 127–144.   https://doi.org/10.1080/13506280444000157

Sheikhi, S., Odobez, J.-M. (2014). Combining dynamic head pose–gaze mapping with the robot conversational state for attention recognition in human–robot interactions. *Pattern Recognition Letters*.

Sugano, Y., Matsushita, Y., & Sato, Y. (2013). Appearance-based gaze estimation using visual saliency. *Pattern Analysis and Machine Intelligence, IEEE Transactions on*, 35(2), 329–341.   https://doi.org/10.1109/TPAMI.2012.101

Sugano, Y., Matsushita, Y., Sato, Y., 2014. Learning-by-synthesis for appearance-based 3d gaze estimation. Presented at the *Computer Vision and Pattern Recognition (CVPR), 2014 IEEE Conference on, IEEE*, pp. 1821–1828.

Sun, Y. (2003). *Hierarchical object-based visual attention for machine vision* (Thesis). Institute of Perception, Action and Behaviour, University of Edinburgh, Edinburgh, UK.

Teufel, C., Alexis, D. M., Clayton, N. S., & Davis, G. (2010). Mental-state attribution drives rapid, reflexive gaze following. *Attention, Perception, & Psychophysics*, 72(3), 695–705.   https://doi.org/10.3758/APP.72.3.695

Tomasello, M. (2008). *Origins of Human Communication*. Boston, MA: MIT Press.

Tomasello, M. (2009). *Why We Cooperate*. Cambridge, MA: MIT Press.

Tomasello, M., Hare, B., Lehmann, H., & Call, J. (2007). Reliance on head versus eyes in the gaze following of great apes and human infants: the cooperative eye hypothesis. *Journal of Human Evolution*, 52, 314–320.   https://doi.org/10.1016/j.jhevol.2006.10.001

Trabelsi, G., Leray, P., Ben Ayed, M., & Alimi, A. M. (2013). Benchmarking dynamic Bayesian network structure learning algorithms (pp. 1–6). Presented at the Modeling, Simulation and Applied Optimization (ICMSAO), 2013 5th International Conference on, IEEE.

Trutoiu, L. C., Carter, E. J., Matthews, I., & Hodgins, J. K. (2011). Modeling and animating eye blinks. *ACM Transactions on Applied Perception (TAP)*, 8(3), 1–17. https://doi.org/10.1145/2010325.2010327

Valenti, R., & Gevers, T. (2012). Accurate eye center location through invariant isocentric patterns. *Pattern Analysis and Machine Intelligence, IEEE Transactions on*, 34(9), 1785–1798. https://doi.org/10.1109/TPAMI.2011.251

Van der Burg, E., Olivers, C. N., Bronkhorst, A. W., & Theeuwes, J. (2009). Poke and pop: Tactile-visual synchrony increases visual saliency. *Neuroscience Letters*, 450(1), 60–64. https://doi.org/10.1016/j.neulet.2008.11.002

Vatikiotis-Bateson, E., Eigsti, I. -M., Yano, S., & Munhall, K. G. (1998). Eye movement of perceivers during audiovisual speech perception. *Perception & Psychophysics*, 60, 926–940. https://doi.org/10.3758/BF03211929

Vertegaal, R., Slagter, R., van der Veer, G., & Nijholt, A. (2001). Eye gaze patterns in conversations: There is more to conversational agents than meets the eyes. In *Conference on Human Factors in Computing Systems* (pp. 301–308). Seattle, WA: ACM Press New York, NY, USA.

Vinayagamoorthy, V., Garau, M., Steed, A., & Slater, M. (2004). An eye gaze model for dyadic interaction in an immersive virtual environment: Practice and experience. *The Computer Graphics Forum*, 23(1), 1–11. https://doi.org/10.1111/j.1467-8659.2004.00001.x

Võ, M. L. -H., Smith, T. J., Mital, P. K., & Henderson, J. M. (2012). Do the eyes really have it? Dynamic allocation of attention when viewing moving faces. *Journal of Vision*, 13(3), 1–14.

Yarbus, A. L. (1967). Eye movements during perception of complex objects. In L. A. Riggs (Ed.), *Eye Movements and Vision* (Vol. VII, pp. 171–196). New York: Plenum Press. https://doi.org/10.1007/978-1-4899-5379-7_8

CHAPTER 8

Automatic analysis of in-the-wild mobile eye-tracking experiments using object, face and person detection

Stijn De Beugher[i], Geert Brône[ii] and Toon Goedemé[i]
[i]EAVISE, ESAT – KU Leuven / [ii]MIDI Research Group – KU Leuven

In this chapter, we discuss a novel method for the analysis of mobile eye-tracking data in natural environments. Mobile eye-tracking systems generate large amounts of continuous data, making manual analysis extremely time-consuming. Available solutions provided by commercially available eye-tracking systems, such as marker-based analysis, minimize the manual labor but require experimental control, making real-life experiments practically unfeasible, and generally only apply to the analysis of objects. Here, we discuss a novel method for the processing of mobile eye-tracking data, based on the integration of computer vision techniques. Using such an approach allows us to automatically detect specific objects, faces and human bodies/body parts in images captured by a mobile eye-tracker. By mapping the gaze data on top of these detections, we gain insights into the visual behavior of recorded participants. As an important step in the integration of this method in the analysis of multimodal interaction, we developed an output format that is compatible with annotation tools such as ELAN, making our software integratable with existing annotations. In this chapter we give an overview of relevant image processing techniques and their application in interaction studies. We also present a thorough comparison between manual analysis and our automatic analysis in both speed and accuracy on challenging, real-life experiments.

Keywords: detection algorithms, computer vision, automatic analysis, software, annotation, multimodal interaction

1. Introduction

The development of mobile eye-tracking systems has opened up the paradigm of eye-tracking to a wide variety of research disciplines and commercial applications. Whereas traditionally, the analysis of eye gaze patterns was largely confined to

https://doi.org/10.1075/ais.10.08beu

controlled lab-based conditions due to technological restrictions (i.c. obtrusive hardware restricting the flexibility of use and potential research questions), mobile systems allow for eye-tracking 'in the wild', without a necessarily predefined set of research conditions. Because of this increased flexibility, research into visual behavior and real-life user experience now extends to natural environments such as public spaces (train stations, airports, museums, etc.), commercial environments (supermarkets, shopping centers, etc.) or to interpersonal communicative settings (help desk interactions, lectures, face-to-face communication, etc.).

The output generated by a mobile eye-tracker typically consists of images captured by the scene camera with the gaze locations laid on top of them. One of the key challenges for this type of pervasive eye-tracking, and mobile eye-tracking in general, is the processing of data generated by such systems. By abandoning the traditional well-controlled lab-based conditions, the data stream generated by the eye-trackers becomes highly complex, both in terms of the objects and scenes that are encountered, and the gaze data that need to be analyzed and interpreted. How can researchers avoid the painstaking task of manually coding large amounts of data, which is extremely time-consuming, without losing the full potential of mobile eye-tracking systems? Recently, several solutions to the analysis problem have been proposed, some of which have been integrated in commercially available systems (cf. Evans et al., 2012 for an overview). The best-known technique is the use of markers to predefine potential *Areas Of Interest* (AOI). These systems, which either use physical infra-red markers (e.g. Tobii Glasses) or natural markers (e.g. SMI Eye Tracking Glasses), determine the boundaries of the *Areas Of Analysis* (AOA), generating a two-dimensional plane within which eye gaze data can be collected for longer stretches of time and generalized across subjects. The output of this type of analysis is often represented in heat maps or opacity maps that highlight the zones within the AOA that received the most visual attention (measured in terms of visual fixations and fixation times). Despite their advantages in comparison to manual analysis, marker-based systems suffer from a range of limitations, as discussed in Brône et al. (2011) and Evans et al. (2012). First, in most implementations there is a need for fixed positions of relevant objects to be tracked, along with a sensitivity to the observer's position. Second, markers work well for objects to be tracked in a series of recordings, but they are not particularly useful for human-human interaction, where gaze behavior may be distributed over multiple individual participants, as well as their respective body parts (focus on face, focus on hand gestures, etc.). These shortcomings of marker-based systems impose limitations on the efficient use of (mobile) eye-tracking in real-life settings with moving subjects, objects and a dynamic interactional environment.

In this chapter, we present an alternative to the AOA-based methods, building on recent studies combining several image processing techniques with eye-tracking data (De Beugher et al., 2012; Toyama et al., 2012; Yun et al., 2013). The basic rationale of the approach presented here is that the scene camera data recorded by eye-tracking glasses are used as a basis for an analysis of objects and object classes (such as humans or human body parts). Once the video data have been processed for relevant objects, the gaze data can be mapped on them, thus rendering statistics for gaze fixations on these objects. One advantage of this approach is that it does not require predefined areas of interest or static objects. For example, objects for which gaze data statistics need to be generated can be selected in the actual video stream, without prior training. The schematic representation in Figure 1 presents the general architecture of our approach. In this chapter we go through the different steps of the approach and describe innovative features in comparison to previous work (De Beugher et al., 2014). In addition, we present validation experiments on challenging real-life experiments.

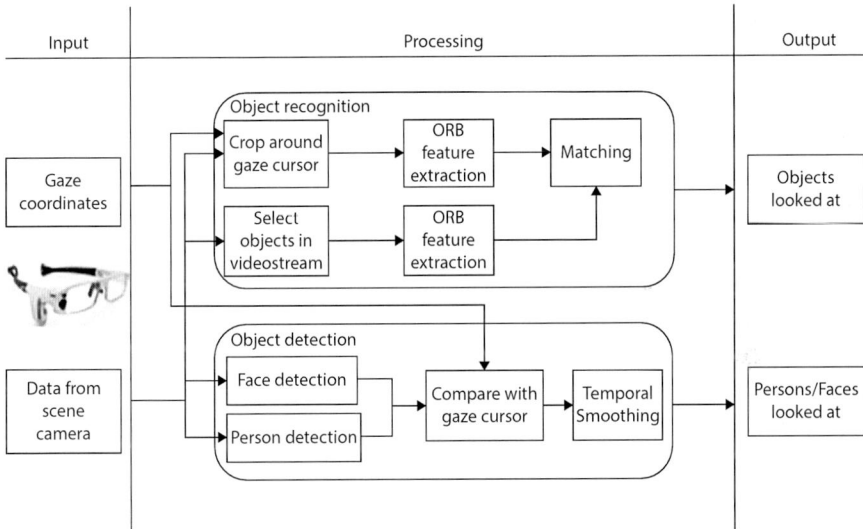

Figure 1. Basic architecture of the approach

In the next section, we discuss the technological background of our approach, including a comparison of different potential feature extraction methods and an overview of face and body detection algorithms. In Section 3, we will clarify our technical approach and in Section 4, we report on our experiments and compare our approach with a traditional manual annotation practice in terms of both accuracy and speed.

2.   Related work

An important distinction in the context of image processing techniques is the one between *object recognition* and *object detection*. Object recognition consists of retrieving a given object that is identical to a trained object in a set of images. Object detection, on the other hand, extends the principle of detecting objects with a known specific appearance towards detecting objects based on a general object class model that allows for intra-class variability. Popular examples of object detection include the detection of human bodies, faces or cars in images. Corresponding examples of object recognition are the identification of specific persons, car brands or types. It is important to note that in the context of image processing, a person is also seen as an "object" to be detected in images.

The next subsections describe a selection of techniques of both object recognition and object detection that are relevant to the application we present in this chapter.

2.1   Object recognition techniques

Object recognition, or finding an object that is identical to a trained one, is traditionally done with *local feature matching techniques*. Recognition methods define local interest regions in an image, based on specific features of the image content, which are described with descriptor vectors. The characterization of these local regions with descriptor vectors that are invariant to changes in illumination, scale and viewpoint enables the regions to be compared across images. Differences between approaches reside in the way in which interest points, local image regions, and descriptor vectors are extracted.

An illustration of a basic object recognition task can be found in Figure 2. Suppose one wants to find out whether the image on the right contains the sign that is presented on the left. In a first step (as can be seen in the upper part of the figure), features are extracted in both images, illustrated by the colored circles. In a second step, as can be seen in the lower part of the figure, the algorithm searches for similar features in both images, as illustrated by the blue lines. Based on the number of correspondences, their confidence and relative positions, one can decide whether or not the sign is in fact present in the second image.

A survey of object recognition methods is given in Tuytelaars & Mikolajczyk (2008), while Mikolajczyk et al. (2005) report comparative experiments. Well-known techniques are the *Scale Invariant Feature Transform* (SIFT; Lowe, 2004) and *Speeded Up Robust Features* (SURF; Bay et al., 2006). Although SIFT and SURF are regarded as state-of-the-art, we opted for a class of more recently developed

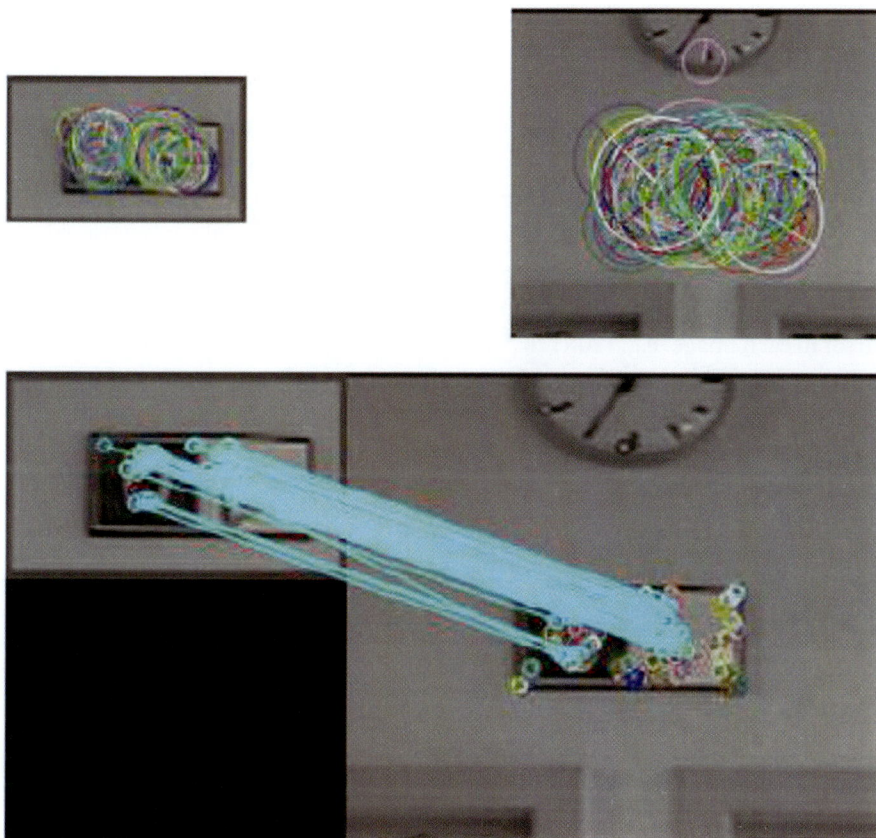

Figure 2. Illustration of basic feature matching. Colored circles represent the features, blue lines represent the matching feature pairs across both images

techniques due to licensing regulations. We compared two competitive alternatives for SIFT and SURF, namely ORB (Rublee et al., 2011) and BRISK (Leutenegger et al., 2011).

The ORB feature descriptor is built on the well-known FAST keypoint detector (Rosten & Drummond, 2005) and the recently developed BRIEF descriptor (Calonder et al., 2010). ORB is a computationally efficient replacement for SIFT and SURF: it has similar matching performance and is less affected by image noise. ORB is suitable for real-time performance since it is faster than both SURF and SIFT. Another competitive approach to keypoint detection (i.e. the detection of points that stand out in the image) and description is Binary Robust Invariant Scalable Keypoints (BRISK). It is as performant as the state-of-the-art algorithms, but with a significantly lower computational cost.

An evaluation of these detectors is presented in Miksik & Mikolajczyk (2012). Although these results demonstrate that BRISK outperforms ORB, we chose to use ORB in our algorithm based on findings from our own experiments. The main reason for this choice is the relevant image size for the analysis. Figure 3 shows the number of keypoints relative to the image size. For our analysis, we are mainly interested in a specific region around the gaze cursor, since we want to calculate the fixations on specific objects and object classes without a full analysis of objects in the broader field of view. As a result, we can crop the scene camera data of the eye-tracker to a smaller Region of Interest determined by the position of the gaze cursor in each image (e.g. 120×120 pixels around the gaze cursor). We observed that applying BRISK to small images often results in an insufficient number of extracted keypoints, and thus does not generate an adequate number of matches, limiting the applicability for our system.

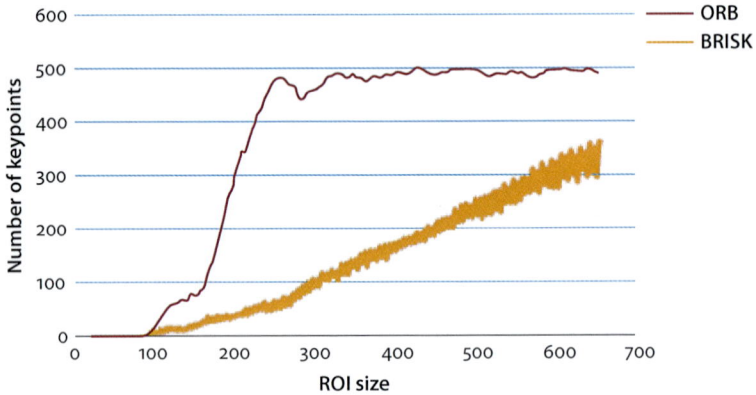

Figure 3. Comparison between ORB and BRISK. The horizontal axis represents the size of the ROI square

2.2   Object detection techniques

Studies in the field of visual behavior have amply shown that visual attention is particularly attracted to other persons (Judd et al., 2009; Van Gompel, 2007) and faces (Henderson, 2003). To broaden the use of our approach, we implemented techniques to automatically detect whether a person looked at another person. We make a distinction between specifically looking at a face, e.g. during talking, and looking at someone from a larger distance. This is relevant because proximity may differ across settings (e.g. short distance in face-to-face conversation vs. longer distance in customer journey experiments), and this difference is taken into account in the analysis.

Since each body or face is unique, it is impossible to apply the previously mentioned object recognition techniques. Object *detection*, on the other hand, can be described as detecting instances of objects of a certain class, in which the appearance of objects may vary, such as humans or faces, and therefore it is particularly suitable for general annotation purposes. A short overview of two robust object detection algorithms is given below.

The technique presented by Viola & Jones (2001) has proven to be a very useful tool to detect faces in natural images. The authors use a set of simple features, Haar wavelets, to decide whether a human face is present in an image. Haar wavelets compute the pixels under black and white rectangles as illustrated in Figure 4. During a training step, in which thousands of face images are presented to the algorithm, an AdaBoosting technique selects automatically which combination of all possible Haar-features is descriptive enough to tell the difference between a face and a non-face. The example in Figure 4 expresses the fact that for most faces the eyes are darker than the bridge of the nose. Thus, when this particular feature overlaps with the "eye-nose-eye" region in a face, it results in a high score. A window

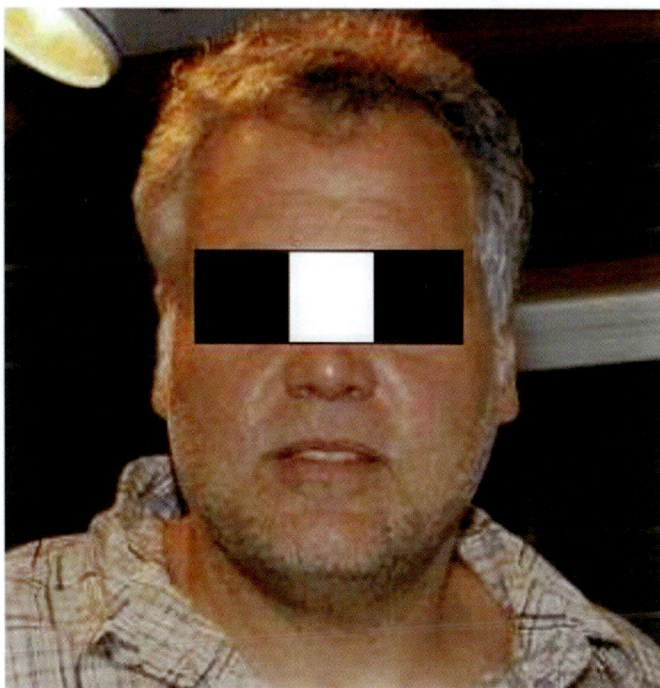

Figure 4. Illustration of a Haar-feature, which is used for face detection. When this feature overlaps with the eye-nose-eye region, it results in a high score due to the fact that the eyes are often darker than the nose

of 24 × 24 pixels is slided over the image, and in each window 6000 of such features are selected to be calculated and validated. Instead of applying 6000 features in each window, which would be time-consuming because of the high processing cost, the concept of a Cascade of Classifiers is introduced. This method groups the features into different stages of classifiers and applies them one at a time. If a window fails at a certain stage, it is discarded in the following stages. If a window passes all the stages, one can assume a face is present in that window. In order to cope with different image sizes, each image is downscaled several times. On each scaled image the above-mentioned actions are applied.

For the detection of full human bodies, rather than only faces, a state-of-the-art detector is the *Deformable Parts Model* (DPM; Felzenszwalb et al., 2010). This approach is a fast and accurate detection technique, which is slightly different from the above-mentioned Haar-based approach. Whereas faces can be identified with a specific pattern of darker and lighter regions, this pattern is not extendable to full bodies because of the variety in clothing people wear. Therefore, it is better to rely on the outline of a human silhouette, of which the edges are computed from an image using gradients. The DPM is built on the work of Dalal & Triggs (2005), who use a single filter on histogram of oriented gradients (HOG) features to represent an object category. This detector uses a sliding window approach, where a filter is applied at all positions and scales of an image. An illustration of such a filter is given in Figure 5a, in which indeed the outline of a human can be perceived. The DPM applies, apart from this root model, several higher-resolution part filters, as shown in Figure 5b and a spatial model for the location of each part relative to the root, as shown in Figure 5c. Such an approach allows for a slight deviation with respect to the root model. Assume, for example, a model for a human body where the training consists of images where both legs are held next to each other. Applying such a model to an image where a person is walking, as can be seen in the left part of Figure 5c, will most likely fail, due to a too large difference between the model and the body pose in the image. The DPM approach, however, allows such a pose using the part models and their allowed deviation. Other full person detectors like *Integral Channel Features* (Dollár et al., 2009) or *Random Hough Forests* (Gall & Lempitsky, 2009) are also frequently-used techniques, but are not applicable in our approach since they are rigid detectors. Such a detector has difficulties with the detection of people making large movements with their arms, like for example during gesturing.

Most of the publicly available models that are trained on the PASCAL and INRIA Person datasets have proven to be very robust in cases where a full body is visible, but sometimes fail when a body is not completely visible (Dollár et al., 2012). Unfortunately, since the scene camera of the eye-tracker has a restricted viewing

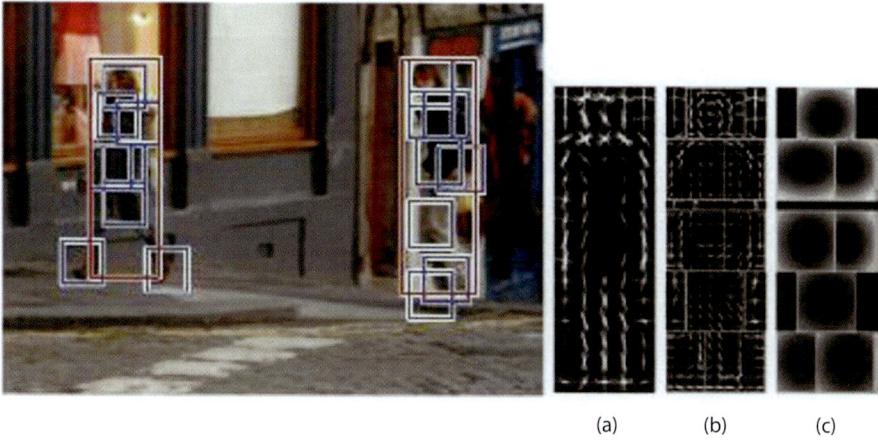

(a)   (b)   (c)

Figure 5. (a) Root model, (b) part models, (c) spatial model of parts

angle, people nearby appear cropped in the image, as illustrated in Figure 6. Since (mobile) eye-tracking experiments are increasingly focusing on the interaction between people in a natural face-to-face setting, a (semi-)automatic annotation systems needs to be able to deal with such images.

Figure 6. Examples of images recorded by a mobile eye-tracker with partial occlusion of the body

3.   Recognition and detection solution for mobile eye-tracking data: A technical description

The input of the algorithm we present here consists of a video stream, captured by the scene camera of an eye-tracker, and a data file that contains the corresponding gaze coordinates. Thus, our software is suitable for the post-processing of an eye-tracking experiment. As explained in the previous section, we apply two different techniques to analyze the eye-tracking data. The first part of this section discusses the implementation of the ORB technique to detect how often and for how long a particular object was viewed. The second part handles the implementation of techniques to count how often and for how long a face or a person was viewed.

3.1   Recognition of specific objects

This part of our approach focuses on how we process eye-tracking data to generate basic statistics for specific objects to be detected. This is done in five steps:

1. Preprocessing step: since we are only interested in the objects that appear close to the visual fixation point, the input images of the scene camera are cropped around the coordinates around the gaze cursor. Based on experiments using a Pupil Pro mobile eye-tracker (Kassner et al., 2014), which captures images of 1280×720 pixels, we chose to crop a ROI of 250×250 pixels around the gaze cursor.

2. The next step consists of selecting objects of interest (for the particular study one is conducting) in the datastream by simply selecting them while the video is playing. The video can be paused to draw a rectangle around the object of interest, after which the video automatically continuous. The objects are then stored in an object database, avoiding the task of manually creating such a database with training images of the objects, as proposed in other approaches (Toyama et al., 2012; De Beugher et al., 2012).

3. The third step consists of searching for correspondences between each cropped frame and each frame stored in the database, using ORB features. We apply a matching algorithm, based on the Euclidean distance to find similar keypoints between each image pair. Furthermore, we also apply several filter techniques to eliminate weak or false matches. First, the distance between the two best matches is evaluated: if this distance is large enough it is safe to accept the first best match, since it is unambiguously the best choice. Second, a symmetrical matching scheme is used, which imposes that for a pair of matches, both points must be the best matching feature of the other. The last step involves a

fundamental matrix estimation method based on RANSAC (Fischler & Bolles, 1981) to remove the outliers. This approach ensures that when we match feature points between two images, we only keep those matches that fall onto the corresponding epipolar lines. An illustration of the keypoint matches is given in Figure 7. The left side of Figure 7a and 7b represents the region of interest as selected by the user (in this case the region of interest corresponds to a presentation screen). On the right side of each image we see a cropped region around the gaze cursor of respectively frame 102 and frame 174 of this particular recording. On the right side of Figure 7a, a part of the region of interest is visible in the cropped region: there are seven corresponding keypoints between the two images, as shown by the blue lines. In Figure 7b, on the other hand, the region of interest is not visible on the right side, thus no corresponding features were found with the exception of one false match.

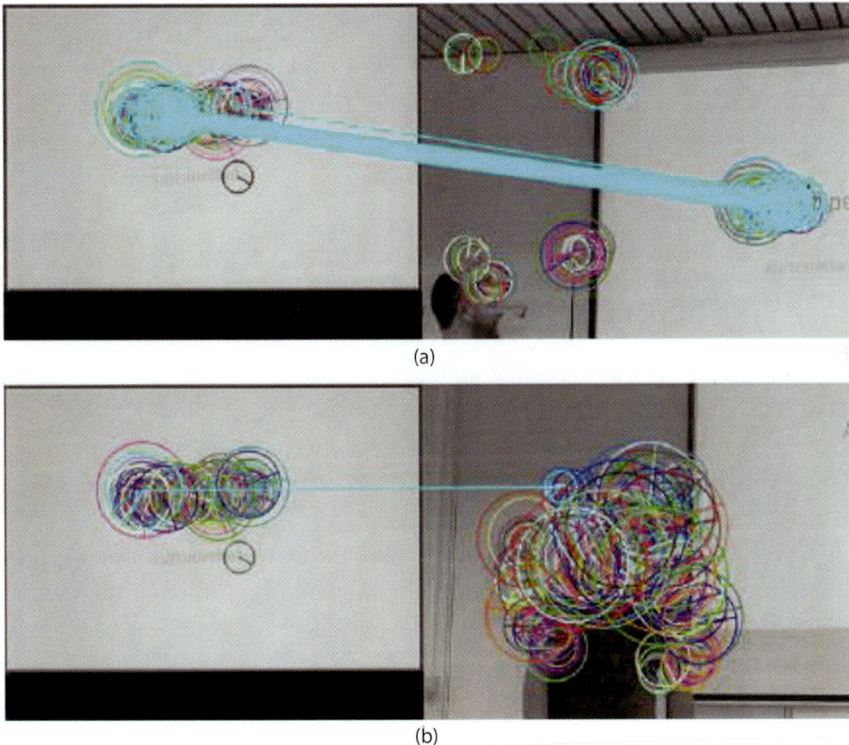

(a)

(b)

Figure 7. Illustration of our feature matching: blue lines illustrate corresponding features. Part (a) represents a valid feature matching, part (b) represents feature matching in which the object of interest is invisible

4. In a fourth step we assign a score S to each pair of images:

$$S = \frac{\sum\limits_{i=1}^{m} d(k_i, k'_i)}{m(\sum\limits_{i=1}^{m} A(k_i) + \sum\limits_{i=1}^{m} A(k'_i))},$$

Where k_i and k'_i stand for the ith keypoint of the corresponding images, m is the total number of matches and $A(k_i)$ the size of the corresponding features. This score S is then used to decide whether a cropped frame exhibits sufficient agreement to one of the frames in the database by comparing S to a tunable threshold.

5. In a fifth and final step we cluster consecutive similar frames into a "visual fixation". We define a visual fixation as a series of images in which the same object was viewed with a minimal duration time. This duration is configurable using a slider, since the length of a visual fixation depends on the task the test person is occupied with. The minimal length factor allows us to remove many false detections, since one can assume that a valid visual fixation should last at least 60 ms (i.e. 2 consecutive frames for a 30 fps camera). If a match between a region of interest and a frame from the recording was found in just a single frame, one can assume that this is an invalid (or too short) visual fixation and therefore it can be discarded.

3.2   Detection of faces and bodies

In the second part of our approach we focus on the detection of faces and human bodies as an important measure in (human-human) interaction analysis. Here we use the algorithms that were developed to detect persons and/or faces in images. By mapping the gaze date on top of these detections, we are able to automatically calculate how often and how long the tracked person looked at another person or more specifically at another face. As explained in the previous section, we use a DPM based approach for the detection of human bodies. Although the standard DPM person model is widely known as a robust and accurate detector, it is not suitable for our approach since persons are mostly not completely visible in the recorded scene camera images (cf. supra Figure 6). To overcome this issue, we trained a new human torso model based on the standard PASCAL VOC dataset.[1] This new model is trained using only the upper 60% of the labeled bounding boxes of human bodies, resulting in a human torso model as illustrated in Figure 8. Our model consists of two components, each belonging to a specific viewpoint. This

---

1. The PASCAL Visual Object Classes Challenge 2009 (VOC2009) Dataset: http://www.pascal-network.org/challenges/VOC/voc2009/workshop/index.html

approach to cope with image border occlusion is also followed by Mathias et al. (2013), but for a channel features detector. To the best of our knowledge, we are the first to use it on a DPM detector. A second advantage of this cropped model is the possibility to use the first component as an upper body (head and shoulder) detector. This model is, as compared to the Haar-cascade model, robust to various poses of the head. Example detections are shown in Figure 9.

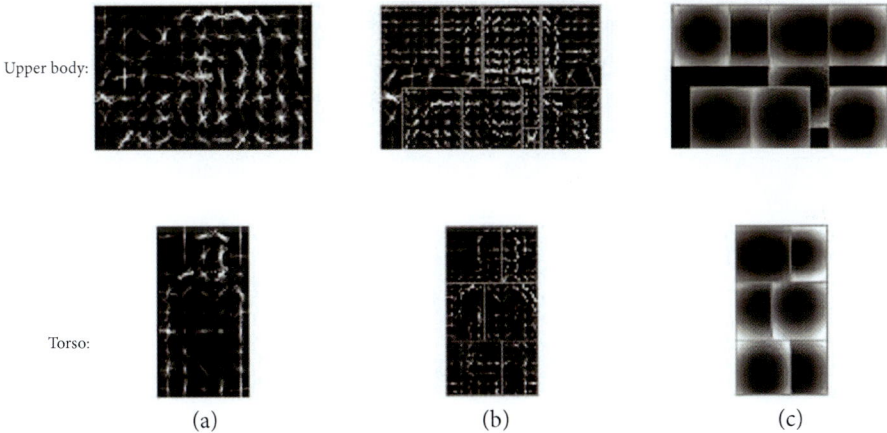

Upper body:

Torso:

(a)   (b)   (c)

Figure 8. Components of the upper body and torso model, each with their own root model (a), part model (b) and spatial model of the parts (c)

Upper body detections

Torso detections

Figure 9. Example of the upper body and torso detection

Next to the human torso and upper body detection, we also perform a human face detection on each image captured by the scene camera of the eye-tracker. For this purpose we use the OpenCV implementation of the Haar-based Viola and Jones (2001) implementation. We utilize two types of face models: one for frontal faces and one for profile faces. Using these models, we can determine the viewing direction of a person appearing in the recorded video.

Instead of applying the above-mentioned steps on each entire frame, we exploit the temporal continuity by applying a tracking-by-detection mechanism. Such an approach reduces the computational cost and can be used to remove false detections. This is done using a Kalman filter (Kalman, 1960), which is a mathematical filter used to predict the position of both face and torso. We use a Kalman filter with the following state vector and update matrix, assuming a constant velocity motion model, such that $x_{t+1} = Ax_t$:

$$x = \begin{bmatrix} x \\ y \\ v_x \\ v_y \end{bmatrix} \qquad A = \begin{bmatrix} 1 & 0 & 1 & 0 \\ 0 & 1 & 0 & 1 \\ 0 & 0 & 1 & 0 \\ 0 & 0 & 0 & 1 \end{bmatrix}$$

where x and y are the position of either the center of the torso or the face and v_x and v_y are the velocity of respectively torso or face. The idea behind this Kalman filter is to predict the location of a detection in a next frame, based on the detections in previous frames. Such an approach allows us to define a smaller region in which most likely the torso and/or face may occur, resulting in a much lower computational cost. Next to reducing the search area, one can also apply the Kalman predictions to fill in missing detections. If, for example, a detection was missing due to occlusion or motion blur, the prediction of the Kalman filter can be utilized.

The above-mentioned approach for the detection of human torsos performs sufficiently well, but there is still room for improvement. We propose a temporal smoothing technique (see Figure 10) using the gaze data to improve the detection rate, thus minimizing both false positives and false negatives. To reduce the number of false positives, we assume that a valid face/person detection should hold for at least a certain time (tunable via a threshold, for example 60 ms or 2 subsequent frames). This criterion substantially reduces the number of false positives (since many false detections occur for a short time). On the other hand, if we find gaps between detection sequences, we can assume those are missing detections. Predicting them will improve the detection rate and thus further reduce the number of false negatives.

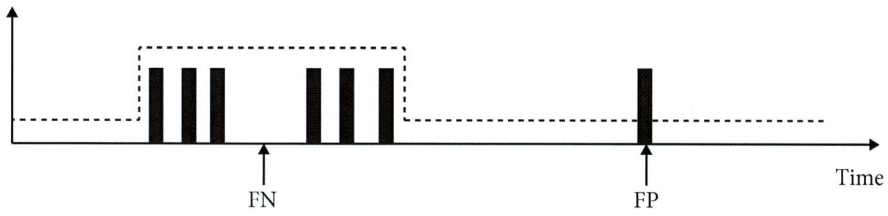

Figure 10. Temporal smoothing detection results. Vertical bars: Real detections, dashed line: Output of the temporal smoothing

3.3   Person reidentification

In the context of human-human interaction analysis, mobile eye-trackers are increasingly being used as a tool in data collection. One of the key measures is the amount of visual focus on co-participants in the interaction (and as a derivative the amount of mutual gaze or eye contact). We are able to automate this analysis using a human torso detection in combination with the gaze coordinates generated by the eye-trackers. In case a human-human interaction experiment involves multiple participants, like for example a triad, one would also like to automatically label which interlocutor the participant is gazing at. An illustration of such an experiment can be found in Figure 11. Here, three persons were equipped with a mobile eye-tracker and the purpose of the experiment is to investigate the visual behavior of each participant as part of the triadic interaction. Figure 11 represents the viewpoint of one of the participants and the red dot illustrates the gaze cursor. In this particular frame, the recorded participant is obviously looking at the person with the yellow T-shirt.

Figure 11. Sample frame of human-human experiment with three participants

We expanded our person detection algorithm with a person re-identification step. Such a re-identification allows us to specify which person a participant is looking at. In Figure 11, it is clear that we could distinguish both persons based on the color of their clothes. We extract this feature using a histogram comparison as shown in Figure 12. First, we select a region around each person as shown in the upper part of Figure 12. This selection is done manually by drawing a rectangle around each person of interest. For each region, we calculate a histogram, which is a graphical representation of the distribution of pixel values. In this particular example, we calculated two target histograms: one histogram of the person wearing the yellow sweater and another histogram of the person wearing the black sweater. In a next step, we apply our person detector as explained above. For each frame where there is overlap between a person detection and the gaze cursor, we calculate a histogram of the detection window. In a last step we compare the target histograms with the histogram of the detection window, as shown in the bottom part of Figure 12. Using the highest comparison score, we are able to identify which person the participant was looking at. The result of this approach is briefly discussed in the following section.

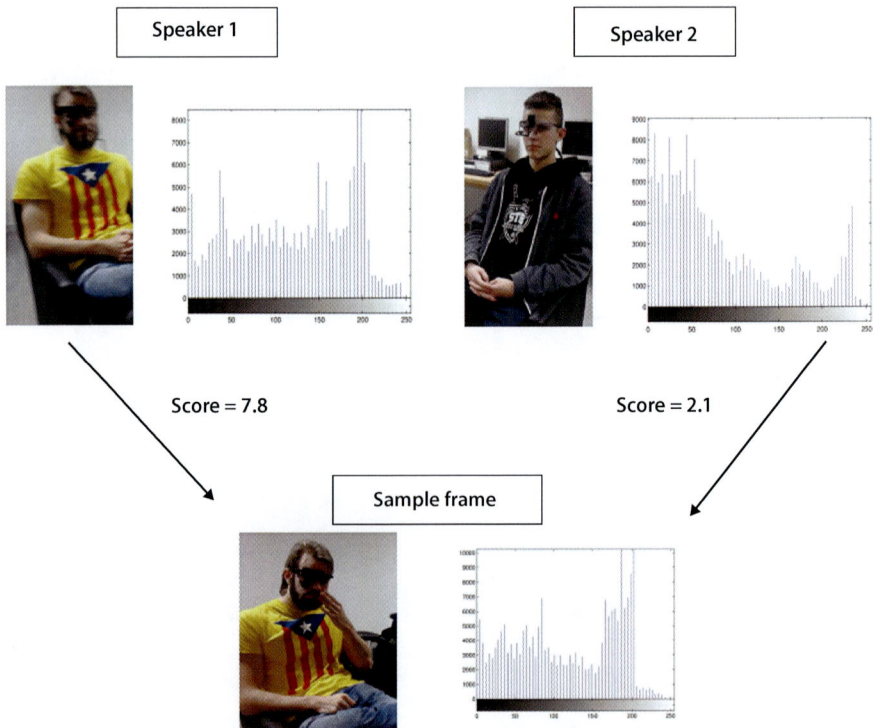

Figure 12. Histogram comparison used for person re-identification

4. Experimental results

In this section we present the results of our automatic analysis software. In order to test our person and object detection scheme on real-life eye-tracking experiments, we recorded a set of data in different settings. These settings included (i) a test person walking through a university campus building and looking for signs, (ii) a subject walking through the streets, while paying attention to traffic and other signs, (iii) a subject attending a presentation given by a lecturer, (iv) one recording of a triad that was conducted as part of a human-human interaction analysis and (v) a larger experiment as a part of which multiple participants visited a museum. In this last experiment, fourteen participants (7 male – 7 female) were recorded while they visited a special exhibition at Museum M in Leuven (Belgium), starting from the ticket counter all the way to the gift shop. The goal of this experiment was to determine the ease-of-use and general user experience of the self-guided tour: signage, information, view time of specific works, etc. In a final experiment (vi) multiple musician duos were equipped with mobile eye-trackers during several rehearsals in order to gain insights into the visual communication in ensemble playing. More information on this last experiment can be found in Vandemoortele et al. (2015, 2016). Recordings were made with Tobii Glasses One, Arrington Gig-E60 mobile systems and Pupil Pro eye-trackers and resulted in several hours of video material.

This section consists of three subsections: in 4.1 we present the results of our object detection algorithm, in 4.2 we discuss the results of both face and person detection and finally in 4.3 we apply the above-mentioned algorithms on real-life eye-tracking experiments in order to show the potential of our approach.

4.1   Object recognition results

In order to test our object recognition technique, we applied it to a set of images, which were captured by a mobile eye-tracker during the above-mentioned experiment (i). This recording was made using an Arrington Gig-E60 mobile eye-tracker, which embeds a scene camera that captures images of 320×240 pixels. As explained in Section 3.1, we crop a region around the coordinates of the gaze cursor in each image of the scene camera. In this experiment we chose to crop a region of 120×120 pixels. We gathered ground truth data by manually labelling a random set of 2000 cropped frames. Since the objective of the particular experiment was to gain insights into the visual impact of signs in a public building, we labeled only the images in which a sign was visible. This resulted in 1284 frames without a label and 716 labeled frames of six different types of signs: two emergency exit signs, pointers to stairs, a plate indicating the location of a fire extinguisher and a toilet sign. In Figure 13, we present the accuracy of our object recognition technique in a precision-recall curve. Such a curve is a frequently used method for presenting the accuracy of object recognition algorithms. The precision (P) is the fraction of retrieved instances that are relevant, while recall (R) is a measure of how many truly relevant results are returned. The mathematical calculation of both (P) and (R) is:

$$P = \frac{T_P}{T_P + F_P} \qquad\qquad R = \frac{T_P}{T_P + F_N}$$

Where T_p stands for true positive, F_p stands for false positive and F_N stands for false negative. When looking at the curve, it is clear that the optimal point corresponds to the upper right corner, yielding a high precision and a high recall. We created this curve by applying a varying threshold on the formula described in step 4 of the procedure (3.1 above). The obtained detection results are satisfactory for most of the objects. However, a large scale variance results in a lower detection rate, as illustrated by the curve of the toilet sign. This problem can be solved by using multiple images of the same object of interest e.g. one image of the toilet sign captured from far away and another image of the same toilet sign captured from nearby.

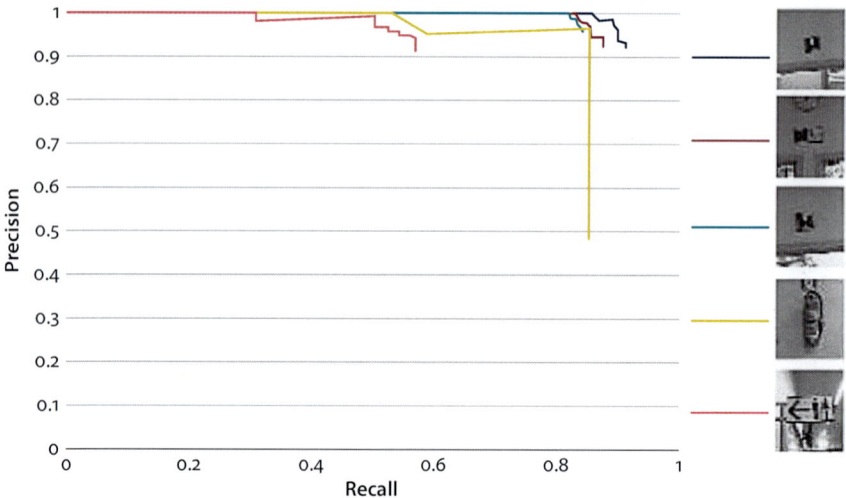

Figure 13. Precision-recall curve of our object recognition technique tested on a set of 2000 images

Next to the accuracy, the computational cost is also of importance. Obviously, it would not be beneficial if the automatic analysis would take as long as the manual counterpart. In Table 1 we show the execution time for a given number of selected objects and a given number of video frames. As illustrated in this table, data of an eye-tracker experiment of 6000 frames (3m 20s of video data) can be processed in a couple of minutes, less than the duration of the video itself even when up to five objects of interest are chosen. These tests were performed on a normal recent desktop PC. The frames we processed had a resolution of only 320 x 240, so applying this software to frames with a higher resolution will have an impact on the computation cost. On the other hand, it is easy to implement this technique on a multi-threaded system in which the processing could be done in parallel.

Table 1. Computational time of the object recognition implementation

# selected objects	2	3	4	5
video of 1 m 6 s	31 s	42 s	54 s	68 s
video of 2 m 13 s	61 s	80 s	104 s	133 s
video of 3 m 20 s	94 s	122 s	162 s	201 s

4.2 Results of face and body detections

The validation of our face and torso detections is done using the same approach as discussed above. First, we chose a set of 3000 consecutive frames captured by the scene camera of an Arrington Gig-E60 mobile eye-tracker during the museum visit (data set (v) mentioned above). In this dataset we labeled each frame in which (a) a person was visible and (b) the participant actually looked at this person (validated using the gaze cursor in each frame). Two types of labels were applied to compose this ground truth: upper body (we manually drew a rectangle around the shoulders-head area) and torso (we manually drew a rectangle around the human torso). Using this labeling, we know in which frames the participant looked at a person and where the person is located in the image. Next, we applied our face and person detector to this dataset and validated the detections using the 50% criterion as proposed in Dollár et al. (2012), which is commonly used to validate object detection algorithms. A detection is considered valid if and only if the bounding box of a detection (as shown by the green rectangles in Figure 9 above) overlaps at least 50% with the ground truth in that particular frame. Since we have two types of ground truth labels, a detection is valid if it corresponds to either an upper body label or a torso label.

In Figure 14 we present a set of precision-recall curves displaying the improvements we have made. These curves are generated by varying a threshold on the detection scores. The red curve shows the performance of the standard VOC 2009 full body model on our dataset. The yellow curve shows the performance of the standard VOC 2009 model in combination with our temporal smoothing approach.

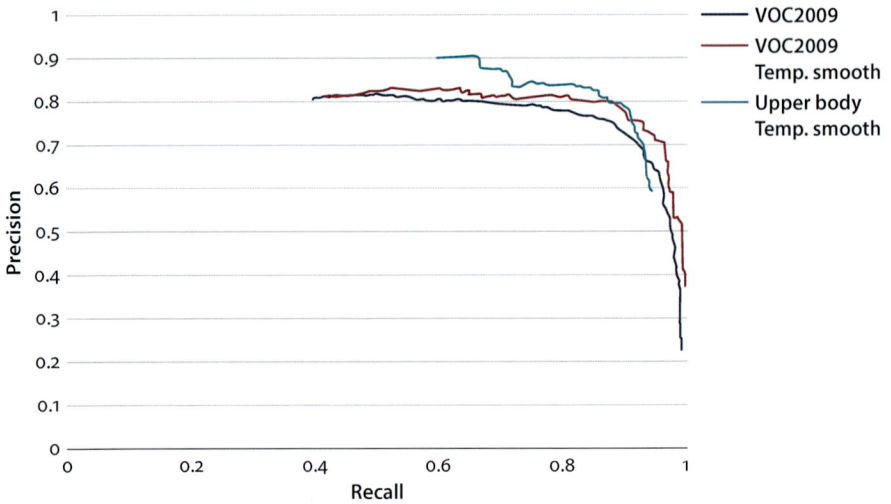

Figure 14. Precision-recall curves of our body detection implementation compared to a standard model

The blue curve shows the new torso model in combination with our temporal smoothing. Mainly in the recall region between 0.8 and 0.9, we reached a significant improvement compared to the standard model.

As mentioned in the previous section, it is possible to use the first component of our model to detect upper bodies, and thus use this model as an additional technique to the Haar-cascade frontal face model. Using the manually drawn upper body labels as described above, we tested the performance of the standard Haar-based face model and our upper body detections. In Figure 15 the results of this comparison are given. The blue dot illustrates the performance of the standard frontal face model. The red graph, on the other hand, represents the performance of our upper body model (thus here only the first component of our newly trained model is used). This graph reveals a large improvement in accuracy as compared to the Haar-based approach. Next to this comparison, we also tested whether it is valuable to combine both approaches. By applying an OR-operation on the detection results of both techniques, we obtain the yellow curve, which performs significantly better.

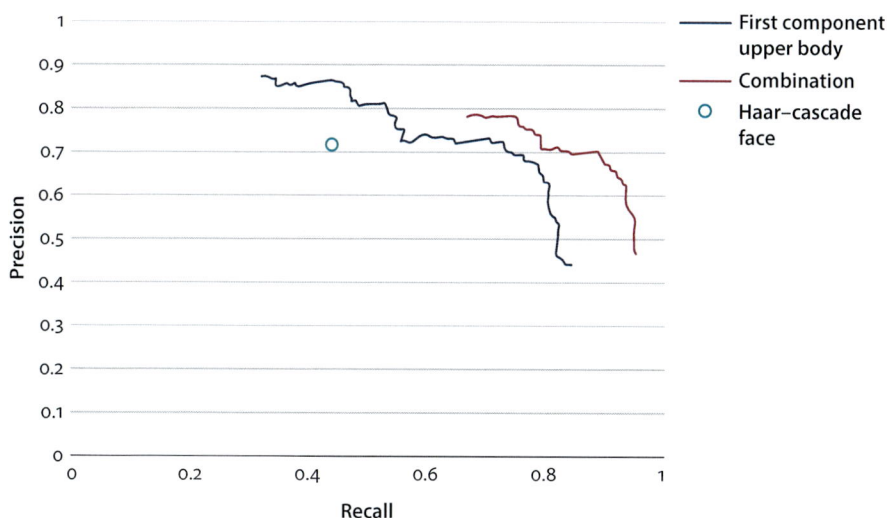

Figure 15. Precision-recall curves of face detection compared to upper body detections

4.3   Combined results of objects, face and body detection

Next to the accuracy of our image processing techniques, it is also important to validate the accuracy and usefulness of our entire system. In order to validate our approach, we used our method to automatically annotate a real-life mobile eye-tracking experiment that was conducted as part of a human-human interaction experiment (dataset (iv) mentioned above). In this experiment a Pupil Pro mobile eye-tracker was used with a scene camera with a resolution of 1280 × 720 pixels. As a validation test, we used our automatic analysis software to process this entire recording. This recording has a duration of 14m 17s and consists of 20568 frames. Initially, we were interested in the visual behavior towards the two interlocutors. This analysis can be performed fully autonomously using our software as described in Section 3.3. During a manual inspection of the video, we noticed that the selected participant tended to look at both a camera tripod and a poster on the wall, typically while speaking. Therefore, we also applied our object recognition software (cf. 3.1) to this recording using two images of the objects of interest. In Figure 16, the four object types are shown: speaker 1, speaker 2, poster and camera tripod.

In order to actually make our automatic analysis software useful for end users (e.g. linguists interested in the use of eye-tracking for multimodal interaction analysis), we also developed an additional tool which transforms our raw data to a file that is compatible with multimodal annotation software tools such as ELAN or ANVIL. Since such tools are widely used, this translation drastically enlarges the applicability of our software. Moreover, this link with annotation software makes it also possible

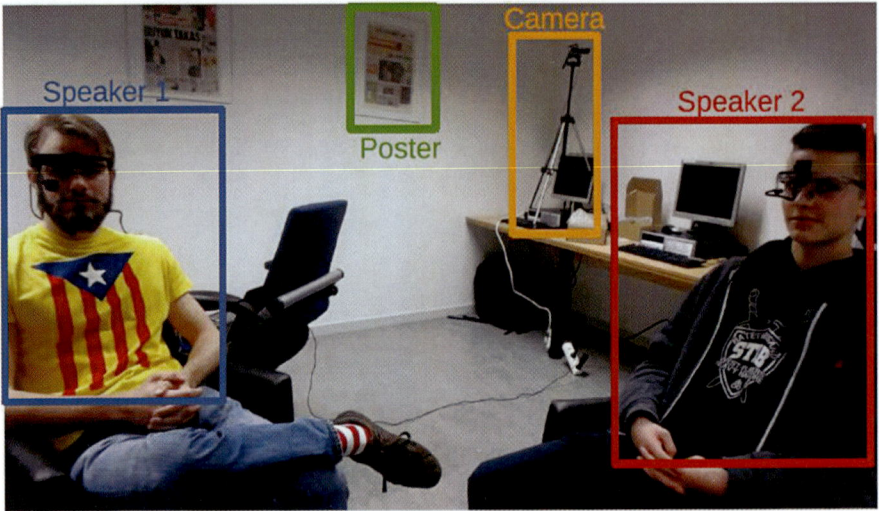

Figure 16. Different objects and persons that were automatically labeled using our software

to again validate our automatic analysis against a manual analysis in order to gain further insights into the accuracy of our system. To achieve this comparison, we removed all the labels of our automatic detections in an ELAN file. Thus, only the segments remain but without any labelling. We then asked an independent annotator to assign a label to each segment. The annotator could choose between the same five categories as our software did. Finally, we compared our automatic analysis with the manual labelling to find out the level of agreement, as shown in Table 2. This table reveals that the level of agreement between the manual and automatic analysis is very high (97.2%). On top of that, the more strict analysis methods such as Scott's Pi or Krippendorff's Alpha (Hayes & Krippendorff, 2007) also report very high levels of agreement. This comparison reveals that our automatic analysis is generally employable for the analysis of mobile eye-tracking experiments.

Next to the accuracy, there is also a significant improvement in analysis time. The automatic analysis of a selection of 90 seconds of video material took approximately

Table 2. Agreement between automatic and manual analysis

	Level
Agreement	97.2%
Scott's Pi	96.0%
Cohen's Kappa	96.0%
Krippendorff's Alpha	96.0%

27 minutes. The manual allocation of labels to the segments in ELAN, which is only a part of the entire labelling job, took about 60 minutes.

As a final step, we performed an analysis of the eye-tracking experiment that was conducted in the museum (v). Here, our goal was to provide an automatic (limited) customer journey analysis and to compare the experience of multiple visitors (thus generalizing over potentially idiosyncratic behavior). As a first step we selected several objects of interest in the recorded data. These include elements that may contribute to the general evaluation of the user experience, such as a booklet with a walking guide, a specific work of art, a story that was written on a wall, etc. On top of that we also applied our face and torso detector on these recordings in order to quantify the number of human-human interactions during the museum visit. An overview of the automatically generated output of our algorithm for the museum experiment is given in Figure 17. In this figure, we present some sections of a visual timeline that was automatically generated using our software. This time-line indicates when and for how long a visitor looked at a specific object or person. This timeline reveals that each visitor -not surprisingly- started his visit at the ticket counter. We also notice that two visitors looked at their route map immediately after buying their ticket, etc. In sum, the analysis provides an immediate linear-temporal overview of fixations on relevant objects of interest. This may then again serve as a useful basis for a more in-depth analysis or for a comparison across subjects. Manually analyzing this type of data, even if only three recordings as in this case, would take a significant amount of time.

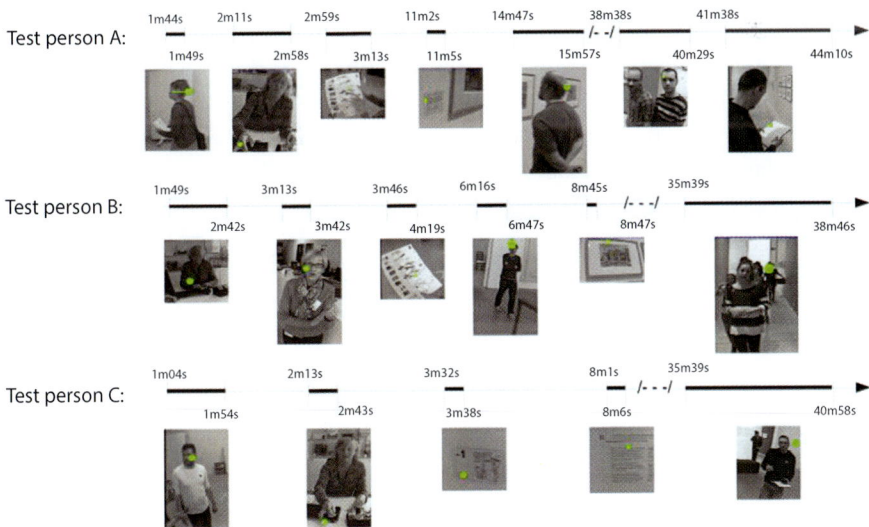

Figure 17. Results of our algorithm applied to the recordings of the museum visit. Each timeline represents a short summary of viewing behavior of a participant

5.   Conclusion and future work

In this chapter we presented an approach to the automatic processing of eye-tracking data based on object recognition, face and person detection. As opposed to Toyama et al. (2012 and De Beugher et al. (2012) we presented an object detection scheme in which a separate training is no longer required. On top of the object detection we presented an approach suited for counting how often and for how long a recorded participant looked at a person or a face. In order to further improve the detection rate we proposed two novelties. The first is a temporal smoothing approach based on the gaze cursor to avoid many false positives and false negatives. The second is the training of a new DPM model, which is designed for torso and upper body detection. We illustrated the accuracy and performance of our approach in the analysis of several experiments. First, the validity of the automatic detection of specific objects was shown in the analysis of an experiment conducted to calculate how often and for how long a specific sign in a public building was looked at. Next, the applicability of the newly trained torso model was proven using the data from an experiment, which was conducted in a museum context. We compared our detection results to a manual analysis and this comparison revealed that our system is highly accurate and that it actually can be used for the analysis of mobile eye-tracking recordings. Finally, we compared several recordings from the museum experiment using our automatic analysis. Next to the various detections methods, we also implemented an integration with commonly used annotations tools. In this integration, we automatically export the detections of both person detection and object recognition to an xml file that is compatible with e.g. ELAN. Our future work includes the implementation of the temporal smoothing approach on object recognition. Furthermore, we plan to apply intelligent sampling, which should avoid the processing of each frame and thus reduce processing time. And as a next logical step, we plan to develop an algorithm to automatically detect hand position and motion in space, which again can be coupled with recorded gaze coordinates (De Beugher et al., 2018).

References

Alves, R., Lim, V., Niforatos, E., Chen, M., Karapanos, E., & Nunes, N. J. (2012). Augmenting customer journey maps with quantitative empirical data: a case on eeg and eye tracking. In *Proceedings of ACM conference on Designing Interactive Systems*, DIS'12.

Bay, H., Tuytelaars, T., & Van Gool, L. (2006). Surf: Speeded up robust features. In *European Conference on Computer Vision*, 404–417.

Brône, G., Oben, B., a Goedemé, T. (2011). Towards a more effective method for analyzing mobile eye-tracking data: integrating gaze data with object recognition algorithms. In *Proceedings of the 1st PETMEI Workshop in Pervasive Eye-Tracking and Mobile Eye-Based Interaction*, 53–56. https://doi.org/10.1145/2029956.2029971

Calonder, M., Lepetit, V., Strecha, C., & Fua, P. (2010). Brief: binary robust independent elementary features. In *European Conference on Computer Vision*, 778–792.

Dalal, N. & Triggs, B. (2005). Histograms of oriented gradients for human detection. In *Computer Vision and Pattern Recognition*, 886–893.

De Beugher, S., Brône, G., & Goedemé, T. (2012). Automatic analysis of eye-tracking data using object detection algorithms. *Proceedings of the 2nd PETMEI Workshop in Pervasive Eye-Tracking and Mobile Eye-Based Interaction.*

De Beugher, S., Brône, G., & Goedemé, T. (2014). Automatic analysis of in-the-wild mobile eye-tracking experiments using object, face and person detection. In *Computer Vision Theory and Applications*, 625–633.

Dollár, P., Tu, Z., Perona, P., & Belongie, S. (2009). Integral channel features. In *Proceedings of the British Machine Vision Conference*, 1–11.

Dollár, P., Wojek, C., Schiele, B., & Perona, P. (2012). Pedestrian detection: An evaluation of the state of the art. *Transactions on Pattern Analysis and Machine Intelligence*, 34(4), 743–761. https://doi.org/10.1109/TPAMI.2011.155

Dubout, C. & Fleuret, F. (2012) Exact Acceleration of Linear Object Detectors. In *European Conference on Computer Vision*, 301–311.

Evans, K. M., Jacobs, R. A., Tarduno, J. A., & Pelz, J. B. (2012). Collecting and analyzing eye-tracking data in outdoor environments. *Journal of Eye Movement Research*, 5(2) 1–19.

Felzenszwalb, P. F., Girshick, R. B., & McAllester, D. (2010). Cascade object detection with deformable part models. In *Computer Vision and Pattern Recognition*, 2241–2248.

Fischler, M. A. & Bolles, R. C. (1981). Random sample consensus: a paradigm for model fitting with applications to image analysis and automated cartography. *Commununications of the ACM*, 24(6), 381–395. https://doi.org/10.1145/358669.358692

Gall, J. & Lempitsky, V. (2009). Class-specific hough forests for object detection. In *Computer Vision and Pattern Recognition*, 1022–1029.

Hayes A. F. & Krippendorff K. (2007). Answering the Call for a Standard Reliability Measure for Coding Data. *Communication Methods and Measures*, 1(1), 77–89. https://doi.org/10.1080/19312450709336664

Henderson, J. M. (2003). Human gaze control during real-world scene perception. *Trends in Cognitive Sciences*, 7(11), 498–504. https://doi.org/10.1016/j.tics.2003.09.006

Jokinen, K., Nishida, M., & Yamamoto, S. (2009). Eye-gaze experiments for conversation monitoring. In *Proceedings of the 3rd IUCS*, 303–308. https://doi.org/10.1145/1667780.1667843

Judd, T., Ehinger, K., Durand, F., & Torralba, A. (2009). Learning to predict where humans look. In *International Conference on Computer Vision*, 2106–2113.

Kalman, R. (1960) A New Approach to Linear Filtering and Prediction Problems. *Transaction of the ASME Journal of Basic Engineering*, 82, 35–45. https://doi.org/10.1115/1.3662552

Kassner, M. and Patera, W. & Bulling, A. (2014) Pupil: An Open Source Platform for Pervasive Eye Tracking and Mobile Gaze-based Interaction. In *CoRR*.

Leutenegger, S., Chli, M., & Siegwart, R. (2011). Brisk: Binary robust invariant scalable keypoints. In *International Conference on Computer Vision*, 2548–2555.

Lowe, D. (2004). Distinctive image features from scale-invariant keypoints. *International Journal of Computer Vision*, 60(2), 91–110. https://doi.org/10.1023/B:VISI.0000029664.99615.94

Mathias, M., Benenson, R., Timofte, R., & Van Gool, L. (2013). Handling occlusions with franken-classifiers. In *International Conference on Computer Vision*, 1505–1512.

Mikolajczyk, K., Tuytelaars, T., Schmid, C., Zisserman, A., Matas, J., Schaffalitzky, F., Kadir, T., & Van Gool, L. (2005). A comparison of affine region detectors. *International Conference on Computer Vision*, 65(1–2), 43–72. https://doi.org/10.1007/s11263-005-3848-x

Miksik, O. & Mikolajczyk, K. (2012). Evaluation of local detectors and descriptors for fast feature matching. In *International Conference on Pattern Recognition*, 2681–2684.

Rosten, E. & Drummond, T. (2005). Fusing points and lines for high performance tracking. In *International Conference on Computer Vision*, 1508–1515.

Rublee, E., Rabaud, V., Konolige, K., & Bradski, G. (2011). Orb: An efficient alternative to sift or surf. In *International Conference on Computer Vision* 2564–2571.

Toyama, T., Kieninger, T., Shafait, F., & Dengel, A. (2012). Gaze guided object recognition using a head-mounted eye tracker. In *Proceedings of the ETRA Conference*, 91–98.

Tuytelaars, T. & Mikolajczyk, K. (2008). Local invariant feature detectors: a survey. *Foundations and Trends in Computer Graphics and Vision*, 3(3), 177–280. https://doi.org/10.1561/0600000017

Van Gompel, R. (2007). *Eye Movements: A Window on Mind and Brain*. Elsevier Science.

Vandemoortele, S., De Beugher, S., Brône, G., Feyaerts, K., Goedemé, T., De Baets, T., & Vervliet, S. (2015). Into the wild: Musical communication in ensemble playing. Discerning mutual and solitary gaze events in musical duos using mobile eye-tracking. In *Proceedings of the SAGA Workshop*.

Viola, P. & Jones, M. (2001). Rapid object detection using a boosted cascade of simple features. In *Computer Vision and Pattern Recognition*, 511–518.

Yun, K., Peng, Y., Samaras, D., Zelinsky, G. J., & Berg, T. L. (2013). Studying relationships between human gaze, description, and computer vision. In *Computer Vision and Pattern Recognition*, 739–746.

PART 3

Case studies

CHAPTER 9

Gaze, addressee selection and turn-taking in three-party interaction

Peter Auer
University of Freiburg

In this paper, I argue that gaze behavior in multiparty interaction is essential for addressee selection and for next-speaker selection by current speaker. The two conversational tasks are related, but – at least in longer turns – not identical and should be distinguished analytically. In multiparty interaction, addressee selection by gaze is a non-trivial issue, as most bodily arrangements make it hard or impossible for the current speaker to look at all (intended) addressees at the same time. As a solution to this problem, current speakers alternatingly look at the co-participants they want to address. For the selection of a next speaker, only the current speaker's gaze during the last phase of the turn is relevant.

Keywords: three-party interaction, turn-taking, next-speakership, conversational analysis, addressee selection

1. Introduction

This chapter offers a first and exploratory investigation of the relevance of gaze for addressee selection and turn-taking in multi-party interaction from a conversation-analytic perspective, using mobile eye tracking technology. Although the relevance of gaze for turn-taking and addressee selection was already demonstrated in Kendon's classic 1967 study and brought into conversation analysis by Ch. Goodwin's equally classic studies (e.g. 1981) a long time ago, follow-up research has remained scarce. It is only in recent years that the topic has re-emerged in conversation analysis thanks to Rossano (2012, also cf. his overview in Rossano, 2013), Streeck (2014) and Holler & Kendrick (2015), among others. However, due to the continuous and strong influence of early work on conversational turn-taking – particularly Sacks, Schegloff and Jefferson's foundational 1974 paper which only mentions non-verbal turn-taking cues in passing – the full relevance of a multimodal approach for the "turn-taking machinery" as described by Sacks et al. has remained underexplored and underappreciated. Since, in addition, much empirical work on

https://doi.org/10.1075/ais.10.09aue

gaze and turn-taking/addresse selection (e.g. by including Kendon's, Streeck's and Rossano's) has dealt with dyadic constellations, the specific conditions under which multi-party conversations are organized with respect to gaze remain to be explored. This paper is a first attempt in this direction, focusing on the speaker in a triadic constellation. Its main point is to argue for a distinction between *speaker gaze for addressee selection and speaker gaze for next-speaker selection*, i.e. for allocating the turn. The addressed participant is not always the one selected as next speaker; particularly in multi-party conversation it is often the case that more than one (often all) participants are addressed by a present speaker but only one is selected/suggested as the next speaker by gaze. As this study will also show, the distinction between other-selection and self-selection as made by Sacks, Schegloff and Jefferson (1974) needs to be reconsidered once gaze is taken fully into consideration.

In the following, various patterns will be discussed by which the gaze of the current speaker either selects addressees or suggests next speakers in three-party conversations. The study is preliminary as it is based on only two interactional episodes of roughly 60 minutes each. In both cases, three German students (three men, three women, respectively) talked to each other while sitting around a table in a room. Participants knew each other well. They had no particular assignment or task. The setting was chosen in order to create a context in which participants' gaze was free to be employed for turn-taking and addressee selection and in which this resource was not systematically needed, e.g., for handling objects or orienting in space. In the latter case, more complex gaze patterns are bound to emerge. Two of the participants in each recording were wearing eye tracking glasses.[1]

Mobile eye tracking glasses not only allow us to locate the participant's focal (foveal) vision, but also record the interaction from the perspective of the speaker. In our case, the interaction was additionally recorded with an external video camera (located at some meters' distance from the group). This means that the encounter was documented by three cameras each showing a different perspective, which were synchronized and displayed on a split screen for analysis, as shown in Figure 1.

In this case, Anni (middle) and Nanni (left in external recording, below) are wearing eye tracking equipment. As can be seen in the upper part of the split screen, Anni is looking at Nanni's face (right upper screen, green cursor), while Nanni is looking at Hanni's face (left upper screen, red cursor). We cannot be sure about Hanni's gaze, since she is not wearing eye tracking glasses, but judging from the direction of her head, she seems to be looking at Nanni.

---

1. We used SMI Eye Tracking Glasses and SMI's iViewETG recording software. The scan path videos were exported using BeGaze software and then analyzed in ELAN. The fact that the third participant did not wear trackers is entirely due to technical restrictions. In this study, only speakers wearing eye tracking equipment will be considered.

Figure 1. Still from split screen representation of one of the recordings

2. Gaze and turn-taking: A short overview[2]

Sacks, Schegloff and Jefferson (1974) describe a "machinery" for turn-taking in conversation that has become a cornerstone of conversation analysis research and beyond. Crucially, their model includes a "turn-allocation" component which is built on three hierarchically ordered steps ("rules") that operate once a "transition-relevant point" has been reached. (The stretch of talk up to such a transition-relevant point is called a "turn-constructional unit", TCU.) In a first step, the current speaker can select a next speaker (current-selects-next); the second step provides the opportunity to self-select for all current non-speakers, among whom the "first starter" will be successful. If neither the current speaker other-selects nor one of the current non-speakers self-selects, the current speaker is given the opportunity to expand the turn.

---

2. Overviews of previous research can also be found in Rossano (2013, p. 315–322), Streeck (2014) and Holler & Kendrick (2015).

Rule (1)(a), most relevant for this study, is formulated in Sacks et al. as follows:

> If the turn-so-far is so constructed as to involve the use of a 'current speaker selects next' technique, then the party so selected has the right and is obliged to take next turn to speak; no others have such rights and obligations, and transfer occurs at that place.   (1974, p. 704)

As the authors further point out,

> [t]he group of allocation techniques which we have called 'current speaker selects next' cannot be used in just any utterance or utterance-type whatever. Rather, there is a set of utterance-types, adjacency pair first parts, that can be used to accomplish such selection; and with the constraint to employ one of those, there are constraints on what a party can say.   (p. 710–711)[3]

A standard technique for selecting a next speaker designated to deliver the second pair part of an adjacency pair is, according to Sacks et al., the use of a name in the function of an address term.

There are several problems with this restriction of the current-speaker-selects-next option to the context of adjacency pairs. Above all, restricting next-speaker selection by current speaker to first adjacency pair parts threatens the independence of the turn-taking machinery from action which Sacks and colleagues insist on. In addition, the dichotomic distinction between one group of actions that have the status of "firsts" and which need to be responded to in adjacent position with a defined second action ("adjacency pairs", such as question/answer or invitation/rejection or acceptance), and another group of actions for which no next actions are projected at all, has been shown to be empirically untenable and should be replaced by a continuum of more or less projecting first actions (see Stivers & Rossano, 2010). Moderately projecting first actions are, for instance, first assessments or tellings.

Sacks et al. are aware of these problems and hint at the possibility that, in addition to what they call the "'obvious' cases" (i.e., first parts of adjacency pairs), there are other contexts in which current-selects-next techniques may be found. Among them, they mention the use of tag questions[4] and "techniques which employ social identities in their operation" (1974, p. 718).[5] But even with these additions, self-selection would remain the only option for a large group of actions by a current speaker.

---

3.   In a later part of their paper, Sacks et al. also count repair initiations among the actions that select a next speaker, i.e. the party whose utterance the repair refers to (1974, p. 717).

4.   Strictly speaking, like all other question formats tag questions are not a next-speaker selection technique but a technique to produce a first pair part which needs gaze or another technique to select its addressee.

5.   In a wide interpretation of "social identities", these techniques can be understood to include those of recipient design for co-participants' background knowledge as well.

Gaze, on the other hand, is available as a resource for turn-allocation in all instances of face-to-face interaction in which participants are able to look at each other, regardless of the action performed by the current speaker. The ubiquity of gaze makes it a perfect candidate for turn-allocation independent of the action performed, and is hence in line with the autonomy of the turn-taking machinery. Note, however, that if gaze is considered a current-selects-next technique, the fact that current speakers almost always gaze at a co-participant in multi-party conversation would make step two of the turn-allocation model (i.e. self-selection) almost vacuous: in most cases, there would be no chance for it to apply. (The only exception would be cases in which the current speaker looks away from all co-participants at the end of the turn; this option, however, seems to be restricted to special sequential environments, such as topic closures.)

The solution for this dilemma suggested here is that gaze does indeed function as a turn-allocation technique, but that its turn-allocating force is weaker than that of address terms attached to first pair parts of adjacency pairs (the context Sacks et al. originally had in mind). Lerner (2003) mentions a possible reason for the special status of gaze: Gaze is an unreliable technique for next-speaker selection – it may not be seen by non-attentive co-participants, particularly when their visual attention is devoted to other interactional tasks. As he points out, the use of second person singular pronouns is a verbal technique to remedy exactly this disadvantage. While the pronoun (as a deictic element) is not able to select one co-participant as next speaker in itself, it attracts the non-speakers' visual attention to the speaker's gaze which then designates the selected addressee as the next speaker. Asking somebody a question by using a second person singular pronoun plus gaze, and asking a question which is open for everybody to answer and gazing at one person is not the same. Combining second person pronouns and gaze is the most efficient current-speaker-selects-next option. If gaze alone is employed, it will be less effective in allocating the turn than gaze combined with a deictic pronoun.

Pre-dating conversation analysis, Adam Kendon already demonstrated the relevance of gaze for turn-taking in a foundational 1967 paper on the role of speaker gaze in dyadic interaction, which can be summarized in his own words as follows (Kendon, 1973, p. 61): "[B]y looking away, just in advance of the speaking, the speaker could signal his intent to claim the floor. [...] while by looking at his partner, and sustaining this look, as he brought his utterance to an end, he could signal his intent to finish. This could thus be a cue to his partner to begin speaking." In support of the second part of this generalization, Kendon observed that "extended" speaker gaze at the recipient toward the end of an utterance was much more frequently followed by the co-participant becoming the next speaker without delay than when gaze was not employed at a possible utterance end (71% vs. 29%; Kendon, 1973, p. 61). The pattern, which is explicitly restricted to what Kendon calls "long utterances" (at least five seconds' duration, "when people are exchanging points of

view comparing experiences or ... exploring one another's knowledge of something",
1973, p. 61), can be illustrated by an example from Kendon's 1967 article:[6]

(1)   (From Figure 1 in Kendon (1967), gaze retranscribed; head movements
      and facial expressions omitted)

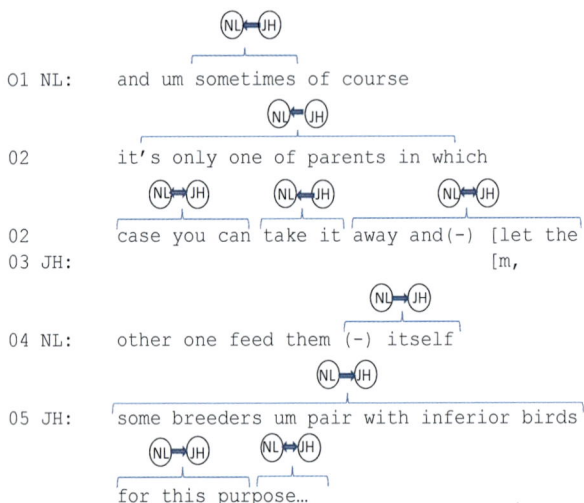

```
                        (NL)◄—(JH)
         01 NL:    and um sometimes of course
                        (NL)◄—(JH)
         02        it's only one of parents in which
                    (NL)►—(JH)  (NL)◄—(JH)        (NL)◄►(JH)
         02        case you can take it away and(-) [let the
         03 JH:                                    [m,
                             (NL)►—(JH)
         04 NL:    other one feed them (-) itself
                         (NL)►—(JH)
         05 JH:    some breeders um pair with inferior birds
                    (NL)►—(JH)  (NL)◄►(JH)
                    for this purpose...
```

Kendon's example has been retranscribed here using a transcription system
adapted from Rossano (2013) in which mutual gaze between NL and JH is sym-
bolized by a two-sided (double) arrow, and one-sided gaze from the speaker at
the hearer or vice versa by a one-sided (double) arrow pointing at the participant
being looked at. Curled brackets mark the approximate duration of a gaze pattern.
(See appendix for details.) Where no gaze is transcribed (as in the beginning of
line 04), the two participants are looking elsewhere. Turn-transition from NL to
JH takes place between lines 04 and 05. Shortly before that, there is a stretch of
talk ((-) *itself*) in which the current speaker looks at the current recipient; the recipient, on the other hand, looks away from the current speaker as he approaches
the end of his turn (all through line 04) and also does so in the beginning of her
turn (beginning of line 05).[7]

---

6.   It should be kept in mind that Kendon studied undergraduates at the University of Oxford
who were unacquainted and told to "get to know one another".

7.   Note that JH produces a recipiency token in line 03, which plays a role in this speaker transition, perhaps for pre-selection by JH. Kendon describes the example as follows: "She utters a
faint "mm," and [...] drops her eyelids over her eyes, tilting her head forward in the next frame.
She continues to look down, even after she begins to speak [...]. This looking away, and other
changes, which occur before she begins to speak, coincide with the beginning of the last phrase
of NL's utterance at the point at which, it may be presumed JH has realized NL is going to finish."

Kendon makes two claims: the first claim is that the current speaker looks at the next speaker when he is about to end his turn; the second claim is that the current recipient looks away before the projectable end of a speaker's turn in order to signal readiness to take the turn. Note that for "short utterances" such as "accompaniment signals, attempted interruptions, exclamations, short answers to questions", Kendon describes different patterns, for instance sustained mutual gaze in "short answers" and "short questions" (1973, p. 76).

To my knowledge, Kendon's second claim (concerning recipient non-gaze to signal claim to speakership after a next possible completion point, i.e. a practice of self-selection) has not been taken up in the literature, and there is no additional empirical evidence for it beyond Kendon's own study. However, his first result (that speaker gaze selects the next speaker) has been replicated, for instance by Streeck (2014). Indirectly, Kendon's finding is also supported by a study by Bavelas et al. (2002) who show that speaker gaze at a recipient prompts a (minimal) "listener's response". As will be argued below, speaker gaze can be understood as offering the turn to a recipient who, by producing a minimal response ("continuer"), declines this offer.

In another important study on gaze in dyadic face-to-face interaction, Rossano (2012) takes a somewhat different perspective from Kendon's in arguing "that gaze in interaction is not organized primarily by reference to turns at talk" but "in relation to sequences of talk and the development of courses of action" (Rossano et al., 2009, p. 191–192). For instance, mutual gaze withdrawal can signal sequence termination. To support his claim, Rossano presents evidence from Italian conversation that the duration and frequency of recipient's gaze at speaker varies with the action performed; for instance, recipients were found to maintain gaze at speakers during tellings, but not questions. Hence, there seem to be restrictions on Kendon's (as well as Goodwin's, 1981) findings, according to which the recipient is required to look at the speaker most of the time. It must be kept in mind here that Rossano's data differ from Kendon's in that participants were mostly handling objects while they were talking, such as photographs they were looking at.[8] This task diminishes the amount of recipient gaze at speakers, as recipients look at the object being talked about instead. Other findings by Rossano show that speakers systematically employ gaze as a way of "mobilizing" a recipient's response (Stivers & Rossano, 2010). If speakers gaze at a recipient towards the end of their turn, it is not only more likely that a response will ensue without delay; it is also observed that an action not responded to can be followed by a speaker's gaze to elicit the missing response (Rossano, 2013, Ch. 3). This finding is in line with Kendon's, as both are evidence for the link between current speaker's gaze and next speaker selection.

---

8. This is a general finding, cf. De Ruiter (2007) for gaze in task-based dialogues (picture task) where gaze is mostly used for this task and not for managing turn-taking. In his data, neither of the participants looked at the other much, i.e. only 7% of the time.

A typical sequence in which all these features can be found is given in the following extract:[9]

(2) (From Rossano et al., 2009, p. 194–195; extract from his ex. 1 = 2PCOMP 9:33). Original transcript. Two participants are looking at photographs taken during a trip to Rome by A

Italian 2PCOMP 9:33

01   (1.0)   ((both participants looking down at pictures))

02 →B: Soccia   quanto   hai pagato per entrar qua.
       Wow   how much have paid for enter here
       Wow how much did you pay to enter here.

03   (0.2)

04   B: Die [ci
                ten
                Te[n

05   A: [Poco. °Un euro. Due euro neanche
          Little. One euro two euro neither
          [Little.° One euro. Not even two euros

06   (.)

07   B: Ah   beh
            Oh   well
            Oh   well

08   (1.9)

---

9.   Transcription as above, but downward arrows included to mark participants' gaze at an object before them, here a photograph.

B asks A how much it cost him to climb up the church tower in Rome shown in the photograph (line 2). During this question, recipient A continues to look at the picture while the speaker raises his gaze from the picture and looks at the recipient (who, although looking down, can see B's gaze being directed at him in his peripheral vision). After a short silence, during which the speaker's gaze at the recipient is sustained, the question is expanded as the speaker suggests an answer, still gazing at the addressee and thereby eliciting an answer/confirmation from him. During the course of this expansion, the recipient raises his gaze and looks at the questioner (line 04). This mutual gaze is sustained through the answer (line 05) and a bit beyond (line 06). Then the questioner produces an acknowledgement token and gazes away. The sequence is dissolved when the co-participant averts his gaze as well (second part of line 07 and line 08).

Kendon and Rossano focus on dyadic interaction, not on multi-party inter-action. In the case of dyadic interaction, the issue is *when* a current speaker relin-quishes the turn and provides an opportunity for the other participant to speak. In multi-party interaction, the issue is also *which* of the co-participants will speak next. Kalma (1992), Lerner (2003) and Tiitinen & Rusuuvuori (2012) have shown that current speakers in multi-party interaction also employ gaze in order to select a next speaker out of various available 'candidates'.

But we need to go one step further. The "participant constellation" (Goffman, 1981) in a given moment of a conversational interaction is not only defined by who is the current (and next) speaker. It also involves the status of the non-speaking participants, which may be that of addressees of the speaker, of recipients, or neither of these two (cf. Clark & Carlson, 1982; Gibson, 2003). While addressee selection is done by the speaker, displays of recipiency are delivered by the recipient. The addressed party should actively display recipiency, but non-adressed parties may do so as well (cf. Holler & Kendrick, 2015; Kidwell, 1997).

The status of an addressee and that of a next speaker as selected by current speaker are often conflated. For instance, Vertegaal et al. (2001) use an experimental setting involving head-mounted eye trackers to measure the average amount of gaze by current speaker at one of three co-participants depending on whether the speak-ers addressed that person (or all three). (A speaker was taken to have addressed a co-participant if s/he said so when watching the recording of the interaction after-wards.) They found that the speaker looked at the addressed co-participant more than three times as often than at any of the other participants. If, on the other hand, the speaker intended to address all three co-participants, the average rate of looking at any one of them diminished substantially, while the total amount of looking at all participants increased. Vertegaal et al.'s study provides solid evidence that gaze is indeed functional for displaying who a current turn is directed at; however, it seems premature to argue on the basis of these results that this pattern will at the same time regulate who is "expected to speak" (2001, p. 301) next.

In the following, the function of gaze for addressee selection and for next-speaker selection will be strictly distinguished analytically, although the two may of course coincide, particularly in short utterances.

3.   Speaker gaze in three-party interaction: Addressee selection and next-speaker selection

If three-party interaction were a mere extension of two-party interaction, speaker gaze would select one particular co-participant both as the addressee and the next speaker of a turn. Each turn would be exclusively directed at one and not the other co-participant, thus selecting this one participant as the next speaker. An obvious case are short questions directed at one party and answered by that party, as in the following extract (3).

As in extract (1), the gaze configuration between the three speakers is schematically represented in topview with double (thick) arrows indicating gaze toward another participant. Two-sided arrows indicate mutual gaze. In addition, simple (thin) arrows are used to mark a participant's gaze away from the co-participants, either at some other point that can be shown in a topdown perspective (solid), or down/up (dotted). If the speaker or hearer looks at their hands or an object, the hand/object is designated by an iconic picture. The curled brackets once more indicate the duration of a given gaze pattern. Movements between fixations are interpolated unless they are slow, which is indicated by a space between the brackets. (See appendix for further details.) The segmental transcription follows GAT2 .[10]

Nanni (sitting left) asks Anni (in the middle) a simple information question, i.e. whether she applied to other universities. (Both Anni and Nanni are presently enrolled at the same university.) The question selects Anni as the only addressed co-participant by the use of a second person singular pronoun (*du*) combined with current-speaker-gaze for selecting the next speaker. Anni is also designated in this way as the *only* legitimate next speaker. While she anwers (in line 05), Nanni sustains her gaze on her. Anni herself averts her gaze toward the end of Nanni's question and continues to look away well into her answer (in line with the pattern described by Kendon, see above, discussion of Extr. 1). Toward the end (on 'emergency option'), she looks back at the questioner.

---

10. A summary of the GAT transcription conventions can be found at the end of Stukenbrock's chapter in this volume.

(3) DREIER-MÄDELS IV: 3:59-4:08/238.635 (seated as in picture 1 above)

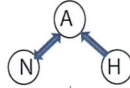

```
01 Nanni: [hast du dir eigentlich damals überlegt auch in KARLSruhe zu
           did you ever consider studying in Karlsruhe then
02 Anni:  [((sips a glass of water                                    ))
```

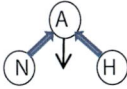

```
03 Nanni: [studieren an der pe ha?
           at the university of education?
04 Anni:  [((puts down glass of water))
```

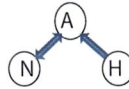

```
05 Anni:  JA,=aber des wär nur so: meine NOTh- (.) lösung;
          yes, but that would have just been like my   emergency   option
```

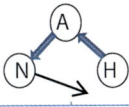

```
05 Nanni: hmHM,
```

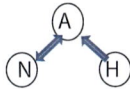

```
06 Anni:  [geWEsen.]

07 Nanni: [NEE ich hab] mich gar nich beWORben.
           no I didn't even apply.
```

During the sequence, the third, non-addressed participant (Hanni, sitting to the right) is not looked at by either Nanni or Anni. Non-addressed conversationalists usually display their participation in such an exchange by looking alternatingly at the momentary speaker (and sometimes, particularly in anticipation of turn-taking by the addressed speaker, also at the recipient; cf. Holler & Kendrick, 2015).[11] However, when this pattern is continued over several sequential steps, a multi-party constellation of four or more people is in danger of desintegrating into different focused interactions (schism), and in a three-party constellation, one of the participants is in danger of being marginalized. The marginalized conversationalist may then withdraw from the currently active dyad by gaze aversion,

---

11. As far as the video allows us to analyse her gaze, Hanni always looks at Anni, i.e. she does not follow the pattern described by Holler & Kendrick 2015.

signalling that s/he is no longer participating, and in an extreme case may become a bystander. If this pattern were dominant, multi-party interaction would be in permanent danger of dissolving into two-party interaction (as indeed argued by Stivers, 2015, and implied by Sacks, Schegloff & Jefferson, 1974, p. 712, who talk about a "last-as-next" bias in conversation). However, this is clearly not what we find. In fact, there is evidence that participants systematically employ practices to avoid schisms or marginalizations of speakers.

The most ubiquitous of these practices during an emerging turn are (1) for speakers to select *different* addressees alternatingly, or (2) to select *all* co-participants as addressees by looking at them alternatingly (Section 4).

In the first case, segments of a speaker's turn are designed specifically for the background knowledge of one participant but not the others, as shown in Goodwin's early work (Goodwin, 1981). Here, "recipient design" (Sacks & Schegloff, 1979) based on background knowledge selects an addressee. This addressee selection is also regularly accompanied by gaze at the speaker for whom the segment is designed. An example is the following:

(4) DREIER-MÄDELS II:0.23

```
01 Anni:    heute hab ich auf meInem em pe: DREI player,
            today on my MP3 player,
```

```
02          (.) in meinem GeSCHENkeordner?
            in my presents folder
```

```
03          (--)weil ich geb meinen em pe: DREI player immer an [so::-
            because I always give my MP3 player to                 like
                                                                [(((gesture
                                                                ,small ˅12))
```

```
            (.) ähm (.) an LEUte weiter un_dann machen die muSI:K drauf?=
            uhm to people and then they put music on it?
```

---

12. The gesture is done with the thumb and the crooked index finger forming a parallel, with the distance between the fingers depicting small size, presumably of the MP3 player.

```
04 Nanni:    ah oKE=ja.
             oh I see=yes.
```

```
05 Anni:     ääh::=      voll die SCHÖne: (.) muSIK entdeckt; (.)
             uhm         I discovered such beautiful music;
```

```
06           vielleicht KENNST du den; (.)
             maybe you know him;
```

```
07           reNE: oBRI:? (-)
```

```
08 Hanni:    [ʔmʔm;]

             [((shakes her head))]
```

Anni begins her turn with a turn segment for which Hanni is the addressee, as shown by her gaze. But before finishing the sentence, i.e. after *today on my MP3 player/ in my presents folder…*, and hence before a possible turn completion point is reached, she inserts a parenthetical turn segment (line 03), which is designed specifically for Nanni. In this parenthetical remark, she explains to Nanni that she often asks other people to transfer music onto her MP3 player, background information apparently not available to Nanni but known to Hanni. During this parenthetical insert, Anni, the speaker, withdraws her gaze from her former addressee Hanni and looks at Nanni (apart from a short word search at the end of line 03, during which she looks down at her hand with which she performs a gesture indicating size, presumably that of the player). Nanni acknowledges this background information, and hence her status as the recipient of that piece of information, in line 04 (*ah oKE = ja.*); but she cannot become the next speaker at this point, since Anni's main line in the news telling is not finished yet, and the initial sentence incomplete. After another short hesitation (beginning of line 05), Anni returns to this main line. The interrupted syntactic construction is continued and completed, and Hanni, the original addressee of the news telling, is once more chosen as its primary addressee through gaze. Lines 06/07 complete the turn by providing the referent (the name of the musician whose music Anni found so beautiful).

Anni mainly talks to Hanni, delivering some news to her (cf. the second person pronoun in the question in line 06); but for a well-defined insertion, she only addresses Nanni who does not have the same background knowledge as Hanni. Hence, the parenthetical insert has a recipient design different from that of the main line of the turn. These different designs do not affect next-speaker selection, however, as the insert does not occur in a position in which turn-taking could become an issue. Addressee selection is an issue, but next-speaker selection is not.

This suggests the following *hypothesis: addressee selection (by gaze) and next-speaker selection (by gaze) are temporally ordered. While addressees may vary during an emerging turn, the co-participant who is gazed at toward the end of a speaker's turn is the one who is selected as next speaker.* There are obvious logical alternatives; for instance, the designated next speaker may be the participant who the current speaker looks at in the beginning of the turn; or it might be the co-participant who is looked at most of the time. These, however, are not chosen by the speakers.

In Section 5 the relevance of turn-final gaze for next-speaker selection will be discussed further. In the next section, it will be shown that speakers systematically work against the reduction of a three-party to a two-party interaction through their gaze behavior.

4.   Speakers regularly address more than one co-participant simultaneously, although only one of them can be looked at at a time

We now turn to the second alternative, i.e. a current speaker wants to select *all* co-participants as addressees for a turn. As a speaker usually cannot look at all co-participants at the same time, the standard technique here is to shift gaze between them.[13] Gaze shift may occur just once or several times within a turn, as required by the turn's length (and presumably by other factors still to be investigated). During the emergence of the turn (other than towards its end), gaze shifts of this kind do not pre-empt next-speaker selection. Any of the addressed co-participants may be suggested as the next speaker by gaze when the current speaker approaches the transition relevant point.

---

13. The theoretically possible alternative of not looking at anybody seems to be rare in our culture.

4.1   Loosely structured sequential contexts

We start with two examples of sequentially weakly projecting turns. Here, the current speaker's action does not project a specific uptake by a co-participant.

In the first example, taken from a conversation among three young men, Roby argues that the rules for volleyball matches are not fair. During his longish turn, Roby repeatedly switches gaze between Koby and Toby. Both of his friends are addressed. They do not seem to share his concerns to the same extent, and it is only in line 16 that Toby responds and produces two agreement tokens. The emerging turn by Roby continues across various intonational phrase boundaries (indicated by line breaks) without being semantically and syntactically complete. It only reaches a first possible completion – and hence a first possible turn transition point – at the end of line 11.

(5) DREIER-Jungs I: 04:21–04:34

```
01    Roby:   [°h des is- (.)
                it is
02            [((raises left hand from rest position on his knee slightly))
```

```
03            [EIgenlich is des- ((gulps))
                actually it is
04            [((circling gesture with left hand, then hand back on knee))
```

```
05            [des kAnn_s eigentlich NICH sein dass du auch; (.)
                it doesn't make sense that you
              [((shrugs shoulders))
```

```
06            nie: während der saison WEISST,=
                never know during the season
```

07   [steigen jetzt FÜNF ab,
       is it five who are relegated
     [((shrugs shoulders))

08   vor allem (wenn de) gegen ABstieg spielst. (-)
       above all when you play against relegation.

09   [manchmal steigen FÜNF mannschaften ab un_dann heißt_s- (.)
       sometimes five teams are relegated and then again they say

10   Toby: [<<ppp>m>

11   Roby: ACH doch nur [drEi; (-)
             oh only three after all

12   Koby: [((smiles))
13

14   manchmal steigt gAr niemand ab;=
       sometimes nobody is relegated

15   [=des_is SO   [lächerlich [ey also;]
       it's so   *ridiculous and*
     [((raises both hands slightly and [lets them fall down))
16   Toby: [ja:, schon,
                                     yes, true

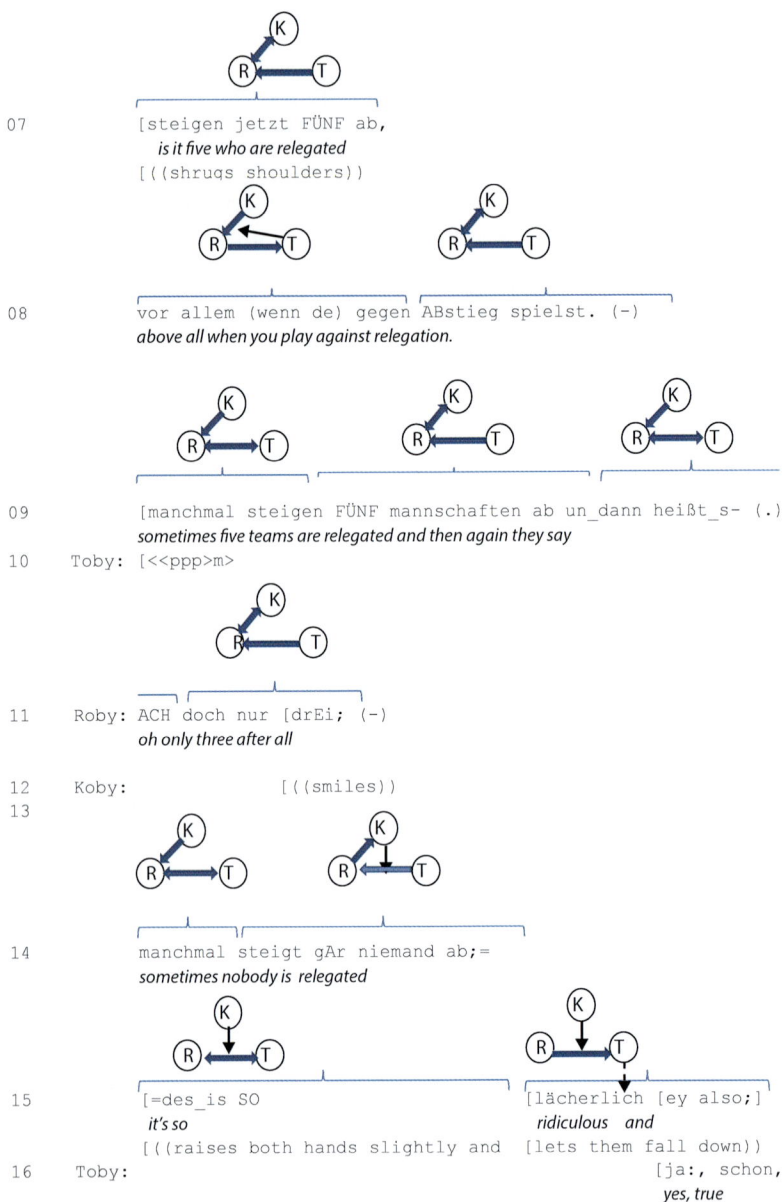

Let us look at Roby's gaze during this phase (lines 0–11). Although both co-participants are looking at him and thereby displaying their availability as recipients, he begins his turn with two restarts accompanied by a gaze shift from Toby to Koby and back again (lines 01–03). The third beginning in line 05 is accompanied by gaze at Toby, but after an intonational break at the end of line 05, Roby shortly looks at Koby during the production of *nie: während der saison* and then back at Toby during the production of the finite verb *weißt* (end of line 06). Probably because Toby looks down at the table for a short time at this moment, Roby again looks at Koby for the production of the complement clause in the format of a direct question (line 07). The turn format up to now projects another negated question which provides the alternative to 'is it five (teams) who are relegated?'. Instead of this alternative, Roby produces a kind of increment ('particularly…', line 08), during which he first gazes at Toby (who looks away) and then again at Koby. At this point, a turn completion point is reached. Toby, the co-participant last addressed by gaze, murmurs a hushed continuer.

The second example that develops in a parallel fashion is from the conversation between the three young women. Nanni is talking about her two brothers, who are very different. The turn is addressed to both Hanni and Anni. Nanni's gaze alternates between the two.

(6) DREIER-Mädels 3, 3:12

```
01 Nanni:   [der (.) Eine der s_FITness jetzt so macht,=
            that one (of my brothers) who now goes to the gym
02 Hanni:   [((holds a water bottle in her hand, ready to
```

```
03 Nanni:   [=der is so_n bisschen domiNANT,
            he is kind of dominating
04 Hanni:   [pour water into a glass))
```

```
05 Anni     [((nods and smiles))
06 Nanni:   [(.) °h= un:d-
                 a:nd
```

```
07 Hanni:   [((starts to pour water))
```

```
08 Nanni:   [(.) ja der andere is halt so [zuRÜCKhaltend;
            well the other one is just like reserved
09                                          [((shoulders jerk back))
10 Hanni:   [((pours water))
```

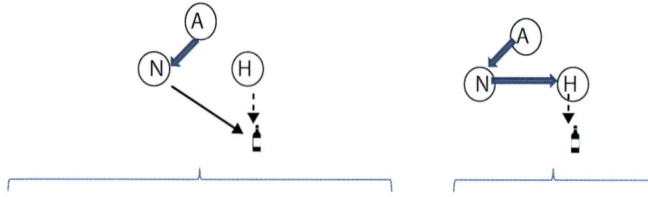

```
11 Nanni:   [un_des <<creaky voice>wa:r>- (.) SCHWIErig; (--)
             and that was                      difficult
12 Hanni:   [((pours water))
```

```
13 Nanni:   in der GRUNDschule so_n bisschen.
             in primary school a little.

14 Anni:    [Mhm.
15 Hanni:   [((screws top on bottle.))
```

```
16 Hanni:   [GLAUB                    ich.
             I can believe that.
17          [((wrinkles nose, while continuing to screw top on bottle))
```

Nanni compares her two brothers. One of them is presented as 'dominant' in lines 01/03. The segment is syntactically complete but ends with rising intonation, therefore projecting more to come. The speaker's gaze is first directed at Anni (line 03, with a short intermitted gaze away into the distance), who receipts the utterance with a nod and a smile. During a micro-pause and an inhalation, Anni turns to Hanni, co-selecting her as the addressee of her turn; however, Hanni at this moment starts to pour water into her glass and therefore has to look down at her hands to coordinate her movements. Nanni therefore cannot secure this recipient's gaze. While she produces the second part of her turn, describing the second more 're-served' brother (08, 11) and his 'difficult' situation, she first looks at Anni and then at Hanni's glass and again at Hanni's face, who still cannot look back (second part of line 11). During the emerging turn up to this point (at which a turn transition might occur), the speaker has looked at one of her co-participants three times and at the other one two times – despite the fact that the latter was not available for reciprocating gaze due to her manipulation of a bottle and glass that needed her visual attention.

As the turn's projecting force is weak, it does not receive immediate uptake (also perhaps because the last looked-at co-participant, Hanni, is still looking at her glass and handling the bottle). Nanni therefore expands it syntactically (cf. the increment 'in primary school a little'), while her gaze turns back to Anni (line 13). Anni responds with a continuer *(Mhm)* and looks away (line 14), thereby proposing to close the sequence. Nanni once again looks at Hanni who now acknowledges Nanni's assessment of her 'reserved' brother's situation as 'difficult' (line 16: 'I can believe that'), thus closing the sequence.

4.2 Tightly structured sequential contexts

Extracts (5) and (6) presented longer turns containing descriptions, tellings or reports leading up to or implicitly expressing an evaluation. Typically, they are internally complex, can be expanded and make no clearly projectable next activity by a co-participant relevant. (In the examples above, co-participants' activities were restricted to acknowledgements, agreements or weak co-assessments.) They can be described as loosely structured sequences. We now look at two extracts in which turn-internal gaze shifts occur in tighter sequential environments.

In the first example, the three Sports students talk about their study program, i.e. whether it is mandatory to include therapeutic gymnastics. Koby claims that this is the case but both Toby and Roby disagree. We focus on Roby's disagreement in lines 03/04/07-09.

(7) DREIER-Jungs I: 15.33-15.43.5

```
01   Koby: die is (.) IMmer mit drin in (vau eff Er)therapie;=
            it is         always included in (VFR) therapy;

02         wenn du en BAChelor machscht;=
            when you do a bachelor;

03   Roby: NEE;=
            no

04         [eben NICH;=
            it isn't
```

```
05     Toby:  [nee,=du kannscht (Dir ja)
               no, you can ( )
06            [((slight headshake))
```

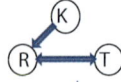

```
07     Roby:  des hab [ICH damals AUCH] gedacht;
               I also used to think that;
08                    [((left hand gesture))]
```

```
09            des war voll der ´FAKE;
              it was totally wrong;
```

Koby's gaze in lines 01/02 is directed at Toby, but it is Roby who contradicts first (line 03) with a simple *nee* 'no',[14] and then reformulates his disagreement in line 04 (*eben nicht* 'it isn't'). Overlapping Koby's second disagreement, Toby also disagrees (05). Explicit disagreements are usually followed by an account, which both disagreeing parties start to deliver now. Toby begins his account in line 05 but breaks off in favor of Roby, who gives his account in lines 07/09, arguing that he also thought that therapeutic gymnastics would be an obligatory part of their study program when he began his studies, but then realized that this was not true. In sequential terms, disagreeing with a speaker means that the turn is addressed at this speaker. Roby contradicts Koby, who is therefore his addressee for this turn on sequential grounds. But at the same time, he uses gaze to integrate Toby in the sequence. This is done by turning from Koby to Toby in the end of line 07, whom he looks at until the end of the extract.

In the second extract, we find the female students talking in a tight sequential context. The topic here is the music streaming platform Spotify. In this sequence Anni is in danger of becoming marginalized, as Hanni and Nanni are talking about a topic she knows nothing about (i.e. regulations for using Spotify before she began using it). We focus on Nanni's turn in lines 06–07.

(8) DREIER-Mädels II 2:23

```
01  Nanni:   FRÜher,
             before,
```

---

14. This case will be discussed below in Section 6.

```
02        war doch mal so_n LImit,
          there was once like a limit
```

```
03        dass man IRgendwie nu:r; (.)
          that you could somehow only
```

```
04        zwanzig [STUNden oder so (.)   [hören durfte,        ]
          listen to twenty hours or so
05  Hanni:           [!STIMMT!;          [!ZE:HN! waren des] doch [nu::r;=
                      right!              ten I think it was only
06  Nanni:                                                        [JA: un
```

```
          dann, (.)
          yes and then
```

```
07        des zÄhlt aber [NICH mehr; ne?]=
          but this isn't the case now any longer; is it?
08  Anni:                [des war noch VOR meiner]   [spOtifypha::se;
                         this was before my spotify phase
09  Hanni:                                           [ja:,
                                                     yes
10        ja DOCH ((…))
          no that's true
```

Nanni remembers that music from Spotify could only be listened to for 20 hours at a go (lines 01–03). She looks at Hanni, who she knows from the previous conversation to have used the streaming platform as well. Hanni agrees enthusiastically and in overlap, displaying her own remembering of the same restriction (04), but immediately goes on to correct Nanni's version (Spotify could only be listened to for 10 hours in her opinion, not for 20; cf. line 05). The turn goes back to Nanni after line 05 to confirm or disconfirm Hanni's correction. Up to this point in the sequence, the two speakers have been linked to each other by mutual gaze. Anni, the third participant, has done what an attentive third party should do (cf. Holler & Kendrick, 2015): she has followed the sequence between Nanni and Hanni by looking at the respective speaker.

Once more in overlap, Nanni confirms the correction and sets out to describe the changes in streaming policy that have taken place in the meantime (line 06, 'yes but then'). During this segment, she looks at Anni, the participant not involved in the sequence so far. Anni at this point is still monitoring Hanni with her gaze. Not finding a gazing recipient, Nanni reorients her gaze toward Hanni in line 07. The segment ends with a question tag (*ne?*), requiring confirmation from Hanni. Before Hanni can provide this next sequential step (which she eventually does with *ja* in line 09), Anni actively intervenes with an overlapping comment that this was all 'before her Spotify phase'.

Other than in extracts (5) and (6), the turns during which speakers in extracts (7) and (8) alternate gaze are short turns that occur embedded into a tightly organized sequential context in which the speakers are involved with one of the other two participants. Nevertheless, they take care to include the third participant as well by looking at him/her at least briefly.

In sum, we have seen that current speakers actively keep a three-party conversation from turning into a two-party conversation by addressing both co-participants by gaze. Multiple-addressee status is achieved despite the fact that a speaker can only look at one co-participant at a time (in the spatial constellation we are dealing with here). Gaze alternation for multiple addressee selection occurs in loose as well as in tight sequential contexts. It is not identical with next-speaker selection on the basis of sequential structure.

5.   The addressee looked at toward the end of a turn constructional unit is given privileged access to the following turn

In the data under consideration here – i.e. three-party conversations in which gaze is free to deal with matters of turn-taking – the co-participant last gazed at in a TCU by the speaker has a privileged status with respect to turn-taking (all other factors being equal). Even if there was multiple addressee selection in the current turn, this co-participant will most often[15] provide the next turn. Examples can be found in extracts 5 (lines 11–12 and 15–16), 6 (lines 03–05 and 13–14), and 8 (lines 04–05, 05–06) above. The verbal response can be a continuer by which the looked-at participant signals that s/he is not interested in taking the turn (i.e. gaze elicits the continuer, cf. Bavelas, Coates & Johnson, 2002) or a full next turn.

In this section, qualitative evidence will be presented for the claim that participants interpret last speaker's gaze as an offer or proposal, and sometimes even as an appeal to take the turn.

---

15.   See Tiitinen & Ruusuvori (2012) as well as Kalma (1992) for quantitative evidence.

5.1 Micro-negotiations of turn-taking by gaze

One piece of evidence can be found in micro-negotiations about who will take the turn. An obvious case are answers to questions. Usually, the co-participant gazed at last answers (first) after a question with multiple addressee design:

(9)   DREIER-Mädels II, 4:395

```
01 Anni:    un da hab ich [des BUCH gelesen-(.)
            and then I read this book
02                        [((presentative hand gesture, held throughout the
                           extract))
```

```
03          eine für VIER?
            one for four?
```

```
04          KENNT ihr des?
            do you (PLURAL) know it
```

```
05 Hanni:   ne:e;(0.5)
            no
```

```
06 Anni:    ni[ch?
            no?
07 Nanni:     [((small headshake))
```

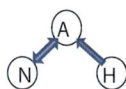

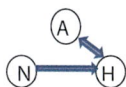

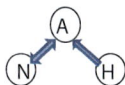

Anni asks whether a certain book is known to her two friends. The question emerges in several steps; in 01/02, the name of the book is presented with try-marked (upward) intonation at the end of the TCU. Anni's gaze is directed at Nanni, who, however, does not respond verbally; Anni then turns to Hanni (line 03) and expands her turn with an explicit question ('do you know it?'). Although the second person plural pronoun in the question selects both co-participants as potential answerers, Anni's gaze is on Hanni. And indeed, Hanni provides the projected second pair part (line 05: *ne:e*). While this answer is produced, Anni turns back to Nanni again and keeps her gaze on her even during the following half-second silence, now selecting her as the answerer. Nanni responds with a faint headshake (line 07). All in all, Anni shifts her gaze twice in order to select answerers in a certain order.

In addition, there is another pattern of micro-negotiation of next speakership involved in this example, this time related to recipient's gaze. As we have seen, Nanni, who is first selected by Anni as the answerer after the try-marked book name in line 03, nevertheless does not take the turn. As a response to Anni's question and gaze, she instead directs her gaze at Hanni (between lines 03 and 04), thereby 'delegating' the role of answerer to her. Averting gaze from the questioner to the co-addressed alternative answerer signals (to the questioner and to the potential other answerer) that Nanni is not able to provide the answer. The same pattern can also be observed in the following extract from the same conversation:

(10)   DREIER-Mädels II, 2:51 (topic: Soundcloud, another streaming platform and alternative to Spotify)

```
01 Nanni:    aber (.) da is doch Immer nu:r so: (.)
             but I think they just have like
```

```
             eh sin doch meIstens nur so RE::mix un sowas o:ben;=oder?
             uhm there're usually only like remixes and things like that on there; aren't there?
```

```
02 Anni:     keine AH[nu:ng.]
             no idea.
03 Hanni:            [ich glaub] (.) SCHON (.) viele:;
                      I think        quite       a few

04           (-) und, (.)
             and

05           ich glaub auch viele nEwcome:::r die: noch Überhaupt nicht

             beKANNT sin;=
             I think also many newcomers who are still not at all known
```

Nanni says she believes that Soundcloud mainly plays remixes of the songs she would like to hear; she finishes her statement with a question tag by which she asks for confirmation of her view (line 01). Her gaze is directed at Anni who is thereby invited to be the next speaker and answerer. However, Anni does not seem to know whether this is true (as she confesses in line 02). She defers the question to Hanni who will eventually confirm Nanni's view, at least tentatively, in lines 03–05. To do so, she averts her gaze from Nanni during Nanni's question tag (*oder*, end of line 01) and turns it toward Hanni. Note that Hanni, the knowing party, does not start to answer immediately after Nanni's request for confirmation, but respects Nanni's gaze which selects Anni, and not herself, as the (first) answerer; only after having been invited by Anni's gaze does she give the answer. This is clear evidence for participants' orientation to gaze as a relevant cue for turn-taking.[16]

As a final example of micro-negotiation of next-speakership, consider the following extract:

(11)   DREIER-Jungs II, 20:32

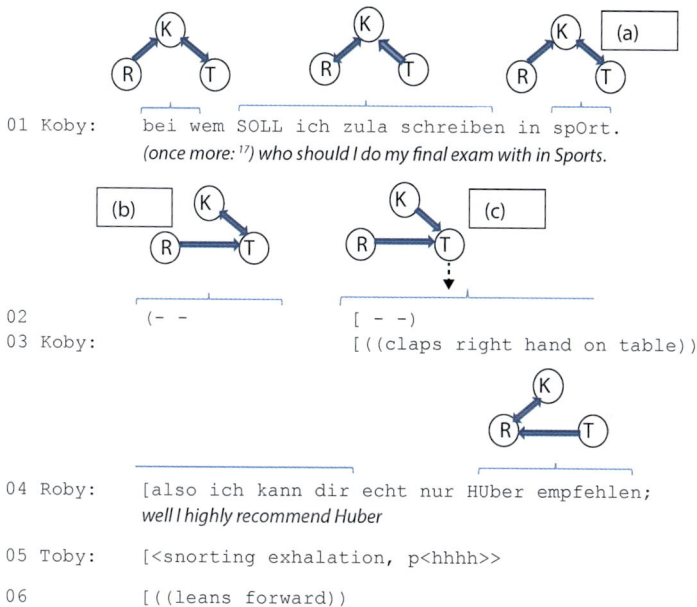

```
01 Koby:    bei wem SOLL ich zula schreiben in spOrt.
            (once more: 17) who should I do my final exam with in Sports.
```

```
02          (- -              [ - -)
03 Koby:                      [((claps right hand on table))
```

```
04 Roby:    [also ich kann dir echt nur HUber empfehlen;
            well I highly recommend Huber

05 Toby:    [<snorting exhalation, p<hhhh>>

06          [((leans forward))
```

Koby's question in line 01 regarding who he should choose as an examiner is accompanied by fast gaze shifts, first from Toby to Roby, and at the end of the turn back to Toby (a). Toby is hence selected as the privileged respondent. However, after about 0.4 seconds during which Koby (as well as the third participant, Roby) keep looking at Toby (b), Toby lowers his gaze and thereby signals that he does not want or does not know how to answer (c). At this point, Roby starts an answer (line 04). Although he is not the invited next speaker, he can answer Koby's question in a legitimate way at this point, as the speaker selected by the current speaker by gaze

---

16. It is worth mentioning that this micro-negotiation takes place before Anni responds verbally in line 02. At this point, Hanni and Nanni have already established mutual gaze.

17. The reading 'once more' is due to the exceptional location of the focal stress on the auxiliary *soll* instead of the canonical stress on the direct object (so-called verum focus).

has visibly declined to do so. Note that the shift from the last gaze constellation in line 01 to the second one in line 02 takes less than a second:

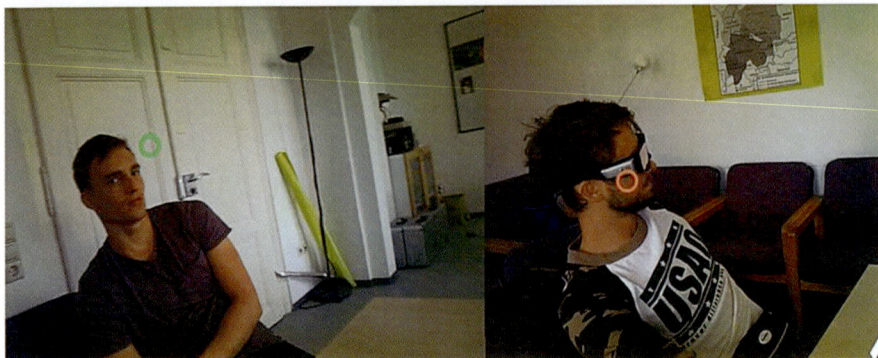

Figure 2a. Koby looks at Toby (left cursor), Roby looks at Koby (right cursor); Toby (left) looks at Koby (not shown). Time 20:39:000

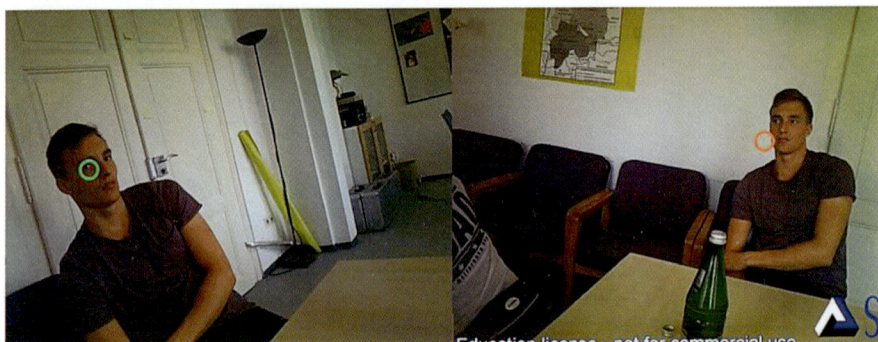

Figure 2b. Koby (left cursor) and Roby (right cursor) both look at Toby. Time 20:39:600

Figure 2c. Koby (left cursor) and Roby (right cursor) look at Toby; Toby looks down. Time 20:39:900

5.2 Gaze and the timing of turn-transition

Exact duration and timing is a highly relevant parameter in determining the effectiveness of a speaker's gaze in choosing a next speaker. In this section, two extracts are considered in which timing differs radically and hence has different conversational effects.

A first observation is that in terminal overlaps, it is regularly the last looked-at party who is responsible for this overlap, not the third participant. In other words: Being looked at seems to be interpreted as a license to start a next turn early. Once more, this shows that participants make use of and orient to gaze as a turn-allocation technique.

(12)   DREIER-Mädels II, 8:05 (about what they wrote in their first diaries)

```
01 Nanni:    ich hab EHer so:; (.) geschrie:ben was ich alles [geMACHT hab.=
             I mostly wrote all those things I did

02 Anni:                                                      [((short laugh))
```

```
03 Nanni:    <<laughing>> nich so meine geFÜ:Hle sondern;> (.)
             not like my feelings but
```

```
04           [°h= ha:]: dann bin ich AUFgestanden;
             well then I got up

05 Hanni:    [((short laughter))
```

```
06 Nanni:    <<laughing>hab geFRÜH:stückt und [so_n zEug oder so.]>

07 Anni:                                      [des is MEIN altes tag-] (.)
                                              this is my old di-

08           mein Erstes tagebu:ch AUCH so.
             my first diary the same.
```

Nanni addresses both Hanni and Anni by gaze when she talks about the things she wrote in her first diary (01–06). The co-participant who is looked at last, however, is Anni (from the end of line 04 onward). Anni indeed takes the turn, and she does so well before Nanni has ended hers, but at a point where the remainder is more or less predictable (see Jefferson, 2004, on such "recognition points"). Of course, for such an early onset to occur, the sequential structure must be one in which terminal overlaps make sense, such as in 'enthusiastic agreements'. But the question of who produces these 'enthusiastic agreements' when several co-participants are addressed is not settled by this sequential structure alone. Rather, the early timing of Anni's turn in 07–08 seems to be licensed by the fact that she is looked at by the speaker toward the end of her turn.

   In Extr. (13), the opposite of a terminal overlap is observed, i.e. a delayed up-take. When the current speaker's gaze remains on a particular co-participant during such a delay, this becomes a particularly strong cue, not only inviting, but also urging the looked-at participant to take the turn:

(13)   DREIER-Jungs II, 9:31 (about the bachelor program the participants are enrolled in)

01 Roby: die gehen ja davon AUS,
            they assume

02   dass du dir Alles was du meTHOdisch mItnimmsch, (-)
            that whatever you learn methodologically

03   im bAchelorstudium alles aus den SPORTarten rausziehst;
            during your bachelor degree, you extract it all from the (different) sports

05   (0.8)

06 Toby: ja, SCHON,
            yes, true

Roby selects both co-participants as his addressees (cf. the gaze shift to Koby in line 02), but toward the end of his turn (line 03), he looks at Toby. Toby, however, does not produce any response but looks away (putting on a 'thinking face') for 0.8 seconds (line 05). During this time, Toby keeps his gaze fixed on him. It is this sustained gaze that finally elicits a response: Toby agrees with Roby's opinion, albeit without much enthusiasm (line 06). Roby's gaze has "mobilized" response (in the sense of Stivers & Rossano, 2010).

6. Why speaker's gaze is not always strong enough to select the next speaker

As shown in the previous section, speaker's gaze at one participant at the end of a turn is an interactionally relevant cue for the selection of next speakers. Nevertheless, there are also cases in which the co-participant selected by current speaker's gaze is not the next speaker; rather, another participant self-selects.[18] Some of these cases can be accounted for by the sequential unfolding of the conversation. An interesting sequential context is, for instance, emphatic agreements.

In the following extract, both co-participants compete (in overlap) for the turn after Anni has delivered a strong assessment, although only one of them (Nanni) has been selected by gaze during the TCU ending. The co-participant who is suggested as the next speaker by the current speaker's gaze – i.e. Nanni – even starts to speak slightly after the non-selected one (Hanni).

(14)   DREIER-Mädels II, 00:53 (about Aubry's music)

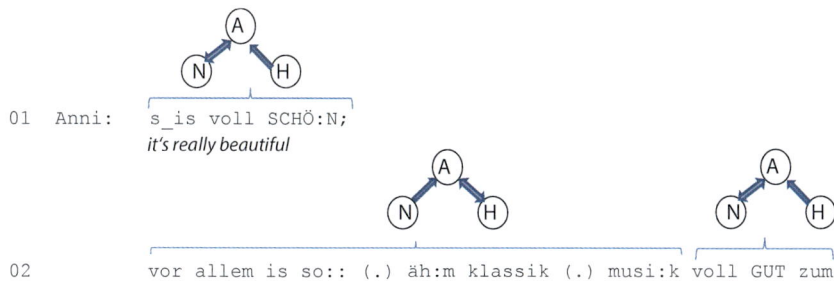

01   Anni: s_is voll SCHÖ:N;
             it's really beautiful

02   vor allem is so:: (.) äh:m klassik (.) musi:k voll GUT zum

---

18. An example for this was already given above (Extr. 8, lines 01–02).

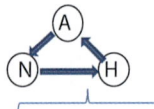

```
                    LERnen. (-)
                    in particular uhm classical music is really good when studying .
```

```
03  Hanni:    j[a: STIMMT;]
               yes, right
04  Nanni:     [(ne:)  STIMMT;]
               (no), right
05             [((nods))
```

Both Hanni and Nanni want to agree with the current speaker, and for one of them to withhold this agreement until the other one has delivered hers (or to even re-frain from delivering it) could be interpreted as disagreement implicative. It seems that the preference for agreements to be delivered quickly wins out here over eye communication: preferred sequential structure overrides gaze.[19]

A similar priority of action over gaze can be observed in the following extract from a place description. It is part of a longer sequence in which Nanni explains the location of a friend's new apartment. Both Hanni and Anni are addressed co-participants and take part in establishing place reference, trying to identify the location:

(15)   DREIER-Mädels III, 6:06-16

```
01 Nanni:    [da is doch dieser BU:CHladen.
             there's this bookshop.
02           [((left hand slightly raised, palm open facing Hanni, held till
             end of line 06))
03 Hanni:    [((right index finger at mouth, 'thinking gesture', until
             beginning of line 10))
```

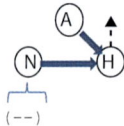

```
04           (--)
```

---

19. It will be noticed, though, that even in this case, there is a slight hitch in the temporal unfold-ing of the sequence which may reflect the privileged status of the last gazed-at speaker: Nanni (who is looked at by Anni at the end of her turn) hesitates slightly to produce her agreement and looks at Hanni during this hesitation (see end of line 02), not at Anni. Hanni then starts about 0.2 seconds before Nanni. This can be interpreted as an instance of micro-coordination in which Nanni suggests that Hanni deliver the first agreement instead of herself, the party who has privileged access to next speakership.

05 Anni: du   [KOMMSCH
              you   *come*

06   [((starts gesture with both hands))

07 Nanni: [dIe
                     the

         geSCHÄFte sin dann [glei?
08   *shops are then just*   [((pointing gesture with right hand
                          waving straight ahead))

09   ähm da ISCH doch [so ne:: (.) STRA   Sse   und [links
         uhm there's this street and left and right there are like shops.

10   [((gesture depicting ,running' street by
                          lateral movement of left hand))
11   [((gesture transforms
                               into two separate
         sin und rechts so geSCHÄFte.   ,putting movements',
                               ,left' and ,right'))

12 Hanni: also eInfach [die die WEIterführt. (-)
         so just the one that leads on.
13   [((gesture with right arm waving to right side))

14   [nach [litten-
         to (name of neighborhood, broken off within word)
15   [((same waving gesture repeated))

16 Nanni: [ja.
         yes.

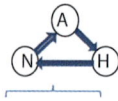

```
17            [genau.
              exactly.

18 Hanni:     [ja.
              yes.
```

Eye communication is highly complex in this extract, as gaze is not only used for turn-taking. Participants also follow some of their gestures by gaze (see lines 05 and 09), and one of them puts on a 'thinking face' among other things by looking up at the ceiling (Hanni in 04, 05). Nevertheless, a gaze pattern is visible that contradicts our claim that the last looked-at participant will take the turn next. During her spatial description, Nanni first looks at Hanni who, instead of acknowledging the place reference to 'that book shop', signals through her facial expression that she cannot identify the referent (lines 01–04). After a short silence and an attempt by Anni to reformulate the place description (which Nanni interrupts), Nanni turns to Anni (07–11). During her next, densely structured multimodal turn component ('uhm there's this street and left and right there are like shops') Nanni mostly looks at Anni, occasionally also at her own gesture and away. Hanni is not addressed by gaze. Nevertheless, it is she who eventually volunteers an understanding check by reformulating Nanni's description (lines 12–14) and who is finally successful in establishing reference.

Again it seems that the task at hand – establishing joint reference – is given priority over speaker's gaze in turn allocation. Both Hanni and Anni are visibly engaged in finding the place reference. Both have been addressed by Nanni. It is the participant who can solve the interactional problem at hand who speaks (first), not the one who was addressed by gaze by the previous speaker toward the end of the turn.

7. Discussion

In this paper, it has been argued that in three-party interaction, gaze is systematically used for addressee selection and for next-speaker selection (turn-allocation). These two functions of gaze overlap, but are not the same. In multi-party conversations, current speakers regularly look at co-participants alternatingly in order to select them as addressees of the turn. For next-turn allocation, on the other hand, it is only the current speaker's gaze at the end of the TCU that counts. More often than not, it is the gazed-at co-participant who will speak next. Gaze at the TCU's end was shown to be used by current speakers to elicit the gazed-at party's production of minimal responses, but also of full next turns. Gaze as a current-speaker-selects-next technique also increases the chances that this co-participant will start speaking before the current speaker has finished the turn (terminal overlap). Sustained gaze at a co-participant who withholds a response after a possible completion point is a particularly efficient technique to elicit this response.

However, it is not always the participant thus selected by the current speaker who takes the turn. For instance, participants who are offered the turn can be observed to 'hand on' the offer to speak to the third party by gaze. In a more competitive vein, a next speaker may self-select even though s/he is not invited to speak by current speaker's gaze. Further research is needed to investigate the sequential contexts in which this happens. It seems that the rule that the last gazed-at co-participant should be the next speaker is rather weak so that the contingencies of sequence structure can license speaker self-selection relatively easily.

Taking gaze into account as a technique for next-speaker selection has several consequences for the turn-taking system as described in conversation analysis. Gaze clearly offers the turn to a co-participant, but when used alone, it is less effective than verbal or multimodal techniques of next-speaker selection (such as the use of names as address terms or second person pronouns in tandem with gaze). Gaze is a ubiquitous resource in face-to-face interaction, and not restricted to turns in which certain actions are performed (such as first parts of adjacency pairs). As such, it shifts the boundary between next-speaker selection by current speaker, and self-selection. Self-selection in the sense of Sacks et al. (i.e. as a hierarchically subordinated option only in play once the current speaker has not used his or her rights to select a next speaker) becomes considerably less frequent. On the other hand, the number of competing cases becomes much higher, since a participant may self-select although the current speaker has gaze-selected another participant as next speaker. As the force of gaze as a selection technique is comparatively weak, the boundary between step (rule) one and two of the turn-taking system becomes blurred.

Acknowledgments

I wish to thank an anonymous reviewer for a number of valuable comments on a previous version.

References

Bavelas, J. B., Coates, L. & Johnson, T. (2002). Listener responses as a collaborative process: The role of gaze. *Journal of Communication*, 52, 566–580. https://doi.org/10.1111/j.1460-2466.2002.tb02562.x

Clark, H. H. & Carlson, Thomas B. (1982). Hearers and speech acts. *Language*, 58, 332–373. https://doi.org/10.1353/lan.1982.0042

De Ruiter, J. P. (2007). Some multimodal signals in humans. In I. Van de Sluis, M. Theune, E. Reiter, & E. Krahmer (Eds.), *Proceedings of the Workshop on Multimodal Output Generation (MOG 2007)*, 141–148.

Gibson, D. R. (2003). Participation shifts: order and differentiation in group conversation. *Social Forces*, 81(4), 1335–1381. https://doi.org/10.1353/sof.2003.0055

Goffman, E. (1981). Footing. In: E. Goffman, *Forms of Talk* (pp. 124–159). Philadelphia: University of Pennsylvania Press.

Goodwin, C. (1981). *Conversational Organization: Interaction between Speakers and Hearers.* New York etc.: Academic Press.

Holler, J. & Kendrick, K. (2015). 'Unaddressed participants' gaze in multi-person interaction: Optimizing recipiency. *Frontiers in Psychology*, 6 (98). https://doi.org/10.3389/fpsyg.2015.00098.

Jefferson, G. (2004). A sketch of some aspects of orderly overlap in natural conversation. In: G. Lerner (Ed.), *Conversation Analysis: Studies from the First Generation* (pp 43–59). Amsterdam: Benjamins. https://doi.org/10.1075/pbns.125.05jef

Kalma, A. (1992). Gazing in triads: a powerful signal in floor apportionment. *British Journal of Social Psychology* 31(1), 21–39. https://doi.org/10.1111/j.2044-8309.1992.tb00953.x

Kendon, A. (1967). Some functions of gaze direction in social interaction. *Acta Psychologica* 26, 22–63. https://doi.org/10.1016/0001-6918(67)90005-4

Kendon, A. (1973). The role of visible behavior in the organization of social interaction. In: M. Cranach & I. Vine (Eds.), *Social Communication and Movement: Studies of Interaction and Expression in Man and Chimpanzee* (pp 29–74). New York: Academic Press.

Kidwell, M. (1997). Demonstrating recipiency: knowledge displays as a resource for the unaddressed participant. *Applied Linguistics* 8(2), 85–96.

Lerner, G. (2003). Selecting next speaker: The context sensitive operation of a context-free organization. *Language in Society* 32, 177–201. https://doi.org/10.1017/S004740450332202X

Rossano, F. (2012). *Gaze behavior in face-to-face interaction.* PhD MPI Psycholinguistics, Nijmegen.

Rossano, F. (2013). Gaze in conversation. In J. Sidnell & T. Stivers (Eds.), *The Handbook of Conversation Analysis* (pp. 308–329). Hoboken: Blackwell Publishing Ltd.

Rossano, F., Brown, P., & Levinson, S. C. (2009). Gaze, questioning and culture. In: J. Sidnell (Ed.), *Conversation Analysis: Comparative Perspectives* (pp. 187–249). Cambridge: CUP. https://doi.org/10.1017/CBO9780511635670.008

Sacks, H., Schegloff, E. A., & Jefferson, G. (1974). A simplest systematics for the organization of turn taking for conversation. *Language* 50(4), 696–735. https://doi.org/10.1353/lan.1974.0010

Sacks, H., & Schegloff, Emanuel A. (1979). Two preferences in the organization of reference to persons in conversation and their interaction. In Psathas, G. (Ed.), *Everyday Language* (pp. 15–21). New York: Academic Press.

Selting, M. et al. (2011). A system for transcribing talk-in-interaction: GAT 2. *Gesprächsforschung* 12, 1–51.

Stivers, T. & Rossano, F. (2010). Mobilizing response. *Research on Language and Social Interaction* 43(1), 3–31. https://doi.org/10.1080/08351810903471258

Stivers, T. (2015). *Conversation is built for two.* Paper presented at 14th IPrA, University of Antwerp, Belgium.

Streeck, J. (2014). Mutual gaze and recognition: Revisiting Kendon's 'Gaze direction in two-person interaction'. In M. Seyfeddinipur & M. Gullberg (Eds.), *From Gesture in Conversation to Gesture as Visible Utterance: Essays in Honor of Adam Kendon* (pp. 35.55). Amsterdam: Benjamins.

Tiitinen, S. & Ruusuvuori, J. (2012). Engaging parents through gaze: speaker selection in three-party interactions in maternity clinics. *Patient Education and counseling* 89(1), 38–43. https://doi.org/10.1016/j.pec.2012.04.009

Vertegaal, R., Slagter, R., van der Veer, G., & Nijholt, A. (2001). Eye gaze patterns in conversation: There is more to conversational agents than meets the eyes. *Proc. SIGCHI Conference on Human Factors in Computing Systems* 3(1), 301–308.

Transcription conventions for gaze (the remainder of the segmental and multimodal transcription follows GAT2, see Selting et al., 2011)

⟹	Direction of gaze from one participant at another.
⟺	Mutual gaze between two participants.
⟶	Gaze not directed at another participant (top-down perspective).
⋮ ↑	Gaze up or down.
⋮	Gaze down at an object (here: the participant's own hands).
🖐	
┌──────┴──────┐	Extension of a gaze constellation with respect to the transcription below it.

Examples:

	K and R mutually gaze at each other, while T looks at R.
	A gazes at N, H gazes at A, N looks away to the right of H.
	R and T look at K, while K looks away between R and T.
	A looks at N, and N looks at H. H looks down at an object (here: at a bottle).

CHAPTER 10

Gaze as a predictor for lexical and gestural alignment

Bert Oben

University College Leuven Limburg / KU Leuven

This chapter provides evidence for the role gaze might have on behaviour at another multimodal level of behaviour, viz. alignment (or copying behaviour) of hand gestures and lexical items. In a corpus of dyadic interactions we demonstrate that gaze behaviour affects alignment behaviour differently at the lexical than at the gestural level: if a speaker is looking at an addressee's face while uttering a target word, this significantly increases the probability that the addressee will use that same later in the conversation. If a speaker is looking at an addressee's face while performing a target gesture, there is no correlation with subsequent gesture production by that addressee. However, if an addressee looked at a gesture made by a speaker, this gesture was significantly more often used by that addressee later in the conversation (compared to situations in which the addressee was not looking at that gesture). We argue that the difference in gaze behaviour between lexical and gestural alignment cases might be explained by the dual function of eye gaze in interaction, viz. gaze for visual perception and gaze for signalling meaning.

Keywords: conversation, dual eye-tracking, alignment, gesture, face-to-face

1. Introduction

1.1   Eye gaze during conversation

Eye gaze can serve many different functions during face-to-face conversation. In the early works on the role of eye gaze in interactional settings (mainly Argyle & Cook, 1976 and Kendon, 1967) the focus was not on the *inter*actional coupling of eye gaze, but on the *intra*personal coupling of it. For example, it was studied how eye gaze correlates with one's own speech, but not how it correlates with the speech or gaze of the conversational partner. More recently however, researchers are investigating interactional aspects of gaze behaviour. A first topic in this respect

https://doi.org/10.1075/ais.10.10obe

is that of shared[1] gaze. One of the basic features of interaction is the joint focus of attention of co-participants. One correlate of this basic feature is shared gaze, i.e. the joint visual focus on relevant aspects of the context (e.g. referents that are the current topic of conversation). This type of gaze alignment in which interlocutors adapt their gaze behaviour to that of their partner has been discussed in several recent studies (Dale et al., 2011; Hadelich & Crocker, 2006; Oben, 2015; Richardson & Dale, 2005; Richardson, Dale & Kirkham, 2007). The research question in these studies typically boils down to 'do interlocutors look at the same thing at the same time?'. The rate and the speed with which interlocutors in a joint task focus on the same referents has been shown to correlate with task performance (Brennan et al., 2008; Neider et al., 2010), shared knowledge (Richardson et al., 2007, 2009) and duration of the conversation (Hadelich & Crocker, 2006; Dale et al., 2011).

A second topic in research on interactional aspects of gaze behaviour (as opposed to intrapersonal aspects), is that of gaze cueing. This can be defined as the effect that cueing a target (i.c. by looking at it) has on the gaze behaviour of an addressee. It is, put colloquially, the fact that looking at something makes other people look at that same thing too. The crucial difference between gaze cueing and the shared gaze described in the previous paragraph, is that gaze cueing can only occur if interlocutors can see each other. Except for Oben (2015), in all of the studies on shared gaze described above, interlocutors were separated from each other, i.e. they were not able to see each other (because they were looking at a computer screen or because they were physically separated). Their shared gaze is a residue of their verbal interaction. Interlocutors are looking at the objects because they are talking about them, not because their conversational partner is looking at them. Crucial to gaze cueing is that interlocutors are fixating an object, not only because of the verbal interaction, but because their partner is fixating that object. Studies on the gaze cueing effect, which date back to early work by Posner et al. (1980), stress its role for joint attention in interaction (Emery, 2000; Frischen et al., 2007). However, these studies still perform their experiments in a non-face-to-face setting in which participants are presented with a photograph or picture of a conversational partner. What these researchers found, is that participants are faster (in terms of reaction time) at targeting an object if that object was first fixated by the pair of eyes in the photograph or picture. Lachat et al. (2012) are the first to test this type of experiment in a face-to-face setting (rather than in on-screen experiments), however without using eye-tracking to obtain gaze data. Gullberg & Holmqvist (2006) and Gullberg & Kita (2009) focus on one specific case of gaze cueing, using head-mounted eye-trackers, viz. the effect a speaker fixating his own gesture has

---

1.   The concept of shared gaze should not be confused with that of mutual gaze. The latter being the phenomenon of eye contact: interlocutors are mutually looking at each other.

on the addressee's gaze behaviour. Both studies reveal that a speaker's gaze at own gestures is a powerful cue for addressees to leave the dominant fixation position (i.e. the face of the speaker) and give overt visual attention to the speaker's gesture.

A third and final relevant interactional aspect of gaze is the effect known as the audience effect. Basically, people behave differently when they know or have the feeling they are being watched. More specifically, studies such as Bateson et al. (2006), Piazza, Bering, & Ingram (2011) and Powell et al. (2012) have demonstrated that people behave more empathically and pro-socially when they are being watched. For instance, they pay more for their drinks, cheat less and donate more to charity, compared to when they are not being watched. This effect is even shown to hold for situations in which no actual human eyes, but (schematically drawn) pictures of eyes on a piece of paper constitute the eye gaze stimulus.

The above-mentioned studies show how eye gaze has an effect on subsequent behaviour: fixating an object makes other people fixate that object too (gaze cueing) and being looked at affects the amount of money people put in a box (audience effect). However, while the studies reported so far do address interactional aspects of gaze behaviour and the influence of gaze on subsequent behaviour, few of them start from a face-to-face experimental set-up. From a methodological point of view, this is where the current chapter fits in and provides a contribution. Content wise, we will zoom in on how eye gaze can account for a very specific phenomenon of face-to-face interaction, viz. alignment behaviour. What is understood by alignment behaviour and how gaze might affect it will be explained in the next section.

1.2   Alignment during conversation

Face-to-face conversation is a matter of coordination and joint action (Clark, 1996). During this act of coordination, interlocutors tend to copy each other at many different multimodal levels. These levels include lexical (Brennan & Clark, 1996; Manson et al., 2013; Pickering & Garrod, 2004), syntactical (Branigan, Pickering & Cleland, 2000; Gries, 2005; Reitter, Moore & Keller, 2006), phonetic (Giles & Powesland, 1975; Lewandowski, 2012; Szczepek Reed, 2010), pragmatic (Roche, Dale & Gaucci, 2010; Zima, 2013), gestural (Bergmann & Kopp, 2012; Kimbara, 2008; Mol et al., 2012) and gaze (Richardson, Dale & Kirkham, 2007; Hadelich & Crocker, 2006; Richardson & Dale, 2005) alignment, and the interaction between those levels (Louwerse et al., 2012; Oben, 2015).

Research on alignment is far from new. For example, the observation that in language learning (both from a phylogenetic and ontogenetic perspective) alignment is crucial, has captured researchers' attention over different centuries (James, 1878; Piaget, 1932; Dominey, 2004). More recently, the phenomenon of alignment is approached from roughly three vantage points. First, in line with Brennan & Clark

(1996), alignment can be considered to be a residue of *interactive grounding*: specific sets of partners reach a temporary agreement about a given (lexical) construal. These *conceptual pacts* are not directly transferable to other new addressees. The upshot is a strong interactional account of conceptualisation: speakers and addressees jointly set up conceptual pacts or shared conceptualisations for the purpose of the ongoing interaction, which result in local (lexical) routines. That this is a dynamic process had already been pointed out by Garrod & Anderson (1987). Based on a data set of subjects playing a maze game, they found conversational partners grow routines in indicating their position in the maze (descriptions using coordinates as in "I'm on C-4" vs path descriptions as in "See the bottom right, go two along and two up. That's where I am."). According to the authors, this *growing* of routines can be taken literally because they observed that this type of alignment was progressive, i.e. it increased as the interlocutors talked longer to each other.

Second, and building on Garrod & Anderson (1987), Pickering & Garrod in their seminal work on *interactive alignment* (2004, 2006) claim that alignment is not based on interactive grounding but that it is automatic, i.e. it is almost entirely based on the input – output mechanism of *priming*. Basically, speakers use a word because they have just encountered it. Using a different word would be suboptimal in terms of cognitive effort: in conversation there is no room for constantly modelling the beliefs of your conversational partner. For example, if a speaker uses "red convertible" to refer to a car in a photograph, the addressee activates the lexical items "red" and "convertible" during the comprehension of that utterance. Because of this rise in activation, addressees will be more likely to use "red convertible" themselves in subsequent language production. Perhaps it is needless to repeat, but it is crucial to keep this in mind, this priming operation runs independently from any other-modelling. According to Pickering & Garrod (2006: 221) the process of activation is "automatic and does not involve a conceptual pact between the interlocutors".

The difference between both interpretations of the same observation (i.e. two interlocutors using the same word) boils down to the difference between *grounding* and *priming*. The interactive alignment theory (Pickering & Garrod) assumes that cross-speaker alignment does not presuppose *shared* conceptualisation, i.e. priming enables interlocutors to efficiently align mental representations without having to tap into additional cognitive resources and without having to model each others' mental states. This priming mechanism is so fundamental that in many cases it would require more cognitive resources to override the basic tendency to align than to adhere to it (Costa, Pickering & Sorace, 2008). To Brennan & Clark, in contrast, other-modelling is crucial in building *common ground*. Speakers design their utterances drawing on previous interaction(s) with their partner, either in the current conversation or even beyond. Alignment to them is not an individual cognitive mechanism, but rather a collaborative process not restricted to the individual mind.

A more recent, third line of research has added a temporal dimension to the field of alignment studies. Studies on interactional synchrony have demonstrated that individuals' verbal and nonverbal behaviour is tightly coordinated in time. These synchronisation patterns have been demonstrated for gaze (Richardson et al., 2007; Hadelich & Crocker, 2006; Cummins, 2011; Lachat et al., 2012), syntactic coordination (Dale & Spivey, 2006), gesture & posture (Shockley et al., 2003; Paxton & Dale, 2013), among others. What is more, synchronization in different semiotic channels (Louwerse et al., 2012) appears to be organized in a dynamic, self-organizing network (Dale et al., 2014; Fusaroli & Tylén, 2015; Fusaroli et al., 2012, 2014; Paxton et al., 2014). In this vein, human interaction is no longer perceived as an alternation of speakers and listeners coding and decoding information (cf. Jakobson, 1960: 353 or Shannon, 1948: 381), but as a complex adaptive system of interlocutors that mutually constrain each other's interactional contributions (Beckner et al., 2009; Fusaroli et al., 2014; Tollefsen & Dale, 2012).

In this chapter the research questions concern the interaction between eye gaze (described in 1.1) and alignment (described in 1.2). We will investigate whether eye gaze can enhance lexical alignment (case study 1) and gestural alignment (case study 2). To be more precise, in terms of gestural alignment, does it matter whether or not a prime gesture has been focussed on by the speaker, by the addressee or by both (cf. gaze cueing)? In terms of lexical alignment, does it matter whether or not speaker and addressee are looking at each other during the utterance of the prime and/or the utterance of the target (cf. shared gaze)? Both case studies with their specific research questions, methodology and results will be presented in two separate sections below.

2. Case study 1: Gaze and lexical alignment

Knowing what people are visually focussing on provides us with information on people's attention, but also on people's mental and emotional states (Jones et al., 2006; Langton et al., 2000; Mathews et al., 2003). In this case study we will focus on the former aspect of attentional states. In digging into the relation between gaze behaviour and speech behaviour we hypothesise that gaze direction influences the degree of verbal alignment. More precisely, if interlocutors fixate each other's face, we expect them to lexically align to each other more frequently. This hypothesis is driven by related studies by, for example, Postma et al. (2013) and Wang et al. (2011, 2014) who found comparable gaze effects for alignment of intonation and hand shape respectively. Chartrand & Bargh (1999) also provide evidence for this hypothesis, but they framed it the other way around: if interlocutors are aligning, they look at each other more often. In one of their experiments a confederate either deliberately mimicked the participants' mannerisms, or he did not. Chartrand

& Bargh report more eye contact in the mimicking conditions, compared to the non-mimicking conditions, which further exemplifies a link between eye gaze and alignment. Even though they did not study eye gaze directly, the findings from Reitter et al. (2006) further highlight the relevance of eye gaze for linguistic alignment: in their corpus study they found more syntactic alignment in corpora of face-to-face settings compared to corpora of telephone conversations.

What -to the best of our knowledge- has not yet been addressed, is the relation between gaze and lexical alignment. Compared to related studies on the interplay between eye gaze and alignment, this case study is discerned by the interactional setting in which we study the phenomenon. Wang et al. (2011, 2014) and Postma et al. (2013) study gaze in a non-communicative setting: participants get to see video images (of either an actor or an avatar) and are explicitly asked to perform a certain type of behaviour. For Wang and colleagues that is producing simple target gestures (viz. opening or closing the hand), for Postma and colleagues it is reproducing simple words (viz. digits between 0 and 10). For both researchers the experimental conditions are twofold: the actor or avatar in the video is either looking at the participant (SpeakerGaze +) or not (SpeakerGaze −). However, what separates the two, is the method of measuring the dependent variable alignment. Whereas Wang et al. (2011, 2014) measure reaction times, viz. between the prime gesture in the video and the target gesture performed by the participant, Postma et al. (2013) measure to what extent there is intonational alignment, viz. in terms of pitch between the prime word in the video and the replication of that word by the participant. In the present case study the dependent variable is lexical alignment, viz. whether or not participants use the same word to refer to the same object. This is crucially different in that participants in our data set are actually talking to each other, face-to-face, and are not instructed to (re)produce certain gestures or words. Although they are performing a task, they are completely free in whether or not, how often, and how they label the target objects under scrutiny (see Section 2.1 for a description of the data set).

A second difference with the studies on the interplay between gaze and alignment reported so far, is that they only consider shared gaze (or the absence thereof) during the prime, when factoring in eye gaze. However, in dyadic interactions, more gaze configurations are possible (see Table 1 in the methods section below). In our data set, both during the utterance of prime and target word, interlocutors are entirely free to fixate whatever they want. In the experimentally controlled studies reported above, the addressee is instructed to always look at the video, and the actor or avatar in the video always performs the same gaze behaviour during the prime as during the target.

Third, and overarching the previous two issues, is the fact that this case study taps into functional and communicative aspects of eye gaze, next to cognitive or social aspects. Because both gaze and alignment behaviour are not elicited or controlled for in our data set, participants will have different reasons to fixate (or not) their partner, and to align (or not) to that partner. However, if participants look at a video in which an actor or avatar is performing a simple gesture or word, and they are instructed to perform a given or a matching gesture or word, those participants have no communicative or functional reasons for their behaviour. Hence, the effect gaze has on the subsequent behaviour can only be cognitively or socially motivated, not communicatively or functionally. We argue that in real, face-to-face interaction, those communicative functions matter as well. To better understand this, we will not only study shared gaze during the prime, but also disentangle the gaze behaviour between speaker and addressee, and prime and target.

Following up on what Chartrand & Bargh (1999) did for mannerisms, we will first study whether shared gaze, viz. eye contact in which interlocutors are fixating each other, correlates with more lexical alignment. Second, and compared to the studies by Postma et al. (2013) and Wang et al. (2011, 2014), we are not only investigating the gaze behaviour of the speaker during the production of the prime, but also the gaze behaviour of the addressee, and the gaze behaviour during the utterance of the target. Postma and Wang and colleagues already found that being looked at (i.e. SpeakerGaze during the prime) correlates with higher or faster alignment rates. This study will add to that observation whether or not fixating the speaker (i.e. AddresseeGaze, either during prime or target) affects alignment rates as well.

The added value of the present study is not as much that we check the effect of gaze for yet another multimodal layer (i.c. lexical alignment), but that we use eye-tracking in a spontaneous face-to-face setting to obtain more fine-grained gaze data in more naturalistic interaction. In doing so, we are not only looking into the cognitive or social underpinnings for the observed alignment behaviour, but also into the functional and communicative ones.

2.1   Method

For this case study we use the InSight Interaction Corpus (Brône & Oben, 2015). This is a multimodal video corpus of face-to-face conversations in Dutch, transcribed and annotated for gaze and gesture. In total, the corpus consists of 15 dyadic interactions of about 30 minutes each, however, for the present study only a subpart of the corpus was used. There are three subparts of the corpus: storytelling, brainstorming and targeted collaborative tasks. The results in this chapter only draw on the latter part of the corpus. The collaborative tasks in the InSight Interaction Corpus are similar to the *diapix* used by Van Engen et al. (2010), in which the interlocutors play 'spot-the-difference' games on the basis of complex drawings. In that study, the interlocutors were asked to identify the differences in the drawings they were both shown (they could not see each other's pictures). The subset of collaborative tasks in the InSight Interaction Corpus differs from the diapix approach in that the animations contain moving images and the interlocutors only get to see the animation once, without being able to look back at it while discussing the differences. More precisely, the tasks in the InSight Interaction Corpus work as follows:

–   two interlocutors are sitting face-to-face;
–   they are each shown an animated video -simultaneously- on a screen in front of them; they can only see their own animation and not the one of their partner;
–   the animations for the two interlocutors are identical except for a few details;
–   immediately after seeing the animation they have to figure out the difference(s) between the videos they just saw;
–   after discussing which are these differences, they are shown a new animation, and so on.

The screenshot below (Figure 1) shows the recording set-up of the InSight Interaction Corpus. On the left is the perspective of an external camera on the interaction. On the right are the videos from the mobile eye-tracking glasses the interlocutors are wearing, with the green dots indicating the visual focus. These three perspectives are edited and synchronised into one video file (from which Figure 1 is a still).

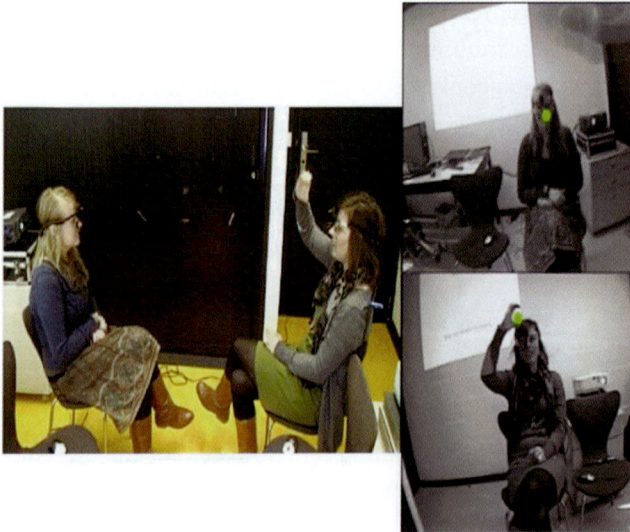

Figure 1. Still from the InSight interaction corpus

2.2 Analysis

To quantify gaze behaviour, we use the annotations from the InSight Interaction Corpus (see method section above). In the corpus, all fixations on the face of the conversational partner are annotated as such and there is no further differentiation between fixations on the eyes, nose or mouth of the partner.

In quantifying lexical alignment we basically want to measure whether or not participants use the same words to refer to the same target objects they are discussing. To measure this type of lexical alignment we take interactional prime-target pairs as our unit of analysis. To illustrate how we define such pairs, consider the example below. In this example the participants are discussing a video animation in which a cat and a dog are performing the actions.

1	S1	First there was a **cat** and a dog.
2	S2	It was a black **cat**.
3		Did you have a black **cat** as well?
4	S1	Yeah.
5	S2	Well they started, the dog was like peeing all the time.
6		[…]
7	S2	And the **pussy** was circling, I guess it was clockwise, was circling round and
8		round a lantern post.
9	S1	In my case the **pussy** was circling, the **pussy** was, I don't know, clockwise or,
10		no I don't remember. But very fast anyway. I couldn't count how many times.
11	S2	The **pussy** was smaller than the dog?

We define prime-target pairs as adjacent lexical references to the target objects in the animation videos that are produced by different speakers. In Figure 2 below, the prime-target pairs for the example above are schematically represented and marked in green rectangles. The second ("cat", line 2) and third ("cat", line 3) lexical reference in the example are adjacent, i.e. there is no other reference to the target object "cat" in between them, but they are produced by the same speaker. Therefore they are not a prime-target pair. Similarly, lexical item one ("cat", line 1) and three ("cat", line 3) do not constitute a prime-target pair either: although they are produced by different speakers, they are not adjacent: there is a reference to the same target object in between them (viz. "cat", line 2). In the example above also "dog" (line 1) and "dog" (line 5) are considered to be a prime-target pair. The "dog" in line 5 and in line 11 are not because they are uttered by the same speaker. Because we only analyse references to target objects, only nouns qualify as potential parts of prime-target pairs. As a consequence, for example, the verbs "circling" in lines 7 and 9 are not part of our analysis (even though they are adjacent and uttered by different speakers).

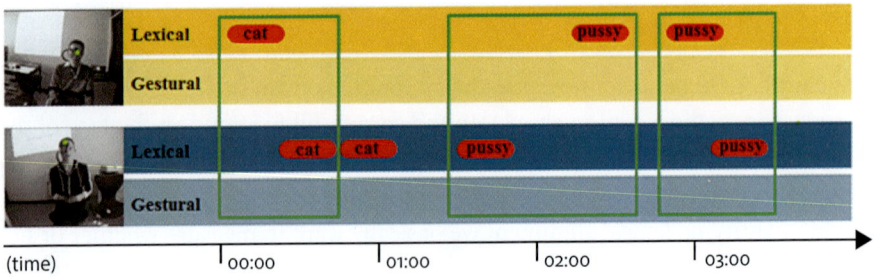

Figure 2. Lexical references to the target object CAT in which all of the prime-target pairs are aligned

To annotate lexical alignment, we identified all the prime-target pairs in the corpus (n = 723) and digitally scored them for alignment: either speakers use the same word or they do not. In the example above, there are three pairs (see green rectangles in Figure 2) that are all aligned. Although annotating lexical alignment is a digital matter, the two lexical items in the prime-target pairs need not necessarily be fully identical in order to be counted as aligned. For example, we discarded diminutives and plurals and regarded cases of "katten" (cats) and "katje" (little cat) as identical and thus fully aligned to the root form "kat" (cat). Only in cases where the root forms in the interactional pair differed (like in "kat" (cat) vs. "poes" (pussy)) we considered the items in the pair as not aligned.

Lexical alignment will be the dependent factor in this case study; gaze the independent. We have already explained how we measure gaze behaviour in terms of fixations on the face, but because of the dyadic conversational situation, four levels of gaze behaviour are relevant:

i.   Gaze behaviour of the speaker during the prime
ii. Gaze behaviour of the speaker during the target
iii. Gaze behaviour of the addressee during the prime
iv. Gaze behaviour of the addressee during the target

At either of these levels the gaze can be directed towards the face of the interlocutor or away from the face. In the example above, all three prime-target pairs are aligned, and there always is eye contact, except for the third pair. In this case the speaker is looking away when he utters the prime, and the addressee is looking away when listening to the target word. Next to gaze behaviour at these four levels, we also calculated eye contact, both during prime and target. Consequently, there is eye contact in the first two pairs and no eye contact in the third pair. Our scoring table for this simple example, then, would look like this:

Table 1. Example coding scheme of resp. the dependent factor alignment,
the independent gaze factors ((i)-(iv)), and the calculated factors for eye contact
during prime and target

	Alignment	(i) Speak prime	(ii) Speak target	(iii) Address prime	(iv) Address target	Eye Contact prime	Eye Contact target
prime-target pair 1	1	1	1	1	1	1	1
prime-target pair 2	1	1	1	1	1	1	1
prime-target pair 3	1	0	1	1	0	0	0
...	...	...	...	...	...	...	...

Using mixed effects models we first want to uncover whether eye contact during
prime or target enhances lexical alignment rates. Second, we look at gaze behaviour in a more fine-grained way, and try to demonstrate how gaze behaviour of
the speaker (focussing on the face of the addressee) or the gaze behaviour of the
addressee (focussing on the speaker's face) during the prime or during the target are
good predictors of whether or not the lexical items in prime and target are aligned.
We use mixed effects models because we maximally want to take into account
idiosyncratic alignment behaviour. Some dyads may systematically align all the
time, or some dyads may produce much more prime-target pairs than others. The
same goes for the target objects that might each typically favour or disfavour lexical
alignment. To avoid taking variation in alignment rates that is due to specific dy-
ads/objects for variation due to our independent factor of gaze behaviour, we treat
dyads and objects as a random factor in our model. Furthermore, to test that our
independent variables are truly independent, we calculated Cramer's V measures
for every possible interaction between the independent variables. None of those
measures exceeded 0.16, which provides evidence against such a collinearity issue
where one independent factor is too good a proxy for another.

2.3 Results

Our research question was whether gaze behaviour during face-to-face interaction
affects lexical alignment. A first relevant result in answering that question comes
from zooming in on the effect of eye contact, i.e. cases where both speaker and
addressee are looking at each other's face at the moment when the target object
is uttered. Our results indicate that the average alignment rate is higher in cases
of eye contact, both during the prime and during the target (Figure 3). If there is
eye contact during the prime, in 91.8% of the cases prime and target are aligned

(compared to 71.3% without eye contact). Similarly, if eye contact occurs during the target there is more lexical alignment (89.9%) than when there is no eye contact (80.9%). A mixed effects model, with dyad and object as random factors (cf. supra), lexical alignment as dependent factor, and eye contact during prime and target as independent factors, shows that the difference in alignment rates between the presence and the absence of eye contact is significant only for the prime ($z = 2.641$, $p = 0.008$) and not for the target ($z = 0.871$, $p = 0.38$). There was no interaction between the two. This means that if both addressee and speaker are looking at each other during the utterance of the prime, chances of the prime-target pair to be aligned are significantly higher. Whether or not there is eye contact during the target, seems to be of little importance in terms of lexical alignment.

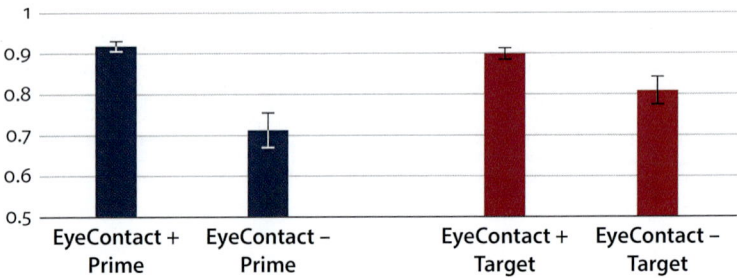

Figure 3. Average lexical alignment rates for cases of eye contact and no eye contact during the utterance of the prime and target. Error bars indicate standard error

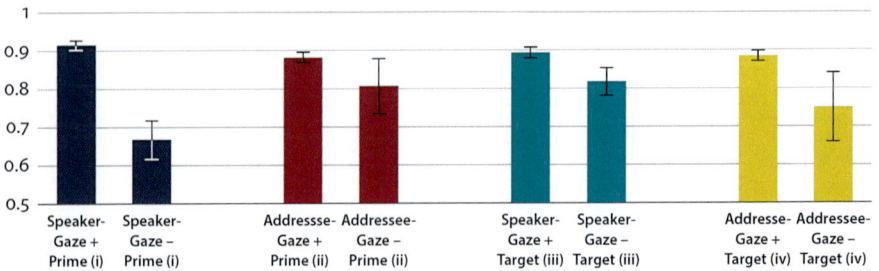

Figure 4. Average lexical alignment rates for gaze levels (i)-(iv)

So far, we have only presented results concerning eye contact. However, our data allow for a more fine-grained analysis. We have already established that eye contact is relevant in predicting lexical alignment, but only during the prime. What we also find is that, more precisely, the behaviour of the speaker during the prime is key. A mixed effects model with dyad and object as random factors, lexical alignment as dependent factor and the factors ((i)-(iv)) concerning gaze behaviour described in

Table 1 as independent factors, shows that the gaze behaviour of the speaker during the prime is the best predictor ($z = 5.074$, $p < 0.001$). No other factors and no interaction between factors reached significance. This means that when a speaker is fixating the addressee while uttering the prime, the addressee will be more likely to align to that prime (alignment rate of 91.5%, see Figure 15), compared to when the speaker averts his gaze during the prime (alignment rate of 66.7%, see Figure 15).

2.4   Discussion

What this case study shows is that gaze behaviour during the prime, and not during the target, significantly affects lexical alignment. If there is eye contact during the utterance of the prime, we observe more lexical alignment. To a large extent, this effect can be explained by the gaze behaviour of the speaker alone: if the speaker fixates the addressee during the prime, that addressee will significantly more often use the same lexical reference during the target, compared to when the speaker does not fixate the addressee during the prime.

These results tie in with previous research on the interplay between gaze and alignment of mannerisms (Chartrand & Bargh, 1999), gesture (Wang et al., 2011) and intonation (Postma et al., 2013). Eye contact, and more specifically SpeakerGaze during the prime, correlates with higher alignment scores. This effect seems to hold true not only under controlled lab settings in which video stimuli of conversational partners are used (Postma et al., 2013; Wang et al. 2011) but also in naturalistic face-to-face interaction. This is an important finding given the wide variety of functions gaze has, and given the very idiosyncratic nature of gaze behaviour during conversations. As reported by Kendon (1967) or Cummins (2011), there is a lot of between-subject variation in gaze behaviour. For example, although participants fixate their partner more during listening than during speaking, different studies (Argyle & Ingham, 1972; Cummins, 2011; Kendon, 1967; Nielsen, 1962) report more variability within the categories "gaze during speech" and "gaze during listening" than between those categories. Some dyads hardly look at each other and other dyads look at each other constantly. Because of this large between-subject variation, the amount of looking at a partner's face is a bad predictor for speakership or listenership. In other words, eye gaze in this example is more dependent on who is talking (between-subjects), rather than whether participants are talking (between-categories). What the results in this case study indicate, is that regardless of this strong speaker-tied variation of gaze during face-to-face interaction, speaker gaze is a good predictor for lexical alignment.

A surplus of this study compared to related work, is that we not only account for the gaze behaviour of the speaker during the prime, but also for addressee gaze, and also for gaze behaviour during the target. This allows us to discriminate between the perception and the production role of gaze. What our results suggest, is that for lexical alignment, the production side of gaze matters more than the perception side. Fixating the speaker (AddresseeGaze) during the prime can be linked to perception, viz. to increased attention to what the speaker is saying. This does not enhance lexical alignment. Fixating the addressee during the prime (SpeakerGaze) can be linked to the production side of gaze, viz. to a signalling function: by looking at his addressee the speaker can highlight that something relevant is going on in his speech signal. This type of gaze behaviour does enhance alignment rates at the lexical level. Related to this issue are the baselines of gaze during speech and during listening. Kendon (1967), Argyle & Cook (1976) or more recently Cummins (2011) found that speakers typically look away while speaking, and listeners typically look at the speaker while listening. Therefore, SpeakerGaze (i.e. speaker fixating addressee) is the marked situation. Gaze aversion is typical for speaking. Looking at the addressee while speaking can thus serve a signalling function. This could explain why SpeakerGaze affects lexical alignment. The other way around, AddresseeGaze (i.e. addressee fixating speaker) does not generate this effect. This might be explained because AddreseeGaze is default for addressees. Addressees look at their speaking partner (nearly) all the time anyway. AddresseeGaze thus does not have the marked, signalling function SpeakerGaze has. Interestingly, the SpeakerGaze effect does not appear to transfer to the target. In related studies (Postma et al., 2013; Wang et al., 2011, 2014) prime and target immediately follow each other and the gaze behaviour during the two is kept constant. In our data this is different: prime and target can (and also do) differ in terms of gaze behaviour. Participants' fixations during prime and target are independent, and the SpeakerGaze effect only resides in the prime. This again hints at the relevance of the signalling function of gaze. Only during the prime can SpeakerGaze have a signalling function. When the participant produces the target word, it is too late for the speaker in the prime (i.e. the addressee in the target) to still use gaze to highlight anything in his initial message. In his role as addressee he can only signal attention to what the speaker in the target is saying. Furthermore, the audience effect that gaze might constitute, does not seem to play an important role in our data. If the social aspect of 'being looked at' would affect lexical alignment, we would expect this to typically (or at least also) occur when producing the target word. However, AddresseeGaze during the target does not affect lexical alignment.

What this case study demonstrates is how gaze enhances alignment. Although there is a lot of idiosyncratic variation in gaze behaviour (Cummins, 2011; Kendon, 1967) and although gaze serves many different functions at the same time (even ranging between mere perception and communicative signalling), we measure an effect of SpeakerGaze on lexical alignment. In our set-up of uncontrolled, spontaneous speech we cannot discriminate between when exactly gaze serves cognitive, social or communicative functions, but we do find evidence that communicative functions of eye gaze, viz. its signalling function, and not cognitive or social functions alone, are good predictors for lexical alignment. What experimentally controlled studies such as Wang et al. (2011, 2014) or Postma et al. (2013) demonstrate, is an immediate and socially or cognitively motivated impact of eye gaze on alignment. This case study reveals there is a mediated and communicatively motived impact as well.

3. Case study 2: Gaze and gestural alignment

Above, we have demonstrated a link between gaze behaviour and lexical alignment. In this case study we will test whether the same link holds true for gaze and gestural alignment. Compared to the previous section, we will roughly use the same set-up and analysis but the crucial difference lies in the type of gaze behaviour we (are able to) measure. For speech, the only relevant gaze behaviour to be measured was "fixating the face" or "not fixating the face". We will do this for gesture as well, and hypothesise that if a speaker looks at the addressee while performing the gesture, the addressee will be more likely to align to that gesture, compared to when the speaker averts his gaze during the gesture production. Because the articulators of gesture, i.e. the arms and hands, are more visible than the articulators for speech, it might also be relevant to measure whether or not speakers and/or addressees fixate those gestural articulators. In other words, we will also study the link between fixation on gestures and gestural alignment, and hypothesise that if speakers or addressees have looked at the gesture in the prime, addressees will be more likely to perform an aligned gesture in the target. This aspect of fixating gestures has already been reported in Oben & Brône (2015), but because it fits in so tightly in this line of reasoning, it will be treated here as well.

In linking gaze behaviour with gesture behaviour, we tie in with studies by Wang et al. (2011, 2014). These researchers found that when addressees are being looked at by a speaker in a video, they are faster at copying the gesture the speaker just performed. However, no such effect was found when speakers fixated their own gesture, i.e. addressees were not faster in copying the gesture if that gesture was fixated by the speaker, compared to when it was not. Perhaps needless to repeat, but we again want to stress that our study crucially differs from Wang et al. (2011, 2014) in two respects. First, our dependent variable is gestural alignment. We study whether or not two gestures in a prime-target pair are the same, whereas Wang and colleagues study the reaction time to a stimulus gesture. Second, the interactional setting is very different. We study gestural alignment in face-to-face conversations, whereas Wang and colleagues study gestural reaction times in non-interactional experimental tasks.

Next to following up on Wang et al. (2011, 2014), the case study in this section also ties in with the work by Gullberg & Kita (2009). In that study participants were asked to watch videos of people telling a cartoon story. The people in the video were talking to a live addressee who was not visible on the video images. During this story telling spontaneous co-speech gestures occurred. The researchers were interested in a subset of target gestures in the videos: gestures encoding spatial events with the speaker either focussing or not focussing on his/her own gestures, and with the spatial information present in the speech or not present in the speech of the story teller. The participants watching the videos were eye-tracked and asked to draw a selection of target scenes in the cartoons after having watched all of the videos. This was done to dig into the information uptake of the target gestures. The crucial question here was whether in the drawing task, fixated gestures (either by the speaker or the addressee) were more adequately drawn, in terms of spatial dynamics, than non-fixated gestures. The main findings, relevant to the present work, in Gullberg & Kita (2009) can be summarised as follows:

i.   Addressees do not focus on many of the speakers' gestures.
ii. If addressees do look at the speaker's gesture, then often that speaker has focussed on his own gesture (i.e. gaze cueing).
iii. If a speaker has looked at his own gesture, the addressee will retain more of the information encoded in that gesture.
iv. If an addressee has focussed on the gesture of the speaker, that addressee will not retain more of the information encoded in that gesture.

Drawing on (i) and (ii), the results above indicate that eye gaze has a strong cueing effect: only if speakers focus on their own gestures, addressees focus at those gestures as well. What (iii) and (iv) demonstrate, is a relation between gaze behaviour and information uptake. If speakers fixate their own gestures, and not if addressees focus on those gestures, the information uptake is higher, i.e. the participants retain more of the spatial information encoded in the gesture. What Gullberg & Kita (2009) do not study, and where this case study fits in, is whether fixations on gestures (either by speaker or by addressee) affect subsequent gesture production. The research questions, then, for this case study can be schematised as follows:

i.   Do interlocutors focus on a minority of their partner's gestures also in face-to-face dialogues?
ii. Is gaze cueing crucial also in face-to-face dialogues?
iii. If speakers or addressees focus on gestures during the prime or the target, are addressees then more likely to align to that gesture in their subsequent gesture production?
iv. If speakers or addressees focus on each other's face (either during the prime or the target), are addressees then more likely to gesturally align?

3.1 Method & analysis

Just as in the previous case study on the relation between gaze and lexical alignment, we use the data from the animation description task in the InSight Interaction Corpus (Brône & Oben, 2015). Since the present study is concerned with the coupling of gesture and gaze, it is important to note that we single out one specific type of gesture, viz. depictive gestures. These are used by the participants to represent the target objects that are present in the animation videos. All other gestures, like emblems or beat gestures, are not part of the data set for the present analysis. In testing our hypotheses, we compare two factors: the alignment between adjacent representational gestures, and the eye gaze of the interlocutors.

To quantify gaze behaviour, we use the gaze annotation from the InSight Interaction Corpus to determine whether or not speakers or addressees are focussing on the target gestures or on each other's faces. The annotation code GEST indicates addressees are fixating the gesture performed by the speaker, OWN indicates speakers fixating their own gestures, and FACE indicates participants fixating their partner's face. Especially in considering fixations on gestures, we need to point out that any study on visual fixations (with or without the help of eye-tracking tools) can only provide positive evidence: if there is a fixation on a given object, we can assume the participant has cognitively processed the visual stimulus. However, if there is no fixation, it cannot be ruled out that the participant still has processed the stimulus. This is due to the human peripheral vision, which allows information uptake without explicit fixations within an angle of 120° (Duchowski, 2007: 29–32). For example, as is clear from eye-tracking research in sign language (Muir & Richardson, 2005), signers hardly ever fixate their interlocutors' hands, while they obviously do 'see' what their conversational partners are expressing with those hands. Because peripheral vision allows perception without fixation, we should take care in how we interpret the data in this case study, but also beyond.

To measure gestural alignment we want to answer the question 'are prime and target gesture aligned?'. This is problematic given the multidimensionality of gesture. For example, if two gestures have the same hand shape and finger orientation but a different palm orientation, can they be considered as fully aligned? In their work on gestural alignment Bergmann & Kopp (2012) acknowledge this multi-dimensionality and calculate gestural alignment on one of five separate gesture features (representation technique, handedness, hand shape, palm orientation, finger orientation and wrist movement). For this study we only use one of those features, viz. representation technique. For the annotation of that feature we adopt the typology of depictive gestures by Streeck (2008: 292–295), who distinguishes gestural depiction methods such as modelling (hand as a token for an object), bounding (hands indicate sides or edges of an object), drawing (fingers draw lines that represent the outline or path of an object), handling (hands enact a prototypical usage of the represented object), etc. By only using representation technique as a basis for our dependent variable of gestural alignment, we miss out on some formal features such as hand shape or palm orientation. However, since we are crucially interested in the question 'are prime and target gesture the same?', adopting a holistic approach and only considering representation technique appears to be justified. In this study we do not want to measure whether gaze behaviour affects palm orientation, but whether it affects gesture production as a whole. If prime and target gesture differ in representation technique, they also differ in many formal features. Which formal features exactly is not the topic of this study.

Measuring gestural alignment is very analogous to our measuring lexical alignment (see 2.2). To illustrate how we compare prime and target gestures, consider the example below. In this example we show how we measure gestural alignment for the target object DOOR. The verbal references to that target object (marked in bold and red) are accompanied by gestural references (marked with red circles in Figure 5).

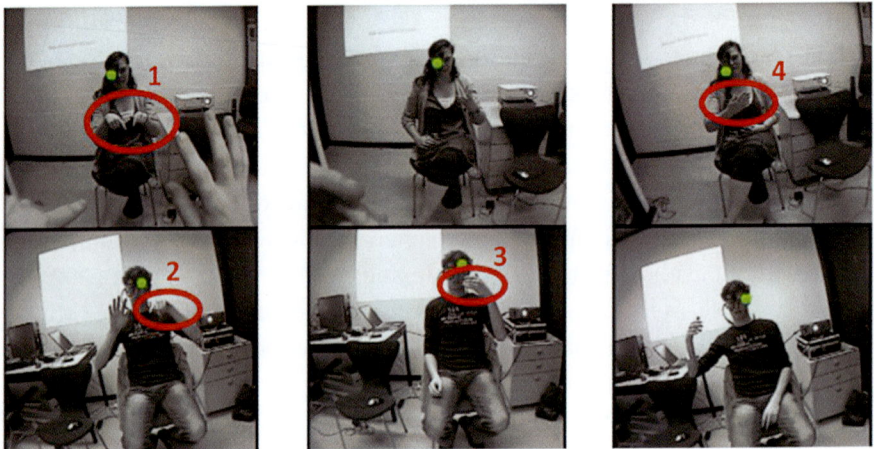

Figure 5.   The target object DOOR is represented four times in this example

1   S2   There's a door [gesture 1].
2   S1   A black door [gesture 2].
3   S2   Yes.
4   S1   Yes, well, a hole [gesture 3].
5   S2   And there's a guy standing in front of the hole [gesture 4] with his hands in his pockets.

In the example above, there are two prime-target pairs (see green rectangles in Figure 6 below). Those pairs are defined as adjacent gestures produced by different speakers. For example, the second and third gesture in the example are adjacent, but they are produced by the same speaker (in this case by the boy, see Figure 5). Similarly, gesture one and three are no prime-target pair: although they are produced by different speakers, they are not adjacent. As mentioned above, in order to label two gestures in a prime-target pair as aligned ones, for this study, we only consider the representation technique (according to Streeck, 2008). This means that for the first interactional pair in the example, we measure alignment in the representation technique 'drawing', although the two gestures are not identical (the most prominent difference being that the girl uses two hands and the boy only one hand). For the second interactional pair, we see a parallel issue: the finger orientation and tension in the hand shape differ between the two speakers, but we still consider it to be an instance of gestural alignment because the representation technique is identical (i.c. modelling).

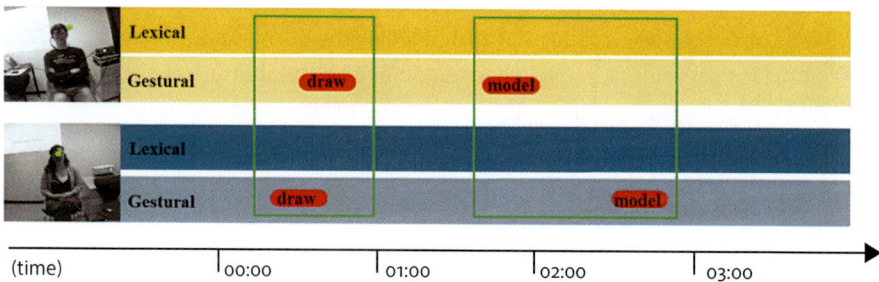

Figure 6. Gestural references to the target object DOOR in which both prime-target pairs are aligned

We identified all prime-target pairs (n = 536) for all of the speakers and coded them for the two factors discussed above: gestural alignment and gaze behaviour. In some prime-target pairs a gaze shift occurs during the production of a prime or target gesture. Because we only want to include pairs in which there either is a full fixation or a full gaze aversion during the entire duration of the gesture, we omitted those gaze shift cases from the data set. From the initial 536 prime-target pairs, we thus keep 417. In the sample conversation above (see Figure 5 and 6), both prime-target pairs are aligned, there is no fixation on own (SpeakerOwnGest) or other (AddresseeGest) gestures during the prime, and participants focus on each other's face (SpeakerGaze & AddresseeGaze) both during the prime and during the target. Our scoring table for this brief example, then, would look like the example given in Table 2.

Table 2. Example coding scheme of the dependent factor alignment
and the independent gaze factors

	Alignment	Speak Gaze prime	Speak Gaze target	Address Gaze prime	Address Gaze target	Speak Own gest	Address gest
pair1	1	1	1	1	1	0	0
pair2	1	1	1	1	1	0	0
...	...	...	...	...	...	...	...

Parallel to the previous section on lexical alignment (see Table 1), we also calculated from the gaze data whether or not there was eye contact during prime and during target, and added that as a factor. We then computed mixed effects models to uncover whether the gaze behaviour of the speaker (focussing on his own gestures or on the addressee's face) or the gaze behaviour of the addressee (focussing on the speaker's gestures or face) are good predictors of whether or not prime and target gestures are aligned. To account for variation in alignment rates that is due to specific dyads or objects we treat dyads and objects as random factors in our models. To account for collinearity issues, we tested every possible interaction between our independent variables and found that none of those interactions exceeded a Cramer's V value of 0.14.

3.2   Results

In answering the first research question (i), we found that also in face-to-face dialogues very few gestures get fixated. In the corpus, on a total of 1770 depictive gestures only 3.7% are fixated by the addressee (AddresseeGest), and 4.0% by the speaker (SpeakerOwnGest). Gullberg & Holmqvist (2006) found 7.4% of AddresseeGest, but because they do not report absolute frequencies and because we restricted ourselves to one subtype of gestures (viz. depictive gestures), we cannot statistically compare the obtained results.

Research question (ii) was on the relation between AddresseeGest and SpeakerOwnGest, viz. the so-called gaze cueing effect. Our data provide evidence of a strong gaze cueing effect: 46.5% of the SpeakerOwnGest fixations are followed by an AddresseeGest fixation. This means that nearly half of the time the gaze cueing is successful. This result appears to be significant: a mixed effects model with AddresseeGest as dependent factor, SpeakerOwnGest as fixed factor and dyad as random factor reveals that the gaze behaviour of the speaker is a good predictor for that of the addressee ($z = 4.85$, $p < 0.001$).

Research question (iii) addressed the relation between gaze behaviour of the speaker or addressee, and gesture behaviour of the addressee. In our data set of 536 prime-target pairs, 80 gestures are fixated by the addressee (AddresseeGest), and 84 gestures by the speaker (SpeakerOwnGest). Our hypothesis that addressees align more to the gestures of the speakers if those speakers focussed on their own gestures was not confirmed. Figure 7 shows there is hardly a difference in alignment scores for the prime-target pairs in which the speaker looked at his own gesture in the prime (SpeakerOwnGest +), compared to when the speaker did not look at his own gesture (SpeakerOwnGest–).

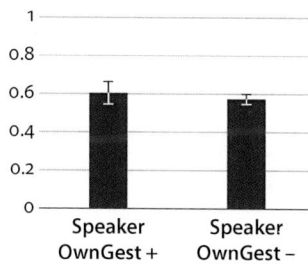

Figure 7. Average alignment rates for speakers fixating their own gestures (SpeakerOwnGest +) and speakers not fixating their own gestures (SpeakerOwnGest–). Error bars indicate standard error

For gaze behaviour on the part of the Addressee we did observe an effect. If addressees have fixated the prime gesture (AddresseeGest +), they align to that gesture in 73.9% of the cases, whereas if there is no such fixation (AddresseeGest–) the average alignment rate is only 55.3% (see Figure 8).

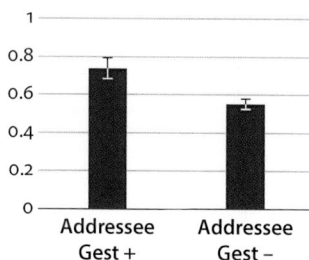

Figure 8. Average alignment rates for addressees fixating the prime gestures (AddresseeGest +) and addressees not fixating the prime gestures (AddresseeGest–). Error bars indicate standard error

Zooming in further on research question (iii), what has not yet been addressed is the relation between SpeakerOwnGest and AddresseeGest. Comparing those two factors creates four possible gaze configurations for which we calculated the average gestural alignment scores. Figure 9 visualises those four configurations: (a) speaker and addressee both fixating the prime gesture, (b) only speaker fixating the prime, (c) only addressee fixating the prime, (d) speaker nor addressee fixating the prime. Figure 10 shows the average alignment scores for those four configurations.

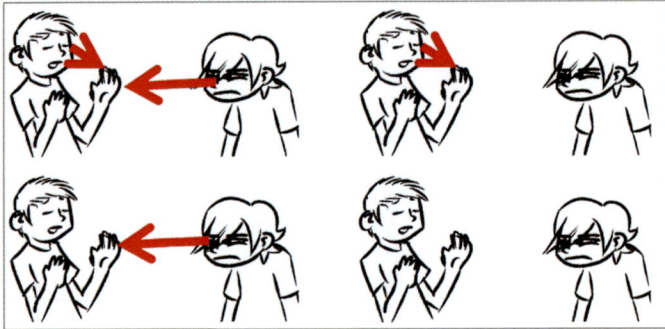

Figure 9. Four possible gaze configurations when combining the two factors SpeakerGaze and AddresseeGaze

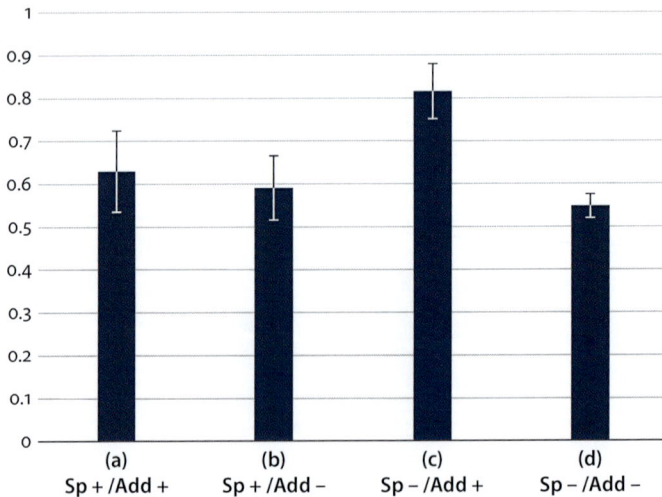

Figure 10. Average scores for gestural alignment across two factors: SpeakerOwnGest (speaker has or has not focussed on his own hand gesture) and AddresseeGest (addressee has or has not focussed on the speaker's hand gesture). Error bars indicate standard error

As was already apparent from the previous results, the average scores in the AddresseeGest + cases ((a) and (c)) are higher than their AddresseeGest– counterparts ((b) and (d)). This means that if addressees have focussed on the speaker's hand gesture, they produce more aligned gestures than if they have not focussed on the speaker's gestures. What stands out here is the SpeakerOwnGest + / AddresseeGest + configuration (a). If both SpeakerOwnGest + (Figure 7) and AddresseeGest + (Figure 8) correlate with higher scores on gestural alignment, then we would have expected the SpeakerOwnGest + /AddresssseeGest + configuration (a) to show the highest alignment scores. Figure 10 shows this is not the case.

To test the significance of the effect of SpeakerOwnGest, AddresseeGest, and the interaction between them, we computed a mixed effects model where gestural alignment was the dependent factor, SpeakerOwnGest and AddresseeOwnGest the independent factors, and dyad and object the random factors. This revealed a significant main effect of AddresseeGest ($z = 2.664$, $p = 0.007$), qualified by an interaction with SpeakerOwnGest ($z = -1.914$, $p = 0.05$). There was an interaction between the factors because only in the SpeakerOwnGest– cases the difference between AddresseeGest + and AddresseeGest– was significant. In the SpeakerOwnGest + cases, there was no such difference. In other words, only when speakers do not fixate their own gestures, it matters (in terms of gestural alignment scores) whether the addressee looks at his partner's gestures. If the speaker does fixate his own gestures, the gaze behaviour of the interlocutor no longer correlates with significantly higher gestural alignment scores.

Unlike what we found for lexical alignment, and answering research question (v), we found no effect of SpeakerGaze or AddresseeGaze (i.e. fixating the partner's face by resp. the speaker and the addressee) on gestural alignment. As is already clear from Figure 11, SpeakerGaze nor AddresseeGaze, either during the prime or during the target, enhances gestural alignment. A mixed effects model with gestural alignment as dependent variable, SpeakerGaze and AddresseeGaze as independent factors and dyad and object as random factors confirmed that none of the independent factors reached significance. Similarly, a mixed effects model with the same dependent and random factors, but eye contact during prime and during target as independent factors, failed to reach significance as well. Together these tests reveal that fixations on the face, regardless of when and by whom, are irrelevant in explaining gestural alignment.

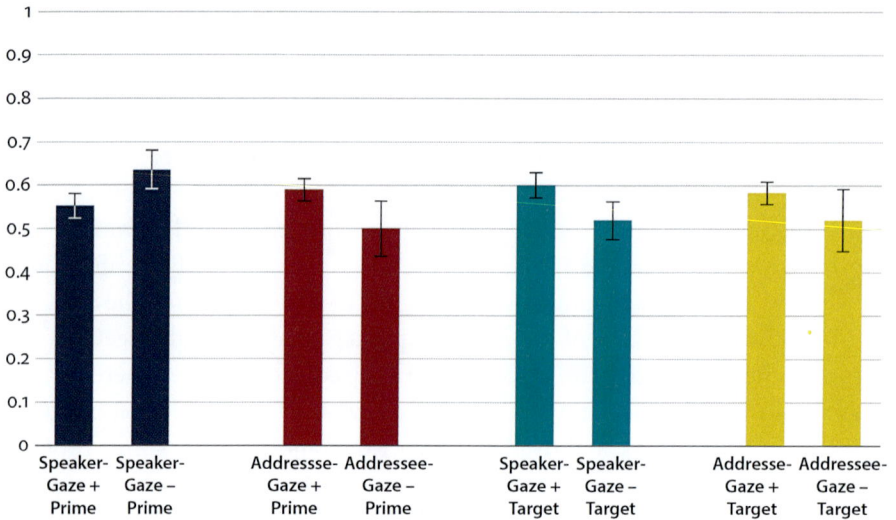

Figure 11. Average scores for gestural alignment for SpeakerGaze and AddresseeGaze during prime and target. Error bars indicate standard error

Summing up the results in this case study we found that:

i.   gestures do not attract a lot of explicit visual attention
ii.   if a speaker looks at his own gesture, the addressee is likely to look at that gesture as well.
iii. if a speaker looks at his own gesture, the addressee is not more likely to copy that gesture (compared to when the speaker does not look at his own gesture).
iv.   if an addressee looks at the gesture of a speaker and the speaker is not looking at his own gesture, the addressee is more likely to copy that gesture.
v.   there is no correlation between gestural alignment and eye contact between speaker and hearer.

3.3   Discussion

Fixations on gesture do not occur often. Only in roughly four percent of the cases or less than one percent of the time participants in our corpus fixated a gesture. However, if it does occur, something happens. First, SpeakerOwnGest and AddresseeGest co-occur often: if a speaker looks at his own gesture, nearly half of the time the addressee does the same thing. This gaze cueing effect was already pointed out (Emery, 2000; Frischen et al., 2007; Lachat et al., 2012), but to the best of our knowledge this is the first account of the phenomenon in which eye-tracking is used in a face-to-face interactional setting. We thus provide evidence that the

observations made in strictly controlled lab settings can be stretched to spontaneous speech.

The second relevant finding of this study pertains to the multimodal relation between fixations on gestures and subsequent gestural behaviour. Regarding this relation, the main results can be summarised as follows: SpeakerOwnGest alone (i.e. the
speaker fixating his own gesture) does not affect gestural alignment, AddresseeGest
(i.e. the addressee fixating the speaker's gesture) does significantly co-occur with
higher scores for gestural alignment, but it only does so in the SpeakerOwnGest–
cases (i.e. when the speaker does not fixate his own gesture). That we did not find
an effect for SpeakerOwnGest ties in with what Wang et al. (2014) found in their
reaction time experiment: addressees looking at actors in a video were not faster in
copying target gestures if those gestures were fixated by the actor, compared to when
they were not fixated. However, our results are quite different from Gullberg and
Kita's (2009) findings. They showed how SpeakerOwnGest did and AddresseeGest
did not have an effect on gestural information uptake. In our study, it appears to be
the other way around. Combining the results of both studies: if a speaker fixates his
own gesture, addressees retain more of the information in that gesture, but they are
not more likely to align in subsequent gesture production. The other way around,
addressees that fixate a prime gesture do not retain more of the information, but
they are more likely to gesturally align to the speaker. This might mean that gesture information uptake and gestural alignment are too disparate phenomena to
be compared. In other words, maybe a higher information uptake does not lead
to more gestural alignment. This assumption, however, is in contraction with the
foundations of priming: if fixating a gesture as an addressee leads to more information uptake, then that should lead to a higher likelihood of gestural alignment
(cf. the notion of activation level in Pickering & Garrod, 2004, 2006). Therefore,
the difference in results between Gullberg & Kita (2009) and this study might be
relevant, and can be explained by the difference in conversational setting: watching
a speaker telling a story in a video in the former study, and a face-to-face collaborative task in the latter. In this vein, the divergent results could be indicative of the
fact that identical gaze events (SpeakerOwnGest and AddresseeGest) serve different
functions in different conversational settings. This interpretation is of course speculative and future research is needed to substantiate this hypothesis.

What then can we conclude from the fixations on gesture in our data set? First,
although gaze appears to be an efficient tool for a speaker to make his addressee
focus on a gesture he is performing (cf. gaze cueing), SpeakerOwnGest is not functional in terms of gestural alignment. Given that fixations on gesture by addressees
and not by speakers correlate with higher gestural alignment scores, it may not
be so surprising that gaze configuration (a), viz. both speaker and addressee are
fixating the gesture, does not correlate with the highest alignment score and that

gaze configuration (c), viz. only the addressee fixating the gesture, does. To make a somewhat simplifying comparison: given that people liking apples get high grades and people liking pears do not get high grades, we would expect people only liking apples (cf. gaze configuration (c)) to get higher grades than people liking both apples and pears (cf. gaze configuration (a)). Comparing the results between gaze configurations (a) and (c), we could hypothesise that addressees may have different reasons for fixating a gesture. One reason would be fixating a gesture because the speaker is fixating the gesture. Here the addressee is being coerced, the gesture fixation is externally triggered. Another reason could be to better process (the physical structure of) the gesture. In this vein the gesture fixation is internally motivated. Perhaps, more than an external trigger, an internal trigger to gesture fixation makes gestural alignment more likely. Of course, whatever the reasons are why addressees fixate gestures, we can only speculate on those reasons in this study due to lack of experimental control. Notwithstanding this speculation, we have at the very least demonstrated that gesture fixation is relevant in explaining gestural alignment in face-to-face conversations. Even amidst the many different functions gaze has, functions that are not evoked or used during experimental, non-dialogic tasks, we measured a significant effect of the subtle interplay between SpeakerOwnGest and AddresseeGest on gestural alignment.

A second main issue we addressed in this case study pertains to the relation between gestural alignment and gaze fixations on the face. For none of the gaze factors we coded, i.e. SpeakerGaze and AddresseeGaze during both prime and target, we found a correlation with higher gestural alignment rates. This is in contrast with what Wang et al. (2011, 2014) found in their reaction time experiments: they found evidence that when SpeakerGaze during the prime occurred, addressees were significantly faster at copying the gesture they just perceived. A factor contributing to the conflicting results could be the effect of distance. In Wang et al. (2011, 2014) prime and target gesture always immediately follow each other. Due to the natural conversation in our study, there is a variable, but crucially a much larger distance between prime and target. The effect of SpeakerGaze during the prime might therefore wear off in many of our prime-target pairs. The absence of an effect for SpeakerGaze is not only in contrast with the results obtained by Wang and colleagues, but also with the previous case study (see 3.1.1) on lexical alignment. Apparently, the gaze behaviour of the speaker during the prime does not matter in terms of gestural alignment rates, but it does in terms of lexical alignment rates.

Combining the results of this case study and the one in 3.1.1 on lexical alignment we see some interesting differences. Whereas lexical alignment is enhanced by gaze behaviour of the speaker, gestural alignment is enhanced by gaze behaviour of the addressee. In the introduction to this case study we noted that gaze can serve both perception and production purposes. We use it to perceive the world around us and to convey meaning during interaction. This dichotomy appears to be relevant in explaining the relation between gaze and multimodal alignment. The production aspect of gaze, viz. the signalling or highlighting function of it, appears to be crucial in explaining lexical alignment. Higher lexical alignment rates correlate with the speaker looking at the addressee during the prime. The perception aspect of gaze, viz. the (cognitive) focus of attention, appears to be linked with gestural alignment. Higher gestural alignment rates correlate with the addressee fixating the speaker's gesture during the prime.

4. Conclusion & future work

In this study we have demonstrated that eye gaze can enhance gestural and lexical alignment. With regard to gestural alignment, we found that when addressees fixate a speaker's gesture, chances are significantly higher that the addressee will use the same gesture in subsequent interaction. However, this effect was only found for cases in which the addressee was fixating the gesture but the speaker was not fixating that same gesture (i.e. his own gesture). With regard to lexical alignment, we found that if a speaker looks at the face of the addressee while lexically referring to one of the target objects in the experiment, that addressee is significantly more likely to use the same lexical reference in subsequent speech (compared to when the speaker does not look at the face of the addressee).

The differences in results between Gullberg & Kita (2009) and Wang et al. (2011, 2014), and the second case study on gaze and gesture are indicative of the many functions of eye gaze in communication and of the intricate relationship between gaze behaviour and alignment. Interlocutors in conversations can fixate their partners or their (partners') gestures for many different reasons: disambiguating, gaze cueing, signalling uncertainty, deictic referencing, etc. Using mobile eye-tracking allows us to measure visual fixations in great detail, but of course without getting direct access to these different conversational functions. Also, we ignored a whole range of parameters that may influence gaze behaviour by interlocutors engaged in face-to-face interaction. McNeill (2006) and Gullberg & Kita (2009) provide an overview of such factors including social status, interpersonal stance, speaker information structure, shared common ground and the physical properties of the gesture. Apart from those factors, also the time difference between the fixation onset and gesture onset, the fixation duration, co-occurring (non-)verbal cues, etc. might be parameters with explanatory potential as well. Unravelling the (relative) effect of those factors in future research will add to a better understanding of the processes underpinning the intricate phenomenon that is alignment.

References

Argyle, M. & Cook, M. (1976). *Gaze and Eye contact*. London: Cambridge University Press.

Argyle, M. & Ingham, R. (1972). Gaze, mutual gaze, and proximity. *Semiotica*, 6, 32–49. https://doi.org/10.1515/semi.1972.6.1.32

Bateson, M., Nettle, D. & Roberts, G. (2006). Cues of being watched enhance cooperation in real-world setting. *Biology Letters*, 2, 412–414. https://doi.org/10.1098/rsbl.2006.0509

Beckner, C., Blythe, R., Bybee, J., Christiansen, M., Croft, W., Ellis, N., Holland, J., Ke, J., Larsen-Freeman, D. & Schoenemann, T. (2009). Language Is a Complex Adaptive System: Position Paper. *Language Learning*, 59, 1–26. https://doi.org/10.1111/j.1467-9922.2009.00533.x

Bergmann, K. & Kopp, S. (2012). Gestural alignment in natural dialogue. *Proceedings of the 34th Annual Conference of the Cognitive Science Society*, 1326–1331.

Branigan, H., Pickering, M. & Cleland, A. (2000). Syntactic co-ordination in dialogue. *Cognition*, 75, 13–25. https://doi.org/10.1016/S0010-0277(99)00081-5

Brennan S., Chen X., Dickinson C., Neider M. & Zelinsky G. (2008). Coordinating cognition: The costs and benefits of shared gaze during collaborative search. *Cognition*, 106, 1465–1477. https://doi.org/10.1016/j.cognition.2007.05.012

Brennan, S. & Clark, H. (1996). Conceptual pacts and lexical choice in conversation. *Journal of Experimental Psychology: Learning, Memory, and Cognition*, 22, 1482–1493.

Brône, G., Oben, B. (2015). InSight interaction: A multimodal and multifocal dialogue corpus. *Language Resources and Evaluation*, 49(1), 195–214. https://doi.org/10.1007/s10579-014-9283-2

Clark, H. (1996). *Using Language*. Cambridge: Cambridge University Press. https://doi.org/10.1017/CBO9780511620539

Chartrand, T. & Bargh, J. (1999). The chameleon effect: The perception-behavior link and social interaction. *Journal of Personality and Social Psychology*, 76, 893–910. https://doi.org/10.1037/0022-3514.76.6.893

Costa, A., Pickering, M. & Sorace, A. (2008). Alignment in second language dialogue. *Language and Cognitive Processes*, 23, 528–556.

Cummins, F. (2011). Gaze and blinking in dyadic conversation: A study in coordinated behaviour among individuals. *Language and Cognitive Processes*, 27, 1525–1549. https://doi.org/10.1080/01690965.2011.615220

Dale, R., Fusaroli, R., Duran, N. & Richardson, D. (2014). The self-organization of human inter-action. In B. Ross (Ed.), *Psychology of Learning and Motivation* (pp. 43–95). Academic Press.

Dale, R., Kirkham, N. & Richardson, D. (2011). How two people become a tangram recognition system. *Proceedings of the European Conference on Computer-Supported Cooperative Work*. Berlin: Springer Verlag.

Dale, R. & Spivey, M. (2006). Unraveling the dyad: Using recurrence analysis to explore patterns of syntactic coordination between children and caregivers in conversation. *Language Learning*, 56, 391–430. https://doi.org/10.1111/j.1467-9922.2006.00372.x

Dominey, P. (2004). Situation alignment and routinization in language acquisition. *Behavioral and Brain Sciences*, 27, 195. https://doi.org/10.1017/S0140525X04270054

Duchowski, A. (2007). Eye Tracking Methodology. *Theory and Practice*. Berlin: Springer.

Emery, N. (2000). The eyes have it: The neuroethology, function and evolution of social gaze. *Neuroscience and Biobehavioral Reviews*, 24, 581–604. https://doi.org/10.1016/S0149-7634(00)00025-7

Frischen, A., Bayliss, A., & Tipper, S. (2007). Gaze cueing of attention: Visual attention, social cognition, and individual differences. *Psychological Bulletin*, 133, 694–724. https://doi.org/10.1037/0033-2909.133.4.694

Fusaroli, R., Bahrami, B., Olsen, K., Roepstorff, A., Rees, G., Frith, C. & Tylén, K. (2012). Coming To Terms: Quantifying the Benefits of Linguistic Coordination. *Psychological Science*, 23, 931–939. https://doi.org/10.1177/0956797612436816

Fusaroli, R., Konvalinka, I. & Wallot, S. (2014). Analyzing social interactions: The promises and challenges of using cross recurrence quantification analysis. *Springer Proceedings in Mathematics and Statistics*, 103, 137–155. https://doi.org/10.1007/978-3-319-09531-8_9

Fusaroli, R. & Tylén, K. (2015). Investigating conversational dynamics: interactive alignment, interpersonal synergy and collective task performance. *Cognitive Science*, 40, 145–171.

Garrod, S. & Anderson, A. (1987). Saying what you mean in dialogue: A study in conceptual and semantic co-ordination. *Cognition*, 27, 181–218. https://doi.org/10.1016/0010-0277(87)90018-7

Giles, H. & Powesland, P. (1975). *Speech styles and social evaluation*. New York: Academic Press.

Gries, S. (2005). Syntactic Priming: A Corpus-based Approach. *Journal of Psycholinguistic Research*, 34, 365–399. https://doi.org/10.1007/s10936-005-6139-3

Gullberg, M. & Holmqvist, K. (2006). What speakers do and what listeners look at. Visual attention to gestures in human interaction live and on video. *Pragmatics and Cognition*, 14, 53–82. https://doi.org/10.1075/pc.14.1.05gul

Gullberg, M. & Kita, S. (2009). Attention to speech-accompanying gestures: Eye movements and information uptake. *Journal of Nonverbal Behaviour*, 33, 251–277. https://doi.org/10.1007/s10919-009-0073-2

Hadelich, K. & Crocker, M. (2006). Gaze alignment of interlocutors in conversational dialogues. *Proceedings of the 2006 Symposium on Eye Tracking Research and Applications*, 38. https://doi.org/10.1145/1117309.1117322

Jakobson, R. (1960). Linguistics and Poetics. In T. Sebeok (Ed.), *Style in Language* (pp. 350–377). Cambridge MA: M.I.T. Press.

James, W. (1878). Brute and human intellect. *The Journal of Speculative Philosophy*, 12, 236–276.

Jones, B., DeBruine, L., Little, A., Conway, C. & Feinberg, D. (2006). Integrating gaze direction and expression in preferences for attractive faces. *Psychological Science*, 17, 588–591. https://doi.org/10.1111/j.1467-9280.2006.01749.x

Kendon, A. (1967) Some functions of gaze-direction in social interaction. *Acta Psychologica*, 26, 22–63. https://doi.org/10.1016/0001-6918(67)90005-4

Kimbara, I. (2008). Gesture Form Convergence in Joint Description. *Journal of Nonverbal Behavior*, 32, 123–131. https://doi.org/10.1007/s10919-007-0044-4

Lachat, F., Conty, L., Hugueville, L. & George, N. (2012). Gaze cueing effect in a face-to-face situation. *Journal of Nonverbal Behaviour*, 36, 177–190. https://doi.org/10.1007/s10919-012-0133-x

Langton, S., Watt, R. & Bruce, V. (2000). Do the eyes have it? Cues to the direction of social attention. *Trends in cognitive sciences*, 4, 50–58. https://doi.org/10.1016/S1364-6613(99)01436-9

Lewandowski, N. (2012). *Talent in nonnative phonetic convergence* (Unpublished doctoral dissertation). Universität Stuttgart, Stuttgart.

Louwerse, M., Dale, R., Bard, E. & Jeuniaux, P. (2012). Behavior matching in multimodal communication is synchronized. *Cognitive Science*, 36, 1404–1426. https://doi.org/10.1111/j.1551-6709.2012.01269.x

Manson, J., Bryant, G., Gervais, M. & Kline, M. (2013). Convergence of speech rate in conversation predicts cooperation. *Evolution and Human Behavior*, 34, 419–426. https://doi.org/10.1016/j.evolhumbehav.2013.08.001

Mathews, A., Fox, E., Yiend, J. & Calder, A. (2003). The face of fear: Effects of eye gaze and emotion on visual attention. *Visual Cognition*, 10, 823–835. https://doi.org/10.1080/13506280344000095

McNeill, D. (2006). Gesture, Gaze, and Ground. *Lecture Notes in Computer Science* 3869, 1–14.

Mol, L., Krahmer, E., Maes, A. & Swerts, M. (2012). Adaptation in gesture: Converging hands or converging minds? *Journal of Memory and Language*, 66, 249–264. https://doi.org/10.1016/j.jml.2011.07.004

Muir, L. & Richardson, I. (2005). Perception of sign language and its application to visual communications for deaf people. *Journal of Deaf Studies and Deaf Education*, 10, 390–340. https://doi.org/10.1093/deafed/eni037

Nielsen, G. (1962). *Studies in self confrontation*. Copenhagen: Munksgaard.

Neider, M., Chen, X., Dickinson, C., Brennan, S. & Zelinsky, G. (2010). Coordinating spatial referencing using shared gaze. *Psychonomic Bulletin & Review*, 17, 718–724. https://doi.org/10.3758/PBR.17.5.718

Oben, B. (2015). *Modelling interactive alignment: a multimodal and temporal account*. [unpublished doctoral thesis]

Oben B., Brône G. (2015). What you see is what you do: On the relation between gaze and gesture in multimodal alignment. *Language and Cognition*, 7(4), 546–562. https://doi.org/10.1017/langcog.2015.22

Paxton, A. & Dale, R. (2013). Frame-differencing methods for measuring bodily synchrony in conversation. *Behavior Research Methods*, 45, 329–343. https://doi.org/10.3758/s13428-012-0249-2

Paxton, A., Abney, D, Kello, C. & Dale, R. (2014). Network analysis of multimodal, multiscale coordination in dyadic problem solving. In P. Bello, M. Guarini, M. McShane & B. Scassellati (Eds.), *Proceedings of the 36th Annual Meeting of the Cognitive Science Society* (pp. 2735–2740). Austin: Cognitive Science Society.

Piaget, J. (1932). *The moral judgment of the child*. Glencoe: The Free Press.

Piazza, J., Bering, J. & Ingram, G. (2011). Princess Alice is watching you: Children's belief in an invisible person inhibits cheating. *Journal of Experimental Child Psychology*, 109, 311–320. https://doi.org/10.1016/j.jecp.2011.02.003

Pickering, M. & Garrod, S. (2004). Towards a Mechanistic Psychology of Dialogue. *Behavioural and Brain Sciences*, 27, 169–225. https://doi.org/10.1017/S0140525X04000056

Pickering, M. & Garrod, S. (2006). Alignment as the Basis for Successful Communication. *Research on Language and Communication*, 4, 203–288. https://doi.org/10.1007/s11168-006-9004-0

Posner, M., Snyder, C. & Davidson, B. (1980). Attention and the detection of signals. *Journal of Experimental Psychology*, 109, 160–174. https://doi.org/10.1037/0096-3445.109.2.160

Postma, M., Brunninkhuis, N. & Postma, E. (2013). Eye Gaze Affects Vocal Intonation Mimicry. *Proceedings of the 35th Annual Conference of the Cognitive Science Society*, 1139–1144.

Powell, L., Roberts, G. & Nettle, D. (2012). Eye images increase charitable donations: Evidence from an opportunistic field experiment in a supermarket. *Ethology*, 118, 1–6. https://doi.org/10.1111/eth.12011

Reitter, D., Moore, D. & Keller, F. (2006). Priming of syntactic rules in task-oriented dialogue and spontaneous conversation. *Proceedings of the 28th Annual Conference of the Cognitive Science Society*, 685–690.

Richardson, D. & Dale, R. (2005). Looking to understand: The coupling between speakers' and listeners' eye movements and its relationship to discourse comprehension. *Cognitive Science*, 29, 1045–1060. https://doi.org/10.1207/s15516709cog0000_29

Richardson, D., Dale, R., & Kirkham, N. (2007). The art of conversation is coordination. Common ground and the coupling of eye movements during dialogue. *Psychological Science*, 18, 407–413. https://doi.org/10.1111/j.1467-9280.2007.01914.x

Richardson, D., Dale, R. & Tomlinson, J. (2009). Conversation, gaze coordination, and beliefs about visual context. *Cognitive Science*, 33, 1468–1482. https://doi.org/10.1111/j.1551-6709.2009.01057.x

Roche, J., Dale, R. & Caucci, G. (2010). Doubling up on double meanings: Pragmatic alignment. *Language and Cognitive Processes*, 27, 1–24. https://doi.org/10.1080/01690965.2010.509929

Shannon, C. (1948). A mathematical theory of communication. *Bell System Technical Journal*, 27, 379–423. https://doi.org/10.1002/j.1538-7305.1948.tb01338.x

Shockley, K., Santana, M. & Fowler, C. (2003). Mutual interpersonal postural constraints are involved in cooperative conversation. *Journal of Experimental Psychology: Human Perception and Performance*, 29, 326–332.

Streeck, J. (2008). Depicting by gesture. *Gesture*, 8, 285–301. https://doi.org/10.1075/gest.8.3.02str

Szczepek Reed, B. (2010). Prosody and alignment: A sequential perspective. *Cultural Studies of Science Education*, 5, 859–867. https://doi.org/10.1007/s11422-010-9289-z

Tollefsen, D. & Dale, R. (2012). Naturalizing joint action: A process-based approach. *Philosophical Psychology*, 25, 385–407. https://doi.org/10.1080/09515089.2011.579418

Van Engen, K., Baese-Berk, M., Baker, R., Choi, A., Kim, M. & Bradlow, A. (2010). The Wildcat corpus of native- and foreign-accented English: Communicative efficiency across conversational dyads with varying language alignment profiles. *Language and speech*, 53, 510–540. https://doi.org/10.1177/0023830910372495

Wang, Y., Newport, R. & Hamilton, A. (2011). Eye contact enhances mimicry of intransitive hand movements. *Biology Letters*, 7, 7–10. https://doi.org/10.1098/rsbl.2010.0279

Wang, Y. & Hamilton, A. (2014). Why does gaze enhance mimicry? Placing gaze-mimicry effects in relation to other gaze phenomena. *The Quarterly Journal of Experimental Psychology*, 67, 747–762. https://doi.org/10.1080/17470218.2013.828316

Zima, E. (2013). *Kognition in der Interaktion. Eine kognitiv-linguistische und gesprächsanalytische Studie dialogischer Resonanz in österreichischen Parlamentsdebatten.* Heidelberg: Universitätsverlag Winter.

CHAPTER 11

Mobile dual eye-tracking in face-to-face interaction

The case of deixis and joint attention

Anja Stukenbrock
Université de Lausanne

In face-to-face interaction deixis, i.e. (the use of) a particular class of linguistic items that have grammaticalised the space-, time- and person-bound structure of the participants' subjective orientation in the speech event (Bühler, 1965[1934]), is intricately connected to visible acts of demonstration (prototypically pointing) and joint attention. A growing body of publications within the field of conversation analysis and research on multimodality acknowledges the central role that pointing plays in acts of deictic reference (Eriksson, 2009; Fricke, 2007; Goodwin, 2003; Kendon, 2004; Kita, 2003; Mondada, 2012a; Stukenbrock, 2009, 2014a, 2014b, 2015). Surprisingly, eye gaze has remained an unexplored area although it serves a variety of crucial functions in the participants' on-line organisation of a joint focus of attention on deictically foregrounded entities in the immediate spatial surroundings (Stukenbrock, 2009, 2010, 2014a, 2014b, 2015). The few existing studies mainly rely on video-recordings that do not allow a precise analysis of eye gaze.

Drawing on innovative mobile eye-tracking technology, my paper explores different forms of gaze behaviour that systematically occur when participants direct their interlocutor's attention to visible entities in the surroundings by means of deictic pointing. My data consists of mobile eye-tracking recordings undertaken with two pairs of eye-tracking glasses worn by participants in non-laboratory, everyday settings ((1) shopping together at a market, (2) searching for a book in a library, (3) conducting an informal conversation). The analysis is based on frame-precisely synchronised split-screen videos consisting of two complementary eye-tracking videos which allow a moment-by-moment reconstruction of the way in which the participants coordinate talk, body movements and gaze in the emergent interaction.

Keywords: mobile eye tracking, deixis, joint attention, gaze, gesture, conversation analysis, multimodality

https://doi.org/10.1075/ais.10.11stu

1.   Introduction

Linguistic research at the intersection of Conversation Analysis (Schegloff, 2007; Sidnell & Stivers, 2013), Interactional Linguistics (Couper-Kuhlen & Selting, 2001) and research on Multimodality (Goodwin, 2000, 2003; Mondada, 2007, 2012a; Streeck, 2009; Stukenbrock, 2009, 2014a, 2014b, 2015), conceptualises verbal interaction as an embodied phenomenon in which speech and visible bodily practices are treated as equally contributing to human understanding.

In the last decades, a wide range of video-analytic research has refined our understanding of how speech combines with other modalities such as gesture, gaze, body movements etc. However, video-recordings often suffer from a lack of precision concerning the participants' gaze behaviour. At the same time, there is a growing recognition of the crucial role that eye gaze plays in the on-line organisation of talk and social interaction (Argyle & Cook, 1976; Goodwin, 1980, 1981; Kendon, 1990; Rossano, 2012; Streeck, 1993, 2002, 2014; Stukenbrock, 2010, 2014a, 2015). Thus far, only very few studies within the paradigm of conversation analysis use mobile eye-tracking technology to study gaze behaviour in more or less naturally occurring interaction (Holler & Kendrick, 2015; Stukenbrock, 2018; Weiss & Auer, 2016).

Eye-tracking methods are also used to examine reference in co-present interaction (Gergle & Clark, 2010, 2011; Hanna & Brennan, 2007; Land, 2006). Psychological and cognitive studies on gaze and reference are undertaken in highly controlled settings, most of them being stationary with the participants seated. However, in everyday life, reference often involves participants on the move (Stukenbrock & Dao, accepted) as well as moving objects. In mobile settings, the temporally unfolding spatial configurations of participants and objects are as relevant as the on-line coordination of speech, movement and perception in these evanescent contextual configurations. Mobile configurations are both shaped by and shaping the participants' use of verbal and embodied resources that cannot be treated separately (De Stefani, 2010; De Stefani & Gazin, 2014; De Stefani & Mondada, 2014; Haddington, Mondada & Neville, 2013).

In order to examine reference and gaze in settings arranged to provide a higher degree of ecological validity, a few studies have begun to use mobile dual eye-tracking technology to compare multimodal reference in stationary and in mobile settings. In a conversation elicitation task (Clark & Gergle, 2010, 2011), dyads of participants in seated (side-by-side, across the table) and standing mobile conditions were asked to discuss LEGO objects according to their likelihood of being replicas of modern art. The results show interesting quantitative differences between mobile and seated participants and underline the role that gaze plays in coordinating participants' attention in multimodal reference both with and without deictic forms. Importantly, mobile pairs seem to use a higher proportion of local deictics for reference than seated participants, but show a lower proportion of gaze overlap (Gergle & Clark, 2011: p. 442). However, the exact gaze patterns of both speaker and addressee as well as the interpersonal coordination of the participants' gaze patterns involved in referring to visible objects remain an open question. Moreover, gesture is not investigated, although it is a key factor in multimodal reference. Establishing joint attention in naturally occurring interaction requires a high degree of coordination of not only speech, gaze and objects but also gesture and body movements in space.

Apart from the fact that mobile eye-tracking studies mostly focus on pre-selected, quantifiable features and do not examine moment-by-moment how participants multimodally establish reference, they also refrain from recording "in the wild". Instead, most studies set up quasi-natural tasks within half-experimental settings in laboratory rooms specifically arranged for the purpose of recording. Thus, they exclude most of what is constitutive of human interaction, most importantly, its endogenous, collective organisation "in naturally occurring social settings" (Schegloff, 1996: p. 167), it is "organized by the co-participants in a locally situated way, achieved incrementally through its temporal and sequential unfolding" (Mondada, 2012b: p. 33).

The following paper presents qualitative analyses of participants' referential practices in naturally occurring interaction across a range of different settings. Ecological validity can be claimed to hold for the conversational and mobile activities to a degree not met by previous studies. At the same time, the data presented here overcomes former deficits of traditional video-recordings as regards reliable and robust observations on the precise location of the participants' gaze and the exact trajectory of their gaze movements.

Starting from an empirically derived model of deixis and joint attention that has been developed on the basis of a large corpus of video-recordings (Stukenbrock, 2009, 2015), this paper expands and refines the results of that study by proposing a differentiated picture of gaze behaviour in acts of deictic reference in the view of mobile eye-tracking data. It claims that deixis in its primordial use in face-to-face interaction is an embodied practice that involves gestural pointing and visual perception. Speech – in the form of grammaticalised expressions termed deictics that encode and create the situational context –, gesture and eye gaze combine in a very specific way: Gaze becomes a means of interpersonal coordination that goes beyond the regulatory functions at work, e.g. in turn-taking. Within deictic referencing acts, eye gaze occupies specific slots and sequential positions that can be claimed to systematically contribute to, create and display a new status of intersubjectivity among the participants vis-à-vis a third entity, i.e. a phenomenon of joint attention.

2.   Data, methodology and challenges

The data for the following analyses consists of mobile eye-tracking recordings undertaken with two pairs of eye-tracking glasses worn by participants in everyday situations. The corpus currently under construction comprises recordings of dyads of participants (1) having an informal conversation, (2) shopping together at a market, (3) searching for a book in a library, (4) constructing a piece of furniture, (5) playing music together.

For each recording, two pairs of mobile eye-tracking glasses (SMI, sampling rate 30 Hz) are used which enables a data collection of the participants' gaze behaviour in non-laboratory, naturally occurring interaction. Each recording results in two individual videos from the participants' eye-trackers. These consist of two complementary scene videos each overlaid with a moving gaze cursor indicating the participant's exact point-of-regard (i.e. his/her foveal gaze direction, cf. for example Duchowski, 2003; Land, 2006). In stationary and in semi-mobile settings, an additional third camera is used to provide an observer's perspective on the activities. The videos are synchronised and exported as a single audio-video file for transcription and analysis. To reconstruct the participants' micro-coordination of speech, gaze and bodily behaviour moment-by-moment, as it emerges on-line, the videos are imported into ELAN (https://tla.mpi.nl/tools/tla-tools/elan/) and manually annotated.

Although mobile eye-tracking is almost exclusively used in experimental research designs within the fields of psychology, cognitive sciences, education and marketing until now (for an overview cf. Horsley et al., 2014), it can also be adapted to the fine-grained multimodal analysis within the paradigm of Conversation Analysis. However, when used for the study of interaction occurring *in situ*, mobile eye-tracking poses a range of challenges. First, when the aim is to reconstruct the "endogenous organization of social activities" (Mondada, 2012b: p. 33), the data cannot be coded automatically. The working phases of verbal transcription and multimodal annotation according to CA standards (Hepburn & Bolden, 2012; Selting et al., 2009) are thus extremely time-consuming. Secondly, recording "in the wild" increases the risk of losing data. Apart from the problems of deteriorating calibration that may result from participants' spontaneous movements (see also Clark & Gergle, 2011), constantly changing light conditions and other external factors may influence the quality of the tracking data as well.

Mobility raises a further problem. In stationary settings, the use of an external third camera that offers a full shot of the on-going interaction does not pose a problem. However, this can often not be done in mobile settings without disrupting the natural flow of the interaction. And yet, in mobile settings, we seem to be more in need of an observer's camera perspective to account for body movements not visible in the participants' scene cameras.

Last but not least, mobility creates problems of non-iconicity in various forms of data and data representation. Non-iconicity occurs almost unavoidably during the process of synchronisation, when the participants' individual recordings have to be allocated definite positions (left/right) in the split-screen video. In the split-screen video, the decisions about the spatial representation are once and for all fixed, whereas the participants on the move constantly change places. They may be walking on the right side of their partner in one given moment and on the left side in the next, they may get into a face-to-back orientation, walking ahead and behind one another, turn around briskly and move in various directions. Once fused into a single split-screen video, however, their individual videos are assigned to fixed positions in the two-dimensional space of the PC screen. Therefore, the spatial location of the participants in the split-screen video and the stills extracted from it will not always correspond to their actual location in space, but may be inverted or non-iconic in various other ways.

Non-iconicity not only affects the visual representation of stills in multimodal transcripts, conference papers and publications, but also the analysability of the data. It constitutes an enormous cognitive and perceptual challenge for the sequential analysis when undertaken not from the observer's perspective provided by a third camera, but on the basis of the dual mobile eye-tracking perspectives that intermittently happen to be represented inversely or non-iconically on the screen. Example (1) (Bib03) illustrates such a case. It shows two participants searching for a book in a library. During their activity, they naturally change places many times. In the sequence under investigation (see Section 4.1), they have re-established a side-by-side arrangement and walk along the floor. However, their momentary spatial arrangement is represented inversely in the split-screen video: The participant who is at present walking on the right hand side appears on the left side of the split-screen video and vice versa. These are moments in which a third camera, though it does not annihilate non-iconicity in the split-screen videos and poses the problem of intrusion, would help to solve analytic problems regarding the participants' bodily configurations and movements in space that are either difficult to access or not visible in the eye-tracking videos at all.

In sum, a range of considerations influences decisions on whether or not to use mobile eye-trackers and whether or not to complement the recordings with additional cameras and how. Schegloff's remarks 20 years ago on the relationship between new technologies and analytic benefits apply as much then as they do today, as with even more sophisticated instruments: "we need to ask what new analytic possibilities are made available by this new technology, and these may follow on the now observational possibilities" (Schegloff, 1996: p. 166).

3.   Deictic practices in face-to-face interaction

3.1   What is deixis?

The term "deixis" derives from the old Greek word δείξις which means 'pointing'. There are various ways in which humans can point: These comprise a large variety of bodily practices (cf. Kendon, 2004; Kita, 2003; Stukenbrock, 2015, 2016) ranging from manual gestures, other body parts such as heads, legs, or even the entire body, to the use of instruments and tools. These may be either specified for pointing or may incidentally be "at hand" (Stukenbrock, 2015). Last but not least, languages have grammaticalised linguistic forms specified for verbal pointing that constitute a class of linguistic items known as deictics.

3.2   Verbal deixis combines with bodily pointing

Significantly, deixis or verbal pointing is often accomplished in combination with bodily pointing. A deictic form and a gesture co-occur to form a multimodal point-ing device used by a speaker to orient her co-participant's attention to a visible entity in the surroundings.

The first theoretician who explicitly acknowledged the central role of gestural pointing in acts of deictic reference and integrated it into his theoretical framework was the German language psychologist Karl Bühler (2011[1934]). Bühler's thoughts on deixis, put forward in his seminal book *Sprachtheorie* (1934), are concerned with the question of how a specific class of linguistic items, deictics, serves to ground the participants communicatively with respect to the dimensions of space, time and person. The personal pronouns "I" and "you", for example, encode the role of the participants in the speech event; local adverbs such as "here" and "there" refer to proximal or distal locations relative to the location of the speaker at the moment of the utterance, and temporal adverbs such as "now", "tomorrow", "soon" etc. refer to moments in time relative to the coding time of the utterance (for more details see Fillmore, 1997; Levinson, 1983).

Bühler distinguishes three modes of pointing: (1) *demonstratio ad oculos et ad aures*, i.e. pointing to visible phenomena in the immediate surroundings, (2) *anaphora*: pointing to elements in the context of speech, and (3) *Deixis am Phantasma*: pointing to absent phenomena available only in the imagination. *Deixis am Phantasma* requires the displacement of the *origo* (Bühler, 2011[1934]) or the indexical ground (Hanks, 1990; Levinson, 2004) into an imagined domain. According to Bühler, we then "deal with the situative phantasy products, the im-agined objects, on and to which 'pointing' takes place within the imagination" (Bühler, 2011[1934]: p. 150). Those imagined entities or phantoms have to be related to spatiotemporal coordinates other than the immediate space of perception within which our body currently dwells (for detailed empirical analyses cf. Stukenbrock, 2012, 2014b, 2015, 2016).

Neither anaphoric pointing nor *Deixis am Phantasma* will be investigated in this paper. Instead, the analysis focuses on *demonstratio ad oculos* and takes up one of Bühler's central concerns. Bühler states that his "main goal" is "to show how the fulfilment of the meaning of deictic words is connected to sensory deictic clues, to show how this fulfilment is dependent on these clues and their equivalents" (Bühler, 2011[1934]: p. 94), an aspect he insists on repeatedly in his book: "I repeat: there is no phonetic deictic sign that could do without the gesture or a sensory guide equivalent to the gesture or, finally, an orientation convention that takes their place. On first hearing, that formulation may seem too involved; but it has the advantage that it includes everything without exception that can properly be called verbal deixis" (Bühler, 2011[1934]: p. 108).

Bühler's emphasis on the crucial role that bodily pointing and visual guidance play for the use of deictics in face-to-face interaction has been confirmed empirically as a key insight by a growing body of research within the field of multimodality (Eriksson, 2009; Fricke, 2007; Goodwin, 2003; Hindmarsh & Heath, 2000; Keevallik, 2013; Mondada, 2007, 2012a; Streeck, 2002; Stukenbrock, 2008, 2009, 2010, 2015). Multimodal studies on deixis demonstrate that using and understanding deictics in interaction is an embodied accomplishment. Reconstructing the participants' practices is therefore an analytic task that implies taking perspectivity and perspective-sharing not solely as a cognitive problem, but as an embodied phenomenon requiring a reciprocal moment-by-moment attunement of talk, gestures, gaze, body movements etc. of the participants in the emergent interaction.

Although there is an agreement that both verbal pointing encoded in the grammatical system of languages (i.e. deixis), and gestural pointing can be conceptualised as communicative means that bring about joint attention (Diessel, 2006; Eriksson, 2009; Goodwin, 2003; Tomasello, 2008; Stukenbrock, 2009, 2015), empirical concerns have largely been absorbed by gestures at the expense of gaze. However, if the creation of joint attention is considered to be one of the central jobs done by deictics and pointing gestures in co-present interaction, eye gaze deserves more systematic and scrupulous examination. In its manifold functions such as looking, seeing, perceiving, scanning etc., eye gaze constitutes one of the most valuable resources for participants to access the world and their co-inhabitants, to interact with them, to see what the other sees and to see whether and when oneself is seen.

When viewed as a central resource for participants in deictic practices, gaze inevitably turns into an analytic resource and object of study for the strand of research pursued by conversation analytic and interactionist approaches to human communication. Within this framework, questions and claims on the role of gaze in deictic practices need to be formulated in a specific way to be made accessible to existing concepts and the methodology of sequential analysis. These claims are put forth in the next section.

3.3   Verbal deixis requests the addressee's gaze

In addition to the Bühlerian claim that verbal deixis combines with gestural pointing (Section 3.2. above), I will argue that local deixis in its primordial use in co-present interaction combines with gesture and, in doing so, necessarily also constitutes a request for gaze. A deictic expression is not only a grammatical form that encodes certain features of the origo/indexical ground, the referent and the relationship between origo and referent or between figure and ground, but in interactional terms, it functions as a summons that makes an answer, i.e. visual attention of the addressee, conditionally relevant.

The idea that turn-initial, as well as turn-internal features in the emergent talk can work as a summons that implements a request for the addressee's gaze has first been formulated by Goodwin in his seminal paper on restarts, pauses and the achievement of mutual gaze in face-to-face interaction (Goodwin, 1981). Goodwin discovers an intricate, systematic relationship between specific vocal actions of the speaker including restarts, pauses and hesitations and the gaze behaviour of the hearer. He argues that restarts and pauses produced by the speaker "act as a request for the gaze of a hearer" so that "the actions of speaker and hearer together would constitute a particular type of summons-answer sequence" (Goodwin, 1981: p. 280). He suggests "the possibility that summons-answer sequences might function not only to provide coordinated entry into a conversation as a whole (Schegloff 1968: 1089) but also to establish the availability of participants toward each other within the turn itself" (Goodwin, 1981: p. 282f., reference to Schegloff in the original).

With respect to different degrees of granularity (Levinson, 2012), it can be observed that a request for gaze, whether implemented by a restart, a pause, a deictic term, an imperative etc. may happen on the level of action no less than within or below the level of action proper. The gestural use of a deictic term is particular in that it by default requires the co-participant to use his eyes and look, first at the speaker to get additional visible information from his bodily displays (e.g. a gesture) and next at the object of interest.

In a congenial way, the name that Bühler (1965[1934]) gave to the first mode of deixis acknowledges the irreducible role of eye gaze in acts of deictic reference. Bühler denominates the first mode of deixis with the Latin expression *demonstratio ad oculos et ad aures*. The term *demonstratio ad oculos* (*demonstratio* = 'pointing' and *ad oculos* = 'to/for the eyes') links the speaker's pointing gesture (the *demonstratio*) to the addressee's eyes (the *ad oculos*). This interpersonal *gesture-eye-link* is condensed in Bühler's terminology.

As will be shown in the empirical analyses, the *gesture-eye-link* (see Section 4.1) is only one of the multimodal relations systematically implemented by participants' gaze behaviour in deictic practices. Like the other relations established by eye gaze, i.e. the *target-eye-link* (see Section 4.2) and the *eye-to-eye-link* (see Section 4.3), it occurs in particular sequential positions and is a contextually sensitive, temporally flexible part of the extremely fine-grained interpersonal coordination that deictic practices both draw upon and accomplish in a systematic way.

4. Analyses: Gaze in deictic practices

The following analyses focus on the different relations between the participants' gaze practices in relation to one another's verbal and embodied practices. In the analyses, P will consistently be used to denote the pointing participant, A refers to his/her co-participant and addressee. Each section concludes with an interim summary that represents schematically the role that P's and A's eye gaze plays in different phases of the pointing action.

4.1 The gesture-eye-link in *demonstratio ad oculos*

When a speaker deictically refers to an entity in the visible surroundings shared with her addressee and uses a pointing gesture to direct the addressee's gaze to the location where the entity is to be found, the embodied practices of the speaker must be attended to by the addressee. If he is not already looking at the speaker, the speaker can employ various verbal and embodied practices to secure the gaze of the addressee, such as explicit summoning devices, body movements, touch etc. The argument put forth in this paper is that the deictic expression in itself constitutes a summons that implements a request for gaze – and a very specific one: It makes clear and contextualises that the addressee is expected to look at the speaker's body, particularly at his gesture or analogous bodily displays that will provide vector information leading his gaze further on towards the relevant location or target.

The first example is one of the rare instances in which a momentary fixation in the eye-tracking data reveals that the addressee A is looking directly at P's gesture before reorienting her gaze to the relevant location. The example is part of the library corpus. The participants have just learned that the library signature for the book they are looking for starts with "A". Consequently, they start searching for the section where book shelves with the shelf mark "A" are installed. We join the participants as they are walking along the hall to re-enter one of the library sections through a glass door. In the transcript, stills from the split-screen video have been inserted and aligned with the stream of speech. The stills correlate temporally with speech syllables given in bold letters in the transcript. In the figures, P's perspective is displayed on the left and A's on the right.[1]

Example (1) DA ist A   (Bib03_00:41:29)

1.   Note that the position of the participants in these stills is non-iconic. Because mobile participants continuously change places, their actual position does not always correspond to the allocation of their videos to the left and right in the split-screen video (cf. Section 2).

At the beginning of the extract, the participants are silently walking towards the glass door. They can be considered to be in an "open state of talk" (Goffman, 1981: p. 134) or "'continuing state of incipient talk'" (Schegloff & Sacks, 1973: p. 325). Figure 1 shows the perspective of our participants as they approach the glass door that separates the floor from the central area of the library. Both can be seen to be looking straight ahead (figure 1/left and right), with P walking slightly ahead of her co-participant, as evidenced in A's scene camera (figure 1/right).

As can be seen in Figure 2, P then opens the right wing of the double door and directs her gaze at the shelves at the far end of the room (figure 2/left: blue tracking circle). In the terminology to be introduced in this paper (Section 4.2), she is looking at the prospective *domain of pointing* (P- > D^P).

While she produces an in-breath that projects upcoming talk (l. 2: °*hh*), P raises her left arm, index finger extended (figure 3 left), and points to the area (figure 4 left) that she is also going to indicate deictically with the local adverb *DA/there* (l. 1: *DA ist A/there is A.*). First, the gesture is visible in her own scene camera (figure 3/left and figure 4/left), before it becomes apparent in the camera frame of her co-participant's recording (figure 4/right).

P's co-participant A slightly begins to turn sideways towards her. A's scene camera shows that she is no longer looking straight ahead through the door and into the library (figure 3/right), but to the side. More precisely, her eye-tracking data consist of saccades and thus reveal that she is moving her gaze towards the speaker P. The movement comes to a momentary halt and turning point, when A sees P's hand with the index finger extended (figure 4/right). In the eye-tracking data, there is a brief fixation almost exactly on the fingertip of P's index finger (figure 4/right); then A's gaze moves back and towards the direction pointed at by P (figure 5/right).

Note that A now comes into sight in P's scene camera. This means that the side-by-side arrangement in which P was slightly ahead of A now develops a different dynamic. Now, it is A who is getting ahead of P who not only points but also holds the door open for A. Holding the door open with her right hand while pointing with her left hand to a distant location can be understood as a multimodal invitation to follow the pointing not just perceptually, but also to take it as a directive to move on to that location.

A complies and enters the room through the glass door first and thus becomes visible in P's scene camera (figure 5–6/left). While walking through the door, A does not focus on a specific location, instead, she keeps scanning the shelves both on the left and on the right side and on the upper and lower levels of the multi-storey room (figure 5–6/right). Note that she has not uttered a response token. By now, she has overtaken her co-participant and is walking slightly ahead of P (figure 6/right).

P, in turn, retracts her pointing gesture and redirects her gaze from the bookshelves (figure 4/left) to her addressee as A enters her field of vision. More precisely, P is looking at the region of A's eyes (figure 5/left). Although the glasses impede direct access to her partner's gaze, P can nevertheless conclude from the vector orientation of A's glasses that she is looking at the far end of the room. The side-by-side-orientation dissolves even more and is reorganised into a face-to-back orientation when A steps through the glass door held open by her partner. P, whose vision now becomes partly blocked by A walking in front of her (figure 6/left), also starts scanning the shelves in the new room (figure 6/left, blue tracking circle on book shelves).

To sum up, the analysis has shown that the pointing participant P is both looking and pointing at the target, while her addressee A, after hearing the deictic adverb (DA), is summoned to redirect her gaze at the pointing speaker, in this case specifically at P's gesture. This constitutes what is conceptualised in this paper as *the gesture-eye-link* in *demonstratio ad oculos*.

This phenomenon cannot always be observed in the eye-tracking data in the form of fixations on the speaker's gesturing body part.[2] Experimental studies on addressees' fixations on gestures and addressees' uptake of gestural information show that there is no direct relationship between addressees' fixations and information uptake, but that both increase when speakers look at their own gestures first (Gullberg & Holmqvist, 2006; Gullberg & Kita, 2009) and thereby draw the addressee's attention to these gestures (Streeck, 1993, 2002). Note, though, that in contrast to the gestures investigated in these studies, speakers do not look at their pointing gestures in deictic reference, but orient their gaze to the target of the gesture. Therefore, speaker-fixation as a means to highlight the relevance of their gesture and to attract the addressee's gaze to it must be ruled out as a factor that increases the likelihood of addressee-fixations on the pointing gestures.

Abstractly, the upshot of the analysis can be represented as in Schema 1. "P" represents the pointing participant, here with the two relevant tiers "gaze" and "gesture". "A" is his/her addressee, only the tier "gaze" is relevant for the moment. Finally, "t" stands for "target":

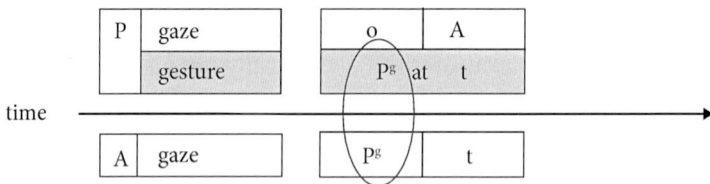

Schema 1. The gesture-eye-link in *demonstration ad oculos*

<hr />

2. As Dao (in prep.) shows in an eye-tracking study on "Blickverhalten bei sprachlichen Lokalisierungen in der Interaktion"('Gaze behaviour and verbal reference in interaction'), participants do not always look at the gesturer's hand, but often directly move on to the domain of scrutiny.

The relevant phase of interpersonal coordination that constitutes the gesture-eye-link as a relevant component of *demonstratio ad oculos*-practices can be described as follows: P is both gazing and pointing at the target object. Simultaneously, A is directing her gaze at P, in this case specifically at P's gesture (noted as P^g). This is the moment denoted by the term "gesture-eye-link".

4.2 The target-eye-link in *demonstratio ad oculos*

Joint attention on a visible object in terms of trackable, interrelated gaze patterns in the interaction between a participant P and her addressee A means that at some point in the emerging interaction, the eye-tracking data should reveal gaze fixations of both P and A on the same target, i.e. the object of shared interest. This can occur simultaneously so that P's and A's synchronised eye-tracking recordings reveal a fixation on the object of shared interest at the very same moment, or it can happen successively.[3] In the latter case, the pointing participant P can be seen to either monitor A's visual attention or to gaze elsewhere.

Typically, the gaze-pattern of a pointing participant P will be organised in such a way that P both points and looks at the target object, then freezes the gesture while reorienting his gaze to his addressee A to monitor her visual attention (Stukenbrock, 2009). When P is able to infer from his co-participant's gaze behaviour that A is also directing her visual attention to the object pointed out to her deictically, P will then look back at the object of interest. The standard gaze-pattern in deictic pointing creates a moment of shared visual attention in an orderly way within the overall multimodal scheme (cf. Stukenbrock, 2009, 2015).

The next extract is an instance of this classical pattern. The example is taken from the market corpus. Two participants, P and A, have just entered the market place and negotiate how to proceed. In the transcript, stills from the split-screen video have been inserted and aligned with the stream of speech. The syllables that the stills correlate with temporally are given in bold letters. In the figures, P's perspective is displayed on the left and A's on the right. In this case, the representation of the participants' perspective in the stills is iconic. P is in fact walking on the left hand side and A on the right.

3. In this paper, the term "sequential" is reserved for the conversation analytic family of terms. In CA terminology, a distinction is made between "sequential organisation" as the more general term referring "to any kind of organisation which concerns the relative positioning of utterances or actions" (Schegloff, 2007: p. 2) and "sequence organisation" as a type of sequential organisation restricted to "the organization of courses of action enacted through turns-at-talk" (Schegloff, 2007: p. 2). *Adjacency pairs* – two type-related turns uttered by different speakers and consisting of a first (initiative) pair-part (FPP) and a second (responsive) pair-part (SPP) – are the basic form of action sequencing and constitute the canonical case of sequence organisation.

Example (2) Kürbis / pumpkin (farmers' market)

```
01   A:    (    ) einmal GUCken,
                 let's see
02         (3.1)
03   A:    soll_ma einmal kurz ähm SCHRÄG laufen?=oder: ähm-
                 shall we just briefly walk across or um
04         (2.8)
```

```
05   P:    jah:;
                 yeah
06         (-)
07   A:    nee?
                 nah
08         (0.9)
09   P:    ha_ja_der ist ja gar nicht so GROß,
                 oh well it isn't that big after all
10   A:    nee;
                 nah
11         das (.) das geht glaub ich SCHNELL;
                 that won't take long I think
```

```
12         (0.9)
13   P:    HIER;
                 here
14         =GUCK mal;
```

```
15         (1.2)
```

```
16   P:    da gibt_s KÜRbisse;
                 there are pumpkins
17   A:    oKAY;
                 okay
```

After having entered the market place, P and A first negotiate the overall course of action (l. 1–11). They finally agree upon A's proposal (l. 03) to walk across the market first. As can be seen in figure 1, while the negotiating process is still emerging, both participants look straight ahead across the market (figure 1/left and right). A, who actually made the proposal to browse the market first, keeps her gaze aligned with that projection, continuing to scan the stalls and surroundings at middle distance (figure 2–3/right). P, however, who has reluctantly complied with the proposal, focuses on a particular class of items on the first stall: pumpkins (figure 2–3/left).

In terms of the concepts to be introduced in this paper, P is looking at an object of interest that will become a *target* within a *domain of pointing*, should he decide to alert his co-participant's attention to it. Indeed, during the pause (l. 12), he keeps his gaze fixed on the pumpkins and then utters the local deictic *HIER/here* (l. 13), followed by an imperative form of a verb of perception: *GUCK mal/look PTCL.* (l. 14). His utterance constitutes the first pair part (FPP) of a multimodal adjacency pair in which the second pair part (SPP) is delivered nonverbally. As a FPP, the summons makes a nonverbal SPP conditionally relevant: namely, that A visibly turns her gaze towards him and directs it to what he is pointing at. Requesting his addressee's gaze exactly at this moment in the emerging interaction means that P transforms the status of the first stall into a place that offers a potential buyable. He thus alters or at least suspends the trajectory of walking across the market first (for a detailed analysis cf. Stukenbrock & Dao, accepted).

During the ensuing pause (l. 15), both participants reorient their gaze. A follows the summons and looks at what P wants her to look at (figure 5/right). P, in contrast, no longer looks at the pumpkins but redirects his gaze at his addressee's face and eyes (figure 5/left), monitoring A's visual attention.[4] The eye-tracking data reveal that at the same moment that P is looking at A (figure 5/left: green tracking circle is on her face and eyes), A's gaze is already oriented at the pumpkins (figure 5/right: blue tracking circle on the pumpkins). This is a noticeable moment in the temporal format within which deictic practices unfold interactionally: the gaze practices employed by the participants systematically lead to a moment of meta-perception, i.e. the moment in which the pointing participant P can perceive his/her co-participant's perception (see Section 4.3). In this case, P orients his gaze at A's gaze so that he can infer from her gaze orientation, whether she is looking at the pumpkins (figure 5/left).

---

4. As Stukenbrock (2009, 2015) shows, this gaze practice regularly occurs in deictic sequences. Drawing on a concept introduced by the German sociologist Niklas Luhmann (1984) who uses the compound noun "Wahrnehmungswahrnehmung" (literally: 'perception's perception') to refer to the phenomenon that *ego* is able to perceive *alter's* perception, this will be termed "perception-oriented perception", "perceiving another person's perception", or "meta-perception" (see also Hausendorf, 2003 who has translated the term into "perceived perception").

When A has turned around, P utters a presentative construction that spells out what his deictic act (l. 13: *HIER/here*) has referred to previously: *da gibt_s KÜRbisse/ there are pumpkins* (l. 16). This utterance now also makes a verbal response conditionally relevant. It contains a local adverb (*da/there*) that both deictically points to an object in the surrounding space and anaphorically refers to and elaborates upon the space previously constructed by the deictic *HIER/here* (l. 13). The utterance is accompanied by a pointing gesture that is performed rather low at waist level (figure 6/right), but quite in line with the addressee's line of vision (figure 6 right: blue tracking circle for A's gaze is in line with P's arm in A's scene video). P is still looking at his addressee who is already looking at the pumpkins.

At the end of the presentative construction, the speaker (P) returns his gaze to the pumpkins. As the eye-tracking data reveal, A continues to look at the pumpkins as well. This, then, constitutes a genuine moment of joint attention created simultaneously. Both the green and the blue tracking circle are located on the pumpkins at the same time (figure 7/left and right).

After this moment of simultaneous joint attention, both withdraw their gaze from the pumpkins (figure 8) and start scanning the stall again. A utters a receipt token (l. 17: *oKAY*) which displays her understanding. However, it also contextualises her ambivalence towards the discovery and foreshadows a dispreferred reaction, followed indeed by a negative assessment (l. 18: *die sind mir zu GROSS/those are too big for me*). This rejects the possibility of considering the item as buyable and obstructs the possibility of a buying transaction.

To sum up, in moments of simultaneous joint attention, both P's and A's eye-tracking video reveal a gaze fixation on the target or object of shared interest at the very same moment in the frame-precisely synchronised split-screen video. Schematically, this can be represented as follows:

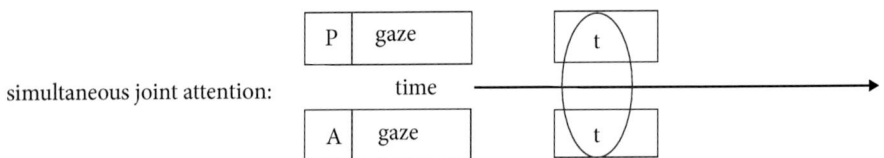

Schema 2. The taget-eye-link in *demonstratio ad oculos*

Note that the concept *target-eye-link* can be said to apply to the pointing participant P who gazes at the target in the first place and does so even before he directs his addressee's attention to it, as well as to the addressee A who follows P's pointing gesture and orients her eye gaze at the target.

However, both in temporal and in interaction-organisational terms, the target-eye-link emerges for P and A in quite different ways and assigns complementary tasks to them. Whereas A may or may not be able to find the target straight away and embark upon a search, P may have to recalculate the triadic relationship between himself, the target and his addressee's visual access to it. To refine the concept of *target-eye-link*, I therefore make two observations. First, the distinction briefly mentioned above between the target and the domain of scrutiny needs to be emphasised and integrated into the model. As Goodwin observes, "a number of different kinds of sign systems, instantiated in different semiotic media, are relevant to the organization of […] [a] point", namely, "the *pointing gesture*" that "points toward a particular place in the surround, a *domain of scrutiny*, where the addressee should look to find the *target* of the point, the particular entity pointed at" (Goodwin, 2003: p. 211, emphasis in the original). Empirical evidence for the endogenous relevance of this distinction can be gained from repair sequences in which the participants interactively work out addressee problems of finding the target within a domain of scrutiny (Goodwin, 2003; Stukenbrock, 2015).

My second observation concerns a specific gaze practice used by the pointing participant before he deictically directs the addressee's gaze to an object of joint attention. As we already noted in Example (2), pointing participants can be seen to first orient themselves in space before they actually initiate a pointing act. This pre-orientation serves both the intra- and interpersonal self-calibration of the speaker P in relation to the target and to the addressee A. It is a gaze practice that is part of the speaker's embodied sensitivity towards the triadic intercorporeal relation that is to be established deictically between himself, his addressee and a phenomenon of the visible world. In order to create a triadic relationship grounded in shared visual perception, P has to ensure that his addressee A has visual access both to his body and to the target of his emerging pointing act. To capture the gaze practice of the pointing speaker P, I differentiate between the *domain of pointing* to denominate the space that P is initially looking at to pre-orient himself with regard to the target, and the *domain of scrutiny* that constitutes the search space that A is looking at when requested to do so by her interlocutor P.

The gaze practice used by pointing participants to pre-orient themselves perceptually is a recurring feature in acts of deictic reference (Stukenbrock, 2009, 2014b, 2015). This could be seen in Example (2) ("Kürbis/pumpkin"), where the pointing participant P looks at the basket with pumpkins (Example (2): figure 2/left, figure 3/left) quite some time before he actually draws his addressee's attention to it. Example (3) is another instance of this gaze pattern. Although the interaction does not occur in a mobile setting, it is included in the data because it illustrates the gaze practice in some detail. It is a sequence taken from an informal conversation between two students in a common room. The participants talk about Christmas decoration. Participant A just complained about her mother's intention to set up a plastic Christmas tree and tells her friend about her reaction to this idea towards her mother. Her friend, participant P, disagrees and points to a plastic tree nearby that is part of the Christmas decoration in the room. The perspective of the third

Example (3) Plastikbaum / plastic tree

```
01 A: <<acc>da ha_ich_gsa_homa_was machen wir mit_m PLAStikbaum;
           then I said look what are we doing with a plastic tree
```

```
02            =ins WOHNzimmer stellen,
              install it in the living room
03            darauf hab ich !GAR! kein bock;
              I would hate that
04            dann [ (…)
              then
```

```
05 P:          [ˀh <<acc>ja aber GUCK_mal;
                    yes but look PTCL
```

```
06            SCHAU mal;
              look PTCL
```

```
07        DESCH AUCH_n plastikbaum;
          that's also a plastic tree
```

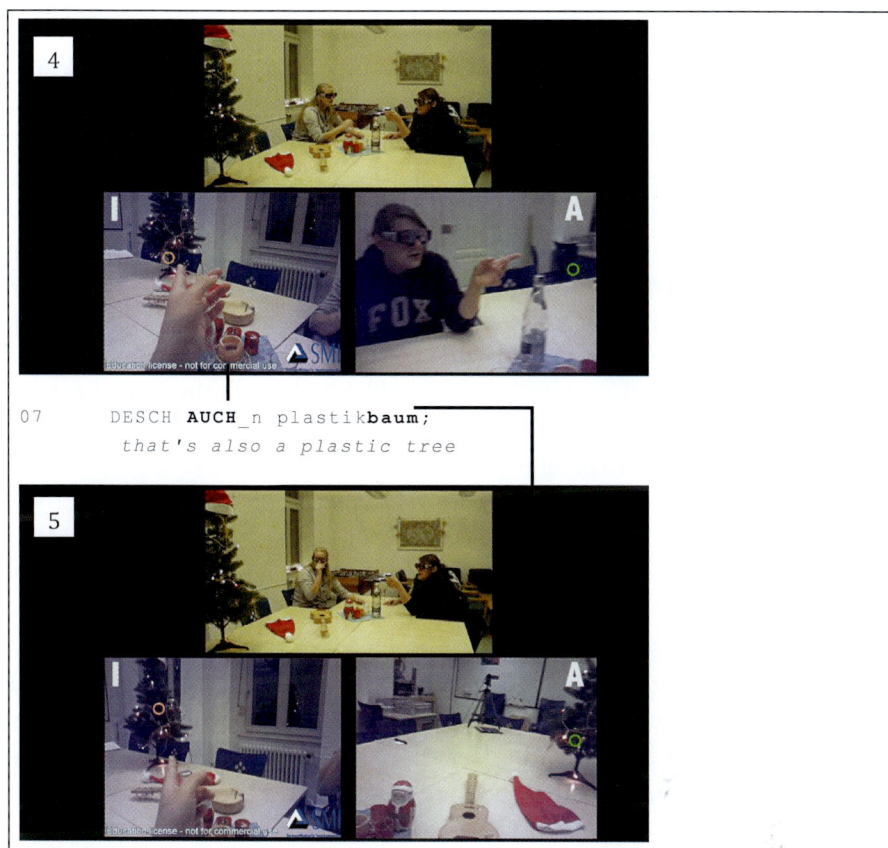

camera placed at the top of the split screen video shows A sitting on the left and P across the table on the right. Whereas P's perspective is displayed on the left, A's perspective is given on the right.

At the beginning of the extract, the participants are engaged in talk. A has just been telling P about her mother's suggestion to buy an artificial Christmas tree this year and reports her reaction to this idea. As she quotes her own words in the narrated situation (l. 1–2), she gazes at her addressee who is listening and looking back at her. Figure 1 (left and right) reveals this moment of mutual gaze (Goodwin, 1981; Kendon, 1990).

After the self-quotation, A continues and utters an assessment (l. 03). She very much dislikes her mother's idea. Conversation analytic research has shown that assessments constitute first pair parts that make a second pair part condition-ally relevant (Pomerantz, 1984), the preference is for agreement. This means that co-participant P is not only expected to utter a second assessment, but also to go along with A's negative evaluation.

However, P's response is designed in such a way that it can be heard as disa-greeing: The particle *ja/yes* is followed by the conjunction *aber/but* that foreshadows disagreement. Instead of disagreeing explicitly with her friend, P draws her attention to an artificial Christmas tree that is part of the decoration by pointing at it. Before she performs the pointing gesture and utters the demonstrative pronoun *DESCH/that* (l. 07), P withdraws her gaze from A and reorients it to the location where the future target of her upcoming pointing gesture is to be found (figure 2/ left: orange tracking circle on the tree).

The gaze shift occurs early: As P takes over the turn by producing an in-breath (l. 05) that overlaps with A's new utterance (l. 04), she no longer looks at her co-participant A, but redirects her gaze to a location in middle distance (figure 2/left: orange tracking circle), i.e. at the plastic tree that she is going to point at in the emerging utterance. A also averts her gaze and looks down at the table (figure 2/ right: green tracking circle).

The perceptual pre-orientation that becomes evident in P's eye-tracking data is an integral part of the pointing participant's multimodal coordination (Stukenbrock, 2009, 2015). The moment when P's gaze arrives at the Christmas tree constitutes a target-eye-link on the part of P, one that occurs within the domain of pointing. This gaze practice primarily serves intrapersonal coordination (Deppermann & Schmitt, 2007), but it can be exploited interactionally for interpersonal coordination as well. For example, pointing participants can be seen to orient their gaze explicitly and perceivably, i.e. publicly displayed, to a location in the surroundings before they manually point to it. Likewise, addressees can be seen to follow their partner's gaze to a future target before the pointing gesture explicitly directs them to that location (cf. Dao, in prep.). Last but not least, pointing participants exploit the mechanism of gaze-following by pointing solely with their eye gaze and/or head without using any manual gestures at all. This practice regularly occurs when the hands are busy with something else (e.g. cooking) or when the pointing has to be accomplished covertly (cf. Stukenbrock, 2015).

As noted above, the gaze practice recurrently used by pointing participants to orient themselves in space before they summon their addressee's attention occurs long before P's hand leaves the resting position to get the gesture under way. P only begins to move her hand as she utters the second of the two summons (l. 06: *SCHAU mal/look PTCL*). P's hand movement is visible in her addressee's scene camera (figure 3/right). The two summons consist of a verb of visual perception in the imperative form (l. 05: *GUCK mal/look PTCL*; l. 06: *SCHAU mal/look PTCL*) that explicitly summons the addressee's gaze before the deictic reference and the pointing are accomplished.

Whereas P's gaze remains fixed on the plastic tree (figure 3/left: orange tracking circle), A redirects her gaze at P's face, more precisely at the region of her eyes (figure 3/right: green tracking circle). When doing so, A can perceive that P is looking elsewhere and use her partner's gaze direction as a vector to extrapolate the target of P's visual attention. But this is by no means certain. Since P's hand has visibly left the resting position, there is an interactional projection at play that P is also going to perform a gesture that A is expected to perceive.

Indeed, as can be seen in figure 4, when P utters the demonstrative pronoun *DESCH/that* (l. 07), she also uses a pointing gesture to direct her addressee's attention to the target. While P is still looking at the tree (figure 4/left), A begins to reorient her gaze away from P (figure 4/right) and towards the domain of scrutiny indexed both by P's gesture and gaze. At the end of P's utterance, A's gaze has arrived at the target, i.e. the object of shared interest (figure 5/right). Since P continues to gaze at the tree (fig 5/left), this moment constitutes a moment of simultaneous joint attention on a visible object.

In this section, the additional term "domain of pointing" has been introduced and contrasted with the term "domain of scrutiny" to conceptualise the space constituted by a recurrent gaze practice deployed by pointing participants as a systematic component of their intra- and interpersonal coordination in deictic practices. Moreover, the concept both theoretically and empirically accounts for the fact that spaces of shared attention emerge gradually and successively in time, moving from subjectively conceived and perceived spaces and phenomena of potentially joint interest to objects of joint attention and interactionally accomplished intersubjectivity.

To sum up, the *target-eye-link* discussed in this section to conceptualise (a) the relation between a speaker P and an object of interest he wants to share, and (b) the relation between the addressee A and an object that P perceives and makes relevant for A by a deictic referencing/pointing act, has proven to be fruitful, but also needed some conceptual refinement. Schematically, the concepts and differentiations introduced in this chapter can be represented as follows:

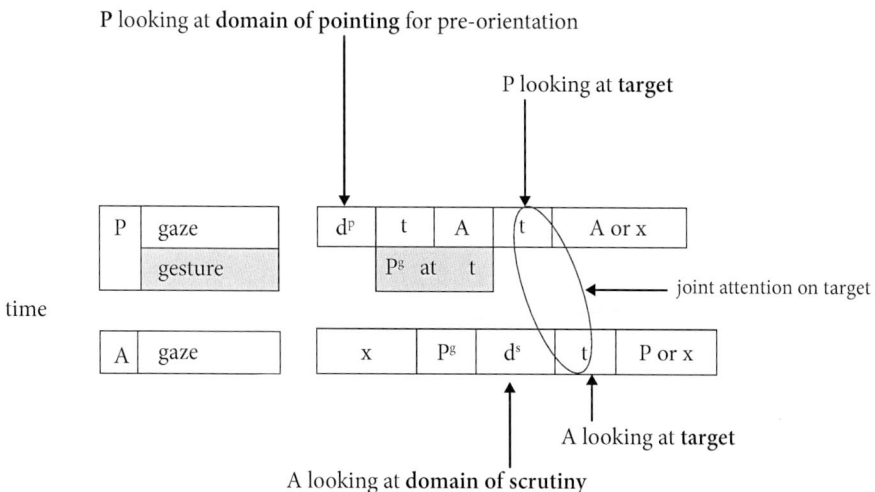

Schema 3. Differentiated view of the target-eye-link in *demonstratio ad oculos*

4.3   The eye-to-eye-link in *demonstratio ad oculos*

Focused interaction – no matter whether it involves deictic practices or not – is characterised by the participants mutually acknowledging and signalling to each other that they have placed themselves "at the disposal of the other for purposes of a mutual eye-to-eye activity" (Goffman, 1963: p. 92). Significantly, Goffman refers to focused interaction as a *face engagement* and emphasises that "[e]ye-to-eye looks [...] play a special role in the communication life of the community, ritually establishing an avowed openness to verbal statements and a rightfully heightened mutual relevance of acts" (Goffman, 1963: p. 92). From a sociological point of view, Goffman ascribes to the eyes a privileged position and unique function among our sense organs, one that is crucially related to the possibility of eye contact: "Of the special sense-organs, the eye has a uniquely sociological function. The union and interaction of individuals is based upon mutual glances. This is perhaps the most direct and purest reciprocity which exists anywhere" (Goffman, 1963: p. 93).

Eye contact or mutual gaze has various functions and occurs at different moments in an emerging interaction (Kendon, 1990; Goodwin, 1981; Rossano, 2012; Streeck, 2014). When Goffman speaks of the "eye-to-eye ecological huddle [that] tends to be carefully maintained, maximizing the opportunity for the participants to monitor one another's perceivings" (Goffman, 1963: p. 95), he is concerned with the nature of face engagements in general. Nonetheless, the observation that the opportunity for mutual monitoring is increased leads to the question of what this monitoring of "one another's perceivings" means specifically in and for deictic practices. For, if the claim holds that verbal deixis is a request for the addressee's gaze, then we would expect specific gaze patterns that deal with the sequential implementation of this request and its correlating next.

The *eye-to-eye-link* in deictic practices means something very specific that is not to be confused with eye contact in the sense of *mutual gaze* or *gaze window* (Streeck, 2014), although this also constitutes an important gaze practice, less with regard to the specificities of deictic practices though, but with regard to turn-taking, action formation etc. (Rossano, 2012). What is special with regard to deixis is the triadic relation and the process of making perception intersubjective, i.e. mutually accessible through perception-oriented perception or meta-perception. This moment of meta-perception already surfaced in Example (2) ("Kürbis/pumpkin") when A turns around to look at the pumpkin and P orients his gaze at her to monitor her visual attention (see Section 4.2, Example (2), Figure 5/left).

The sequential analysis of the last example "fett DRAN/in bold" focuses on the moment in which the pointing participant P can see, by looking at her addressee's eyes, that A is looking at the target of the pointing gesture. The participants, two freshmen searching for a book in the library, have just asked the library staff (L) about the location of a library signature they have not been able to find. They turn away from the library desk to resume their search.

Example (4) fett DRAN/in bold   (Bib03_00:46:49)

```
01    A:    also::
            PTCL
02    L:    (also [HIER HINten) die TREppe hoch,
            PTCL here in the back up the stairs
03    P:          [also HIER;
                   PTCL here
04          (--)
05    A:    geNAU;
            right
06          oKEE;
            okay

07    L:    [(...........)
```

```
08    P:    [GUCK_ma hIer stehts auch fett DRAN;
            look PTCL here it's also written in bold
```

```
09          (1.3                                              )
10    A:    ha;
```

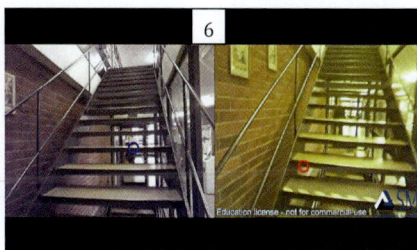

```
11    P:    ha;
            ha
12    A:    ((giggles))
13          (-)
14    A:    DANkeschö::n;
            thank you
15          (2.0                                              )
```

After the two women have left the library desk, A utters the discourse marker *also::/ so* (l. 01) to relaunch the search. From afar, the library staff who must be monitoring the two girls, reformulates the instruction previously given at the desk by adapting it to the trajectory projected by the students' movement (l. 02: *also HIER HINten die TREPpe hoch/PTCL here in the back up the stairs*). In partial overlap with the staff's instruction, P begins to speak also using the discourse marker *also* followed by the deictic adverb *HIER/here* (l. 03). The clarification process will not be described in greater detail here. It is brought to a close when P discovers a sign on a glass door. The sign indicates the sub-unit of the library (*Germanistische Linguistik*/'German Linguistics') they were looking for.

Upon discovering the sign, P utters a summons (l. 08: *GUCK_ma/look PTCL*) followed by the deictic adverb *hIer/here* (l. 08). The deictic is accompanied by a pointing gesture performed with an open hand palm vertical (for details about gesture shapes cf. Kendon, 2004; Stukenbrock, 2015) and directed at the door sign. At the same time, P keeps looking at the sign (figure 1/right: red tracking circle). Simultaneously, A's recording reveals that P is now within the camera frame of her addressee A (figure 1/left) whose gaze is likewise oriented at the sign (figure 1/left: blue tracking circle). Since P is not looking at her partner, she cannot know that A has discovered the sign as well. P then lowers her arm, reorients her gaze and, by reaching for the doorknob and aligning her gaze with the movement, projects that she will open the door (figure 2/left). At the end of her utterance, with her left hand already on the doorknob (figure 3/left), P turns towards A and focuses on her partner's eyes (figure 3/right: red tracking circle on A's eyes/glasses). She can then see and infer from the visual orientation of her partner that A is looking at the relevant sign at that very moment. A's eye-tracking data reveal that her gaze is indeed fixed on the sign (figure 3/left: blue tracking circle on the third line of the sign).

The moment in which a pointing participant directs her gaze to the addressee's eyes to monitor her visual attention constitutes what is here conceptualised as the *eye-to-eye-link* in *demonstratio ad oculos*. More precisely, since this is not a dyadic moment of mutual gaze or eye-contact, but a triadic one in which the pointing participant P perceives that her co-participant A is perceiving a third entity (i.e. the target of the deictic referencing act), the phenomenon under investigation would more suitably be called an *eye-to-eye-to-target-link*.

Interestingly, after having perceived her co-participant's perception, P looks back at the door sign (figure 4/right: red tracking circle on the sign again), whereas A now withdraws her gaze from the sign and directs it at P's eyes (figure 4/left: blue tracking circle on P's eyes/glasses) thus mirroring the previous moment of an eye-to-eye-(to-target)-link in a kind of role reversal. The one who has been perceived before now takes over the role of the perceiver.

In what follows, the two participants also verbally mirror each other. First, A utters a response cry (l. 10: *ha*) that displays the changed epistemic state vis-à-vis the way-finding problem followed by P repeating the response cry (l. 11: *ha*) and thus audibly sharing the affective stance also incorporated in A's initial response cry. This is additionally displayed facially when the two participants reciprocally exchange glances and smiling faces (figure 5/left and right). Afterwards, they establish a side-by-side orientation and jointly walk up the stairs (figure 6/left and right).

To sum up, claims hitherto made about the role of perceiving the other's perception in deictic reference on the basis of video analyses (Hausendorf, 2003; Stukenbrock, 2009, 2015) can now be validated more exactly with mobile dual eye-tracking data. We can observe with an extremely high degree of granularity that a very fine intercorporeal attunement between the participants is at play that enables them to converge on the moment in which A looks at the target and P manages to see A looking at the target. That we use our own and the other's gaze in a meta-perceptual way[5] to "monitor one another's perceivings" (Goffman, 1963: p. 93) proves gaze to be an enhancer of intersubjectivity *par excellence*.

The results of the empirical analyses on the eye-to-eye-link in deictic practices can be schematically represented as follows:

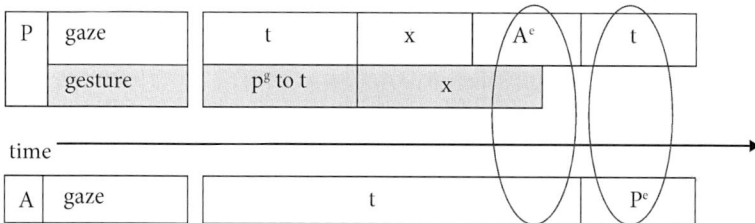

P	gaze		t	x	A^e		t
	gesture		p^g to t		x		

time →

| A | gaze | | t | | | P^e | |

Schema 4. The eye-to-eye-(to-target-)link in *demonstratio ad oculos*

In the sequence, P first gazes and points at the target, then reorients her gaze to the door (noted in the schema as "x") and reaches with her hand for the doorknob, before she finally looks at her addressee A. When she does so, she can see that A is also looking at the target. A has already been looking at the target for quite a while. Sequentially, this is not always the case. On the contrary, in cases in which the pointing participant establishes a new focus of attention, the addressee A has to look at P and his gesture first before she can find the target (see Section 4.1). What is important for the phenomenon discussed here is the moment in which P perceives A's perception, i.e. when P monitors A's eye gaze (noted as A^e) and sees that A is looking at what P wants her to look at. Interestingly, in this example, a mirror effect

---

5. Note that gaze following constitutes a gaze practice that serves various functions: We can use another person's gaze direction to find out what he/she is looking at and thus also focus on a new area of interest, or we can use our co-participant's gaze orientation to monitor his/her attentional state regarding a phenomenon we pointed out to him/her.

occurs when P reorients her gaze to the target and A, inversely, looks back at P. Her gaze fixation is on P's eyes (P^e). She can gather from P's visual orientation that P is looking at the target again. This marks the transition from the orientation seeking sequence to the stance taking sequence in which both humorously acknowledge that they had been blind to the fact that the solution to their way-finding problem was hiding in plain sight.

5.   Conclusion: On eye-tracking natural gaze practices in *demonstratio ad oculos*

Based on dual mobile eye-tracking data recorded 'in the wild', the empirical analyses presented in this study examine gaze practices that are systematically implemented when participants refer deictically to visible entities in their surroundings. Importantly, the analytic focus has been both on the gaze practices of the pointing speaker P, as well as on those of his addressee A. These gaze practices have not been studied apart from other practices, but in their intricate relationship to speech and other embodied practices, particularly pointing gestures, body movements, participant configurations and movements in space.

By recording pairs of mobile participants in naturally occurring interaction, the study has aimed to test the novel technology of mobile eye-tracking within a research paradigm – conversation analysis – that has put forth methodologically and theoretically compelling reasons for *in situ* studies of human interaction in order to study "the rational properties of indexical expressions and other practical actions as contingent ongoing accomplishments of organised artful practices of everyday life" (Garfinkel, 1967: p. 11).

One of the most important observations that needs to be made is that mobile eye-tracking videos do not represent the participants' perspective in a naturalistic way. An eye-tracking video gives an artificial picture frame of the participant's camera that reduces his/her view technically to a rectangular window onto the world and literally cuts out an important amount of perceptual information that participants gain through peripheral vision. It omits quite a large amount of contextual information that the participants have access to and that researchers also need in order to examine the wider spatial context. At least in stationary settings, this problem can easily be solved by using an additional observer's camera.

Although mobile eye-tracking recordings do not offer a naturalistic, emic representation of the participant's view, they do present a new participant-centred visual perspective on what emerges online in spatially situated, space building embodied interaction. Recording naturally occurring human interaction with mobile eye-tracking glasses creates entirely new sets of data that differ radically from the observer's or third person perspective in traditional video recordings. These data force us to both open up and confine our analytic view to the ego-perspective of each recorded participant and at the same time allow us to get inside the interpersonal dynamics on an unprecedented micro-analytic level. Moreover, mobile eye-tracking data also challenge our video-analytic practices and invite us to search for, discover and make use of new and alternative sources of information in the eye-tracking videos beyond fixations and saccades such as, for example, constantly changing and oblique angles of the scene camera, varying temporal and spatial dynamics of camera movements as the participants move their head, torso and entire body, walk, sit down, get up, turn around etc.

The detailed analyses on gaze practices in deictic reference presented in Section 4 have shown that gaze plays a prominent role in the interpersonal coordination of the participants' speech, gesture, body orientation and movements in space. The following gaze practices form constitutive parts of deictic reference in face-to-face interaction and occur systematically at specific moments in the accomplishment of joint attention on a visible phenomenon. They have been conceptualised as *the gesture-eye-link, the target-eye-link* and *the eye-to-eye-link* in *demonstratio ad oculos* and can be refined as follows:

First of all, establishing a *target-eye-link* is an indispensable component of both P's and A's gaze practices in deictic reference:

P ·······➤ t   = P looking at target
A ·······➤ t   = A looking at target

The term "target-eye-link" is a catchy phrase that condenses, but also simplifies the detailed analyses of how P and A use their eyes in deictic reference. On the micro-level of analysis on the temporal unfolding of deictic referencing acts, it has become evident that the pointing participant P first orients him-/herself in space before he/she actually deictically refers and gesturally points to a visible phenomenon he/she wants to share with his/her co-participant A. He/she looks at the *domain of pointing* first in order to access the visibility of the target both to him-/herself and to his/her co-participant at the moment in which he/she will be pointing to it. This pre-orientation can come very early:

P ·······➤ d^P = P looking at the domain of pointing

Likewise, the addressee A, when being led by P's pointing gesture to find a target in the surroundings, will first look at what has been termed the "domain of scrutiny" (Goodwin, 2003) before actually identifying the target of the point. Finding the target within the domain of scrutiny can become problematic at times:

A ·······➤ d^s = A looking at the domain of scrutiny

Joint attention is a crucial component in deictic reference to visible phenomena in face-to-face interaction. It does not consist of P looking at the domain of pointing and A at the domain of scrutiny. Instead, it has to be conceived of as both participants being perceptually oriented to the same phenomenon. This constitutes the visible target of the pointing act and enables the addressee to identify the referent:

P ·······► t   = P looking at target
A ·······► t   = A looking at target

P and A may happen to gaze at the target simultaneously, when P, after having monitored A's reaction to his pointing act and seeing that she looks at the target, turns his gaze to the target as well; or it may occur at different moments in the emerging interaction.

The second important dimension of gaze practices in *demonstratio ad oculos* is *the gesture-eye-link* that takes various forms. Of course, being visually oriented to the co-participant is crucial in face-to-face interaction in general. At times, P will be looking at A and A at P with moments of mutual gaze, and other moments in which one is gazing at the partner when the partner is looking elsewhere (Goodwin, 1981; Kendon, 1967, 1990; Rossano, 2012; Streeck, 2014). The dimensions of the *body-eye-link* that are constitutive for the interpersonal coordination in multimodal reference can be specified as follows: Beyond A looking at P and P looking at A in an unspecified way, A can be observed to look at P's body, and even more specifically, at his gesture:

A ·······► P^g = A looking at P's gesture

The third dimension that is constitutive for the way in which gaze practices are systematically organised for the specific purpose of deictic reference has been termed "the eye-to-eye-link" in *demonstratio ad oculos*. As in turn-taking and other actions and activities, P and A can be seen to orient their gaze at their co-participant's eyes. When A and P reciprocally look at each other's eyes simultaneously, a moment of mutual gaze occurs:

A^e ◄···············► P^e = A looking at P's eyes and P looking at A's eyes simultaneously

Mutual gaze is nothing in particular with regard to deictic reference, nor is looking at the co-participant's eyes when he/she is gazing elsewhere. What is specific about the interpersonal coordination of gaze in *demonstratio ad oculos* and distinguishes it from other gaze practices in face-to-face interaction, is the fact that deictically embedded gaze practices are designed to gather information about the co-participant's perception vis-à-vis a third entity – the phenomenon of joint attention. This makes them uniquely suited for the interactional accomplishment of joint attention constituting a triadic intercorporeal relation that involves a timing and spacing of embodied action, perception and cognition. Confirming and refining former work on deixis and gaze (Stukenbrock, 2009, 2010, 2015), the eye-tracking analyses presented here identify systematic moments that mark a heightened perceptual interest of ego in alter's perceivings, i.e. an other-oriented meta-perceptual use of perception. This interest of the participants is put to practice and displayed by their other-gaze-oriented gaze and thus also becomes accessible to the sequential analysis of embodied conduct:

A ┄┄┄► P^e = A looking at P's eyes
P ┄┄┄► A^e = P looking at A's eyes

When A gazes at P's eyes in *demonstratio ad oculos*, this occurs after and in response to A having been summoned to look at P by a deictic form that "is connected to sensory deictic clues" (Bühler, 2011[1934]: p. 94) and thus requires A to gather additional information from P's gesture and/or gaze orientation. A will therefore be looking at P's gesture and/or alternatively at his gaze direction.

P, on the other hand, can be systematically observed to look at A and particularly at her eyes right after he has uttered a deictic request for A's gaze. Getting A's gaze is not an end in itself as it is in the production of restarts and pauses in order to attract the addressee's visual attention (Goodwin, 1981), but a means to direct the addressee's attention to a third entity via an embodied pointing device, most often a manual gesture. P will therefore carefully coordinate his bodily behaviour with the perceived conduct of his addressee A to make sure that A can see his gesture, when A turns to him and follows his gestural instruction to look at the target. P's monitoring of A, his gazing at A's gaze is thus aimed at perceiving whether A perceives what P wants A to perceive, so that joint attention and intersubjectivity arise as an interactional accomplishment.

Note, however, that P does not always turn his gaze to A to monitor her visual orientation with regard to the target of his pointing act. When participants are intensively involved in manual tasks and both know that this absorbs their entire visual attention, gaze practices designed to monitor the co-participant's perception are dispensed with. These cases are particularly prominent in the IKEA corpus, where participants build furniture together and are very much involved with material objects and construction tasks at hand (Stukenbrock, in prep.). In other words, gaze practices that are meta-perceptually oriented at the co-participant's visual perception not only occur in particular positions, but are also activity-sensitive (Stukenbrock, 2015).

In order to put the detailed observations on the interrelatedness of dialogically emerging gaze patterns in deictic reference together to get the whole picture, we finally need to come back to the role that language and, more specifically, that deictic forms play in the overall organisation of the participants' multimodal reference practices. In this paper, two related claims have been put forth: first, that verbal deictics are combined with (pointing) gestures to direct the co-participant's attention to visible phenomena in the surroundings, and secondly, that the use of deictics in face-to-face interaction consequently constitutes a request for the co-participant's gaze. This means that within the deictic referencing act, a multi-modal summons-answer unfolds that occupies a systematic position and implements recurrent gaze patterns of P and A that are activity-sensitive, contextually adapted and temporally fine-tuned to their emerging verbal and kinesic practices. Schematically, the deictic form can be integrated as in Schema 5:

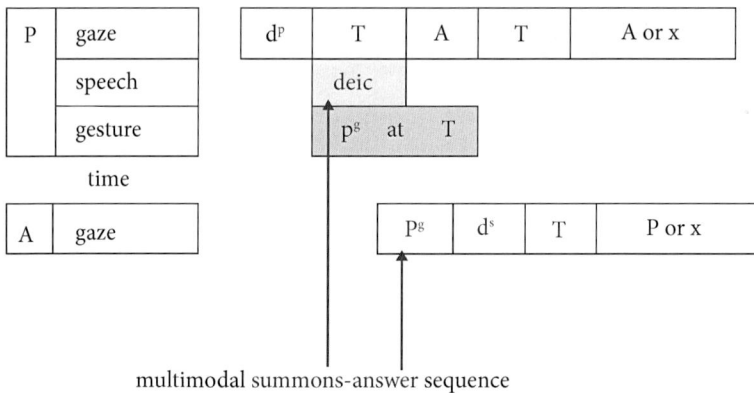

multimodal summons-answer sequence

Schema 5. Gaze practices in *demonstratio ad oculos*

Acknowledgments

I thank the anonymous reviewer for a critical reading and insightful comments on the manuscript. I would also like to thank Anika Kamilla Clausen for checking my English and for proofreading.

References

Argyle, M. & Cook, M. (1976). *Gaze and Mutual Gaze*. London: Cambridge University Press.
Brooks, R. & Meltzoff, A. N. (2014). Gaze following: A mechanism for building social connections between infants and adults. In M. Mikulincer & P. R. Shaver (Eds.), *Mechanisms of social connection: From brain to group* (pp. 167–183). Washington, D.C.: American Psychological Association. https://doi.org/10.1037/14250-010
Bühler, K. (1965 [1934]). *Sprachtheorie. Die Darstellungsfunktion der Sprache*. Stuttgart: Gustav Fischer Verlag.
Bühler, K. (2011 [1934]). *Theory of Language. The Representational Function of Language*. (translated by D. F. Goodwin in collaboration with A. Eschbach). Amsterdam, Philadelphia: John Benjamins. https://doi.org/10.1075/z.164

Clark, A. T. & Gergle, D. (2011, September). *Mobile Dual Eye-Tracking Methods: Challenges and Opportunities*. Paper presented at DUET 2011: Dual Eye Tracking Workshop at ECSCW 2011, Aarhus, Denmark.

Clark, A. T. & Gergle, D. (2012, February). *Know what I'm talking about? Dual eye-tracking in multimodal reference resolution*. Paper presented at DUET 2012: Dual Eye Tracking workshop at CSCW 2012, Bellevue, WA.

Clark, H. H., Schreuder, R. & Buttrick, S. (1983). Common Ground and the Understanding of Demonstrative Reference. *Journal of Verbal Learning and Verbal Behavior*, 22(2), 245–258. https://doi.org/10.1016/S0022-5371(83)90189-5

Couper-Kuhlen, E. & Barth-Weingarten, D. (2011). A system for transcribing talk in interaction. GAT 2. English translation and adaption of Selting. Margret et al. (2009): Gesprächs-analytisches Transkriptionssystem 2. In *Gesprächsforschung – Online-Zeitschrift zur verbalen Interaktion*, 12, 1–51.

Couper-Kuhlen, E. & Selting, M. (2001). *Studies in Interactional Linguistics*. Amsterdam: John Benjamins.

Dao, A. N. (in prep.). *Blickverhalten bei sprachlichen Lokalisierungen in der Interaktion*. PhD thesis Freiburg/Br.

Deppermann, A. & Schmitt, R. (2007). Koordination. Zur Begründung eines neuen Forschungs-gegenstandes. In R. Schmitt (Ed.), *Koordination. Analysen zur multimodalen Interaktion* (pp. 15–54). Tübingen: Narr.

De Stefani, E. (2010). Reference as an interactively and multimodally accomplished practice. Organizing spatial reorientation in guided tours. In M. Pettorino et al. (Eds.), *Spoken Communication* (pp. 137–170). Newcastle upon Tyne: Cambridge Scholars Publishing.

De Stefani, E. & Gazin, A. -D. (2014). Instructional sequences in driving lessons: Mobile partic-ipants and the temporal and sequential organization of actions. *Journal of Pragmatics*, 65, 63–79. https://doi.org/10.1016/j.pragma.2013.08.020

De Stefani, E. & Mondada, L. (2014). Reorganizing mobile formations: When 'guided' partici-pants initiate reorientation in guided tours. *Space and Culture*, 17(2), 157–175. https://doi.org/10.1177/1206331213508504

Diessel, H. (2006). Demonstratives, joint attention, and the emergence of grammar. *Cognitive Linguistics*, 17(4), 463–489. https://doi.org/10.1515/COG.2006.015

Duchowski, A. T. (2003). *Eye Tracking Methodology. Theory and Practice*. Berlin: Springer. https://doi.org/10.1007/978-1-4471-3750-4

Eriksson, M. (2009). Referring as Interaction: On the Interplay Between Linguistic and Bodily Practices. *Journal of Pragmatics*, 41, 240–262. https://doi.org/10.1016/j.pragma.2008.10.011

Fillmore, C. (1997). *Lectures on Deixis*. Stanford, CA: CSLI Publ.

Fricke, E. (2007). Origo, Geste und Raum. Lokaldeixis im Deutschen. *Berlin: de Gruyter*.

Garfinkel, H. (1967). *Studies in Ethnomethodology*. Englewood Cliffs, Nj: Prentice-Hall.

Gergle, D. & Clark, A. T. (2010). *Effects of Shifting Spatial Context on Referential Form*. Paper presented at the 20th Annual Meeting of the Society for Text and Discourse.

Gergle, D. & Clark, A. T. (2011). See What I'm Saying? Using Dyadic Mobile Eye-Tracking to Study Collaborative Reference. *Proceedings of CSCW* (2011), 435–444.

Goffman, E. (1963). *Behavior in Public Places. Notes on the Social Organization of Gatherings*. New York: The Free Press.

Goffman, E. (1981). *Forms of Talk*. Philadelphia: University of Pennsylvania Press.

Goodwin, C. (1980). Restarts, Pauses, and the Achievement of a State of Mutual Gaze at Turn-Beginning. *Sociological Inquiry*, 50(3–4), 272–302. https://doi.org/10.1111/j.1475-682X.1980.tb00023.x

Goodwin, C. (1981). *Conversational Organization: Interaction Between Speakers and Hearers.* New York: Academic Press.

Goodwin, C. (2000). Action and embodiment within situated human interaction. *Journal of Pragmatics*, 32, 1489–1522. https://doi.org/10.1016/S0378-2166(99)00096-X

Goodwin, C. (2003). Pointing as Situated Practice. In S. Kita (Ed.), *Pointing. Where Language, Culture, and Cognition Meet* (pp. 217–241). Mahwah, NJ: Erlbaum.

Gullberg, M. & Holmqvist, K. (2006). What speakers do and what addressees look at. Visual attention to gestures in human interaction live and on video. *Pragmatics and Cognition*, 14(1), 53–82. https://doi.org/10.1075/pc.14.1.05gul

Gullberg, M. & Kita, S. (2009). Attention to Speech-Accompanying Gestures: Eye Movements and Information Uptake. *Journal of Nonverbal Behavior*, 33, 251–277. https://doi.org/10.1007/s10919-009-0073-2

Haddington, P., Mondada, L. & Neville, M. (2013). *Interaction and Mobility. Language and the Body in Motion.* Berlin, Boston: de Gruyter. https://doi.org/10.1515/9783110291278

Hanks, W. F. (1990). *Referential practice. Language and lived space among the Maya.* Chicago: University of Chicago Press.

Hanna, J. E. & Brennan, S. E. (2007). Speakers' eye gaze disambiguates referring expressions early during face-to-face conversation. *Journal of Memory and Language*, 57, 596–651. https://doi.org/10.1016/j.jml.2007.01.008

Hausendorf, H. (2003). Deixis and speech situation revisited. The mechanism of perceived perception. In F. Lenz (Ed.), *Deictic Conceptualisation of Space, Time and Person* (pp. 249–269). Amsterdam: John Benjamins. https://doi.org/10.1075/pbns.112.13hau

Hepburn, A. & Bolden, G. (2012). The Conversation Analytic Approach to Transcription. In J. Sidnell & T. Stivers (Eds.), *The Handbook of Conversation Analysis* (pp. 57–76). Wiley: Blackwell. https://doi.org/10.1002/9781118325001.ch4

Hindmarsh, J. & Heath, C. (2000). Embodied reference: A study on deixis in workplace interaction. *Journal of Pragmatics*, 32(12), 1855–1878. https://doi.org/10.1016/S0378-2166(99)00122-8

Holler, J. & Kendrick, K. (2015). Unaddressed participants' gaze in multi-person interaction: Optimizing recipiency. *Frontiers in Psychology*, 6(98), 1–14.

Horsley, M., Eliot, M., Knight, B. A. & Reilly, R. (Eds.) (2014). *Current Trends in Eye Tracking Research.* Heidelberg: Springer. https://doi.org/10.1007/978-3-319-02868-2

Keevallik, L. (2013). Here in time and space: Decomposing movement in dance instruction. In P. Haddington, L. Mondada & M. Nevile (Eds.), *Interaction and Mobility. Language and the Body in Motion* (pp. 345–370). Berlin, Boston: de Gruyter. https://doi.org/10.1515/9783110291278.345

Kendon, A. (1967). Some function of gaze-direction in social interaction. *Acta Psychologica*, 26, 22–63. https://doi.org/10.1016/0001-6918(67)90005-4

Kendon, A. (1990). *Conducting Interaction. Patterns of Behavior in Focused Encounters.* Cambridge, New York: Cambridge University Press.

Kendon, A. (2004). *Gesture. Visible Action as Utterance.* Cambridge: Cambridge University Press. https://doi.org/10.1017/CBO9780511807572

Kita, S. (Ed.) (2003). *Pointing. Where Language, Culture, and Cognition Meet.* Mahwah, NJ: Erlbaum.

Land, M. F. (2006): Eye movement and the control of actions in everyday life. *Progress in Retinal and Eye Research*, 25, 296–324. https://doi.org/10.1016/j.preteyeres.2006.01.002

Levinson, S. C. (1983). *Pragmatics.* Cambridge: Cambridge University Press.

Levinson, S. C. (2004). Deixis. In L. R. Horn (Ed.), *The handbook of pragmatics* (pp. 97–121). Oxford: Blackwell.

Levinson, S. C. (2012). Action Ascription and Formation. In J. Sidnell & T. Stivers (Eds.), *The Handbook of Conversation Analysis* (pp. 103–130). Wiley: Blackwell. https://doi.org/10.1002/9781118325001.ch6

Luhmann, N. (1984). *Soziale Systeme. Grundriß einer allgemeinen Theorie.* Frankfurt/M.: Suhrkamp.

Mondada, L. (2007). Multimodal Resources for Turn-Taking: Pointing and the Emergence of Possible Next Speakers. *Discourse Studies*, 9(2), 195–226. https://doi.org/10.1177/1461445607075346

Mondada, L. (2012a). Deixis: an integrated interactional multimodal analysis. In P. Bergmann, J. Brenning, M. Pfeiffer & E. Reber (Eds.), *Prosody and Embodiment in Interactional Grammar* (pp. 173–206). Berlin, Boston: de Gruyter. https://doi.org/10.1515/9783110295108.173

Mondada, L. (2012b). The Conversation Analytic Approach to Data Collection. In J. Sidnell & T. Stivers (Eds.), *The Handbook of Conversation Analysis* (pp. 32–56). Wiley: Blackwell. https://doi.org/10.1002/9781118325001.ch3

Pomerantz, A. (1984). Agreeing and disagreeing with assessments: Some features of preferred/ dispreferred turn shapes. In J. M. Atkinson & J. Heritage (Eds.), *Structures of social action: Studies in conversation analysis* (pp. 57–101). Cambridge: Cambridge University Press.

van Quine, W. O. (1960). *Word and Object.* Cambridge: Technology Press of the Massachusetts Institute of Technology.

Rossano, F. (2012). *Gaze Behavior in Face-to-Face Interaction.* Nijmegen: Max Planck Institute for Psycholinguistics Series.

Schegloff, E. A. (1968). Sequencing in Conversational Openings. *American Anthropologist*, 70(6), 1075–1095. https://doi.org/10.1525/aa.1968.70.6.02a00030

Schegloff, E. A. (1996). Confirming Allusions: Toward an Empirical Account of Action. *American Journal of Sociology*, 102(1), 161–216. https://doi.org/10.1086/230911

Schegloff, E. A. (2007). *Sequence Organization in Interaction.* Cambridge: Cambridge University Press. https://doi.org/10.1017/CBO9780511791208

Schegloff, E. A. & Sacks, H. (1973). Opening Up Closings. *Semiotica*, 8, 289–327. https://doi.org/10.1515/semi.1973.8.4.289

Selting, M. et al. (2009). Gesprächsanalytisches Transkriptionssystem 2 (GAT 2). *Gesprächsforschung – Onlinezeitschrift zur verbalen Interaktion*, 10, 353–402.

Sidnell, J. & Stivers, T. (Eds.) (2013). *The Handbook of Conversation Analysis.* Wiley: Blackwell.

Streeck, J. (1993). Gesture as communication I: Its coordination with gaze and speech. *Communication Monographs*, 60, 275–299. https://doi.org/10.1080/03637759309376314

Streeck, J. (2002). Grammars, Words, and Embodied Meanings: On the Uses and Evolution of So and Like. *Journal of Communication*, 52(3), 581–596. https://doi.org/10.1111/j.1460-2466.2002.tb02563.x

Streeck, J. (2009). *Gesturecraft. The manu-facture of meaning.* Amsterdam, Philadelphia: John Benjamins. https://doi.org/10.1075/gs.2

Streeck, J. (2014). Mutual gaze and recognition: Revisiting Kendon's "Gaze direction in two-person conversation". In M. Seyfeddinipur & M. Gullberg (Eds.), *From Gesture in Conversation to Visible Action as Utterance. Essays in honor of Adam Kendon* (pp. 35–55). Amsterdam/ Philadelphia: Benjamins.

Stukenbrock, A. (2008). "Wo ist der Hauptschmerz?" – Zeigen am eigenen Körper in der medizinischen Kommunikation. *Gesprächsforschung – Online-Zeitschrift zur verbalen Interaktion*, 9, 1–33.

Stukenbrock, A. (2009). Referenz durch Zeigen: Zur Theorie der Deixis. *Deutsche Sprache*, 37, 289–315.

Stukenbrock, A. (2010). Überlegungen zu einem multimodalen Verständnis der gesprochenen Sprache am Beispiel deiktischer Verwendungsweisen des Ausdrucks "so". *InLiSt –Interaction and Linguistic Structures*, 47, 1–23.

Stukenbrock, A. (2012). Imagined spaces as a resource in interaction. *Bulletin Suisse de Linguistique Appliquée*, 96, 141–161.

Stukenbrock, A. (2014a). Take the words out of my mouth: Verbal instructions as embodied practices. *Journal of Pragmatics*, 65, 80–102. https://doi.org/10.1016/j.pragma.2013.08.017

Stukenbrock, A. (2014b). Pointing to an 'empty' space: *Deixis am Phantasma* in face-to-face interaction. *Journal of Pragmatics*, 74, 70–93. https://doi.org/10.1016/j.pragma.2014.08.001

Stukenbrock, A. (2015). *Deixis in der face-to-face-Interaktion*. Berlin, Boston: de Gruyter.

Stukenbrock, A. (2016). Deiktische Praktiken: Zwischen Interaktion und Grammatik. In A. Deppermann, H. Feilke & A. Linke (Eds.), *Sprachliche und kommunikative Praktiken* (pp. 81–126). Jahrbuch 2015 des Instituts für Deutsche Sprache. Berlin, Boston: de Gruyter.

Stukenbrock, A. (2018). Forward-looking: Where do we go with multimodal projections? In A. Deppermann & Jürgen Streeck (Eds.), *Modalities and Temporalities: Convergences and divergences of bodily resources in interaction*. Amsterdam: Benjamins, 31–68.

Stukenbrock, A. (in prep.). Divergent foci of visual attention in joint projects.

Stukenbrock, A. & Dao, A. N. (accepted). Joint attention in passing. What dual mobile eye-tracking reveals about gaze in coordinating embodied activities on a market.

Tomasello, M. (2008). *Origins of Human Communication*. Cambridge/Massachusetts: MIT Press.

Weiß, C. & Auer, P. (2016). Das Blickverhalten des Rezipienten bei Sprecherhäsitationen. *Eine explorative Studie. Gesprächsforschung – Online-Zeitschrift zur verbalen Interaktion*, 17, 132–167.

Conventions for the transcription gaze behaviour

Throughout the analyses, P is consistently used for the pointing participant and A for his or her co-participant or addressee.

The target-eye-link
The target-eye-link which means that P or A looking at the object of interest is differentiated as follows:

P - > d^p	= P looking at domain of pointing
A - > d^s	= A looking at domain of scrutiny
P - > t	= P looking at target
A - > t	= A looking at target

The body-eye-link, more specifically the gesture-eye-link
A - > P^b	= A looking at P's body
A - > P^g	= A looking at P's gesture

The eye-to-eye-link
A - > P^e	= A looking at P's eyes
P - > A^e	= P looking at A's eyes
P^e < = > A^e	= A looking at P's eyes and P looking reciprocally at A's eyes

GAT 2 transcription conventions

(GAT2, **Selting et al. 2009**; for the English translation cf. Couper-Kuhlen &
Barth-Weingarten 2011)

Sequential structure

[ ]	overlap and simultaneous talk
=	immediate continuation with a new turn or segment, latching

In- and outbreaths

°h / h°	in-/outbreaths of approx 0.2–0.5 sec. duration
°hh / hh°	in-/outbreaths of appr. 0.5–0.8 sec. duration
°hhh / hhh°	in-/ outbreaths of appr. 0.8–1.0 sec. duration

Pauses

(.)	micro pause, estimated, up to 0.2 sec. duration appr.
(-)	short estimated pause of appr. 0.2–0.5 sec. duration
(--)	intermediary estimated pause of appr. 0.5–0.8 sec. duration
(---)	longer estimated pause of appr. 0.8–1.0 sec. duration
(0.5)/(2.0)	measured pause of appr. 0.5 / 2.0 sec. duration

Segmental conventions

and_uh	cliticizations within units
uh, uhm, etc.	hesitation markers, so-called "filled pauses"
:	lengthening, by about 0.2–0.5 sec.
::	lengthening, by about 0.5–0.8 sec.
:::	lengthening, by about 0.8–1.0 sec.
?	cut-off by glottal closure

Laughter

haha, hehe, hihi	syllabic laughter
((laughs))	description of laughter and crying
< < laughing > >	laughter particles accompanying speech with indication of scope

Continuers

hm, yes, no, yeah	monosyllabic tokens
hm_hm, ye_es, no_o	bi-syllabic tokens
ʔhmʔhm	with glottal closure, often negating

Accentuation

SYLlable	focus accent
sYllable	secondary accent
!SYL!lable	extra strong accent

Final pitch movements of intonation phrases

?	rising to high
,	rising to mid
–	level
;	falling to mid
.	falling to low
<<surprised>>	interpretive comment with indication of scope
<<f>>	forte, loud
<<ff>>	fortissimo, very loud
<<p>>	piano, soft
<<pp>>	pianissimo, very soft
<<all>>	allegro, fast
<<len>>	lento, slow
<<cresc>>	crescendo, increasingly louder
<<dim>>	diminuendo, increasingly softer
<<acc>>	accelerando, increasingly faster

Other conventions

(xxx), (xxx xxx)	one or two unintelligible syllables
(may i)	assumed wording
((…))	omission in transcript

CHAPTER 12

Displaying recipiency
in an interpreter-mediated dialogue
An eye-tracking study

Jelena Vranjes, Hanneke Bot, Kurt Feyaerts and Geert Brône
KU Leuven

This chapter discusses the findings of a study that used mobile eye-tracking in the context of a naturally occurring interpreter-mediated dialogue. This type of interaction is particularly interesting for the study of gaze and other (non-)verbal resources, as the primary interlocutors have no or limited access to each other's languages and have to rely on the interpreter and other modalities for the successful accomplishment of the social interaction. The aim of the study was to examine the role of gaze in the multimodal displays of recipiency (backchannel responses) in one interpreter-mediated therapeutic encounter. Our study reveals asymmetrical gaze patterns of the three participants while listening to the ongoing talk. The analysis also shows that backchannel responses are found on different levels of communication and between all participants in an interpreter-mediated conversation. Moreover, this contribution demonstrates how eye-tracking technology can help us reveal specific micro-events between the participants in the conversation, which can strengthen our understanding of the interpreter-mediated talk as a joint action.

Keywords: eye gaze in interaction, multimodality, backchannel responses, mobile eye-tracking, interpreter-mediated dialogue, psychotherapy

1. Introduction

In contrast to monolingual forms of conversation, interpreter-mediated dialogues are typically conducted between two primary participants, who have no or limited access to each other's language, and the interpreter. Traditionally, the view of interpreting was determined by the 'transfer' model of communication (Wadensjö, 1998) in which the interpreting process was viewed as the production of 'texts' and the role of the interpreter was reduced to that of a mere translation-machine.

https://doi.org/10.1075/ais.10.12vra

More recently, however, the process of interpreting is viewed as an 'interaction' in which all participants – including the interpreter – collaborate in the construction of social action (Wadensjö, 1998; Angelelli, 2004). Rather than just rendering the primary participants' utterances – as suggested in the work of Goffman 1981 and Edmondson 1986 – the interpreter's participatory role is oriented towards facilitating participation and managing the turn system in function of the communicative goals of the interaction, without disrupting his/her professional role (Gavioli, 2012; Baraldi & Gavioli, 2012; Mason, 2012). Moreover, Bot (2005: 112) remarks that interpreter-mediated dialogues are situated somewhere in between a dialogue and a trialogue: although the interpreter as a third party is actively involved in the talk by taking every second turn, (s)he has a different role in the conversation from the two primary interlocutors. Therefore, the conversational mechanisms in this type of interactions need to be studied in their own right.

One of the challenges for the primary parties who are talking via the interpreter is to establish direct communicative contact (by responding directly or providing direct feedback) and to develop mutual understanding (Linell, Wadensjö & Jönsson, 1992). Likewise, it is difficult for the interpreter to reproduce verbal feedback of the primary participants due to the "temporal and spatial delay" between the speaker's and the recipient's turns (Englund Dimitrova, 1997). Thus, it is assumed that participants in an interpreter-mediated dialogue provide and receive little verbal feedback during the interaction (see also Linell, Wadensjö & Jönsson, 1992). However, as any form of face-to-face communication, interpreter-mediated talk is characterized by its visibility and simultaneity (Clark, 1996), and requires collaboration on every level of communication. Multimodal resources such as gaze and gestures are then of particular importance in this kind of complex interaction (Pasquandrea, 2011).

It seems that particularly gaze direction has an important function in signaling conversational attention and facilitating turn management in face-to-face interpreter-mediated dialogue. Despite a growing number of studies focusing on eye gaze in interpreter-mediated interaction (Bot, 2005; Pasquandrea, 2011, 2012; Mason, 2012; Davitti, 2013; Krystallidou, 2014; Davitti & Pasquandrea, 2016), there is still systematic research to be done on the gaze direction of all participants and its concurrent interaction with speech and other modalities. This study aims at making a contribution in this direction by using mobile eye-tracking technology, which allows for a highly detailed analysis of gaze in ongoing communication.

In this chapter, we will present a case study on the multimodal display of recipiency in one naturally occurring interpreter-mediated therapeutic encounter. This is – to our knowledge – the first study using mobile eye-tracking in a face-to-face dialogue interpreting setting. First, we will analyze how the participants display recipiency during the speaker's turns and try to link these patterns to their respective (social) roles within this institutional setting. Second, we will discuss the participants' use of backchannels during the conversation. And finally, we will discuss the role of gaze in producing and eliciting backchannel responses in this specific interpreter-mediated encounter.

2. Recipiency in face-to-face (monolingual) interaction

Face-to-face interactions are characterized by a high degree of reciprocity between speakers and listeners (Bavelas et al., 2002). During ongoing utterances, listeners manifest their continued attention and understanding in a multimodal way: by orienting their gaze towards the current speaker, nodding or shaking their head and producing listener signals such as "mm hm" or "yeah". Such listener signals have been called *accompaniment signals* (Kendon, 1967), *backchannel responses* (Yngve, 1970), *listener responses* (Dittmann and Llewellyn, 1968; Bavelas et al., 2002) and *acknowledgments* (Clark & Brennan, 1991) in the literature. They can be defined as "actions [both audible and visible] that indicate the person is attending, following, appreciating, or reacting to the story" (Bavelas et al., 2002: 574). Through the use of backchannel responses, the listeners display no intention of taking the turn at talk (Clark & Brennan, 1991; Gardner, 2001). In addition, backchannel responses have an important role in the emerging story of the speakers (Goodwin, 1981; Stivers, 2008). As shown by Bavelas et al. (2002), for example, speakers need their recipients' listener responses to be able to tell their stories well. Thus, backchannel responses are essential in the process of communication.

From the existing literature on backchannel responses, it becomes clear that this notion covers a broad spectrum of tokens that are not always clearly defined (Drummond & Hopper, 1993; Gardner, 2001). In line with Gardner (2001:2-3), we include the following listener practices in our study of backchannel responses: continuers (e.g. 'mm hm'), acknowledgments (e.g. 'yeah'), newsmarkers and other newsmarker-like objects (e.g. 'Oh'), assessments (e.g. 'great'), collaborative completions and nonverbal vocalizations and kinesic actions (see Table 1 below). Although backchannels have traditionally been studied mainly on the verbal level, a number of researchers have argued for including the nonverbal or embodied signals as well (Kendon, 1967; Goffman, 1981; Goodwin, 1981; Clark & Brennan, 1991; Gardner, 2001). More recently, a series of studies has focused on the collaborative and multimodal displays of recipiency (Bavelas et al., 2002; Allwood & Cerrato, 2003; Bertrand et al., 2007; Ford & Stickle, 2012). Bavelas et al. (2002) argue for an "integrated message model", according to which co-occurring verbal and nonverbal listener responses work together to convey meaning. Similarly, Allwood & Cerrato

(2003) report that gestural listener responses (such as head nods) mostly co-occur with short vocal or verbal responses, together with which they perform a related or complementary function. Furthermore, it was shown that eye gaze has an important role in seeking and providing listener responses in face-to-face communication (Kendon, 1967; Goodwin, 1981; Bavelas et al., 2002; Stivers & Rossano, 2010; De Kok & Heylen, 2012).

Table 1. The typology of backchannel responses (Gardner 2001)

Continuers:	function to hand the floor* back to the immediately prior speaker (e.g. *Mm hm, Uh huh*);
Acknowledgments	claim agreement or understanding of the prior turn (e.g. *Mm, Yeah*);
Newsmarkers, and other newsmarker-like objects:	mark the prior speaker's turn as newsworthy in some way (e.g. *Really?*, the change-of-state token *Oh*, the "idea-connector" *Right*);
Change-of-activity tokens	mark a transition to a new activity or a new topic in the talk (e.g. *Okay, Alright*);
Assessments:	evaluate the talk of the prior speakers (e.g. *Great, How intriguing, What a load of rubbish*);
Brief questions	for clarification or other types of repair, which seek to clarify mishearings or misunderstandings (e.g. *Who?, Which book do you mean?*, or the very generalized *Huh?*);
Collaborative completions:	whereby one speaker finishes a prior speaker's utterance (e.g. A: *So he's moved into …* B: *commercial interests*);
Many **nonverbal vocalizations** and **kinesic actions**	(e.g. sighs, laughter, nods and head shakes).

* Gardner's (2001) definition here is somewhat contradictory, because the listener does not take the floor by producing continuers, but rather signals to the current or immediately prior speaker that (s)he may continue.

Gaze direction is crucial for the display of recipiency in face-to-face interaction. Interlocutors employ their gaze to display attention and (dis)engagement (Goodwin, 1981) and their participation status within the given interaction (see also Rossano, 2013). By orienting their gaze to the speaker, listeners show that they are acting as hearers to the speaker's utterance (Goodwin, 1980). In addition, early work by Kendon (1967) revealed an asymmetrical gaze pattern in face-to-face interaction that is dependent on the interlocutors' participation roles: while listening, people sustain their gaze at their interlocutor for a longer period of time than when they are speaking. Thus, there seem to be norms associated with listener's gaze behaviour in social interaction. Goodwin (1980) formulated these norms in a set of rules, stating that (a) a speaker should obtain the gaze of his recipient during the course of a turn at talk, and that (b) a recipient should be gazing at the speaker when the speaker is gazing at the hearer. Rossano (2013) went one step further by showing that some activities, such as tellings, "require more sustained gaze by the recipient toward the speaker" than others.

In the following, we will discuss the use of listener responses in the context of an interpreter-mediated dialogue and their connection with (mutual) gaze.

3.   Recipiency in interpreter-mediated interaction

3.1   Verbal backchanneling

According to Wadensjö (1998: 236) "one of the 'trouble sources' typical of interpreter-mediated interaction is that mutual feedback between the primary parties is delayed and often non-existent". As they have little or no knowledge of each other's language, the primary participants are dependent upon the interpreter, whose task is not only to create shared understanding, but also to establish contact and rapport between the primary parties (Linell, Wadensjö & Jönsson, 1992). Thus, the interpreter's involvement within an interaction is not the same as that of the primary participants. The interpreter's participation status has often been discussed in terms of Goffman's (1981) participation framework (see Wadensjö, 1998; Pöchhacker, 2012), according to which the interpreter's speaker mode can be described as that of an 'animator' or 'author', whereas speaking as the 'principal' (i.e. the party that is committed to the expressed stance and beliefs) is usually reserved for the primary speakers.[1] Concerning the interpreter's reception role, the interpreter can be either fully or partially ratified (Krystallidou, 2014) as addressee. Moreover, Gavioli (2012: 201) points out that "while interpreters are not the main recipients of talk, they are most often (…) the *first* recipients of the interlocutors' talk; therefore, there must be some way in which they negotiate their 'recipiency'" (Gavioli, 2012: 201).

Very few studies have focused on the backchanneling behavior of the participants in an interpreter-mediated dialogue. Linell, Wadensjö & Jönsson (1992) studied verbal feedback as indicators of communicative contact between the interlocutors in a large corpus of interpreter-mediated dialogues in legal and medical contexts. They report a low incidence of listener responses between the interpreter and the primary parties, as well as between the primary parties themselves. In

---

1.   However, as observed by Wadensjö (1998: 93), the reality is more complex: "Participating in face-to-face interaction interpreters can be, and regularly are, flexible in modes of speaking and listening, and thus relate to what others utter in ways that display different aspects of self".

addition, they suggest that backchannel responses such as continuers are "dysfunc-tional from the point-of-view of the interpreter's task", whose main focus is to un-derstand and memorize what is being said (Linell, Wadensjö & Jönsson, 1992: 133). Gavioli (2012), on the other hand, analyzed verbal backchannel responses (what she refers to as 'minimal responses') in a corpus of audio-recorded interpreter-mediated doctor-patient encounters. She points out, among other things, that the interpret-er's backchannel responses have an important coordinating function and offer a window into the interpreter's 'interpreting' activity. However, these studies were limited to the verbal or vocal displays of recipiency.

3.2   Gaze as an instrument in multimodal backchanneling

Englund-Dimitrova (1997) included head nods and gaze direction in her study of listener responses in doctor-patient interaction. She observes that the communica-tive contact in interpreter-mediated dialogues is a collective construction (Englund Dimitrova, 1997: 157):

> It is usually recommended that users of interpreters look at the other interlocutor instead of looking at the interpreter. This means that whilst one of them is speaking, the other probably feels more or less forced to take an active listening role, even if he does not understand what is being said. This also means that even in interpreted discourse there may be feedback from one interlocutor when the other is speaking.

In her data, she found that interpreters can produce nods to display themselves as attentive listeners and to encourage the current speaker, thereby acting as a 'deputy listener' (Englund Dimitrova, 1997: 163). Thus, the interpreter "has the opportunity to encourage interlocutors to a certain extent" to make their message clear. At the same time, she warns that the interpreters should limit their feedback in line with their professional role.

Much work still needs to be done in order to understand the role and multi-modal dynamics of backchannel responses in interpreter-mediated talk. In this study, we focus on the role of gaze direction in relation to listeners' backchannel responses in one interpreter-mediated encounter. For several decades after Lang's (1978) pioneering study, the role of eye gaze received no attention in the studies of interpreter-mediated talk. It is only in the recent years that we have witnessed a growing number of – mainly qualitative – studies on the role of gaze direction in this setting. In her study of interpreter-mediated psychotherapeutic sessions, Bot (2005) has analysed gaze patterns with reference to turn management. She observes that gaze behaviour in interpreted therapeutic encounters is essentially different from what is found in monolingual talk (as described by Goodwin 1981). Pasquandrea (2011, 2012) shows how eye gaze and posture function in the establishment of mutual involvement and coordination of joint actions in interpreted doctor-patient interactions. Also within the setting of medical interactions, Krystallidou (2014) discusses the role of eye gaze and body orientation as a means of participant inclusion and exclusion in interpreter-mediated dialogue. Mason (2012) combined a qualitative and a quantitative approach in his detailed study on the role of gaze direction in interpreter-mediated immigration hearings. He shows how eye gaze is involved in process monitoring, regulation (turn-taking) and interactive positioning of the participants, by scrutinizing gaze patterns of two participants (the immigration officer and the interpreter) during the immigration interview. Furthermore, Davitti (2013) and also Davitti & Pasquandrea (2016) investigated the role of eye gaze in interpreted parent-teacher meetings as a contextualization cue and as a means of establishing or negotiating the participation framework.

Nevertheless, as noted by Mason (2012), there is still systematic research to be done on the gaze direction of all participants and its concurrent interaction with speech and other modalities in interpreter-mediated talk. However, research in this field is faced with different challenges. First, it is extremely challenging to gain permission to video record naturally occurring interpreted encounters due to their often sensitive and confidential nature (Mason, 2012; Pöllabauer, 2004). Second, even when the recording is made by using one or even two (see Pasquandrea, 2011, 2012; Davitti, 2013) video cameras, it remains difficult to register detailed gaze information (for example, rapid gaze shifts) of all participants and at the same time capture other semiotic channels, such as gesture and posture. Third, videos do not always allow a detailed study of interlocutors' mutual gaze and errors can occur when making judgments of gaze from video recordings (Argyle & Cook, 1976; Streeck, 2009). In order to overcome some of these limitations, we made use of mobile eye-tracking technology (see Section 4 for a full description of the method).

The case study described in this chapter focuses on the displays of recipiency in one particular institutional setting: an interpreter-mediated therapeutic encounter. Apart from the studies by Wadensjö (2001) and Bot (2005), very little systematic research has been conducted on interpreting in the context of mental health. Moreover, this setting is particularly interesting for the study of backchannel responses. As argued by Gerhardt and Beyerle (1997, see also Gardner, 2001: 378) "a crucial type of therapeutic work is accomplished through [the use of response tokens], but that this work has gone unrecognized due to the (…) bias toward verbal interventions". During the encounter, the therapist is oriented towards the patient in a non-intrusive way in order to provide space for a patient to open out with his/her telling (Gardner, 2001: 34). Through the therapeutic process, the therapist and the patient create an intersubjective field, "an emergent field of shared understandings regarding each other's actions and the worlds of momentary experience that these actions embody" (Peräkylä, 2013). However, in interpreted encounters, the therapist has no direct access to the patient's talk and relies heavily on the relaying work by the interpreter. Bot (2005: 79) argues that "the interpreter [is] a person who, through his presence, also helps to form a therapeutic reality. The essence then is the interaction between the therapist, patient and interpreter." Moreover, the hierarchical relation that exists in this type of dialogue (the therapist being the 'chair' of the session and the patient being submitted to the conversation flow) makes it interesting to see how this relation is maintained in the presence of an interpreter.

Building on the research done by Bot (2005), we ask the following questions: how do the participants in an interpreted therapeutic encounter display recipiency? Can we find any differences? What is the directionality of their backchannel signals? And finally, what is the role of eye gaze in the processes of providing and eliciting listener responses? Although the present study is of an exploratory nature, we hope to contribute to the almost non-existent literature on the multimodal displays of recipiency in a face-to-face interpreter-mediated talk.

4.   Method and data

For this study, we recorded a naturally occurring interpreted therapeutic encounter at a mental health institution in the Netherlands. The patient was a Russian-speaking asylum seeker with a very limited knowledge of Dutch. At the moment of recording, he had been in therapy in that institution for several months. The Dutch-speaking therapist had very limited understanding of Russian. Both the therapist and the patient were accustomed to speaking in the presence of an interpreter. As therapeutic sessions can sometimes be stressful for the patient, we agreed with the therapist to record a session that was at the end of the patient's treatment. A professional interpreter was present to relay the utterances of the primary parties from one language into the other. The interpreter had 20 years of experience in mental healthcare and was positively evaluated by the therapist. The conversation lasted about 47 minutes, of which 32 minutes were analyzed in detail. All three participants knew each other prior to the recording session. The study was approved by the KU Leuven ethics committee, the institution's ethics committee and all participants agreed to be recorded by signing a written informed consent (in Dutch and in Russian), which ensured their anonymity and stated how the data were going to be used and presented.

The recording took place in the therapist's consultation room. The participants were seated in a triangular formation around a small table, as preferred by the therapist, with the patient in the middle, the interpreter on the right and the therapist on the left side of the patient (see Figure 1).

Each participant wore a head-mounted eye-tracker, which enabled us to follow and study the interaction through the eyes of the participants, as it were. The eye-tracking paradigm is already being used in different domains of linguistic research; psycholinguistics, cognitive linguistics and interactional linguistics (e.g. Gullberg & Kita, 2009; Jokinen, 2010; Holler & Kendrick, 2015; Brône & Oben, 2015; Oben & Brône, 2015; see also Auer and Stuckenbrock, this volume). This paradigm is interesting as it allows for a highly detailed analysis of gaze points (fixations) and eye movements (gaze shifts) in ongoing communication, both as a measure of cognitive processing (Duchowski, 2007) and as an active communicative signal (for example, in providing feedback).

The participants were told that they could move their hands and head freely during the conversation. In addition, a scene camera was positioned on the other side of the room to provide a profile shot of the interaction (see Brône & Oben, 2015). The recording equipment was set up prior to the conversation, so that the eye trackers could be calibrated immediately upon the arrival of the therapist, interpreter and the patient (in that particular order). During the conversation, the researchers were waiting in an adjacent room. At the end of the session, a short interview with the participants was conducted, in which they were asked about their background and impressions about the encounter.

All four video recordings were synchronized in Adobe Premiere Pro into one single video (Figure 1). This video was then imported into the video annotation tool ELAN (Wittenburg et al., 2006) where it was coded for gaze direction and (verbal/vocal and embodied) backchannel responses. In addition, the conversation was transcribed into Russian and Dutch and the Russian parts were translated into Dutch.

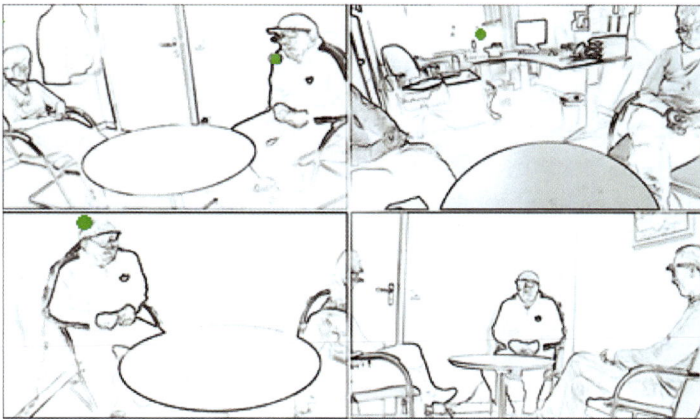

Figure 1. Three dynamic internalized perspectives and the profile shot. Green dots indicate the gaze direction of each of the participants

We distinguished following types of backchannel responses in our data, as proposed in Gardner (2001): continuers, acknowledgments, newsmarkers, change-of-activity tokens, assessments, collaborative completions and nonverbal feedback (see Table 1).[2] Cases that were not easily attributable to one of the categories were presented to and discussed with a second coder. We then grouped the backchannels according to their modality in (1) vocal or verbal backchannels, (2) nonverbal backchannels (e.g. head nods occurring on their own) and (3) combined backchannels (which represent contiguous gestural and vocal listener responses, e.g. "yeah" accompanied by a head nod). Following Bavelas et al. (2002: 574), we treated "simultaneous or very closely sequential behaviors as a single listener response as long as their meaning was the same or complementary". In sum, we were interested to see how many backchannel responses are situated on the nonverbal level, as previous research on the use of response tokens has focused mainly on the verbal or vocal listener responses.

In the following analysis, we focus on the displays of recipiency by each participant in the interpreter-mediated encounter. In a first step, we analyze how the participants display recipiency with their eye gaze during speaker's turns, by linking those patterns with their respective (social) roles within this institutional setting. In the second step, we discuss the participants' use of backchannels within this encounter. And finally, we discuss the role of gaze in producing and eliciting backchannel responses in this interpreter-mediated encounter.

5.   Analysis

5.1   Distribution of visual attention

For the purpose of this study we focused on the gaze direction of the participants while listening. We distinguished three relevant regions of interest (ROI's) for each participant, namely, (i) the face of speaker A, (ii) the face of speaker B, (iii) elsewhere in the consultation room (wall, table, door etc.). Figure 2 shows the therapist's distribution of visual attention during the patient's and the interpreter's turns. Similar to Mason (2012), we made an additional distinction between the 'Interpreter's turn in Dutch (NL)' and the 'Interpreter's turn in Russian (RU)' in the assumption that the understanding of the language will have an influence on the gaze direction of the two primary participants.

---

2.   Gardner (2001) also includes brief questions in his overview of backchannels. These, however, were not found in our data.

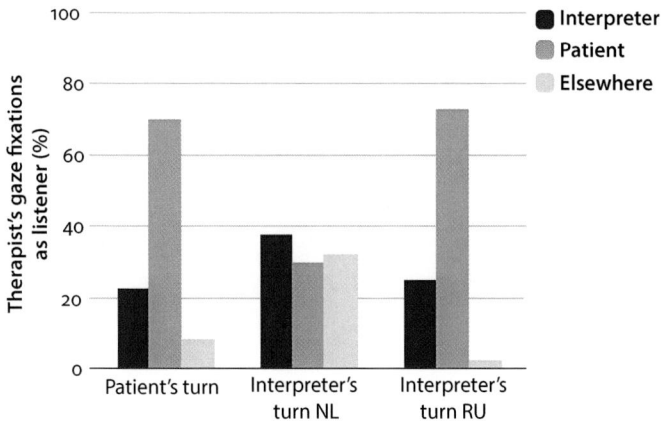

Figure 2. Therapist's distribution of visual attention while listening

Our results reveal that, when the interpreter is addressing the patient in Russian ('Interpreter's turn RU), the therapist tends to look at the patient and not at the current speaker (see also Bot, 2005; Mason, 2012). Although this behaviour is rather unusual in monolingual communication, it is not surprising in the context of psychotherapy (see also Bot, 2005: 137). By orienting his gaze on the patient, the therapist monitors the patient's potentially important embodied displays of understanding or (dis)agreement (for example smiles, nodding) and at the same time displays participation or engagement in the interpreter's turn. Interestingly, when/while the interpreter is rendering the patient's talk to the therapist in Dutch ('Interpreter's turn NL'), the therapist tends to shift his gaze from the interpreter to the patient. We will discuss this gaze pattern in relation to the therapist's back-channeling behaviour (what we refer to as 'dual feedback') and in relation to the ongoing discourse later on in this chapter.

During the patient's turns, the therapist mostly gazes at the patient, despite the fact that he has very limited understanding of the Russian language. However, he shifts his gaze towards the interpreter when he projects a transition relevance place, i.e. a point in the conversation where turn transfer from current speaker to the next may occur (see also Sacks et al., 1974), or when he wants to see if the patient's telling elicits any kind of nonverbal response by the interpreter (personal communication).

The distribution of the interpreter's gaze fixations while listening is shown in Figure 3. The interpreter is the only one who has access to both languages during the interaction. While the patient is speaking, the interpreter's visual attention is almost exclusively oriented toward him. A similar pattern was reported by Mason (2012), who found that the interpreters were more oriented toward the asylum

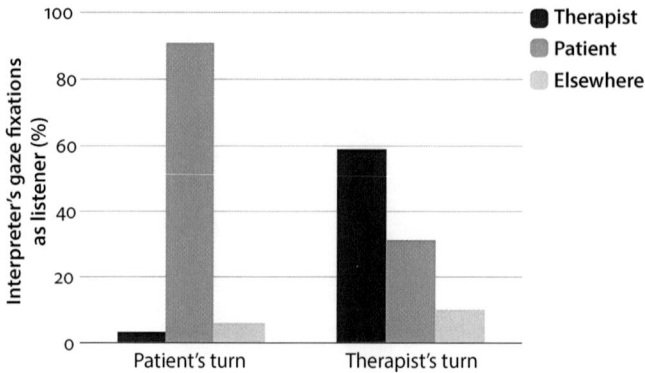

Figure 3. Interpreter's distribution of visual attention while listening

seekers during the immigration hearings. During the therapist's turns, she mostly gazes at the therapist, but she also regularly shifts her gaze to the patient.

After the interpreter has finished with rendering the patient's utterance to the therapist, she tends to shift her gaze back to the patient (in 76% of her turn-ends), even though in most instances the therapist takes the next turn. This is somewhat surprising, as one would expect that the interpreter orients her attention to the other primary speaker who is about to take the turn or has already started producing it. We can assume that, in this way, she is able to monitor and anticipate if the patient wants to resume his turn. Thus, the interpreter clearly displays orientation toward the weaker[3] party in this conversation.

The patient's distribution of visual attention is represented in Figure 4. While the therapist addresses the patient in Dutch by orienting his gaze towards him, the patient tends to look elsewhere in the consultation room. Even when the interpreter is addressing him in Russian, the patient displays a tendency to orient his gaze away from her. These results show that the degree of patient's displayed recipiency and engagement in the therapeutic encounter is much lower than that of the therapist and the interpreter.

We also find that the patient tends to orient his gaze toward the interpreter when she is speaking in Dutch, although he had very limited understanding of the language (a similar gaze behaviour was reported by Davitti, 2013). In this way,

---

3.   We chose to talk about the 'weaker' instead of 'power-less' (Merlini & Favaron, 2005; Mason, 2012) participant, because the latter term would imply that the patient has no power over the organization of turn-taking. That is not the case, as both the interpreter and the therapist are fully oriented towards the patient during the encounter, monitoring his every action and giving him interactional space to come out with his telling.

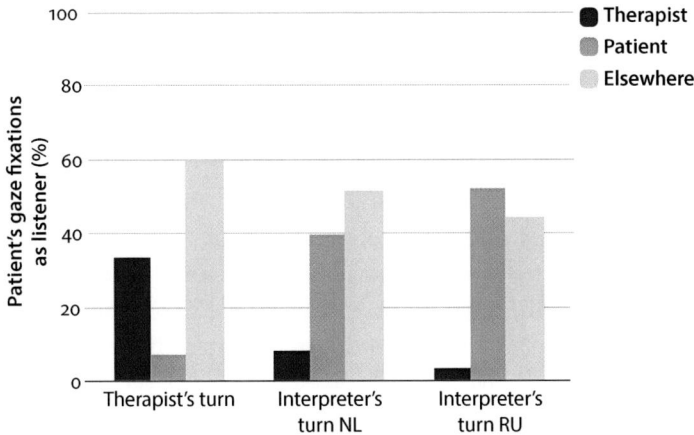

Figure 4. Patient's distribution of visual attention while listening

it might have been more difficult for him to pick up any visual displays of recipiency from the therapist. This observation is somewhat different from what Bot (2005: 140) found in her data, where the patient "does not treat the [interpreter] as an ordinary speaker most of the time, but focuses on the listener, i.e. the therapist, or turns his gaze away from the participants".

5.2   Listener responses

In the following, we discuss the participants' use of backchannel responses during the encounter.

It becomes clear that the patient's low display of engagement during the conversation is also manifest in the low frequency of his listener responses (Table 2). Therefore, the further analysis will focus on the interpreter's and the therapist's use of backchannel responses.

Table 2. Frequencies for the backchannel responses (verbal & nonverbal) during speakers' turns

Listener	Speaker				
	Therapist	Interpreter NED	Interpreter RU	Patient	Total
Interpreter	1	/	/	75	76
Therapist	/	136	4	19	159
Patient	3	4	6	/	13

We find that the interpreter provides listener responses almost exclusively during the patient's turns (Table 2). Thus, the interpreter displays active involvement in the patient's narrative, as it requires more listener-support and participation. In contrast to what was observed by Gavioli (2012), the interpreter in this talk provides no backchannel responses during the therapist's turns. Apparently, the therapist does not display any need for listener support from the interpreter during his turn. While speaking, he directs his gaze more at the patient (66% of his gaze fixations) than at the interpreter (14%), thus treating the patient as the 'real' recipient of his utterances. Therefore, the interpreter's gaze and backchanneling behaviour is indicative of the structural asymmetry of this triadic interaction.

The therapist in this conversation displays a very high level of participation and engagement during the interpreter's turns (Table 2). In total, the therapist produces 159 backchannel responses. Although most of them are produced during the interpreter's turns in Dutch, we also find listener responses produced by the therapist during the patient's turns in Russian. These listener responses are either a sign of recognition or understanding of the patient's utterance, or have a mere aligning function with respect to the ongoing structure of the interaction (for example, nodding to the patient's displayed intention to hold the floor).

In addition, we considered the modality of the listener responses provided by the interlocutors (Table 3). A formal distinction was made between nonverbal backchannels (for example head nods), verbal or vocal backchannels (for example "mh hm", "yeah", "okay") and combined backchannels (for example, a nod accompanied by "yeah"). Moreover, we analysed if listener's backchannel responses were produced following mutual gaze with the current speaker.[4] What becomes evident is that both the therapist and the interpreter use nonverbal backchannels (mainly head nods) most frequently as backchannel responses in this therapeutic talk. For the interpreter, nodding is a non-interruptive way of displaying conversational attention and encouraging the patient to continue speaking. Her head nods co-occur in most cases with mutual gaze with the patient (Table 3) (see also Englund Dimitrova, 1997).

---

4. The speaker to whom the interpreter provided backchannel responses was the patient in 99% of the cases (see Table 2). The therapist, on the other hand, provided backchannel responses both during the interpreter's and the patient's turns (Table 2).

Table 3. The interpreter's and therapist's backchannels with or without mutual gaze with the speaker

	Backchannels	Mutual gaze	No mutual gaze	Total
Interpreter	Nonverbal	28 (74%)	10 (26%)	38
	Verbal/vocal	8 (53%)	7 (47%)	15
	Combined	22 (96%)	1 (4%)	23
Therapist	Nonverbal	53 (66%)	27 (34%)	80
	Verbal/vocal	10 (29%)	25 (71%)	35
	Combined	27 (61%)	17 (39%)	44

Interestingly, the therapist's nods are in 43% of the cases accompanied by a gaze shift from the interpreter to the patient. As an example, consider the therapist's gaze behavior in the following extract (the green dot represents the therapist's gaze fixation).

```
1   Interpreter    .h # dat (.) dat     kl*opt
                   .h that (.) that's true

    therapist                            *repeated nods--->
```

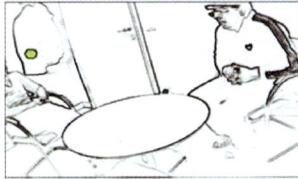

```
    fig.
                   #fig.1
```

```
2   Interpreter    u:h# daar kan ik ook niks mee:.
                   uh    I can't    also do anything with it.

    therapist      ------------------------------------->
```

```
    fig.
                   #fig.2-3
3   Interpreter       (-)*
    therapist      --->*
```

```
4    Interpreter      En   daarom   [wil ik]  nu #eigenlijk liever
                      and that's why I would now actually rather



     fig.



                               #fig.4


5    Patient                     [(да) ]
                                 (yeah)
6                     iets anders heb[ben (.)]
                      talk about something else
7    Therapist                      [ *ja* ]
                                     yeah
     therapist                      *nod*
```

Here, the interpreter is rendering the patient's utterance in the first person pronoun and gazing at the therapist. At line 1 the therapist starts producing a series of big nods. These nods are accompanied by the therapist's gaze shift (line 2) from the current speaker toward the patient, who occupies the position of the 'principal' (Goffman 1981) in the exchange. The patient also shifts his gaze toward the therapist (line 2), who is still nodding and directing his gaze at him. Their mutual gaze ends when the patient produces a backchannel ("yeah") at line 5 (see also Bavelas et al. 2002).

This example shows that with gaze, the therapist indicates the 'principal', whose views are being expressed by the interpreter. In combination with nodding, the therapist thus claims understanding of the primary speaker's stance (see also Stivers, 2008). In total, 52 instances of this type of feedback were found in our data. The frequency and regularity of this pattern suggest that it is some sort of a multimodal routine. We will refer to this nodding in the mid-turn position accompanied by a gaze shift from the current speaker to the other interlocutor as *dual feedback*. In some cases, nodding can occur in combination with vocal feedback such as 'yeah' or 'mm hm', thus making it a complex multimodal routine. We can say that through dual feedback, the therapist manages multiple actions at the same time: he addresses both 'speakers' with his gaze, while indicating his understanding with head nods.

In the last part of our analysis we focused on the relation between mutual eye gaze and backchannel responses. To test whether there is a significant dependency between feedback and mutual gaze between the listener and the speaker we conducted a Chi-square test. Our Chi-square test revealed that occurrence of feedback differed significantly by the presence or absence of mutual gaze (χ^2 = 20.19, df = 2, p < 0,001). In other words, there was a significant association between the occurrence of feedback and mutual gaze. Cramer's V was.28 which indicates a relatively strong association (Rea & Parker, 1992).

6. Discussion

The analysis of gaze data in a naturally occurring interpreter-mediated encounter reveals that all participants display recipiency and engagement in a multimodal way, both by focusing their gaze at each other and by producing verbal and nonverbal backchannel responses during the ongoing talk. The therapist and the interpreter used most often non-interruptive displays of recipiency, such as head nods. We also found multimodal displays of recipiency between the primary interlocutors, despite their limited understanding of each other's language (see also Englund-Dimitrova 1997). Thus, even during the moments when the listeners appear silent, they were nonverbally (through their gaze and head nods) involved with the ongoing discourse.

In addition, we observed differences in the displays of recipiency between the participants. In line with the observations by Bot (2005), we found that the therapist is clearly more oriented toward the patient. By gazing at him and providing (dual) feedback, the therapist seemed to be working towards the establishment of an intersubjective field (Peräkylä, 2013) between himself and the patient. Moreover, during the patient's turns, the therapist regularly shifted his gaze to the interpreter. In this way, the therapist was actively monitoring the conversational flow and was able to anticipate moments of possible turn completion or turn transfer between the interpreter and the patient.

The interpreter was also much more oriented toward the weaker party in the encounter (see Englund Dimitrova, 1997). This might be due to the fact that the patient's narrative requires more listener-support. As was shown, the interpreter's nonverbal backchannel responses (head nods, smiles) were not provided randomly during the patient's turn, but co-occurred in most cases with mutual gaze with the patient. In contrast to what was reported by Bot (2005), the patient was more oriented toward the interpreter and treated her as a 'real' participant in this conversation by gazing at her during her turns.

Through a detailed analysis of gaze direction during the conversation, we found some evidence of collaboration at the micro level between the interlocutors: there seemed to be a significant relationship between visual contact (mutual gaze) and nonverbal backchannels (head nods) during the conversation. Also, eye gaze helped the participants to manage multiple actions at the same time, as illustrated with the therapist's *dual feedback*-patterns.

What also needs to be considered here is the potential influence of the eye-trackers on the participants' behavior. In the immediate post-interview with the participants, the interpreter and the therapist stated that they were 'fairly aware' of the fact that they were wearing the eye-tracker during the encounter; the patient on the other hand declared that he had 'almost no awareness' of the eye tracker during the conversation. It is thus difficult to establish the level of intrusiveness of the recording equipment in the course of interaction. As it was a naturally occurring therapeutic encounter in a psychotherapeutic institution, each of the participants was there of set purpose: the therapist was oriented toward the realization of specific goals in that therapeutic session (personal communication), the interpreter was focused on her task of relaying the talk and the patient might also have had his own agenda for his last session. However, it would be interesting to conduct the study over a longer period of time and – if possible – record several subsequent sessions using the same technology.

In this exploratory study we aimed to show that a detailed analysis of gaze can help us reveal interesting micro-phenomena in interpreter-mediated dialogue. Furthermore, a detailed analysis of gaze, bodily conduct and speech can contribute to our understanding of dialogue interpreting as a *mediated trialogue*. In addition, this study has presented the mobile eye-tracking paradigm as a new approach to the study of dialogue interpreting. We have demonstrated that the eye-tracking paradigm is not confined to controlled experimental environments, but can also be used to study interaction in naturally occurring events. Moreover, the study illustrates some opportunities of the eye-tracking paradigm for other settings as well, such as in sign language interpreting, in which eye gaze and multimodality play an even more important role.

Appendix. Transcription conventions

Speech is transcribed according to GAT2 (see Selting et al., 2009). Conventions for the multi-modal transcription are adopted from Mondada, see http://icar.univ–lyon2.fr/projets/corinte/bandeau_droit/convention_icor.htm).

[ ]	simultaneous speech
(.)	micropause (shorter than 0.2 seconds)
(–)	short pause (duration between 0.2. and 0.5 seconds)
.h	in-breath
(text)	unclear or dubious words
:	lengthening or prolongation of a sound (sound stretch)
*	delimits gestures by the therapist
*--->	the action described continues across subsequent lines
--- > *	until the same symbol is reached
#	symbol # specifies the exact moment at which the image refers. This is done by inserting the symbol both on the line of the talk and on the line dedicated to the image (fig. in the margins)

References

Allwood, J. & Cerrato, L. (2003). A study of gestural feedback expressions. In P. Paggio et al. (Eds.), *Proceedings of the First Nordic Symposium on Multimodal Communication*, 7–22.

Angelelli, C. V. (2004). *Revisiting the Interpreter's Role: A Study of Conference, Court, and Medical Interpreters in Canada, Mexico, and the United States*. Amsterdam: John Benjamins. https://doi.org/10.1075/btl.55

Argyle, M. & Cook, M. (1976). *Gaze and Mutual Gaze*. Cambridge: Cambridge University Press.

Baraldi, L. & Gavioli, C. (2012). Understanding coordination in interpreter-mediated interaction. In L. Baraldi, & C. Gavioli (Eds.), *Coordinating Participation in Dialogue Interpreting* (pp. 1–22). Amsterdam/Philadelphia: Benjamins Publishing. https://doi.org/10.1075/btl.102.01intro

Bavelas, J., Coates, L. & Johnson, T. (2002). Listener responses as a collaborative process: The role of gaze. *Journal of Communication*, 52, 566–580. https://doi.org/10.1111/j.1460-2466.2002.tb02562.x

Bertrand R., Ferré, G., Blache, P., Espesser, R. & Rauzy, S. (2007). Backchannels revisited from a multimodal perspective. *Proceedings of Auditory-Visual Speech Processing 2007 (AVSP2007) 2007*, Kasteel Groenendaal, Hilvarenbeek, The Netherlands.

Bot, H. (2005). *Dialogue Interpreting in Mental Health*. Amsterdam and New York: Rodopi Publishers.

Brône, G. and B. Oben. (2015). InSight Interaction. A multimodal and multifocal dialogue corpus, *Language Resources and Evaluation*, 49, 195–214.

Clark, H. H. (1996). *Using Language*. Cambridge: Cambridge University Press. https://doi.org/10.1017/CBO9780511620539

Clark, H. and Brennan, S. (1991). Grounding in communication. In L. B. Resnick, J. M. Levine, & S.D. Teasley (Eds.), *Perspectives on socially shared cognition* (pp. 127–149). Washington: APA Books.

Davitti, E. (2013). Dialogue Interpreting as Intercultural Mediation: Interpreter's use of upgrading moves in parent-teacher meetings. *Interpreting*, 15(2), 168–199. https://doi.org/10.1075/intp.15.2.02dav

Davitti, E. & Pasquandrea, S. (2016). Embodied participation: What multimodal analysis can tell us about interpreter-mediated encounters in pedagogical settings. *Journal of Pragmatics*, 107, 105–128.

De Kok, I. & Heylen D. (2012). Analyzing nonverbal listener responses using parallel recordings of multiple listeners. *Cognitive Processing*, 13, 499–506. https://doi.org/10.1007/s10339-012-0434-3

Dittmann, A. & Llewellyn, L. (1968). Relationship between vocalizations and head nods as listener responses. *Journal of Personality and Social Psychology*, 9(2), 79–84. https://doi.org/10.1037/h0025722

Drummond, K. & Hopper, R. (1993). Back channels revisited. Acknowledgment tokens and speakership incipiency. *Research on Language and Social Interaction*, 26, 157–178.

Duchowski, A. (2007). *Eye Tracking Methodology: Theory and Practice*. London: Springer-Verlag.

Englund Dimitrova, B. (1997). Degree of Interpreter Responsibility in the Interaction Process in Community Interpreting. In S. E. Carr (Ed.), *The Critical Link: Interpreters in the Community* (pp. 147–164). Amsterdam/Philadelphia: Benjamins. https://doi.org/10.1075/btl.19.17eng

Ford, C. E. & Stickle, T. (2012). Securing recipiency in workplace meetings: Multimodal practices. *Discourse Studies*, 14(1), 11–30. https://doi.org/10.1177/1461445611427213

Gardner, R. (2001). *When Listeners Talk: Response tokens and listener stance*. Amsterdam: J. Benjamins Publishing. https://doi.org/10.1075/pbns.92

Gavioli, L. (2012). Minimal responses in interpreter-mediated medical talk. In L. Baraldi & C. Gavioli (Eds.), *Coordinating Participation in Dialogue Interpreting* (pp. 201–228). Amsterdam/ Philadelphia: Benjamins Publishing. https://doi.org/10.1075/btl.102.09gav

Gerhardt, J. & Beyerle, S. (1997). "What if Socrates had been a woman? The therapist's use of acknowledgment tokens (*mm-hm, yeah, sure, right*) as a nonreflective means of intersubjective involvement". *Contemporary Psychoanalysis*, 33(2), 367–410. https://doi.org/10.1080/00107530.1997.10746995

Goffman, E. (1981). *Forms of Talk*. Philadelphia: University of Pennsylvania Press.

Goodwin, C. (1980). Restarts, pauses, and the achievement of a state of mutual gaze at turn-beginning. *Sociological Inquiry*, 50, 272–302. https://doi.org/10.1111/j.1475-682X.1980.tb00023.x

Goodwin, C. (1981). *Conversational Organization. Interaction between Speakers and Hearers*. New York, London.

Gullberg, M. & Kita, S. (2009). Attention to speech-accompanying gestures: Eye movements and information uptake. *Journal of Nonverbal Behaviour*, 33, 251–277. https://doi.org/10.1007/s10919-009-0073-2

Holler, J. & Kendrick, K. H. (2015). Unaddressed participants' gaze in multi-person interaction: Optimizing recipiency. *Frontiers in Psychology*, 6, 1–14. https://doi.org/10.3389/fpsyg.2015.00098

Edmondson, W. J. (1986). Cognition, conversing and interpreting. In J. House, & S. Blum-Kulka (Eds.), *Interlingual and Intercultural Communication* (pp. 129–138). Tübingen: Gunter Narr.

Jokinen, K. (2010). Non-verbal signals for turn-taking & feedback. *Proceedings of 7th International Conference on Language Resources & Evaluation* (LREC) *International Universal Communication Symposium.*

Kendon, A. (1967). Some functions of gaze-direction in social interaction. *Acta Psychologica*, 26, 22–63. https://doi.org/10.1016/0001-6918(67)90005-4

Krystallidou, D. (2014). Gaze and body orientation as an apparatus for patient inclusion into exclusion from a patient-centred framework of communication. *The Interpreter and Translator Trainer*, 8(3), 399–417.

Lang, R. (1978). Behavioral aspects of liaison interpreters in Papua New Guinea: some preliminary observations. In D. Gerver & H. W. Sinaiko (Eds.), *Language Interpretation and Communication* (pp. 231–244). New York/London: Plenum Press. https://doi.org/10.1007/978-1-4615-9077-4_21

Lerner, G. H. (2003). Selecting next speaker: The context-sensitive operation of a context-free organization. *Language in Society*, 32, 177–201. https://doi.org/10.1017/S004740450332202X

Linell, P., Wadensjö, C. & Jönsson, L. (1992). Establishing Communicative Contact through a Dialogue Interpreter. In A. Grindsted, & J. Wagner (Eds.), *Communication for Specific Purposes – Fachsprachliche Kommunikation* (pp. 125–142). Tübingen: Gunter Narr Verlag.

Mason, I. (2012). Gaze, positioning and identity in interpreter-mediated dialogues. In L. Baraladi, & C. Gavioli, C (Eds.), *Coordinating Participation in Dialogue Interpreting* (pp. 177–199). Amsterdam/Philadelphia: Benjamins Publishing. https://doi.org/10.1075/btl.102.08mas

Merlini, R. & Favaron, R. (2005). Examining the "voice of interpreting" in speech pathology. *Interpreting*, 7(2), 263–302. https://doi.org/10.1075/intp.7.2.07mer

Oben, B. & Brône, G. (2015). What you see is what you do: On the relation between gaze and gesture in multimodal alignment. *Language and Cognition*, 7(4), 546–562. https://doi.org/10.1017/langcog.2015.22

Pasquandrea, S. (2011). Managing multiple actions through multimodality: Doctors' involvement in interpreter-mediated interactions. *Language in Society*, 40(4), 455–481. https://doi.org/10.1017/S0047404511000479

Pasquandrea, S. (2012). Co-constructing dyadic sequences in healthcare interpreting: A multimodal account. *New Voices in Translation Studies*, 8, 132–157.

Peräkylä, A. (2013). Conversation Analysis in Psychotherapy. In J. Sidnell & T. Stivers (Eds.), *The Handbook of Conversation Analysis* (pp. 251–274). Malden: Wiley-Blackwell.

Pöchhacker, F. (2012). Interpreting participation. Conceptual analysis and illustration of the interpreter's role in interaction. In L. Baraldi, & C. Gavioli (Eds.), *Coordinating Participation in Dialogue Interpreting* (pp. 201–228). Amsterdam/Philadelphia: Benjamins Publishing. https://doi.org/10.1075/btl.102.03poch

Pöllabauer, S. (2004). Interpreting in asylum hearings: Issues of role, responsibility and power. *Interpreting*, 6(2), 143–180. https://doi.org/10.1075/intp.6.2.03pol

Rea, L. M. & Parker, R. A. (1992). *Designing and conducting survey research*. San Francisco, CA: Jossey– Bass.

Rossano, F. (2013). Gaze in Conversation. In J. Sidnell & T. Stivers (Eds.), *The Handbook of Conversation Analysis* (pp. 308–329). Oxford: Wiley-Blackwell.

Sacks, H., Schegloff, E. A. & Jefferson, G. (1974). A simplest systematics for the organization of turn-taking in conversation. *Language*, 50, 696–735. https://doi.org/10.1353/lan.1974.0010

Selting, M. et al. (2009). *Gesprächsanalytisches Transkriptionssystem 2 (GAT 2). Gesprächsforschung – Online-Zeitschrift zur verbalen Interaktion*, 10, 353–402.

Streeck, J. (2009). *Gesturecraft – The manufacture of meaning.* Amsterdam/Philadelphia: John Benjamins.

Stivers, T. (2008). Stance, alignment and affiliation during story telling: when nodding is a token of preliminary affiliation. *Research on Language in Social Interaction*, 41, 29–55. https://doi.org/10.1080/08351810701691123

Stivers, T. & Rossano, F. (2010). Mobilizing Response. *Research on Language and Social Interaction*, 43(1), 3–31. https://doi.org/10.1080/08351810903471258

Wadensjö, C. (1998). *Interpreting as interaction.* London and New York: Longman.

Wadensjö, C. (2001). Interpreting in Crisis: The Interpreters Position in Therapeutic Encounters. In I. Mason (Ed.), *Triadic Exchanges. Studies in Dialogue Interpreting* (pp. 71–85). Manchester: St. Jerome Publishing.

Wittenburg, P., H. Brugman, A. Russel, A. Klassmann & Sloetjes, H. (2006). ELAN: a Professional Framework for Multimodality Research. In: *Proceedings of LREC 2006, Fifth International Conference on Language Resources and Evaluation.*

Yngve, V. H. (1970). On getting a word in edgewise. In *Papers from the Sixth Regional Meeting of the Chicago Linguistic Society* (pp. 567–577). Chicago: Chicago Linguistic Society.

Index